Research Methods
for Managers

Dr John Gill, before his retirement, was Reader in Management at Sheffield Business School, Sheffield Hallam University. He has experience of the supervision of management research projects from diploma to doctorate. He has been a member of the (then) Social Science Research Council's Management and Industrial Relations Committee and the Research Committee of the CNAA. He was chair of the Research Degrees Sub-Committee of the Business and Management Board of the CNAA and chair for eight years of the (then) Sheffield City Polytechnic's Research Degrees Committee.

Dr Phil Johnson is Professor of HRM at The School of Management, Sheffield University. He has undertaken and published research mainly in the areas of epistemology, methodology, managerial control, managing change and business ethics. He has recently undertaken management research projects sponsored by ESRC and EPSRC. He has experience of the supervision of management research projects from first degree to doctorate.

Dr Murray Clark is a Principal Lecturer in Organization Behaviour and Research Methodology at Sheffield Business School, Sheffield Hallam University. He is also Director of the DBA programme. Prior to embarking upon an academic career he was a senior manager with the National Coal Board. He has undertaken and published research mainly in areas of leadership, trust and methodology. He has experience of the supervision of management research projects from first degree to doctorate.

Research Methods
for **Managers** 4th Edition

John Gill | Phil Johnson | With Murray Clark

Los Angeles | London | New Delhi
Singapore | Washington DC

First published 1991
Second edition published 1997
Third edition published 2002
Reprinted 2003, 2005 (twice), 2006
This fourth edition published 2010

SAGE Publications Ltd
1 Oliver's Yard
55 City Road
London EC1Y 1SP

SAGE Publications Inc.
2455 Teller Road
Thousand Oaks, California 91320

SAGE Publications India Pvt Ltd
B 1/I 1 Mohan Cooperative Industrial Area
Mathura Road
New Delhi 110 044

SAGE Publications Asia-Pacific Pte Ltd
33 Pekin Street #02-01
Far East Square
Singapore 048763

Library of Congress Control Number: 2009930376

British Library Cataloguing in Publication data

A catalogue record for this book is available from the British Library

ISBN 978-1-84787-093-3
ISBN 978-1-84787-094-0 (pbk)

Typeset by C&M Digitals (P) Ltd, Chennai, India
Printed and bound in Great Britain by TJ International Ltd, Padstow, Cornwall
Printed on paper from sustainable resources

Summary of contents

338309

Contents

Preface to the fourth edition

We introduced the preface of the first edition of this book by making clear that its inception lay in our concern that the teaching of research methods to management and business students was hampered by a suitable text book. One of the key developments in the past 15 or so years has of course been the publication of a number of excellent texts that are aimed precisely at these students and provide invaluable aids for project and dissertation work. Nevertheless, where we would argue that this book is distinctive is that it attempts to meet certain objectives with regard to the choices that people make in their methodological engagements.

We have a number of objectives. First, we wish to address key philosophical matters that are basic to any real understanding of the methodological approaches to management research. Perhaps whatever choices management researchers make around methodology, the most important thing for us is that we make those choices consciously by engaging in critical reflection upon the philosophical presuppositions that inevitably influence how any research is undertaken. Second, we attempt to make the text very practical in that examples and exercises are drawn from management and business. Finally, we wish to ensure that the text will enable students to take their first steps in project work confident that they are on firm ground in their choice of methodological approaches.

We also wish to challenge the widespread advocacy of particular approaches to management research as being 'the best'. Advocacy of one approach or another, often irrespective of context or philosophical stance, is still unfortunately commonplace in business and management research. These debates are frequently acrimonious, probably reflecting fundamental cultural, ideological and disciplinary differences as well the defensiveness arising from the need to advance careers in the light of peer evaluation and recognition. Our position is to make clear that there is a wide array of different approaches to management research and all have particular advantages and disadvantages whilst articulating various philosophical commitments. They are thus vulnerable to various kinds of criticism which researchers must take into account when making methodological choices. However, our view is also that management research can only benefit from broadening the philosophical repertoires available so that those methodological choices are also made on an informed basis rather than by default. By exposing the reader to these various philosophical debates we hope that people not only gain understanding of their own stance but also that of others working in the field.

Since the third edition we have received feedback from many researchers, educators and students and we have tried to use this information to update and produce this edition yet maintaining the book's original orientation. Hence, this new edition has involved a complete rewriting of many of the chapters in the third edition and the inclusion of several completely new chapters. While we have included some new examples of management research in practice, one of our key tasks has been to try to keep pace with the philosophical developments which seem to have impacted upon management research. This new sensibility (see Willmott, 1998) sits relatively comfortably with the stance of previous editions as it entails noticing, evaluating and being suspicious of the relationship between the researcher and the 'objects' of research. As such, it has had major implications for methodologies like action research and ethnography which we have tried to capture in this new text. Simultaneously this new sensibility has significant implications for how management research should be evaluated. Again we have tried to correct typographical errors and obscurities in the text. We have also updated it to introduce new ideas, technologies and references which have become available since the third edition. Of course the usual disclaimers apply!

The material presented in this book has been discussed with many people over the years, with colleagues, academics elsewhere, and by managers and students. We particularly acknowledge the following: Chris Argyris, Peter Ashworth, Tony Berry, Anna Buehring, Cathy Cassell, Chris Clegg, John Darwin, Joanne Duberley, Steve Fineman, Philip Frame, David Golding, Dan Gowler, Chris Hendry, Rita Johnston, Karen Legge, Clive Ley, Tom Lupton, John McAuley, Ian McGivering, Ian Mangham, Stuart Manson, John Morris, Joe Nason, Andy Neely, Roy Payne, Nigel Slack, Ken Smith, Stuart Smith, Paul Stokes, Gillian Symon, Ian Tanner, Pat Terry, Doug Thacker, David Tranfield, Don White and Sue Whittle. We also gratefully acknowledge the help of Natalie Aguilera at SAGE who has encouraged and guided us through the difficulties of preparing material for publication. We also would like to thank Marianne Lagrange, formerly of Paul Chapman Publishing, who originally supported our work in the 1990s.

John Gill
Phil Johnson
Murray Clark
June 2009

Aims and purposes of the book

This book is designed to help those about to undertake research in business and management either in connection with their jobs as managers or as a research project requirement as part of a taught course at undergraduate or postgraduate levels. It will also be particularly appropriate to those working for master's and doctoral degrees by research.

In our experience, students undertaking a research project have most difficulty deciding which approach or strategy to use to address the research problem they have set themselves; and then how to employ methods of data collection in undertaking fieldwork, frequently in organizations.

We aim, therefore, to provide an introductory text to enable students to make an informed start on project work. With such help they are not only likely to be made more aware of the appropriateness of the range of available approaches to research but are also more likely to be in a better position to justify their choices and evaluate their subsequent findings.

The book presents students with a wide range of approaches to management research and their philosophical bases sufficient to be readily applicable to managerial problem-solving. Many of the references in this book are available in the following library reference collection, *Business and Management Research Methodologies*, edited by Johnson and Clark (2006) and published by SAGE.

Please see http://www.uk.sagepub.com for further details.

Guided tour

Welcome to the guided tour of
Research Methods for Managers,
4th Edition. This tour will take you
through the main sections and
special features of the text.

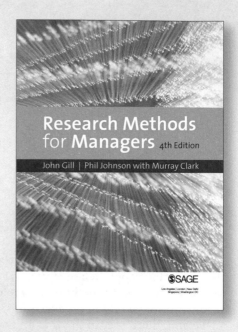

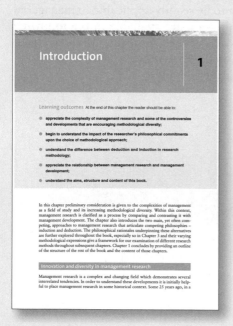

Learning outcomes: A clear set of bullet
pointed learning objectives are provided at
the beginning of each chapter.

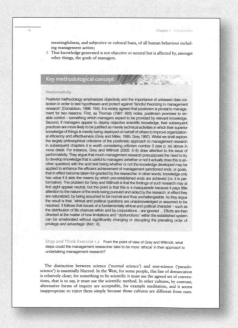

Key methodological concept: Helpful
boxed sections that look in closer detail at a
methodology under discussion.
Stop and Think Exercise: Exercises are
provided throughout the chapters to help the
reader engage and think further about the
concepts being discussed.

98 Chapter 5 Action research

changing things to solve or ameliorate problems, as an integral part of the research, Lewin thought that theory was pivotal to guiding how those problems were understood and acted upon by the action researcher. Moreover by enabling intervention into everyday problems Lewin thought that action research also enabled hypothesis testing and that the action research process itself thereby enabled the refinement of theory and the evolution of new theory (see Marrow, 1969: 128).

Management research example The Tavistock Institute and early action research

At roughly the same time as Lewin's work, and virtually unconnected with these developments in North America, there was significant growth of action research in the UK. As in North America, the roots of this growth were to be found in the Second World War, during which psychologists, anthropologists and psychiatrists of a psychoanalytic orientation came together in multidisciplinary teams to work on a number of problems. During and just after the war a number of successful action research programmes were conducted in personnel selection and the treatment and rehabilitation of returning prisoners of war.

This work led to the formation of the Tavistock Institute of Human Relations, which was composed of people of various social science backgrounds but with the shared objective of attempting to find ways by which social science could contribute to finding solutions to some of the pressing social problems of the post-war period so as to 'improve both organizational effectiveness and dignity' (Passmore, 2006: 38). Although the term 'action research' was not specifically used by workers at the Tavistock Institute until the 1960s, almost all their work was problem centred, entailed a long-term involvement with clients with a focus upon their perceived needs and involved helping with the implementation and monitoring of changes.

In the management field probably the best-known early work in this tradition is by Jaques (1951), based on research in the Glacier Metal Company (discussed later in this chapter); Sofer (1961) in further education; Wilson (1961) in Unilever; and Trist et al. (1963), working in the Durham coalfield. Topics included planned organizational change, the analysis of tasks in organizations and the relationship of the organization to its environment, and the analysis of absenteeism, accidents and alienation as symptoms of organizational malfunction. In almost all cases the researchers included very full accounts of their fieldwork methods, especially the day-to-day interactions between researcher and client, and the contexts in which the work was carried out as being major influences on the change process. The work was guided throughout by a strong orientation towards the study of the research process and in particular to the relationships that developed between researcher and client and the extent to which these helped or inhibited utilization of findings. In more recent work, psychoanalytic ideas have become less prominent, although the analogy of the psychoanalytic situation, where the client is confronted with the researcher's perception of what in reality is occurring, is still a feature of much of the work in this tradition.

Management research example: Concepts and theories are given context through the inclusion of 'real life' examples that will assist in the overall understanding and awareness of the topics covered.

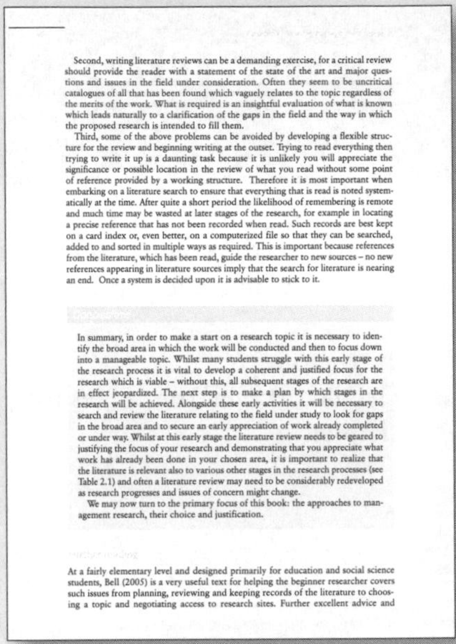

Second, writing literature reviews can be a demanding exercise, for a critical review should provide the reader with a statement of the state of the art and major questions and issues in the field under consideration. Often they seem to be uncritical catalogues of all that has been found which vaguely relates to the topic regardless of the merits of the work. What is required is an insightful evaluation of what is known which leads naturally to a clarification of the gaps in the field and the way in which the proposed research is intended to fill them.

Third, some of the above problems can be avoided by developing a flexible structure for the review and beginning writing at the outset. Trying to read everything then trying to write it up is a daunting task because it is unlikely you will appreciate the significance or possible location in the review of what you read without some point of reference provided by a working structure. Therefore it is most important when embarking on a literature search to ensure that everything that is read is noted systematically at the time. After quite a short period the likelihood of remembering is remote and much time may be wasted at later stages of the research, for example in locating a precise reference that has not been recorded when read. Such records are best kept on a card index or, even better, on a computerized file so that they can be searched, added to and sorted in multiple ways as required. This is important because references from the literature, which has been read, guide the researcher to new sources – no new references appearing in literature sources imply that the search for literature is nearing an end. Once a system is decided upon it is advisable to stick to it.

In summary, in order to make a start on a research topic it is necessary to identify the broad area in which the work will be conducted and then to focus down into a manageable topic. Whilst many students struggle with this early stage of the research process it is vital to develop a coherent and justified focus for the research which is viable – without this, all subsequent stages of the research are in effect jeopardized. The next step is to make a plan by which stages in the research will be achieved. Alongside these early activities it will be necessary to search and review the literature relating to the field under study to look for gaps in the broad area and to secure an early appreciation of work already completed or under way. Whilst at this early stage the literature review needs to be geared to justifying the focus of your research and demonstrating that you appreciate what work has already been done in your chosen area, it is important to realize that the literature is relevant also to various other stages in the research processes (see Table 2.1) and often a literature review may need to be considerably redeveloped as research progresses and issues of concern might change.

We may now turn to the primary focus of this book: the approaches to management research, their choice and justification.

At a fairly elementary level and designed primarily for education and social science students, Bell (2005) is a very useful text for helping the beginner researcher covers such issues from planning, reviewing and keeping records of the literature to choosing a topic and negotiating access to research sites. Further excellent advice and

Conclusions: Draws together and summarizes the chapter discussion and re-emphasizes the most important points.
Further reading: Suggestions and information on relevant readings from books and journal articles to provide a deeper understanding of the issues raised.

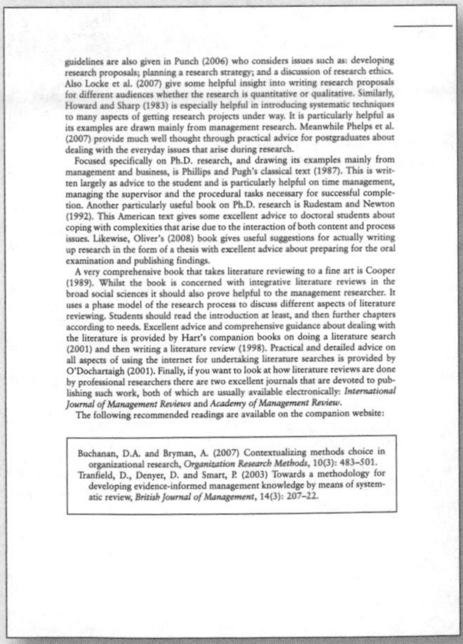

guidelines are also given in Punch (2006) who considers issues such as: developing research proposals; planning a research strategy; and a discussion of research ethics. Also Locke et al. (2007) give some helpful insight into writing research proposals for different audiences whether the research is quantitative or qualitative. Similarly, Howard and Sharp (1983) is especially helpful in introducing systematic techniques to many aspects of getting research projects under way. It is particularly helpful as its examples are drawn mainly from management research. Meanwhile Phelps et al. (2007) provide much well thought through practical advice for postgraduates about dealing with the everyday issues that arise during research.

Focused specifically on Ph.D. research, and drawing its examples mainly from management and business, is Phillips and Pugh's classical text (1987). This is written largely as advice to the student and is particularly helpful on time management, managing the supervisor and the procedural tasks necessary for successful completion. Another particularly useful book on Ph.D. research is Rudestam and Newton (1992). This American text gives some excellent advice to doctoral students about coping with complexities that arise due to the interaction of both content and process issues. Likewise, Oliver's (2008) book gives useful suggestions for actually writing up research in the form of a thesis with excellent advice about preparing for the oral examination and publishing findings.

A very comprehensive book that takes literature reviewing to a fine art is Cooper (1989). Whilst the book is concerned with integrative literature reviews in the broad social sciences it should also prove helpful to the management researcher. It uses a phase model of the research process to discuss different aspects of literature reviewing. Students should read the introduction at least, and then further chapters according to needs. Excellent advice and comprehensive guidance about dealing with the literature is provided by Hart's companion books on doing a literature search (2001) and then writing a literature review (1998). Practical and detailed advice on all aspects of using the internet for undertaking literature searches is provided by O'Dochartaigh (2001). Finally, if you want to look at how literature reviews are done by professional researchers there are two excellent journals that are devoted to publishing such work, both of which are usually available electronically: *International Journal of Management Reviews* and *Academy of Management Review*.

The following recommended readings are available on the companion website:

Buchanan, D.A. and Bryman, A. (2007) Contextualizing methods choice in organizational research, *Organization Research Methods*, 10(3): 483–501.
Tranfield, D., Denyer, D. and Smart, P. (2003) Towards a methodology for developing evidence-informed management knowledge by means of systematic review, *British Journal of Management*, 14(3): 207–22.

Readings available on website: A selection of relevant journal articles to assist in gaining more in-depth and detailed knowledge. These articles are available on the companion website *www.sagepub.co.uk/gillandjohnson*

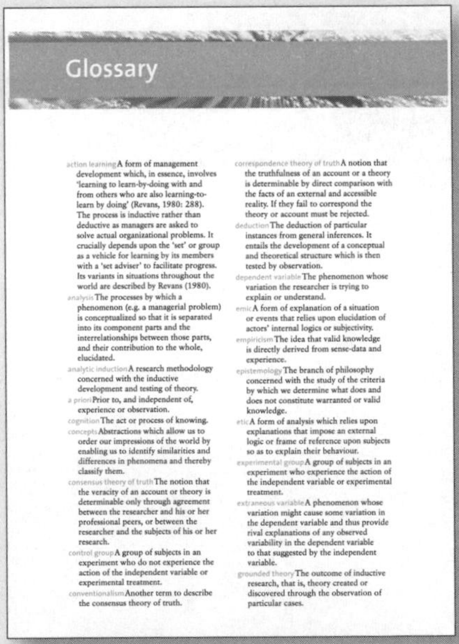

Glossary

action learning A form of management development which, in essence, involves 'learning to learn-by-doing with and from others who are also learning-to-learn by doing' (Revans, 1980: 288). The process is inductive rather than deductive as managers are asked to solve actual organizational problems. It crucially depends upon the 'set' or group as a vehicle for learning by its members with a 'set adviser' to facilitate progress. Its variants in situations throughout the world are described by Revans (1980).
analysis The processes by which a phenomenon (e.g. a managerial problem) is conceptualized so that it is separated into its component parts and the interrelationships between those parts, and their contribution to the whole, elucidated.
analytic induction A research methodology concerned with the inductive development and testing of theory.
a priori Prior to, and independent of, experience or observation.
cognition The act or process of knowing.
concepts Abstractions which allow us to order our impressions of the world by enabling us to identify similarities and differences in phenomena and thereby classify them.
consensus theory of truth The notion that the veracity of an account or theory is determinable only through agreement between the researcher and his or her professional peers, or between the researcher and the subjects of his or her research.
control group A group of subjects in an experiment who do not experience the action of the independent variable or experimental treatment.
conventionalism Another term to describe the consensus theory of truth.
correspondence theory of truth A notion that the truthfulness of an account or a theory is determinable by direct comparison with the facts of an external and accessible reality. If they fail to correspond the theory or account must be rejected.
deduction The deduction of particular instances from general inferences. It entails the development of a conceptual and theoretical structure which is then tested by observation.
dependent variable The phenomenon whose variation the researcher is trying to explain or understand.
emic A form of explanation of a situation or events that relies upon elucidation of actors' internal logics or subjectivity.
empiricism The idea that valid knowledge is directly derived from sense-data and experience.
epistemology The branch of philosophy concerned with the study of the criteria by which we determine what does and does not constitute warranted or valid knowledge.
etic A form of analysis which relies upon explanations that impose an external logic or frame of reference upon subjects so as to explain their behaviour.
experimental group A group of subjects in an experiment who experience the action of the independent variable or experimental treatment.
extraneous variable A phenomenon whose variation might cause some variation in the dependent variable and thus provide rival explanations of any observed variability in the dependent variable to that suggested by the independent variable.
grounded theory The outcome of inductive research, that is, theory created or discovered through the observation of particular cases.

Glossary: A detailed glossary of terms is provided at the end of the book – an essential reference point!

Companion website

Be sure to visit the companion website at www.sagepub.co.uk/gillandjohnson to find a range of teaching and learning materials:

For instructors:
- Detailed **PowerPoint** slides for each chapter.

For students:
- Selected **online journal readings** available to accompany each chapter.
- An **online glossary** that covers all the relevant terms in the book.

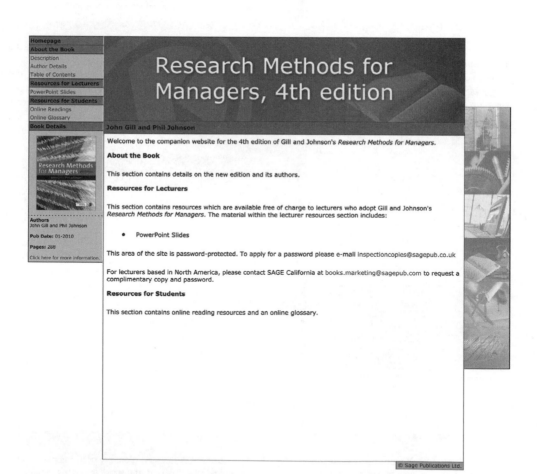

Issues and processes in management research

Part I

Introduction

Learning outcomes At the end of this chapter the reader should be able to:

- appreciate the complexity of management research and some of the controversies and developments that are encouraging methodological diversity;

- begin to understand the impact of the researcher's philosophical commitments upon the choice of methodological approach;

- understand the difference between deduction and induction in research methodology;

- appreciate the relationship between management research and management development;

- understand the aims, structure and content of this book.

In this chapter preliminary consideration is given to the complexities of management as a field of study and its increasing methodological diversity. Within this context, management research is clarified as a process by comparing and contrasting it with management development. The chapter also introduces the two main, yet often competing, approaches to management research that articulate competing philosophies – induction and deduction. The philosophical rationales underpinning these alternatives are further explored throughout the book, especially so in Chapter 3, and their varying methodological expressions give a framework for our examination of different research methods throughout subsequent chapters. Chapter 1 concludes by providing an outline of the structure of the rest of the book and the content of those chapters.

Innovation and diversity in management research

Management research is a complex and changing field which demonstrates several interrelated tendencies. In order to understand these developments it is initially helpful to place management research in some historical context. Some 25 years ago, in a discussion of the historical development of management studies, Whitley (1984a, b) described it as being in a fragmented state; as a field characterized by a high degree of task uncertainty and a low degree of co-ordination of research procedures and strategies between researchers who undertake research in an ad hoc and opportunistic manner. This apparent situation led Pfeffer (1993, 1995) to argue, by using economics as an exemplar to be copied, that management research must develop consensus through the enforcement of theoretical and methodological conformity. As he argued, such a paradigmatic convergence may increase the social standing of the discipline and thus should assure more access to scarce resources, whilst easing its methodological development. However, in a reply to Pfeffer, Van Maanen (1995a) argued that if management research followed Pfeffer's recommendations the resultant enforced conformity would create what amounted to a 'technocratic unimaginativeness' which could drive out tolerance of the unorthodox and significantly reduce our learning from one another. During the intervening years, management students have been confronted by much controversy about the most appropriate approaches to the study of management as an academic discipline. Of course, it is debatable how far these controversies have actually reconfigured management research practice as it may be argued that there is a dominant orthodoxy within management research which is maintained by very powerful institutional pressures. Nevertheless, the dominance of this mainstream in management research is being resisted by numerous management researchers and indeed has been under attack on a number of fronts (see Symon et al., 2008). To some extent the development of these controversies has been due not only to the emergence of different schools of management thought but also to the development of different approaches to research methodology, especially so in the social sciences. Indeed, since the first edition of this book in 1991, there seems to have been an increasing methodological diversity amongst those who undertake what can be broadly classified as management research – although it is important to note that quantitative methods still dominate much of what is published in prestigious academic journals.

Whilst it remains accurate to say that the diversity in management research has been exacerbated due to its multi-disciplinary (Brown, 1997) and inter-disciplinary (Watson, 1997) nature and its position at the confluence of numerous social science disciplines (e.g. sociology, psychology, economics, politics, accounting, finance and so on), other forces are clearly at play which have promoted methodological innovation and change. For instance, this increasing diversity might also be explained by the 'coming of age' of qualitative and interpretive methods (see Prasad and Prasad, 2002) which may be seen as arising in response to certain perceived limitations in conventional management research and thereby presents a significant challenge to, and critique of, the quantitative mainstream of management research. However, qualitative management research is itself characterized by an expanding array of methodologies that articulate different, competing, philosophical assumptions which have significant implications for how management research should be (Johnson et al., 2006), and is (Johnson et al., 2007), evaluated by interested parties. Simultaneously, there has been the development of an array of critical approaches to the study of management usually going under the umbrella term 'critical management studies'. This influential development, in part, arises out of a philosophical and methodological critique of the assumed objectivity and neutrality of the quantitative mainstream but also aims to generate what are presented as emancipatory forms of research that challenge the status quo in contemporary organizations by exposing and undermining dominant managerial discourses whose content is often just taken-for-granted by organizational members and thereby assumed to be natural and unchallengeable (see Fournier and Grey, 2000; Grey and Willmott, 2005; Kelemen and Rumens, 2008). Of course such developments open questions about who is the intended audience for management research. For instance, is management research about:

1 addressing the presumed pragmatic concerns and presumed business needs of practising managers, or,
2 is it about investigating and understanding the structures and processes of oppression and injustice, that are taken to be part of organizing in a capitalist society, whose main beneficiaries and victims are often these social actors labelled managers?

Any cursory inspection of management research would suggest that a great deal of it published in prestigious academic journals adopts, often by default, the first orientation noted above. Unlike our second orientation above, it adopts the view that management research must be relevant in the sense that it helps managers to manage more efficiently and effectively by enhancing their ability to cope with the problems that assail contemporary organizations by improving the technical content of managerial practice based upon rigorous analysis using social scientific theory rather than common sense. However, many commentators (e.g. Tranfield and Starkey, 1998; Keleman and Bansal, 2002) have noted some irony here in the sense that the channels by which this research is disseminated, and often the language used, all tend to reflect the institutional incentives, intellectual requirements, interests, and concerns of academia rather than the needs of management practitioners, whoever they might be. Nevertheless, many management researchers (e.g. Heckscher, 1994; Osbourne and Plastrik, 1998; Kalleberg, 2001; Johnson et al., 2009) have pointed to how the nature of managerial work, and the roles available to managers, may indeed be fundamentally changing under the impact of the organizational changes driven by a possible shift from bureaucratic forms of command and control to post-bureaucratic forms of organizational governance. The latter are usually characterized as flatter, less hierarchical, more networked and flexible organizations wherein employees are necessarily empowered to use their discretion to cope with a more volatile and uncertain workplace and requires managers capable of facilitating the participation of self-directed employees in decision-making (Tucker, 1999): something which further requires the evolution and deployment of managers' research skills at work (Hendry, 2006).

Of course the second orientation noted above is much more associated with critical management studies, which often overtly rejects a managerially orientated approach partially on the basis of a desire to enhance the democratic rights and responsibilities of the relatively disempowered majorities of members of work organizations: an approach that has significant methodological implications but which also is an outcome of a philosophical challenge to mainstream management research (which we shall consider later in this book) which seems to reflect Whitley's (1984b: 387) criticism that management research had adopted 'a naïve and unreflecting empiricism'. For Whitley, the solution to this problem required freeing researchers from lay concepts and problem formulations and by providing them with a more sophisticated understanding of the epistemological and sociological sciences.

In sum, there are a range of forces at play which have created a trajectory in management research that seems to be one of increasing methodological diversity and innovation, much of which uses varying philosophical critiques of the quantitative mainstream as a starting point to legitimate the methodological changes that are deemed to be necessary.

One of the major themes of this book is that there is no one best methodological approach but rather that the approach most appropriate for the investigation of a given research question depends on a large number of variables, not least the nature of the research question itself and how the researcher constitutes and interprets that question. Research methodology is always a compromise between options in the light of tacit philosophical assumptions, and choices are also frequently influenced by practical issues such as the availability of resources and the ability to get access to organizations and their memberships in order to undertake research.

Making methodological choices

In this book we will advance criteria for choice of methodology by reviewing the major approaches to management research and, through examples, their appropriateness to finding answers to particular research questions. Therefore, one key aim of this work is to illustrate the different means by which business and management research is undertaken by presenting some of the variety of methodologies that are potentially available to any researcher. In attempting to meet our key aim we are also concerned to illustrate that the research methods available to the management researcher are not merely neutral devices or techniques that we can just 'take off shelf' to undertake a particular task for which they are most suited. Such a perspective implies that it is the nature of the research question, and what phenomenon is under investigation, which should pragmatically dictate the correct research method to use since different kinds of information about management are most comprehensively and economically gathered in different ways. Whilst at first sight this stance seems to have much to offer, and of course the nature of the research question being investigated is methodologically important, it can simultaneously deflect our attention from what we see to be a key issue: that the different research methods available to the management researcher also bring with them a great deal of philosophical baggage which can remain unnoticed when they are classified as constituting merely different data collection tools that can be chosen to do different jobs. Therefore, management researchers need to be aware of the philosophical commitments they make through their methodological choices, since that baggage has a significant impact not only upon what they do, but also upon how they understand whatever it is that they think they are investigating in the first place.

For instance (see Figure 1.1), the decision to use deductive research methods (for example, experiments, analytical surveys, etc.) that are designed to test, and indeed falsify, previously formulated theory through confronting its causal predictions about human behaviour with empirical data gathered through the neutral observation of social reality, tacitly draws upon an array of philosophical assumptions and commitments that are contestable yet so often remain taken-for-granted. Even a cursory inspection of the management field would show that such methodological choices are common place yet, by default, also involve the decision not to engage through alternative means: alternatives that in themselves articulate different philosophical commitments, e.g. to build theory inductively out of observation of the empirical world that focuses upon the operation actors' everyday culturally derived subjective interpretations of their situations in order to explain their behaviour theoretically. As we will see in Chapter 3, there are significant philosophical differences between these

Figure 1.1 | Deduction vs induction

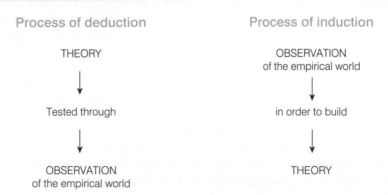

two approaches, to a degree initially centred upon what each assumes to be the key influences upon human behaviour and the forms that it takes as well as how those influences are best investigated by researchers.

The point is that whilst we cannot avoid making philosophical commitments in undertaking any research, a problem lies in the issue that any philosophical commitment can be simultaneously contested because they are merely assumptions that we have to make. This is because the philosophical commitments which are inevitably made in undertaking research always entail commitment to various knowledge-constituting assumptions about the nature of truth, human behaviour, representation and the accessibility of social reality. In other words there are always tacit answers to questions encoded into what is called the researcher's pre-understanding. These answers are:

- about ontology (what are we studying?)
- about epistemology (how can we have warranted knowledge about our chosen domains?)
- and about axiology (why study them?).

Those answers always have a formative impact upon any methodological engagement. Quite simply we cannot engage with our areas of interest without having answers already to those questions. The philosophical assumptions we make in dealing with these questions implicitly present different normative specifications, justified by particular rationales, for management research regarding what it is and how it should be done. But significantly these assumptions also impinge upon a further crucial area – how should we judge, or evaluate, the findings and quality of any management research? Here there is the persistent danger that particular evaluative criteria, deriving from particular philosophical traditions within management research, are inadvertently applied to all management research regardless of its particular philosophical stance. This is a particularly important issue as it could mean that the outcomes of some management research may be inappropriately and unfairly evaluated: an issue we shall explore in the later chapters of this book.

The notion that methodological choices regarding how to do research always involve philosophical choices that need to be excavated is supported by some recent developments in management research. For instance, since the early 1990s, there has been much discussion of the notion that in order to understand ourselves as social science researchers we must reflexively engage (see Holland, 1999; Newton, 1999; Weick, 1999; Alvesson and Deetz, 2000; Johnson and Duberley, 2003) with ourselves through thinking about our own thinking and how those beliefs have repercussions for our engagements with our areas of interest. According to Chia and Morgan such vigilance must also embrace management education through the inculcation of 'an intimate understanding of the way ... management knowledge ... is organized, produced and legitimized' (1996: 58) – an agenda which has become all the more important with the increasing 'managerialization of the world' (Alvesson and Deetz, 2000: 209). Although this 'new sensibility' (Willmott, 1998) has many implications for management research, several commentators have emphasized how it entails noticing, and being suspicious of, the relationship between the researcher and the substantive focus of his/her research. This involves reflecting upon how those often tacit, unacknowledged, pre-understandings impact upon:

- how those 'objects' of research are conceptually negotiated and constituted by the researcher;
- what kinds of research question are then asked by the researcher;
- how the results of research are methodologically arrived at, justified and presented to audiences for consumption;
- how those results are then, or should be, evaluated by interested parties.

Such increased awareness regarding the philosophical choices made by management researchers, either consciously or by default, might serve to broaden the philosophical repertoire available to both management researchers and practitioners so that alternatives to the current mainstream are also understood and appreciated rather than being just discounted as outlandish eccentricities not worthy of serious contemplation, never mind use. The choices we always have to make in doing research can then be based upon a fuller consideration of the ever present alternatives rather than inadvertently limiting the focus of these decisions, by default, to that which is conventionally seem as 'normal' and thus incontrovertible. Mutual understanding is paramount here.

This book attempts to support this 'new sensibility' and, simultaneously, to bridge the gap between academic and managerial views of what constitutes appropriate research by offering challenges to both the academic community and the practising manager.

The management research process and management development

Harvey-Jones (1989: 240), in his bestselling book *Making it Happen*, advised managers when setting about tasks to distinguish content from process. What he meant by this is that it is helpful conceptually to separate the content of the task from the way the task is accomplished; that is, to separate the content (what) from the process (how). Research methods on this analysis are then primarily concerned with how (process) to tackle tasks (content).

Despite the variety of approaches to management research they all, in essence, share a problem-solving sequence that may serve as a systematic check for anyone undertaking research at whatever level. At this point we introduce a cautionary note in qualification. An idealized representation of the research sequence will help the naïve researcher at this stage to review the research process as a whole and make a start; however it rarely accords with actuality. It should be borne in mind that 'the research process is not a clear-cut sequence of procedures following a neat pattern but a messy interaction between the conceptual and empirical world, deduction and induction occurring at the same time' (Bechhofer, 1974: 73).

Nevertheless, the seven-step sequence proposed by Howard and Sharp (1983) which builds on earlier work by Rummel and Ballaine (1963), may be found particularly useful (see Figure 1.2), and is referred to again in the next chapter.

Figure 1.2 | The research sequence (adapted from Howard and Sharp, 1983) © The Management of a Student Research Project, by John A. Sharp, John Peters and Keith Howard (1983), Gower Publications Ltd.

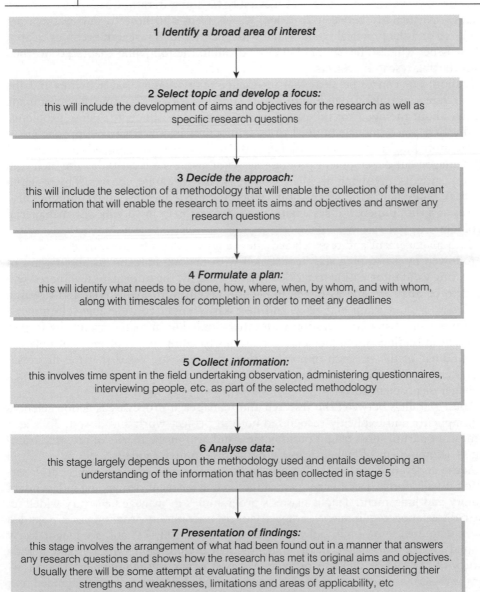

1 Identify a broad area of interest

2 Select topic and develop a focus:
this will include the development of aims and objectives for the research as well as specific research questions

3 Decide the approach:
this will include the selection of a methodology that will enable the collection of the relevant information that will enable the research to meet its aims and objectives and answer any research questions

4 Formulate a plan:
this will identify what needs to be done, how, where, when, by whom, and with whom, along with timescales for completion in order to meet any deadlines

5 Collect information:
this involves time spent in the field undertaking observation, administering questionnaires, interviewing people, etc. as part of the selected methodology

6 Analyse data:
this stage largely depends upon the methodology used and entails developing an understanding of the information that has been collected in stage 5

7 Presentation of findings:
this stage involves the arrangement of what had been found out in a manner that answers any research questions and shows how the research has met its original aims and objectives. Usually there will be some attempt at evaluating the findings by at least considering their strengths and weaknesses, limitations and areas of applicability, etc

These seven steps should be useful to all students at whatever level they are undertaking project work, from diploma to doctorate. It is recommended that each step in the sequence be given equal attention if time is to be saved in the longer term. For example, it is commonplace for people to be able to identify a broad area of interest but find it difficult to select a topic within that area that is researchable and often give insufficient attention to defining clearly the focus of research. Unless it is dealt with early in the development of the research, this issue can completely hamstring further progress down the seven-step sequence. However, sometimes a lack of clarity may only become apparent at later stages of the process, either when planning the project or deciding on methods of collecting data. As a consequence time may be lost recycling to earlier stages of the sequence or the work may fail to meet its objectives. Nevertheless, there will inevitably be some iteration between the seven stages – particularly between 2, 3, and 4 – as ideas and how to pursue them are explored and the practicality and viability of the intended research becomes clearer. These issues will also be explored in more detail in the following chapter, concerned with starting research projects.

It should of course be clear that in essence many managerial activities and the research process outlined in Figure 1.2 are similar. Notwithstanding the point made earlier about the need for reflexivity when it comes to conceptualizing 'problems' in the first place, managers need to be competent in investigative approaches to decision-making and problem-solving and this has been recognized in practically all management development programmes and business education by the inclusion of project work involving problem-solving as part of taught courses. The research process, while being the means of developing knowledge and understanding, also serves as a disciplined and systematic procedure of help in solving any managerial problem.

Both management and research activities require a decision as to what to do; this is followed by a planning stage concerned with making judgements about ways of collecting valid information to tackle the issue. Finally, the information gathered will need to be analysed and assessed, and action taken. Both managerial and research processes are uncertain and risky, and necessarily entail considerable self-initiated endeavour involving co-operation with others and skill in managing all the factors inherent in finding and implementing solutions to complex problems. Not only are the findings of the research important, then, but it is suggested that the processes of systematic discovery have clear benefits to the manager's self-development as a manager or problem-solver.

These parallels between the research and managerial processes as action sciences are implicitly and explicitly recognized both in project work and dissertations as a significant part of most taught programmes, and also in the merits of research training as a component of higher degree programmes in management.

At the undergraduate level in business and management a research project or dissertation usually forms a significant part of the final assessment demanding independent inquiry and judgement. Taught master's programmes in management vary widely in their dissertation requirements. Some relatively uncommon programmes are guided by an action learning philosophy pioneered by Revans (1971) and are taught solely around project work based in the student's own organization. More usually a wide variety of MBA, MSc and MA programmes exist where the requirement is generally for the dissertation to be completed, through independent research usually guided by a supervisor, in about six to eight months part time or around 4 months full-time as part of a largely taught programme of study. Nevertheless, in most cases the dissertation forms a significant part of the assessment and is almost invariably preceded by a taught research methods component.

Typically a postgraduate master's level dissertation aims to allow the student to develop and demonstrate powers of rigorous analysis, critical inquiry, clear expression and independent judgement in relation to an area of business and management activity. Simultaneously there will always be an emphasis upon the student demonstrating methodological competence in the sense that the student can:

- systematically justify the choice of approach to collecting data deployed;
- competently undertake any data collection;
- be able to analyse that data and make sense of its implications for the dissertation's aims, objectives and research questions;
- demonstrate an understanding of the strengths and weaknesses of the approach used with reference to findings;
- demonstrate an appreciation of the applicability of any findings, often with particular reference to any managerial implications either within the organization studied or more generally – and very often both.

Many postgraduate dissertations are based on an in-depth investigation into a managerial problem within the student's own organization or a client organization where the student is not a direct employee. However, the most usual requirement is for more than just problem-solving typical of management consultancy since it requires the student to stand back from the problem, conceptualize it and explore its wider implications for other managers outside the particular case.

Some taught master's programmes designed for specialists, such as operations researchers, HRM and organization development practitioners, may make even greater demands on students in terms of the dissertation requirement. The time devoted to the dissertation may be as much as one third of that spent on the taught programme accounting for as much as 60 out a total of 180 credits. Commonly such dissertations are concerned with the student's management of a consultancy project where the student is required not only to find a solution to a particular problem but also to reflect on the consulting approach and the problems of implementation with regard to any identified remedial changes to the organization. For instance, the philosophy supporting the research methods component of such a master's programme in organization development is outlined by a colleague who advocates respect for data, the appropriateness of the research strategy to the problem confronted and the use of a hermeneutic approach to encourage a more reflexive understanding of the theories and philosophies of management held by both managers themselves and by self-aware researchers in order to comprehend organizational change-management issues and cope with the consulting process more effectively (McAuley, 1985; see also Darwin et al., 2002).

On other types of postgraduate programme students may have the choice to undertake more issue-centred research. This is where an issue relevant to management practice is investigated in order to determine its incidence and/or its causes across a number of different social and organizational contexts in order to answer specific research questions determined from the relevant literature rather than resolve a particular client's organizational problems.

The requirements for master's degrees undertaken solely by research (e.g. M.Phil.) and doctoral projects are similar except that the doctorate is a much more demanding piece of work requiring an independent and original contribution to knowledge.

In both degrees, however, there is a heavier emphasis upon demonstrating method-ological competence and most significantly a need to demonstrate an understanding of research methods appropriate to the chosen field and a requirement for students to defend their final theses by oral examination. At this final stage attention is given to the quality of the methodology; the thoroughness of the bibliographic search; the depth of the analysis and conclusions; and the standard of the presentation of the thesis. Finally, the extent of the contribution to knowledge is assessed: clearly, the contribution made by the master's thesis will be of some importance and will probably at least serve as a reference work. Work at master's level is, however, to be distinguished from the doctorate by the requirement placed on the latter to provide a distinct and original contribution to knowledge.

We now turn to the broad approaches or strategies to management research cov-ered in this book. It is clear that methodological choices are determined not only by the nature of the topic being investigated and the resources available but also by the particular training and socialization processes to which the researcher has been exposed which have a significant formative impact upon any pre-understanding thereby sometimes severely limiting any decision-making process regarding meth-odological choice. It will therefore be helpful at this point to diagnose your own predispositions towards particular research approaches, by doing Stop and Think Exercise 1.1.

Stop and Think Exercise 1.1   Self-diagnose your research approach

Say whether you agree or disagree with the following statements by placing a tick (agree) or a cross (disagree) in the box against each statement.

1 Quantitative data are more objective and scientific than qualitative data. ☐
2 It is always necessary to define precisely the research topic before data ☐
   collection.
3 Of all methods the questionnaire is probably the best by which to collect ☐
   objective data on management topics.
4 Field experiments such as the Hawthorne Studies effectively determine ☐
   cause and effect relationships.
5 A good knowledge of statistics is essential for competence in all ☐
   approaches to management research.
6 A case study is an inappropriate way to undertake management research ☐
   as it cannot be generalized.
7 Anthropological methods are obviously fine as a means of studying exotic ☐
   tribes but have little utility in management research.
8 Laboratory experiments, such as studies of decision-making in groups, ☐
   should be used more widely in management research as they can be
   closely controlled by the researcher.
9 Research into management issues is best achieved through the ☐
   accumulation of quantitative data.
10 As a management research method, participant observation is too prone ☐
    to researcher bias to be valid.

Method of scoring: For the method of scoring, see the instructions at the end of this chapter.

Approaches to management research

It has been suggested that a common stereotype firmly held by managers is to regard researchers as remote, ivory-tower individuals working on issues of little practical relevance. This stereotype, by analogy with the 'boffin' scientist, may of course be partly defensive and serve to preserve managers from the study of difficult philosophical concepts necessary for a comprehensive understanding of research methodology (Gill, 1986; Gill et al., 1989; Grey and Mitev, 1995; Johnson and Duberley, 2000).

Managers are not alone in this, for most people associate the word 'research' with activities that are substantially removed from daily life and which, it is assumed, usually take place in a laboratory. Further, research – and its connection in many minds with 'science' – is often understood to refer to the study of problems by scientific methods or principles deriving from the natural or physical sciences. Management is no exception and there is an influential body of writers who all apparently believe that science is basically a way of producing and validating knowledge which can be applied to managerial problems without too much difficulty. For example, House (1970), in discussing 'scientific' investigation in management, suggests that in order to be objective there is a requirement of public demonstration to prevent the construction of theories and the formulation of general laws on the basis of inadequately tested hypotheses (see also Donaldson, 1996; Hogan and Sinclair, 1996). The requirement of demonstration is satisfied, he believes, when the research design includes:

1 a priori hypotheses that specify causal predictions of relationships between variables that may be then tested empirically through data collection;
2 a priori criteria that can be used to measure the acceptability of those hypotheses;
3 isolation and control of the variables under investigation so as to enable testing; and
4 methods of quantitatively measuring and verifying the variables in the investigation.

Whilst we shall explore the logic underpinning this deductive approach to research, and how it has been criticized in much more detail in Chapters 3 and 9, it is worth stating here that this is also a 'positivist' approach which remains predominant in management research (see Alvesson and Willmott, 1996; Alvesson and Deetz, 2000; Symon et al., 2008). Whilst there are many important aspects to positivism, for the time being it is worth noting that positivists usually suggest that management research methodology has to be essentially similar to that used in the natural and physical sciences in order to emulate its evident successes. As Hogan and Sinclair (1996) also argue, positivist methods allow the checking of the validity of their findings through replication. The findings are therefore pivotal to promoting organizational effectiveness and efficiency by providing verified guides to managers' interventions into their organizations. However, the assumptions on which this normative view is based have been challenged on at least three main grounds:

1 That there is no single method which generates scientific knowledge in all cases.
2 That what may be an appropriate method for researching the natural or physical world may be inappropriate in the social world given the inherent

meaningfulness, and subjective or cultural basis, of all human behaviour including management action.

3 That knowledge generated is not objective or neutral but is affected by, amongst other things, the goals of managers and the pressuppositions of researchers themselves.

Key methodological concept

Performativity

Positivist methodology emphasizes objectivity and the importance of unbiased data collection in order to test hypotheses and protect against 'fanciful theorizing in management research' (Donaldson, 1996: 164). It is widely agreed that positivism is pivotal to management for two reasons. First, as Thomas (1997: 693) notes, positivism promises to enable control – something which managers expect to be provided by relevant knowledge. Second, if managers appear to deploy objective scientific knowledge, their subsequent practices are more likely to be justified as merely technical activities in which their superior knowledge of things is merely being deployed on behalf of others to improve organizational efficiency and effectiveness (Grey and Mitev, 1995; Grey 1997). Whilst we shall explore the largely philosophical criticisms of the positivistic approach to management research in subsequent chapters, it is worth considering criticism number 3 (see pp. 193–200) above in more detail. For instance, Grey and Willmott (2005: 5–6) draw attention to the issue of performativity. They argue that much management research presupposes the need to try to develop knowledge that is useful to managers (whether or not it actually does this is another question) with the acid test being whether or not the knowledge developed may be applied to enhance the efficient achievement of management sanctioned ends, or goals, that in effect become taken-for-granted by the researcher. In other words, knowledge only has value if it aids the means by which pre-established ends are achieved (i.e. it is performative). The problem for Grey and Willmott is that the findings of such research may at first sight appear neutral, but the point is that this is a masquerade because it pays little attention to the nature of the ends being pursued and aided by the research: in effect they are naturalized, by being assumed to be normal and thus unchallengeable. As they argue the result is that, 'ethical and political questions are unacknowledged or assumed to be resolved. It follows that issues of a fundamentally ethical and political character – such as the distribution of life chances within and by corporations – are ignored ... Efforts are then directed at the matter of how limitations and "dysfunctions" within the established system can be ameliorated without significantly changing or disrupting the prevailing order of privilege and advantage' (ibid.: 6).

Stop and Think Exercise 1.2   From the point of view of Grey and Willmott, what steps could the management researcher take to be more 'ethical' in their approach to undertaking management research?

The distinction between science ('normal science') and non-science ('pseudo-science') is essentially blurred. In the West, for some people, this line of demarcation is relatively clear; for something to be scientific it must use the agreed set of conventions, that is to say, it must use the scientific method. In other cultures, by contrast, alternative forms of inquiry are acceptable, for example meditation, and it seems inappropriate to reject them simply because those cultures are different from ours.

Moreover, the conventions we agree to are simply those which have proved useful in the past. If these conventions, and so our scientific process, cease to be successful, however, it would be time to re-evaluate them. An exponent of this view, from 'management science' or operations research, believes that the extreme complexity of managerial problems, and attempts to apply natural scientific methodology to real-world, essentially social problems, have been responsible for the limited success of management science (Checkland, 1981, 1991).

Similarly, Bygrave (1989) endeavoured to account for what he regards as the unhelpful tendency for researchers to use the methods of the physical sciences in the context of research into entrepreneurship. He pointed out that many of the key contributors to business strategy have educational backgrounds in engineering, natural science and mathematics and are steeped in Newtonian mechanics at a very impressionable age. Amusingly he makes a plea for less 'physics envy' in approaches to research into the emerging field of entrepreneurship. As Van Maanen has more recently commented in his critique of positivism, 'we display more than a little physics envy when we reach for covering laws, causes, operational definitions, testable hypotheses and so forth' (1995a: 133–43). In relation to this issue of 'physics envy', now undertake Stop and Think Exercise 1.3.

Stop and Think Exercise 1.3   What are the main characteristics of the behaviour of the phenomena studied by physicists (i.e. physical things) as opposed to the behaviour of the phenomena studied by management researchers (i.e. human beings)? How are they different and if so what may be the implications for how we might study them? How does this relate to what you found out about yourself during Exercise 1.1? How do these differences relate to the issue of performativity in the natural and social sciences?

The main contemporary criticisms of positivism have been well summarized by Burrell and Morgan (1979: 255) as follows:

> Science is based on 'taken for granted' assumptions, and thus, like any other social practice, must be understood within a specific context. Traced to their source all activities which pose as science can be traced to fundamental assumptions relating to everyday life and can in no way be regarded as generating knowledge with an 'objective', value-free status, as is sometimes claimed. What passes for scientific knowledge can be shown to be founded upon a set of unstated conventions, beliefs and assumptions, just as every day, common-sense knowledge is. The difference between them lies largely in the nature of rules and the community which recognises and subscribes to them. The knowledge in both cases is not so much 'objective' as shared.

Accordingly, we may need to change our conception of science to one of problem-or puzzle-solving, where science is simply regarded as a problem-solving process which uses certain conventions in that process (Kuhn, 1970; Morgan, 1993). In this respect Pettigrew's (1985a) view of problem-solving as a craft may be inadvertently misleading because if researchers are regarded as 'tool users rather than as tool builders then we may run the risk of distorted knowledge acquisition techniques' (Hirschheim, 1985: 15). An old proverb says 'for he who has but one tool, the hammer, the whole world looks like a nail'. For the most part, the way we currently practise much research in management leads directly to that view, but times are changing and increasing awareness of, and sensitivity to, the various assumptions we inevitably make in undertaking any research should further facilitate these challenges to the positivist mainstream of management research.

In view of these concerns it is unsurprising that there are a number of approaches to management research and several ways of classifying them as a means to clarify the available approaches to research. This book aims to present and discuss certain key methodological approaches to management research and their underlying philosophical rationales.

The rationale and structure of the book

Management research may be classified according to its purpose. On the one hand, it may primarily be concerned with solving theoretical issues; something capable of wide generalization but difficult to achieve. On the other hand, it may be much more policy-orientated by being concerned with solving a very specific practical problem in one company; this may be achieved more readily but may be seen to have little application outside the particular case. Simultaneously, research may be classified according to the broad methodological approach taken to achieving its purposes. It is primarily with regard to these different approaches that this book is concerned. The book is not primarily concerned with such issues as selecting and justifying the research topic or with literature searching and reviewing except in so far as these activities may interact with decisions about the methodological approach to the investigation. To that extent, these issues are outlined in the Chapter 2. In the same way, means of presenting research findings will not be considered in any detail. Rather, we propose to address the methodological issues entailed in the various approaches to managerial research and managerial problem-solving. While to some extent we will at times be prescriptive, we hope to avoid a 'cookbook' approach with an emphasis on how research can be done by discussing many examples of how management research is actually done.

In Figure 1.2 we outlined the research process and within this process we will be particularly concerned, to varying degrees, with stage 3, deciding the approach or strategy; stage 4, formulating the plan; stage 5, collecting data; stage 6, interpreting and analysing the data; and stage 7 evaluating one's own findings and those of others. The variation in methodological approach to management research, outlined in this chapter, provides some degree of structure to the chapters that follow. In Chapter 2 we begin by offering some help to the new researcher who wishes to make a start. Then, in Chapter 3, we address the important role of theory in underpinning practical research activities. We believe this is fundamental to understanding, especially so for vocationally orientated management students, who may be inclined to regard some philosophical matters basic to any real appreciation of methodological issues as unnecessarily theoretical and academic. Here we explore the differences between deduction and induction in much more detail and how these competing logics have a different role for theory in undertaking research which impacts upon the nature of methodologies that may be deployed. We then initially turn to deductive methodologies in the subsequent chapters.

Deductive methodologies largely form the mainstream of management research: but it is through an array of largely philosophical, but varied, critiques of this mainstream, that alternative approaches usually begin their methodological trajectories. So in Chapter 4 we begin with looking at the laboratory or 'true' experiment – often seen as the gold standard of deductive approaches. We trace how the logic of the experiment is taken out of laboratory conditions in the form of the quasi-experiment which looks at naturally occurring events. In either case there is some reliance upon highly structured methods derived from those used in the natural sciences. These, as has been mentioned above, have as their basis a hypothesis testing process using standardized instruments and controls and most usually generate quantitative data.

In Chapter 5 we turn to forms of action research which, as with quasi-experiments, sometimes borrow the logic of experimentation but this methodology applies that logic to naturally occurring settings outside the laboratory. In this case, however, the solution of the problem, frequently some aspect of organizational change, is both an outcome of the research and a part of the research process itself, and used to identify further remedial interventions by the researcher. In doing so, action research may or may not involve experimental control groups. Action researchers would often claim both to solve idiosyncratic problems for clients and simultaneously to add to the stock of general knowledge about change processes. However, whilst the methodological origins of action research certainly lie in positivism and experimental logic, over the years it has developed into various participatory and emancipatory forms that have steadily distanced themselves, philosophically and methodologically, from these earlier beginnings.

Survey approaches, the subject matter of Chapter 6, vary in terms of their aims. All surveys use some form of questionnaire to measure phenomena important to the aims of the research. However, some types of survey only try to describe the features of a population whereas others attempt to test already formulated theory deductively using complex statistical analyses in order to simulate the logic of the experiment by asserting control over the variables of interest which have been operationalized by the questionnaire format.

In Chapter 7 we present ethnographic approaches as an example of qualitative research. Firmly within the inductive tradition, qualitative methods usually express a particular philosophical critique of those working deductively that claim that the latter impose an external causal logic upon phenomena that have their own internal logics, deriving from the cultures to which people defer and refer in making subjective sense of their experience of the variable social context in which they socially construct meaningful action. There is, then, in this approach an emphasis on the analysis of subjective accounts which are generated by 'getting inside' situations and often involving the investigator in the everyday flow of life of the people who are being investigated (see Burrell and Morgan, 1979: 5–6). Emphasis is on generating theory grounded in empirical observations which take account of actors' meaning and interpretational systems in order to explain by understanding that subjective domain. However, qualitative methods have been most open to reconfiguration by the philosophical distancing some researchers have adopted in relation to positivism – these issues are taken up, more fully, in Chapter 8.

In Chapter 8 we return to the issue of how our methodological choices are influenced by our implicit and explicit philosophical commitments which we cannot avoid making in undertaking any research. Here we will try to describe the emergence of several key attacks upon the philosophical stance underpinning positivism and consider some of their methodological implications whilst trying to encourage the reader to attempt to interrogate their own philosophical preferences in relation to these developments. One key issue raised by the increasing methodological diversity of management research, and which has partially developed in response to these philosophical debates and controversies, is the vexed issue of evaluating management research. This is taken up in our concluding Chapter 9. The aim of this chapter is to consider different ways in which the quality of management research may be evaluated. However, this is a problematic issue because, since management research is so variable, 'quality' becomes a variable issue and therefore a somewhat elusive concept. There is a real danger that criteria used to judge the quality of the positivist mainstream of management research, that have embedded in them particular philosophical commitments, are assumed to be universally applicable and thus are used inappropriately to evaluate research adopting commitments at odds with those of the mainstream: a serious issue especially if you are on the receiving end of such unfair judgements! So, in this chapter, not only do we discuss different ways of evaluating management research, but also look at how within a positivist framework multi-method approaches, such as the case study, attempt to deal with what are often presented as the inherent strengths and weaknesses that particular methods have built into them, by combining methods in a single study. We trace from this debate philosophical shifts that lead to alternative criteriologies to that presented by the mainstream of management research.

Conclusions

It will be clear from the foregoing that one of our main aims in this book is to challenge the physical science model as the only approach to knowledge acquisition, particularly for management studies. Often one finds that many researchers are committed to a particular school of thought or methodology, either because it has affinity with the academic discipline from which they have originally come, or because of a combination of habit and conviction. It is very often the lack of understanding of the precise nature of alternatives and their philosophical rationales that generates a great deal of criticism and cynicism, some of which may be justified, but more often may be embedded in prejudice and misunderstanding. We hope that an informed debate on the methodological rationales and philosophical assumptions of alternative approaches to management research, together with the implications of such issues for how we evaluate the findings of management research will contribute to a greater understanding and awareness of others.

However, it is important here to emphasize a cautionary note regarding the nature of the research process illustrated in this chapter. Whilst it is always helpful to conceptualize the research process as a series of logically directed steps, this does not of course provide a description of the way in which research is actually conducted. Rather like the managerial process, which sometimes was idealized by textbooks as a logical, orderly one of planning, controlling and the like (Mintzberg, 1973), we must be very careful not to overly idealize the research process in a manner that ignores the often messy nature of actual research in practice. This warning is best summarized by the quotation from Becker below and it is always worth bearing in mind when planning any research.

As every researcher knows there is more to doing research than is dreamt of in philosophies of science, and texts in methodology offer answers to only to a fraction of the problems one encounters. The best laid research plans run up against unforeseen contingencies in the collection and analysis of data; the data one collects may prove to have little to do with the hypothesis one sets out to test; unexpected findings inspire new ideas. No matter how carefully one plans in advance, research is designed in the course of its execution. The finished monograph is the result of hundreds of decisions, large and small, made while the research is under way and our standard texts do not give us procedures and techniques for making those decisions ... It is possible, after all, to reflect on one's difficulties and inspirations and see how they could be handled more rationally the next time around. In short one can be methodological about matters that earlier had been left to chance and improvisation and thus cut down the area of guesswork. (Becker, 1965: 602–3, quoted in Kulka, 1982)

Method of scoring Exercise 1.1

Count each tick as a plus and each cross as a minus. Subtract ticks from crosses. The greater your minus score the more you are disposed towards inductive research approaches and, conversely, the greater your plus score the more you are disposed towards deductive approaches. The nearer your score is to zero, the more flexible you are likely to be when making methodological choices.

Further reading

The philosophical debate between Pfeffer (1993) and Van Maanen (1995a) about the relevance of natural science methodology to management research illustrates two very different perspectives regarding management research which have significant methodological implications which are explored throughout the rest of this book. The nature of the diversity in management research is outlined and explained by Hardy and Clegg (1997) with specific reference to an array of philosophical disputes that continue to impact upon how research is undertaken. Methodological innovations, in the domain of qualitative methods, that have developed in response to some of those philosophical disputes, are explored by Prasad and Prasad (2002). Meanwhile Willmott (1998) provides an interesting account of the development of approaches to management research that question the prevailing positivist consensus and its somewhat technocratic agenda: a critique that is further developed through the evolution of Critical Management Studies which is comprehensively reviewed by Keleman and Rumens (2008) and in an edited collection of essays by Grey and Willmott (2005). For an analysis of how researchers methodologically react to institutional pressures to conform to the quantitative mainstream of management research the reader should turn to Symon et al. (2008). Finally, for an extremely useful overview of the factors that impact upon how researchers make choices about research methods the reader should turn to Buchanan and Bryman (2007). In this article they argue how the choice of research method is not just influenced by the aims of the research and the researcher's own philosophical commitments, but also by a combination of other factors, including those deriving from significant characteristics of the field of research including various institutional pressures, and other personal attributes of the researcher.

These journal articles are freely available on the companion website (www.sagepub.co.uk/gillandjohnson):

Fournier, V. and Grey, C. (2000) At the critical moment: conditions and prospects for critical management studies, *Human Relations*, 53(1): 7–32.
Grey, C. and Mitev, N. (1995) Management education: a polemic, *Management Learning*, 26(1): 73–90.
Symon, G., Buering, A., Johnson, P. and Cassell, C. (2008) Positioning qualitative research as resistance to the institutionalization of the academic labour process, *Organization Studies*, 29(10): 1315–36.

Starting management research

2

Learning outcomes At the end of this chapter the reader should be able to:

- **understand the processes and complexities of selecting and justifying a research topic;**

- **take initial steps with regard to planning the research;**

- **understand the importance of knowing and summarizing the literature in a field of interest;**

- **understand how to begin a literature search;**

- **understand how to undertake a literature review.**

This chapter considers some preliminary matters essential to making a start. These are the selection and justification of the topic, planning the project and reviewing the literature. The rest of the book is then devoted to methodological issues. Nevertheless, it is of course recommended that the whole book should be read at least once before starting a research project.

As we explained in Chapter 1, this book is primarily concerned with offering guidance on the appropriate approach to take to a particular research topic. From experience we have discovered that this matter is generally the most problematic for the researcher. However, we also suggested earlier that research invariably proceeds in roughly the sequence outlined in Figure 1.2, and such a systematic procedure is clearly a useful way of clarifying matters at the outset. However, as also mentioned, it should be recognized that these stages are usually not so clear cut in practice and frequently may be recycled; for example, both the topic and the approach taken to address it may be modified iteratively as the work is planned and action taken.

Primarily, then, in this book we will be concerned with selecting the research approach, and collecting and analysing data and evaluation research findings; that is stages 3 to 7 in the sequence in Figure 1.2, and these matters will be the main concern of later chapters.

Topic selection

Until a topic for the research is identified the work cannot of course start. This obvious point is made to emphasize that so much research, particularly for research degrees, founders because students do not take a systematic approach to topic selection. At the risk of complicating this matter at so early a stage, there are fundamentally two ways of formulating research topics. One is by analysing the literature, formally stating the problem and the major questions, and only then collecting relevant data; the other suggests that this way of formulating problems tends to stifle questions that a more open-ended approach to the topic might stimulate. Both ways have merit and choice depends upon the research approach(es) selected. Broadly speaking, action research and most qualitative approaches exert open-ended constraints on formulating problems while programmed constraints are placed on those using surveys and experiments. Brewer and Hunter (1989) suggest that multi-method strategies may help overcome these constraints upon problem formulation, and we will consider this matter in more detail in Chapter 9.

Students may of course be allocated a research topic. This is less likely in projects that are part of taught programmes in business and management, where students are generally encouraged to find their own topics with some supervisory help since negotiating various stakeholders about the focus of research and about gaining access to organizations is often considered to be a key part of the learning process. Nevertheless, much depends on the disciplinary traditions and the immediate research setting. For example, if the student is working as a member of a research team this may entail fitting into an existing programme of research. Further, in such areas as the natural sciences and engineering the student apparently has less influence in topic selection than is commonly the case in the social sciences (Young et al., 1987: 21).

On the other hand, topic selection may be a somewhat risky process if left entirely to the student, and it would seem that an arrangement whereby student and supervisor work together to define the topic is ideal. There is otherwise a danger that, through lack of experience, topics chosen solely by students may prove impracticable, or alternatively, that the student who is allocated a project will feel no sense of ownership and commitment.

Sources of research topics

Topics may arise in a number of ways. For example, many part-time students in business and management derive topics from their work experience often in consultation with hierarchical superiors. In effect they offer to work as internal consultants on some problem in their own organization and then, when studying at, say, master's level, stand back from the work so that it becomes generalizable to other cases.

Topics may also arise from articles in academic and professional journals, and ideas for research may be stimulated by reports in the media, where an unsupported assertion may provide a fruitful line of inquiry. Such assertions are not confined to the media; authorities in the field may also make assertions which are not well founded. For example, an established researcher may assert that capital budgeting techniques are used not for decision-making but only as a control mechanism – an assertion that may be readily tested by accumulating research evidence from practitioners.

Experts or authorities will frequently write articles or make speeches commenting on the absence of research in a particularly fruitful area and in the same way committee reports may also refer specifically to the need for research in an area under investigation.

Groups of managers at local meetings of professional bodies, such as the Chartered Institute of Personnel and Development, may also be useful sources of research ideas and access to research them. Such suggestions do need to be regarded with a degree of caution, for practitioners are often unaware of research that has already been done, but nevertheless they may often be a useful starting point for a research inquiry.

Research projects in management have also often originated from consultancy, where research questions have arisen in the course of the work. An example was consultancy in a large, nationally known chemical complex to help management commission a technically very sophisticated plant, where the research issues were concerned with the staff's resistance to implementing the new technology. Consultancy helped clarify the topic area as well as lend credibility to the research group in their search for funding in a competitive field in which they previously had little experience.

Finally, many theses and dissertations contain suggestions for further research. Journal articles sometimes refer to the need for further work and since these appear only a year or so after the study they are generally more up to date than books.

Some characteristics of a good research topic

In looking for a research topic certain important characteristics need to be kept in mind. It is unlikely that all these can be satisfied and each student will place them in a different order of priority, but all the following factors should be checked against each topic proposed.

Access   The possibility of access is generally a fairly easy matter to assess. Nevertheless, students often start with ideas for projects where accessibility will clearly prove difficult if not completely impractical. For example, a Ph.D. project to investigate the role of personnel departments in acquisitions and to make comparisons between the UK and North America clearly posed insurmountable problems of accessibility, not least because of the unwillingness of organizations to provide access to such sensitive and traumatic events. Further, and probably for the same reasons, secondary data seemed sparse – but this took a little longer to assess before the topic was drastically revised. In addition, of course, such a topic was also probably too broad, a common fault and one we will address below.

Similarly, topics concerned with, for example, redundancy, competitive markets or managerial stress, while potentially interesting and useful research areas, may be difficult to access. One internationally known research worker once told one of the authors that one of the fundamental problems in carrying out investigations into managerial stress was to gain access to individuals to interview. After many rejections the conclusion was reached that many managers were too stressed to talk to him about it! It has sometimes been cynically remarked that the potentially most rewarding research topics are often those which are also most inaccessible and often considerable ingenuity and persistence may be required to research further in such areas.

However, it should also be borne in mind at this stage that, as Drummond (1989) has pointed out, the use of lateral thinking to concentrate on objectives rather than on obstacles to gaining access to data is a useful technique. In this regard, she provides an example from her own Ph.D. research, which seemed to demand access to coercive organizations such as prisons. Much time and wasted effort were taken up trying to gain access to such organizations through official channels, when a focus on what was actually needed to meet the research aims led to fresh thoughts on how to obtain the necessary data. It was found instead to be comparatively easy to obtain access to released inmates through the National Council for the Care and Resettlement of Offenders, to enable the completion of questionnaires. Similarly, Spencer (1980) gained access to non-executive directors by interviewing some who performed the role part-time in the course of their work as business school academics and were as a consequence probably more sympathetic to a researcher working for a Ph.D.

Achievable in the time available   With limited time available there is a temptation to select a topic before doing the preliminary groundwork suggested here; this temptation should be resisted and time will be saved in the long run.

In general the time taken to accomplish a piece of research is frequently underestimated. The time actually spent on the project is lengthened by delays due to such matters as illness, domestic pressures and part-time work; and, for part-time students, by job changes and pressures. There is a further potential difficulty for students undertaking research part-time in their own organization. While it may be advantageous for the research to be undertaken as part of their normal duties, there may be difficulties if the research depends on the researcher's superior and the organization remaining unchanged throughout the period of the work. Such a case occurred in research being conducted in a region of the National Health Service, where an original plan, based on strategies largely determined by a powerful superior, had to be changed radically following organizational changes. Fortunately, the research design was flexible and the researcher sufficiently resilient to regard such changes as an opportunity rather than a hindrance. This of course frequently has to be the approach in research concerned with complex problems in the relatively uncontrolled conditions found in organizations.

These potential delays are made more manageable by drawing up a research plan, which will indicate the phases of the research and the dates for its completion; an example is given later in this chapter.

Symmetry of potential outcomes   A way of reducing the risk entailed in any project is to try to ensure that, whatever the findings from the work, the results will be equally valuable; this is known as symmetry of potential outcomes.

For example, a research project to explore the effects on managers' careers of holding a postgraduate qualification in a management subject would have symmetrical potential outcomes. If no correlation were found this would be at least as interesting and important as if there were found to be a high correlation. On the other hand, an example of a non-symmetrical outcome might be research which aimed to investigate a possible link between psychoanalytical factors, such as the mid-life crisis, and the personality of the entrepreneurial individual. Establishing such a relationship would clearly be an interesting and potentially useful contribution, but if no relationship were found the result would not be nearly as interesting. The matter of symmetry is particularly important in doctoral studies, where the contribution to knowledge is a principal criterion for the award and the risk entailed in a relative lack of symmetry needs to be minimized.

Student capabilities and interest   This seems an obvious point: clearly, a student with strong capabilities in the behavioural sciences and low numeracy should hesitate before choosing a topic, needing, for example, complex statistical analysis even though it might otherwise be a good one. Similarly, a student with poor descriptive writing skills might be unwise to embark on an ethnographic study.

Finally, it is obviously important for the student to be able to sustain interest in work which may continue for long periods; in the case of higher degrees for a number of years. In these circumstances it is essential that the topic be of particular interest to the student. Thus, the student should carefully assess his or her interests and abilities to ensure they match the proposed research project.

Financial support   In most student projects it is usual for the matter of financial support to have been resolved before the project begins but, even then, there are frequently problems for full-time students in ensuring continuity of support; for example, the curious rules of the research councils (e.g. Economic and Social Research Council) sometimes cause problems of continuity for the researcher.

It is therefore particularly important for the matter of cost to be examined before a topic is finally selected; the lack of funds for travelling, expensive equipment or subsistence may prejudice a successful outcome.

Value and scope of the research   In projects which form part of taught courses the value of the work may usually be judged primarily by its suitability in demonstrating sufficient research competence or problem-solving ability to fulfil the criteria judged necessary to pass the course. For a higher degree by research, both problem-solving ability and research competence are needed and, additionally, the findings should add to the general body of knowledge without necessarily being of value to the community at large.

There are, however, several reasons why the value of the research should be considered when topics are selected. Both students and supervisors are likely to be more highly motivated if the work has obvious value and examiners, too, are likely to be more interested and award higher marks if the work is clearly making a contribution to the solution of a significant problem. Furthermore, there is growing concern by government and public funding bodies that publicly funded research should be devoted to problems judged to be important and of practical application.

Closely related to the issue of value is the extent to which the topic has the scope to challenge current beliefs, to be surprising and to affect public policy. For example, personal research for a higher degree into risk-taking by decision-makers had considerable scope, particularly when it was fortuitously discovered that decisions taken by groups were apparently more risky than the same decisions taken by individuals. The implications of such findings, if confirmed, were clearly enormous and led to considerable research activity (Brown, 1965: Ch. 13).

Findings with this degree of scope will rarely present themselves to the student researcher but topics low in both surprise and value should if possible be avoided and the search continued for topics which better meet these criteria.

Techniques for generating research topics

When defining a research area most researchers move from a wide field to a manageable topic using some of the criteria mentioned above. We suggested earlier that such criteria are best applied systematically, and the same is true when narrowing down what may be a rather vague list of early ideas into something capable of being researched. On the other hand, some researchers may have already defined their topics and, while this may at first sight seem ideal, the work may be impractical or have already been done; either way, the inexperienced researcher may not be aware of the position.

Techniques which may be used to clarify topics owe much to work on creativity by, for example, De Bono (1971), Parnes et al. (1977) and Miller (1983).

Simplistically, one might start by using brainstorming methods to provide a list of first thoughts in a particular topic area and then reviewing items on the list by deciding what is meant by each idea. For example, if it were proposed to investigate managerial stress in a particular organization, questions which might arise in a non-evaluated, brainstormed list might be:

1   What is managerial stress?
2   How is it to be identified?
3   Do 'managers' include 'supervisors'?
4   Might some managers be more stressed than others?
5   Will this be a function of the individual?
6   Or of the job?
7   Or of the supervisory style?
8   Might the investigation be focused on particular departments?
9   If so, which?
10 Does stress increase at particular times?
11 Is it possible to predict stressful events?
12 What remedial measures may be appropriate?
13 Is managerial stress openly discussed in organizations?

The next step with such a list is to analyse it carefully and ensure that it is clear what is meant by the terms used and what is to be discovered and why. In this way the aims and objectives of the study will become clearer, as will the tasks which require to be performed; irrelevant topics will also stand a better chance of being eliminated at this stage.

As well as checklists some authors (e.g. Howard and Sharp, 1983) suggest a more systematic approach to topic generation, by the use of particular techniques employed in the management of research and development (Jantsch, 1967). Such techniques have as their foundation the use of analogy, which may usefully indicate a line of inquiry by its resemblance to the one under consideration, or it may suggest a methodology that, having been employed in one field, may be applied to another. An example of the former was useful in suggesting approaches to consultants who were studying the implementation of computer-aided design into small businesses. Such a specialized topic had apparently had little research attention but when looking into related fields, such as the implementation of high technology in large manufacturing companies, it became clear that advances made there could, by analogy, provide useful insights in the field under study. Similarly, the methodology used to study marketing managers (Grafton-Small, 1985) was helped by analogy with the methods used by Watson (1977) in his study of personnel managers.

Other analogy-based techniques that may be employed to generate topics are forced relationships, attribute-listing, relevance trees and morphological analysis. Most of these techniques are best performed in a group, where the synergy introduced by an effective group process usually stimulates creativity. While research is often thought of as an individual effort, particularly in relation to student research projects, the usefulness of working in groups at particular stages of the work should not be underestimated.

Table 2.1 Morphological analysis

Objective	Method	Target
Exploratory	Experiments	Individuals
Exploratory	Quasi-experiments	Protessional group
Clarification	Action research	Department
Theory	Surveys	Interdepartment organization
Problem-solving	Case studies	Multiple
Conceptual	Longitudinal	Interorganization
Predictive	Ethnographic	National

Forced relationships involve attempting to relate anything in one's awareness to the problem at hand. It may be a particularly useful technique when an individual is temporarily bogged down and needs to be helped to bring back a flow of ideas.

Attribute-listing, another technique to aid the flow of ideas, involves identifying particular aspects, or attributes, of the research area and then focusing on one of them.

Relevance trees are used to suggest ways of developing related ideas from a broad starting concept. As groups of related ideas are produced it becomes possible to identify manageable research areas. Relevance trees are therefore particularly useful for producing alternative areas for research or for helping to bring into focus otherwise vague ideas for a research topic.

Morphological analysis applies the notions of attribute-listing and forced relationships in a matrix, with the purpose of generating a large number of alternative ideas. For example, a morphological analysis of types of management research projects might produce three lists of attributes under factor headings as shown in Table 2.1. Different research projects can then be generated by taking one attribute from each of the three columns. For example, an exploratory survey might be made of a professional group to define some research issues.

Such an analysis can be useful in offering insights and may be of particular help in focusing a topic, although it is advisable to keep the number of factors low as morphological analysis is capable of producing a large number of alternatives.

All these techniques create many alternatives, which are of course useful only when carefully evaluated. (The ideal creative individual may be the manic-depressive who generates ideas in his or her manic phase and evaluates them later!)

Planning the project

In their book, *How to Get a PhD*, Phillips and Pugh (1987) refer to the need for planning as a means of overcoming some of the main difficulties inherent in such a large individual undertaking. What they have to say is also true of many difficulties.

These difficulties stem from initial enthusiasm, perhaps leading to over-ambitious projects, followed by periods of alienation as the earlier excitement diminishes, deadlines become increasingly irksome and the boredom of concentrating on a particular project for a long period becomes predominant. There are periods of feeling stuck, often towards the middle of the research, and other times when the work proceeds speedily and purposefully, especially when the end of the work is in sight. While all this may seem part of the very nature of such endeavour, the remedy for many of these problems is to manage time carefully by systematic timetabling and planning.

People often run into trouble because they are unable to identify a manageable focus for their research topic. Translating the bright idea into a set of research aims and objectives will make research not only easier in that it is more manageable, but also better in that from the outset you will have a clearer idea about how you will undertake your research, who it might involve, where it might be undertaken, and when you need to do things. This might sound obvious but, regardless of the level at which students are working, it is often a lack of focus which causes people difficulties. Thinking through the what, how, who, where and when will also avoid the problem that often student research is much too over ambitious given the resources available. This is why virtually all research projects are best set out in the form of a proposal, which will generally be a summary of the researcher's more detailed plan. Some experienced researchers advocate the use of network analysis, a technique often applied to the planning of construction projects and which seems easily applicable to research work, particularly if students are already familiar with this approach (Howard and Sharp, 1983: 48).

The essentials of a research plan are contained in the questions asked, for example, in most universities' application forms to register a higher degree, and are implicit in the demand to submit a research proposal on well organized postgraduate and undergraduate courses that have a dissertation component. Candidates are asked to define their field of interest, then their aims and finally a plan, clarifying the proposed phases of the work, with dates; outlining the state of current knowledge and how the proposal intends to add to that knowledge; and, finally, the methods that will be used to research the topic. For example, a Ph.D. proposal (Noble, 1989) was structured as follows:

Management research example: Organizational design and the implementation of office information systems (Noble, 1989)

Title: Organizational Design and the Implementation of Office Information Systems

Aim: To identify the effects of different organization design strategies on the implementation and successful exploitation of office systems.

What is Known: The exploitation of office information systems is much less than anticipated in the early 1980s, in part because senior management are unsure of the strategic benefits of office automation, where to start, or how to manage the change process (Prince Waterhouse 1988/89). Research on the organizational effects of office automation has focused on the introduction of word processing and the work and attitudes of typists and secretaries (Wainwright and Francis, 1984). Less is known about the effects of computerized office systems on interdepartmental relations and organizational structure and performance, (Olson and Lucas, 1982). The researcher will focus on the managerial issues involved in the successful introduction of new technology which seem to depent on the interaction of technical and organizational factors and the quality of the implementation process (Marcus and Robey, 1983).

Plan of work

Phase One

1–4 Months
Literature searching on the nature and types of office systems: the strategic use of information technology, implementation approaches and methodologies and qualitative research methods. Literature searching to continue throughout the project but particularly intense throughout this period.

1–6 Months
Comparison of implementation methodologies used by consultants, vendor and user organizations, with particular attention to organizational design implications.

Locating and entering six organizations which have recently implemented office systems.

6–12 Months
Three of the six organizations accessed in depth.

Phase Two

9 Months
Literature survey to be exended to analogous topics such as the management of innovation and methodological approaches widened to include. For example, Pava (1983): Mumford et al. (1985): Checkland (1981): and Eason (1989). Survey results analysed.

Fiedwork in the three organizations to continue and to be three additional sites to represent differing implementation approaches and organization types.

An original contribution to knowledge is expected to lie in the relationship between technology and organization structure: the role of different management strategies in determining the outcome of technical change: and the identification of those environments and organizational constraints which inhibit the use of 'best practice'.

Phase Three

7 Months
Completion of Ph.D. thesis. Word processing and editing.

Methods

Research methods will be employed to build up case material from which generalizations will be made.

Semi-structured interviews will be conducted with senior management, IT staff, users, and heads of user departments.

Documents such as, for example, training manuals will be analysed.

A postal survey of 250 managing directors of leading UK companies will be conducted to discover the state of the art. i.e. the relevance of office systems to business strategy and the problems encountered in introducing it.

References

Checkland, P. (1981) *System Thinking Systems Practice,* Chichester Wiley.

Eason, K. (1989) *Information Technology and Organisational Change.* Taylor and Francis.

Marcus, M. L. and Robey, D. (1983) *The Organisational Validity of MIS. Human Relations* 3, 6, 203–206.

Mumford, E. et al. (eds.) (1985) *Research Methods in Information System.* Elsevier Science Publishers BV.

Olson, M. H. and Lucas, H. C (1982) The impact of office automation on the organization: some implications for research and practice. *Communications of the ACM*, 25. 11. Nov.

Pava, C. (1983) *Managing New Office Technology: an Organisational Strategy.* The Free Press.

Price Waterhouse (1988/9) Information Technology Review.

Wainwright, J. and Francis, A. (1984) *Office Automation. Organisation and the Nature of Work.* Gower.

Clearly, then, planning is an important factor in determining the effectiveness and efficiency with which research is carried out. It is especially useful and motivating for students when stages in the work can be identified and dates agreed with supervisors. As with all plans, it will need to be revised from time to time but with an adequate plan progress can be assessed at any time, problems are more likely to be foreseen and contingencies can be taken care of.

Reviewing the literature

Whatever its scale, any research project will necessitate reading what has been written on the subject and gathering it together in a critical review which demonstrates some awareness of the current state of knowledge on the subject, its limitations and how the proposed research aims to add, or contribute, to what is known. Indeed, one of the criteria for any research degree is to demonstrate a critical awareness of background studies and matters relating to the thesis.

What is a literature review?

The aim of the literature review is to demonstrate the researcher's familiarity with existing knowledge of the subject area and to provide insights in the field. As such, it has been argued that reviewing the literature is in itself a 'research activity' that can make a contribution to knowledge (Easterby-Smith et al., 2008). More generally, it is seen as a way of developing a rationale for the significance of the research and importantly where it will lead. An effective review will present the case and the context for the proposed research and it is, therefore, 'important to demonstrate the relationship of the work to previous research in the area' (Lee and Lings, 2008: 78).

The review, however, has purposes other than to simply demonstrate knowledge of previous work in the field and the research methods literature offers many opinions as to the multiple purposes of the review. For example, apart from providing the background to the research and identifying contemporary debates, issues and questions in the field, Ridley (2008) suggests it may be used to provide definitions to clarify how terms are being used in the context of the research and it may be used to show how your work extends, challenges or addresses a gap in work in the field of interest.

Whatever the case, at a general level we can identify a number of important outcomes of a well conducted literature review.

- It helps to describe a topic of interest and refine either research questions or directions in which to look;
- It presents a clear description and evaluation of the theories and concepts that have informed research into the topic of interest;
- It clarifies the relationship to previous research and highlights where new research may contribute by identifying research possibilities which have been overlooked so far in the literature;
- It reviews opinions and provides insights into the topic of interest that are both methodological and substantive;
- It helps discover strategies and methodologies appropriate to the research question and objectives;
- It presents the theoretical and methodological contexts for the proposed study which demonstrates why it is important and timely;

- It demonstrates powers of critical analysis by, for instance, exposing taken for granted assumptions underpinning previous research and identifying the possibilities of replacing them with alternative assumptions;
- It justifies any new research through a coherent critique of what has gone before and demonstrates why new research is both timely and important;
- The extent and form of this depends upon whether a deductive or inductive research strategy (discussed in Chapter 3) has been adopted.

Clearly it is important to start reviewing the relevant literature from the outset of research – even when the topic of interest is still unclear. Indeed, the review of the literature will help to refine a focus, help to identify gaps in prior studies which new research might fill, and most importantly enable the researcher to set conceptual boundaries on what is relevant. Moreover, Easterby-Smith et al. (2008) identify three discernable features of a literature review:

1 There needs to be critical engagement with previous research such that gaps in the theory and knowledge are identified;
2 It should not recount knowledge and ideas already written about, but should build progressively towards the research questions to be addressed in the study;
3 The review is not a one off thing – it is ongoing throughout study.

So whilst literature searches and reviews usually take place early in the research sequence, keeping up to date with the literature on the topic of course continues throughout the period of the research. As mentioned earlier, most projects will have a section that gives an overview of the existing theory that underpins the research, however, this is not the only area where literature needs to be reviewed. Table 2.2 (based on Hart, 1998) summarizes the different uses of the literature throughout the research project.

Table 2.2   Research report: use of literature

1. Introduction	Show aims, objectives, scope, rationale and design features of the research. Rationale is usually supported by references to other works which have already identified the broad nature of the problem.
2. Literature Review	Demonstrate skills in library searching: show command of the subject area and understanding of the problem; justify research topic, design and methodology through a coherent critique of what has gone before.
3. Methodology	Show appropriateness of techniques used to gather data and methodological approaches employed. Relevant references from literature are often used to show understanding of data collection techniques and methodological implications, and to justify their use over alternative techniques.
4. Findings and discussion	Show command of the subject area and understanding of the problem; justify and validate the credibility of findings. Develop convincing arguments for relevance of finding. Discussions usually supported by references to other works that have already identified similar results or other interesting issues.

Adapted from Hart, C. (1998) *Doing a Literature Review*. Sage.

Engaging with the literature is a good way to start to develop your research questions and aims. For example, you may have an interest in effective Human Resource Management or developing commitment, but how do you develop a researchable issue? In this case, Lee and Lings (2008) suggest that you need to adopt an emerging strategy. You start to read widely. Once you have, and thereby clarified your interest in the field you can then use a more directed strategy, the subject of the next section.

Undertaking the review

Clearly, in any research the relevant literature is used to perform different functions within a single piece of research. Nevertheless, as Hart shows in Table 2.2, much of this is about demonstrating and justifying the nature, focus, methodology and contribution of the research in question. Here we shall focus upon the use on the literature in row 2 of Table 2.2 where a key question relates to how to approach the review of a particular area, that is, what type of review is appropriate? Writing the literature review can be a difficult exercise as Lees and Lings (2008: 97) suggest, 'you need to provide some kind of added value to the literature', that is the literature review should make 'an intellectual contribution to your research project'.

The literature review needs to be structured around your research aims and there is a need to synthesize the literature through identifying and developing relevant themes or patterns in that literature. It should lead to a focusing of the research problem through a theoretical conceptualization of the topic, such that the review either articulates prior formulated theory and in doing so justifies the hypotheses which you are going to test (deductively) through the collection of data, or articulates the concepts/embedded problems, which you are going to (inductively) explore in the field and thus constitute what are called 'sensitizing concepts' that in effect are directions in which to initially look when conducting fieldwork that aims to generate theory out of observation and data collection (see Chapters 3 and 7). Regardless of these important issues you need to plan your literature review and, in particular, how you are going to conduct the search of the relevant literature.

Planning the literature search

1 *Identify the topic and focus.* This entails being very clear about what it is you are going to research because this sets some initial parameters for your literature search and thereby makes it more manageable. Start to focus your search as conceptual clarity develops and set parameters accordingly.

2 *Identify and define key terms.* Usually your research will link together several phenomena, sometimes in the form of a research question. Usually these phenomena are indicated by the use of an abstract concept (see Chapter 3). For instance, you might be interested in researching the extent of employee organizational commitment in post-bureaucracies. This immediately raises several definitional issues which need to be sorted out. For instance, does the term employee include or exclude managers? Does it refer to part-time as well as full-time employees? Do you have a clear idea of what you mean by post-bureaucracy – are other terms used for this kind of organization – such as high performance organization? The same goes for organizational commitment. Basically you need to have a clear idea of what you might mean by these terms so that you can define the limits of the literature research.

3 *Define the parameters of the literature research and determine key words.* This is vitally important. In our example there is a huge literature upon

either organizational commitment or post-bureaucracy. There is a much smaller literature that combines the two. Obviously you would need to examine very closely any literature that specifically investigates both organizational commitment and post-bureaucracy together as this is the most relevant for you. But you would also need to look at the literature specifically about just organizational commitment as well as that which looks at just post-bureaucracy. Other parameters for the literature search that would need some thought are issues like: time frame (how far back do you go); sector (public or private sector or both); geographical location: is this relevant or important to your literature search. The aim is to create a list of possible terms, or key words, that you can use in your literature search.

4 *Identify possible literature sources.* Here you need to think about whether or not the materials you are going to search are limited to journal articles available electronically and therefore easier to search (and access) via key words, or does it include books, theses, bibliographies, etc. Be very careful here, often some very important research has been published as chapters in edited books, etc. and thus may not come up in an electronic search of journal articles.

5 Once you have begun the literature search be sure to *record and evaluate* the bibliographic details and content of the literature sources you access and try to assess its importance (see Stop and Think Exercise 2.1). Develop a flexible structure for your search at an early stage – then you know where things go. Use references given in the literature you have reviewed to guide you to new sources or sometimes to reconfigure your parameters of the search.

Stop and Think Exercise 2.1   Identify two or three key words that capture an area of interest, e.g. post-bureaucracy and organizational commitment. Enter these words into one of the search programmes available in your academic library such as Academic Google. Choose from the list of articles, books and papers that will appear an article which seems to be very important in your area and which has some empirical content. Have a go at summarizing the content of each these articles in terms of the following questions:

> What are the aims and objectives of the article?
> What does their literature review claim about the area they are investigating?
> What is the theoretical stance of the article, including any hypotheses that are presented for testing or any sensitizing concepts that are articulated?
> What is the methodology used by the authors and how have they justified the chosen approach?
> What did they find?
> How important are these findings for your area of interest?
> What are the strengths and weaknesses of the reported research?

Structuring of a literature review

Whilst searching the literature is an important aspect of any literature review, a literature review is not merely a description or list of published sources. Rather it should articulate your own considered opinion which does not take anything that is written at face value: a critical stance upon the different themes and orientations evident in the literature which is defended and justified. Arriving at such a position involves an attempt at demonstrating how the relevant literature fits together and/or varies, through outlining its substantive and methodological content and relating different writings to each other and exposing their differences and similarities whilst evaluating their evident strengths and weaknesses. From these discernible patterns there has to be an attempt to show how the literature informs and justifies the intended research whilst initially indicating how that research will simultaneously contribute to, and perhaps even move beyond, that existing literature either substantively, or methodologically or philosophically – or even all three! This should involve you developing a personal position upon what you have read, which you have justified through argument by exposing the taken-for-granted assumptions, values and theories that other writers inevitably project onto their subjects of interest and thereby influence what they argue or find. In doing so you too will be making assumptions but it is best to articulate and try to defend them in the review, thereby justifying your position and demonstrating that you can articulate and understand the choices you have made. In other words, a well done literature review entails an attempt at interpreting the information gathered and presented such that there is a clear structure of how the different elements fit together so that the intended research focus, aims, objectives, questions, etc. are clearly positioned in relation to that existing literature and arises out of a critique of that literature. In doing so you will set the context of your own research and demonstrate that you understand the relevant literature. Naturally this raises the issue of how can such a tall order be accomplished?

At the beginning of any literature review it is very important to state the aims listed in Table 2.3 This is a useful check list for anyone beginning to write a literature review and it sets key parameters for what should follow.

Having defined the aims and parameters of the literature review in its introduction, usually reviews start with a general description of the relevant literature which compares and contrasts the work of key researchers in the area. Often there will be a chronological structure here that illustrates the development of the field from its inception through to the latest research. This narrative structure is used to outline the different ways in which the topic has been studied highlighting methodological variation as well as to summarize key findings. The emphasis here is to identify patterns or themes within the literature and to present some form of critical evaluation that serves to justify the aims and objectives of your own research.

The review of previous related research should also help you to identify key concepts and variables relevant to the research which may have been defined by researchers in different ways and thus inconsistently reported – something you may need to try to resolve in the literature review. With the development of this picture of

Table 2.3　Main components of an introduction to literature review

Aim	Means
To announce the topic of your review	A clear and concise statement
To state the purpose of your review	A careful explanation of what you aim to achieve
To explain the relevance of your review	An indication of its importance to your research, theoretically and methodologically
To establish your credibility	Information on why you should be seen as competent to write about the topic

Adapted from Hart, C. (1998) *Doing a Literature Review*. Sage.

the different ways in which the topic has been studied usually there is an attempt to narrow the focus of the review down to work that is most relevant to your research topic in order to position your research substantively and methodologically in relation to this existing literature. In doing so there should be opportunities to highlight those issues where your research will provide additional, or indeed alternative, insights thereby further justifying your research project by elaborating the nature of its predicted contribution to the field.

However, it is important to emphasize that the outcome of your literature review should vary according to whether or not your intention is to conduct deductive or inductive empirical research. With a deductive approach the role of the literature review is to critically review existing knowledge and to enable an exploration of the relationships between different variables or constructs of interest. The primary aim is to develop hypotheses from the review that are testable by collecting data (see Chapter 3). Thus, a literature review may end with articulation hypotheses or predictions which you wish to test out in the situation under study. Indeed, at the end of the literature review you should be able to say: 'This is the exact study which needs doing in order to move this area forward'. However, with inductive research the purposes of the literature review are rather different. Whilst the issues of contextualization and justification in relation to an existing body of knowledge outlined by the literature review are equally important, inductive approaches are concerned with developing a pre-understanding of the substantive area of interest that provides a starting point for research in terms of what are called sensitizing concepts (see Chapter 7). In a sense these are foreshadowed guidelines for research which may be of help to the researcher during fieldwork rather than the precise hypotheses for testing of the deductive approach.

Good literature reviews will vary significantly in style and content. However poor literature reviews tend to share one or more of the following problems:

- A lack of organization and structure;
- A lack of focus and coherence indicating that the aims of the research have not been thorough and thus the topic has not been clearly defined;
- Much too repetitive and verbose rather than being incisive in its description and critique of the literature;
- A failure to cite influential research in the field under investigation;
- A failure to outline recent developments in the field under investigation;
- A failure to critically evaluate cited research thereby become a mere description of the literature rather than a review;
- Citing irrelevant research because there is no focus to the intended research;
- An over dependence on a restricted number of literature sources;
- An over–use of web-based references and hence the danger of using literature of a dubious provenance.

At this stage it is appropriate to make three important cautionary points. First, it is not uncommon for researchers to become bogged down in reading the literature so that it not only becomes a means of avoiding the tough process of writing but also often seems to become unhelpful in advancing original ideas, as the student becomes submerged in those of other people and thereby loses their own power and authority. Accordingly, the state of the literature search needs to be kept under close review, in consultation with supervisors and colleagues, to avoid becoming over concerned with other people's work at the expense of creativity.

Second, writing literature reviews can be a demanding exercise, for a critical review should provide the reader with a statement of the state of the art and major questions and issues in the field under consideration. Often they seem to be uncritical catalogues of all that has been found which vaguely relates to the topic regardless of the merits of the work. What is required is an insightful evaluation of what is known which leads naturally to a clarification of the gaps in the field and the way in which the proposed research is intended to fill them.

Third, some of the above problems can be avoided by developing a flexible structure for the review and beginning writing at the outset. Trying to read everything then trying to write it up is a daunting task because it is unlikely you will appreciate the significance or possible location in the review of what you read without some point of reference provided by a working structure. Therefore, it is most important when embarking on a literature search to ensure that everything that is read is noted systematically at the time. After quite a short period the likelihood of remembering is remote and much time may be wasted at later stages of the research, for example in locating a precise reference that has not been recorded when read. Such records are best kept on a card index or, even better, on a computerized file so that they can be searched, added to and sorted in multiple ways as required. This is important because references from the literature, which has been read, guide the researcher to new sources – no new references appearing in literature sources imply that the search for literature is nearing an end. Once a system is decided upon it is advisable to stick to it.

Conclusions

In summary, in order to make a start on a research topic it is necessary to identify the broad area in which the work will be conducted and then to focus down into a manageable topic. Whilst many students struggle with this early stage of the research process it is vital to develop a coherent and justified focus for the research which is viable – without this, all subsequent stages of the research are in effect jeopardized. The next step is to make a plan by which stages in the research will be achieved. Alongside these early activities it will be necessary to search and review the literature relating to the field under study to look for gaps in the broad area and to secure an early appreciation of work already completed or under way. Whilst at this early stage the literature review needs to be geared to justifying the focus of your research and demonstrating that you appreciate what work has already been done in your chosen area, it is important to realize that the literature is relevant also to various other stages in the research processes (see Table 2.1) and often a literature review may need to be considerably redeveloped as research progresses and issues of concern might change.

We may now turn to the primary focus of this book: the approaches to management research, their choice and justification.

Further reading

At a fairly elementary level and designed primarily for education and social science students, Bell (2005) is a very useful text for helping the beginner researcher covers such issues from planning, reviewing and keeping records of the literature to choosing a topic and negotiating access to research sites. Further excellent advice and guidelines are also given in Punch (2006) who considers issues such as: developing research proposals; planning a research strategy; and a discussion of research ethics. Also, Locke et al. (2007) give some helpful insight into writing research proposals for different audiences whether the research is quantitative or qualitative. Similarly, Howard and Sharp (1983) is especially helpful in introducing systematic techniques to many aspects of getting research projects under way. They are particularly helpful as their examples are drawn mainly from management research. Meanwhile Phelps et al. (2007) provide much well thought through practical advice for postgraduates about dealing with the everyday issues that arise during research.

Focused specifically on Ph.D. research, and drawing its examples mainly from management and business, is Phillips and Pugh's classical text (1987). This is written largely as advice to the student and is particularly helpful on time management, managing the supervisor and the procedural tasks necessary for successful completion. Another particularly useful book on Ph.D. research is Rudestam and Newton (1992). This American text gives some excellent advice to doctoral students about coping with complexities that arise due to the interaction of both content and process issues. Likewise, Oliver's (2008) book gives useful suggestions for actually writing up research in the form of a thesis with excellent advice about preparing for the oral examination and publishing findings.

A very comprehensive book that takes literature reviewing to a fine art is Cooper (1989). Whilst the book is concerned with integrative literature reviews in the broad social sciences it should also prove helpful to the management researcher. It uses a phase model of the research process to discuss different aspects of literature reviewing. Students should read the introduction at least, and then further chapters according to needs. Excellent advice and comprehensive guidance about dealing with the literature is provided by Hart's companion books on doing a literature search (2001) and then writing a literature review (1998). Practical and detailed advice on all aspects of using the internet for undertaking literature searches is provided by O'Dochartaigh (2001). Finally, if you want to look at how literature reviews are done by professional researchers there are two excellent journals that are devoted to publishing such work, both of which are usually available electronically: *International Journal of Management Reviews* and *Academy of Management Review*.

This journal article is freely available on the companion website (www.sagepub.co.uk/gillandjohnson):

Buchanan, D.A. and Bryman, A. (2007) Contextualizing methods choice in organizational research, *Organization Research Methods*, 10(3): 483–501.

The role of theory in management research

3

Learning outcomes At the end of this chapter the reader should be able to:

- understand what is meant by the term theory and identify what theories are and what they enable us to do;

- understand the relationship between theory and management practice;

- differentiate deductive approaches to management research from inductive approaches;

- appreciate the variety of methods used in management research;

- understand the rationale for the rest of this book.

In this chapter we introduce a series of debates about philosophical issues pertinent to the role of theory in management research. The different positions and competing rationales articulated in these debates implicitly underpin the only too evident variation in how management research is undertaken. Hence, an understanding of these debates is pivotal to enabling an understanding of how management research is variably undertaken in practice. First, this chapter identifies what theories are and then briefly explores the interrelationship between theory and management practice, making the point that there is nothing so practical as a good theory. Second, it then covers the philosophical foundations of inductive and deductive methodological approaches to research, wherein the relationship of the research to theory varies, and compares their competing underlying rationales. Third, using the inductive–deductive frame of reference, the chapter concludes by initially describing and explaining the variety of research methods used in management research; methods which form the foci for subsequent chapters.

The methodological importance of theory

Key methodological concept

Theory

A scheme or system of ideas or statements held to explain a group of facts or phenomena; a statement of general laws, principles, or causes of something known or observed (Oxford English Dictionary).

Trying to understand the relationship between theory and management research methods is a very complicated task which we are going to undertake in stages starting with this chapter. Here we shall argue that the varying role of theory in management research is of fundamental significance in understanding why management researchers approach their research in very different ways. By collecting data in different ways, some management researchers are trying to test theory through observation whilst others are trying to create, or discover, theory through observation. In other words, these different theoretical aims lead directly to the deployment of different methods by which management research is undertaken. Largely these different theoretical aims express deeply held philosophical assumptions about how it is best to explain the various aspects of human behaviour which management researchers are interested in. However, the importance of theory to us goes beyond an initial understanding of such methodological variation. For instance, although we might not be immediately aware of it, our everyday lives are fundamentally interwoven with our use of theory. Here we shall argue that theories influence how we understand and explain what is going on around us and how we practically do things. One important aspect of this 'theory-dependent' character relates to the way in which the various practical activities in which we routinely engage might be seen as involving regular attempts at creating, applying and evaluating theory – even though we might not necessarily usually notice this aspect of our practices.

Here it is important to emphasize that our use of the term 'theory-dependent' must not be confused with the term 'theory-laden'. Although the two are intimately related, the latter specifically refers to the way in which the prior theories of the observer are taken to influence how he or she engages with, and makes sense of, the world. That is, as Norwood Hanson (1958: 7) famously claimed, 'there is more to seeing than meets the eyeball'. Thus, the issue of how observation may be 'theory-laden' raises the problem that perhaps there is no independent or neutral point from which an observer might occupy and objectively observe the 'facts' of the world and thus all knowledge is knowledge from particular points of view or even paradigms (see Burrell and Morgan, 1979; Schultz and Hatch, 1996) or schools of thought (Ofori-Dankwa and Julian, 2005). The methodological implications of the possibly 'theory-laden' nature of observation are considered in later chapters of this book, especially Chapter 8. Meanwhile, we shall use the term 'theory-dependent' to specifically refer to the way in which practical activities which human beings undertake, in all circumstances, involve the use of theory in various ways. This everyday variation in the use of theory, which we all deploy, has a direct relevance to the kinds of research methods used by social scientists generally and management researchers specifically.

Theory and practice

To many readers, particularly those who might perceive themselves as 'practical people', the claim that all our everyday practical activities are theory-dependent might seem an absurd assertion. Often such a view is expressed in the lament of vocationally orientated management and business students that particular courses are too 'theoretical', or 'academic', and hence irrelevant to the 'real' world of their chosen careers. By implication, academics are seen to occupy 'ivory towers' that are far removed from the professional activities of practising managers. Intriguingly this lament resonates with the archaic Platonic–Aristotelian view that theoretical knowledge was knowledge acquired for its own sake, rather than for some practical use.

Indeed, both Plato and Aristotle had severed theory from practice in the sense that they distinguished between episteme (genuine theoretical knowledge that was an end in itself) and doxa (opinions or beliefs suitable only for the conduct of practical affairs). However, for many commentators such a view tended to endow a submissiveness on the part of people to nature's vagaries because it divorced knowledge from practice and hence stymied our ability to develop and use our knowledge to intervene and assert practical control over our natural environments. Episteme, which had a higher social status and perceived value, was more about passive contemplation of the world rather than about directing interventions to promote desirable change. To some extent this view of knowledge and science eventually lost its dominance during the seventeenth and eighteenth centuries with the arrival of a new version of the scientific enterprise articulated by people such as Francis Bacon (Tiles, 1987; Johnson and Duberley, 2000). This alternative philosophical stance emphasized the necessity for science to provide knowledge and theory for the control of nature through the discovery of regularities or patterns which allowed for the prediction of, intervention into, and manipulation of, nature to meet human needs. Moreover, as we shall try to demonstrate, the conception of theory as being divorced from practice is grounded in a misunderstanding of what theories are and what they enable us to do. We shall now try to illustrate the fundamental importance of theory in relation to practice.

During our everyday lives we all regularly attempt to understand the events that occur around us. For instance, in regard to the social behaviour of the people with whom we have regular contact, whether colleagues at work or friends and neighbours, we routinely have expectations (i.e. predictions) about the way they will behave in particular circumstances. These expectations are closely tied to explanations of why they behave in the ways that they do. These expectations and explanations might concern rather mundane events such as a friend's change in mood, or the behaviour of particular groups of colleagues at work, or even more personally distant events such as the performance of the national football team or the apparent nationwide increase in the incidence of particular types of criminal behaviour. Regardless of the particular focus of these expectations and explanations, when the former are not fulfilled or when the latter appear to be wrong, we will often reflect upon recent events and experiences and thereby begin to generate new webs of explanations and expectations that help us understand and cope with the events that impact upon us (Law and Lodge, 1984: 125). This process might result in our changing the way in which we do things, such as how we relate to friends or communicate with colleagues at work in particular circumstances. It might also lead us to suggest remedial strategies for dealing with perceived social problems which, for instance, we think the government ought to implement. It also involves our creation, application and evaluation of theory.

Figure 3.1 | Kolb's experiential learning cycle. Adapted from Kolb et al., 1979: 38. Kolb, David A., Osland, Joyce S., Rubin, Irwin M., *Organizational Behaviour: An Experimental Approach*, 6th edition © 1995, p. 49. Reprinted by permission of Pearson Education Inc., Upper Saddle River, NJ.

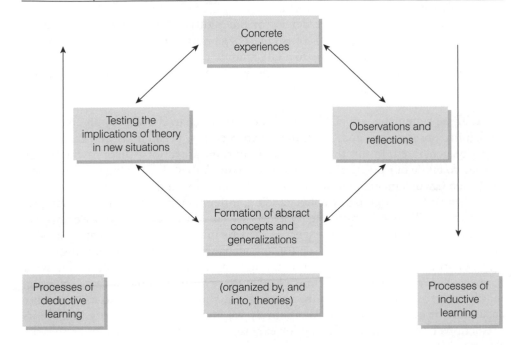

For Kolb et al. (1979), although their terminology is somewhat different, the above processes are linked to how human beings learn and can be diagrammatically represented by the model in Figure 3.1. According to Kolb, learning might start *inductively* with the experience of an event or stimulus, which the individual then reflects upon in trying to make sense of it. This might lead to the generation of explanations of how or why what was observed actually happened in the way it did – explanations that can then be used to form an abstract rule or guiding principle that can be extrapolated (or generalized) to new situations similar to that already experienced. Alternatively, for Kolb, learning can start *deductively* at this point where such an abstract rule is merely inherited from other people by the learner, along with its web of explanations and expectations, and is subsequently applied by that learner and thereby practically tested out. In either case, whether the rule is received from others or generated out of the prior personal experience and reflection, its testing in new situations creates a source of new experiences which enable consequent reflection, observation and ultimately new rules.

Kolb et al. (1979) also suggest that particular individuals might emphasize particular elements of the learning cycle to the neglect of others due to the presence of particular predilections into which they have been previously socialized: for example, the emphasis may be a product prior to education and/or professional training.

For our purposes here, what is very significant about the processes described in Figure 3.1 is that they might be seen as attempts at constructing, using and testing or evaluating explanatory statements, or theories, about what is going on around us. As Friedman (1953) puts it, such theories might be seen as 'filing systems' which allow observations to be used for explaining past and predicting (i.e. they create expecta-tions about) future events. For instance, consider the following statements/views:

1 The notion that a friend's evident irritability is due to his or her inability to get sufficient sleep the previous night.
2 The claim that the relative demise of the Scottish National Football team is due to too few indigenous Scottish players gaining experience of playing in the Scottish Premier League due to a large number of foreign imports.
3 The idea that improved training provision will create a more productive, reliable and satisfied workforce.

These three statements are all theories. They are all characterized by an attempt at explaining observations and, from those explanations, predictions or expectations might be generated. In this they reveal an important aspect of a theory – that it can be used to guide our practical actions, e.g. if we do A then B will happen, if we don't do A then C will happen. In other words, the formulation and application of theory is at the heart of our attempts at understanding, influencing, or controlling, what goes on around us. Taking the third theory above, we could thus claim that if we improve a workforce's training we should expect an increase in employee productivity, reliability and satisfaction: an important issue for any manager attempting to get things done through other people. By actually attempting to do this, and then by observing what happens, we can evaluate the accuracy of that theory. An outcome of that evaluation may be a retrospective change in the nature of the third theory so as to make it more accurately fit our observations. Alternatively we might reject the theory because its predictions have not been borne out by experience and observation. Conversely the theory might be supported by what is observed as happening and therefore con-sidered to be useable in other organizational situations. For instance, if the second theory was correct it could give the English Football Association forewarning about what could be happening to its own international team and provide an indication of what might be done to mitigate the effects of the problem.

Indeed, it is this latter process of evaluating and changing theory which is so often haphazard and imprecise, that for some commentators (for example, Kidder and Judd, 1986: 5) separates science from common sense. Basically, it is claimed that 'science' entails deliberate and rigorous searches for bias and invalidity through sys-tematically testing theory – research processes which a range of commentators have noted to be remarkably lacking when it comes to management's appropriation of organizational recipes often deriving from 'management gurus' (Huczynski, 1993) or copied from the apparent practices of other institutions (Scott and Meyer, 1994; Cappelli et al., 1997).

Stop and Think Exercise 3.1   Dr Snow and the Broad Street Pump
In Soho, London, 1854. There was a devastating outbreak of cholera. By 10 September, 500 people had died, increasing to 616 people by the end of that month. Dr John Snow was investigating the causes of the outbreak in a desperate attempt to prevent further deaths. However, at first he could see no pattern in the trajectory of the cholera epidemic's incidence that might indicate its source. For instance, who was dying came from diverse social and economic backgrounds and seemed to live all over the Soho area. However, upon further investigation, he noticed that of the 70 workers at the Broad Street Brewery none had died, neither had any

of their families been infected with cholera. The fact that the workers at the brewery received a free ration of beer which they took home and shared with their families and hence did not drink the local water made Dr Snow suspect that contaminated water may have been at fault. This was a controversial explanation at the time. His suspicions began to centre on the Broad Street Pump which supplied most of the people in Soho with water. An exception to this was the Poland Street Workhouse which had its own supply of water and therefore inmates did not drink water from the Broad Street Pump. At the time of his investigation no one had suffered from cholera at the Poland Street Workhouse. His suspicions were further confirmed when he discovered that some wealthy people who lived outside the Soho area had also died from cholera but they had got their servants to fetch water from the Broad Street Pump, rather than locally, because they believed the water tasted better. Despite considerable local opposition, Dr Snow eventually managed to get the Broad Street Pump shut down. The outbreak of cholera promptly ceased. It was later discovered that a nearby sewer had been leaking into the groundwater accessed by the Broad Street Pump.

In relation to Kolb's learning cycle, what was Dr Snow doing in his analysis and subsequent intervention?

Theories and hypotheses

*Theory is to be judged by its predictive power for the class of phenomena which it is intended to 'explain'.... the only test of the **validity** of a hypothesis is comparison of its predictions with experience. Friedman, 1953: 8, emphasis in original*

Now, to elaborate upon the above examples, it is necessary to consider more closely what a theory is and attempts to do. Although the terms 'theory' and 'hypothesis' are often used interchangeably, in its narrowest sense the term theory usually refers to a linguistic framework that is advanced so as to conceptualize and explain the occurrence, or non-occurrence, of a particular social or natural phenomenon. In other words:

1 a theory is an abstract conceptual framework which allows us to explain why specific observed regularities happen;
2 in doing, a theory defines or categorizes aspects of the world and relates these phenomena together in terms of cause and effect relationships which explain why what we have observed has actually happened;
3 usually a theory will also specify situations in which it does, or does not, apply, thereby setting boundaries to where it is applicable as an explanation;
4 in contrast a hypothesis is more specific yet also speculative: a hypothesis makes a precise prediction about what should happen, in particular conditions, if the underlying theory is an accurate representation and explanation of the phenomena in question – predictions that are testable through observation (i.e. the collection of specific data).

Stop and Think Exercise 3.2   In relation to Dr Snow's work in Soho – what was his theory and what was his hypothesis that allowed him to test his theory?

So any hypothesis presents an assertion about the relationship between two or more concepts in an explanatory fashion. Concepts are the building blocks of theories and hypotheses in that they are 'abstract ideas which are used to classify together things sharing one or more common properties' (Krausz and Miller, 1974: 4).

For instance, in the third theory above (see p. 42), 'improved training', 'productive', 'reliable' and 'satisfied' are all concepts. Moreover, we can see that this third theory links together these concepts in an explanatory way. Such explanations are usually causal – that is, they state that one aspect of our world causes, or leads to, another (see Pratt, 1978: 65–7, for an elaboration of what is meant by 'cause' and its importance); that the action or behaviour of phenomenon A causes, or leads to, specific responses in the behaviour of phenomenon B (i.e. in the third theory, improved training causes or leads to a more productive, reliable and satisfied workforce); from this we can predict that if we were to improve training for certain people in the workforce we should observe that they become more productive, reliable and satisfied either in comparison to what they were before and/or in comparison to other employees who have not experienced the provision of enhanced training.

An alternative example might be a hypothetical assertion that:

1 the adoption of a participative management style causes or leads to increased job satisfaction among the manager's subordinates; and

2 increased job satisfaction causes or leads to increased productivity.

From 1 and 2 we might infer that:

3 the adoption of a participative management style should cause, or lead to, increased productivity amongst the manager's subordinates.

Obviously any theory would normally state the underlying reasoning behind the postulated associations between management style, job satisfaction and productivity by locating its assertions in a critical review of the relevant literature. Although this example seems deceptively simple, hypotheses can be much more complex, not only in terms of being interlinked with other hypotheses but also by bringing in qualifying concepts that limit the causal relationship to particular classes of phenomena, e.g. A causes B only in conditions of C. For instance, we could rewrite our initial hypothesis that the adoption of a participative management style causes increased productivity among subordinates by limiting its applicability to conditions where subordinates are motivated primarily by the desire for intrinsic rewards. By implication, where those conditions do not apply, neither do the hypothetical assertions put forward by, or deduced from, the theory.

In trying to understand and explain the social and natural phenomena that surround us, and in our attempts at making decisions about what to do in particular circumstances, nobody escapes making or assuming these kinds of theoretical linkages. Every intentional act, every regularly undertaken practice, can be seen as an attempt to attain or create some desired state of affairs or conversely avoid the undesired. This implies the belief on the part of the actor that a causal relationship exists between his or her decision, or act, and the state of affairs he or she desires. In this sense, much of our everyday social lives and our work activities are in essence theory-dependent activities. Now this clearly illustrates the conjectural and practical aspects of theory, since people act in accordance with their expectations about, or indeed their prejudices about, what will, might, or should, happen in particular circumstances. Such conjectures are often derived from, and hence generalized from, our

Figure 3.2 | Theory and management control

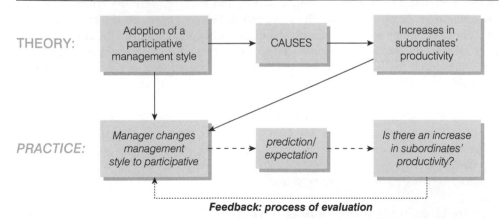

THEORY:

Adoption of a participative management style → CAUSES → Increases in subordinates' productivity

PRACTICE:

Manager changes management style to participative - - - → prediction/ expectation - - - → Is there an increase in subordinates' productivity?

Feedback: process of evaluation

impressions regarding what has previously happened in what we take to be similar circumstances. Thus, even the most mundane activity, such as walking down a street, might be considered in terms of an actor applying theoretical assertions, virtually without thinking about them in a conscious fashion, that are usually borne out by being able to accomplish that activity. Often it is only when we become aware that our expectations, that are grounded in such tacit or taken-for-granted knowledge, have not been met (perhaps due to the intervention of some capricious circumstances) that we begin consciously to re-evaluate the webs of causal relationships that have previously been used to orientate and enable our practical actions. Out of this re-evaluation we may begin to generate a new theory to account for the previously unconsidered, or unencountered, anomalies. So, to paraphrase Douglas (1970: 80–103), such tacit knowledge is ordered and reordered according to the ebb and flow of situations. In Kolb et al.'s (1979) terms we are inductively and deductively learning.

Theory and management control

So it is evident that theories are a means by which we generate expectations about the world; often they are derived from what we have perceived to have happened before and thus they influence (tacitly or otherwise) how we set about future interactions with our world(s). Moreover, it is also evident that if we have the expectation that by doing A, B will happen, then by manipulating the occurrence of A we can begin to predict and influence the occurrence of B. In other words, theory is clearly enmeshed in practice since explanation enables prediction which in turn enables us to assert control over what happens or does nor happen (see Figure 3.2 above) – or at least it proffers the potential for doing such things.

In recent years many commentators, from an array of different perspectives, have all argued that there is an inextricable relationship between management and the control of the behaviour of subordinates so as to ensure that the latter accomplish particular tasks (e.g. Braverman,1974; Mant, 1977; Kunda, 1992; Johnson and Gill, 1993; Du Gay, 2000). If this is so, the importance of theory so as to enable such a control process is only too evident. Indeed, as Pugh (1971: 9) has claimed, every managerial act rests upon 'assumptions about what has happened and conjectures about what will happen; that is to say it rests on theory'.

As we have implied above, managers in their everyday activities rely upon both theories deriving from their 'common sense' and theories deriving from social science research. Although, as we shall see, the differences between the two are subtle and complex, many social scientists would ostensibly claim that the differences relate primarily to the extent to which social science research incorporates the overt and rigorous search for bias (Cook, 1983: 82), while common sense is much more imprecise and haphazard. In a similar vein, Kidder and Judd claim that

> social scientists look for biases and pitfalls in the processes used to support and validate hypotheses and submit their conclusions to the scrutiny of other scientists who attempt to find biases that were overlooked. The casual observer or ordinary knower often gathers evidence in support of hypotheses without being aware of or worried about the biases inherent in the process. (1986: 18)

As we have already noted, the danger in uncritically and unreflectively acting upon common-sense theories and hypotheses of the casual observer may be that one entraps oneself in the current 'traditions' or 'fads' dominant among the social groups to which we belong or defer to, at work or elsewhere. Although these traditions and fads may at first sight appear plausible as they 'create order out of disorder' (Huczynski, 1993: 198) with regard to the complex problems with which any manager has to cope, the potential for creating the problems associated with 'groupthink', so vividly described by Janis (1972), whereby decision-makers (amongst other things) fail to identify and evaluate options and information which might threaten to undermine the prevailing group consensus, is only too evident.

These issues provide a very useful starting point for considering the processes by which social science theories are constructed, evaluated and justified. In other words, what are the sources of such theories and hypotheses, and how do we set about judging rigorously whether or not these theories and hypotheses are 'true' and hence appropriate for our use? Different answers to these questions enable us to distinguish between different social science research methods. Pivotal to understanding these issues is the need to differentiate between those research methods that are deductive and those that are inductive.

Deduction

As illustrated by Figure 3.3, deduction entails the development of a conceptual and theoretical structure prior to its testing through empirical observation of the facts 'out there' in the world through data collection. As the reader may realize, deduction in this sense corresponds to the left-hand side of Kolb's experiential learning cycle (see Figure 3.1) since it begins with abstract conceptualization and then moves on to testing through the application of theory so as to create new experiences or observations. As we shall show later in this book, certain research methods, such as the various forms the experiment takes, certain types of survey and some forms of action research, all follow deductive logic – however, how they do this varies considerably.

To some researchers working within the deductive tradition, the source of one's theory is of little significance. Popper (1967: 130–43), for example, claims that it is the creative element in the process of science that is essentially unanalysable. Obviously we would not recommend this stance – usually it is very important to be able to justify why you think a particular theory, or hypothesis, is worth testing by

Figure 3.3 | Processes of deductive logic

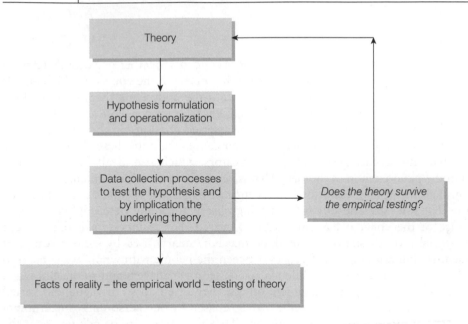

undertaking a critical review of the relevant literature that legitimizes your research (see Chapter 2). Nevertheless, according to Popper, what is most important here is the logic of deduction and the operationalization process, and how this enables the subsequent testing of the theory through its confrontation with the empirical world. Essentially the process of deduction might be divided into the following stages.

The use of concepts and hypotheses

First, the researcher must decide which concepts represent important aspects of the theory or problem under investigation. As we have already implied, concepts are abstractions that allow us to select and order our impressions of the world by enabling us to identify similarities and differences, e.g. 'efficient', 'social class', 'authoritarian', 'satisfied', 'manager', and so on. Concepts are linguistic devices that people regularly use to make sense of their worlds by signifying a particular phenomenon in terms of its perceived common features and its differences with other phenomena thereby allowing users to convey a sense of meaning during communication with others. In other words, a concept is an abstraction that enables us to give order to our otherwise chaotic sensory impressions by enabling the categorization of certain aspects of our experience. Everyone regularly does this in making sense of what is going on around us and in articulating those impressions to other people. However, how an abstract concept is construed and used in everyday sense making may vary because the definitions in-use are often implicit, tacit, and emergent, rather than explicitly formulated. This may create confusion during everyday debate and discussion since different people may be talking about different phenomena and not realize this because the same conceptual label is being deployed – yet it actually refers to different things. In social science research such abstractions, and the potential dissensus they can create, are problems that need to be resolved through what is called operationalization.

Operationalization is the process whereby precise and accessible definitions of phenomena are created.

Operationalization

As we have seen, hypotheses link two or more concepts together in a causal chain – a set of untested assertions about the relationship between the concepts which entails precise predictions about what should happen if the underlying theory, from which the hypothesis have been deduced, holds. However, since concepts are abstract they are not readily observable, and therefore the asserted relationships between concepts provided by the theory are not open to empirical testing until these abstractions are translated into specific observables, or indicators, which also ideally measure variation in the phenomenon of interest. That is, they have to be operationalized.

Through the operationalization of an abstract concept it becomes defined in such a way that rules are laid down for making observations and determining when an instance of the concept has empirically occurred. For instance, take the concept 'managerial level or status' – something that is regularly used by some researchers to identify similarities and differences between the people with whom we come into contact, e.g. line managers, middle managers, senior managers and so on. But when people use this concept to categorize others, they often do so in vague and varied ways. For instance, the term 'middle manager' used by one person may mean something very different when used by another. They may appear to be talking about the same things when in fact they are not: for example, one person might mean people in a certain income bracket, someone else may identify 'middle manager' with accent or educational background, but not income, others may be referring to a particular hierarchical level and span of control within organizational arrangements. Essentially, what these people are doing is operationalizing a concept in different ways and hence creating different meanings which cause confusion because people do not have an overt agreement about what they refering to in their use of particular concepts.

Therefore, by creating rules for making observations we are making a clear definition of what it is we are going to observe and how we are going to observe it. In this we create indicators, or measures, which represent empirically observable instances of, and variations in, the concept(s) under investigation. That is, we overtly link the abstract concept to something that is observable and whose variation is measurable.

Management research example Defining and operationalizing the concept of empowerment

During the last two decades, the use of the concept empowerment has permeated the language of business leaders and the remedial prescriptions of popular business press commentaries upon contemporary organizational issues (e.g. Block, 1987; Clutterbuck, 1994; Robinson, 1997; Cloke and Goldsmith, 2002).

However, the concept is replete with ambiguity and amenable to a variety of interpretations in practice. Spreitzer (1995) noted this growing interest but observed that the lack of a measure of empowerment had deterred substantive research on empowerment and its causes – a gap she attempted to fill by operationalizing the concept. Through an exhaustive review of the literature available at the time she then argues that organizational researchers in the past had focused upon empowering managerial practices but had not grappled with the effects of those practices upon employees. Hence, her focus was upon employees' psychological experience of empowerment in developing a systematic definition of empowerment. By drawing upon a sparse literature she then defines psychological empowerment in terms of a set of four cognitions (1995: 1443–4):

Meaning: the value of a work goal or purpose judged in relation to an individual's own ideals or standards;

Competence: the individual's belief in his or her capability to perform activities with skill;

Self-determination: an individual's sense of having choice in initiating and regulating actions such as making decisions about working methods, pace and effort;

Impact: the degree to which an individual can influence strategic, administrative or operating outcomes at work.

Spreitzer then notes that '[t]he four dimensions … combine additively to create an overall construct of psychological empowerment. In other words, the lack of any single dimension will deflate, though not completely eliminate, the overall degree of felt empowerment … empowerment is a continuous variable; people can be viewed as more or less empowered, rather than empowered or not empowered' (1995: 1444). In her research she then used a separate scale to measure each of the four dimensions of empowerment which were administered to respondents in her sample of middle managers. Each dimension was further operationalized via three statements (illustrated below, 1995: 1994–5) and the extent of respondents' agreement with each

statement was measured and recorded using a seven-point Lickert Scale.

Meaning
The work I do is very important to me.
My job activities are personally meaningful to me.
The work I do is meaningful to me.

Competence
I am competent about my ability to do my job.
I am self-assured about my capabilities to perform my work activities.
I have mastered the skills necessary for my job.

Self-determination
I have significant autonomy in determining how I do my job.
I can decide on my own how to go about doing my work.
I have considerable opportunity for independence and freedom in how I do my job.

Impact
My impact on what happens in my department is large.
I have a great deal of control over what happens in my department.
I have significant influence over what happens in my department.

Consider the way in which Spreitzer has defined and operationalized the concept empowerment – are there any problems with conceiving empowerment in terms of how people subjectively feel with regard to their own experiences at work? What are the assumptions Spreitzer is making about the phenomenon empowerment? Are these assumptions viable?

The linking rules, that is, the rules about when and where an observable instance of the concept has empirically occurred, are called operationalizations (see Figure 3.4). The point of these rules is that, by using the same indicators of a concept, and by standardizing the recording of the results of any observation, it should be possible to have a 'reliable', or consistent, measure of the relevant concept.

Figure 3.4 | Operationalizing abstract concepts

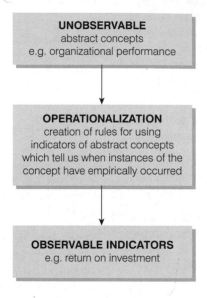

So at the heart of deductive approaches to management research is the process of operationalization because it enables the construction of clear and specific instructions about what and how to observe which in a sense can establish a consensus about what it is we are investigating. This enables the testing of hypotheses and theories by confronting them with the empirical data, which is then collected. In this testing, priority is given to what are considered directly observable phenomena and behaviour: things, events or activities which are publicly observable and hence can be corroborated and agreed upon by other observers. This emphasis upon the control of potential bias through replication by others has thus led to attempts to create standardized procedures for undertaking observation that can be followed exactly by those other researchers. This has in turn created the tendency in this approach to dismiss the analysis of the subjective or intangible since these kinds of phenomena, it is often claimed, cannot be directly observed in an unproblematic fashion and hence any findings cannot be corroborated through the replication of the research by other researchers. However, there is a great deal of choice regarding how we operationalize concepts such as 'organizational performance' and it may be instructive at this point to try Stop and Think Exercise 3.3.

Key methodological concept

Empiricism

Empiricism is a philosophical position which has a long history which does not directly concern us here (see Johnson and Duberley, 2000 for a description of empiricism's historical development). It has been the basis of much scientific thinking and practice in that empiricism articulates an important commitment: if a phenomena cannot be directly observed using our senses (i.e. touch, sight, hearing, smell) we must question whether or not it exists. Phenomena which cannot be directly observed through our senses probably do not exist and are most likely the result of myth, superstition or fantasy (e.g. gods, ghosts, demons, extraterrestrials, the paranormal, etc.). The point is, according to empiricism, the social and natural science must be limited to explaining phenomena that are directly observable whilst avoiding bias on the part of the scientist through the deployment of the most appropriate research methodology. Empiricism assumes, therefore, that provided the correct methodology is rigorously deployed it is possible to objectively observe the real world 'out-there' without contaminating what we find during the act of observation.

Stop and Think Exercise 3.3   In Figure 3.4 the abstract concept that we have attempted to operationalize is organizational performance. Obviously this is a very important concept for both management researchers and practitioners and has been the focus of much research especially when evaluating the impact of various changes and developments in management practices. Here we have operationalized organizational performance in terms of return on investment.

1   What assumptions have been made about business organizations, and the different groups of people who make them up, in how organizational performance has been operationalized in Figure 3.4?
2   Identify some alternative ways of operationalizing organizational performance.
3   How might these alternative indicators affect what is found in management research which for instance explores the relationship between certain management practices and organizational performance?
4   What does your answer to question 3 tell you about the objectivity of deductive research methodology and how it controls potential bias?
5   What does your answer to question 4 tell you about the strengths and weaknesses of empiricist philosophical commitments in practice?

Testing theory

The outcome of the above operationalization process is the ability to test: where the assertions or predictions put forward by the hypothesis are compared with the 'facts' collected by observation. Often, within the deductive tradition, once tested and if corroborated the theory is assumed to be established as a valid explanation. Those explanations are often termed 'covering-law explanations' in that the observations or variables to be explained are covered by the assertions about those phenomena contained within the theory. However, since these covering-law explanations posit regular relationships between those variables, which hold across all specified circumstances, they not only explain past observations but also predict what future observations ought to be like. Take the example: 'water boils when heated to 100° centigrade, at sea level, in an open vessel'. This covering-law not only explains what has happened when water is heated to 100° centigrade in such circumstances but it also predicts what will happen if water is subjected to those conditions. They also help us practically by providing a guide for our activities. However, it is usually the statistical version of the covering-law, whereby the relationships asserted by the theory have only some degree of probability of obtaining across all circumstances, which has generally been adopted by social scientists working within this deductive tradition.

So far we have used the term 'corroboration' in a fairly unproblematic fashion; but what is possible in, and what is meant by, corroboration, has been open to considerable dispute. Here we must turn to some of the debates that have taken place, and are continuing, in that branch of philosophy that has a concern with science: the 'philosophy of science'. As we shall show many of the methods used in management research articulate a particular stance within the philosophy of science so without some understanding of these debates it is difficult to fully understand why some researchers do the things that they do when conducting management research.

What we are alluding to here has often been generally called 'Hume's problem of induction' (Hume, 1739–40/1965). This problem arises because the testing of a theory inevitably involves a finite number of observations undertaken by researchers. Even if every observation that is made confirms the assertions put forward by a theory, logically we can never be certain whether some future observations might demonstrate instances in which the theory does not hold. In other words, we can never verify a theory and say that it applies everywhere, or prove it to be true in a universal sense, because we cannot extrapolate what we have observed so far to unobserved instances without contradicting the empiricist scientific commitment of limiting our claims about the world to what is observable. Future instances, by definition, have not been observed. This problem plagued scientific research until Sir Karl Popper, a famous philosopher, appeared to provide a viable solution. This philosophical solution is important because it is directly articulated by many of the research methods used today by management researchers, how they report their findings and the kinds of claim they make. Moreover, it also has a direct bearing upon management practice.

Popper's hypothetico-deductive approach

Popper, in perhaps one of his most famous contributions to the philosophy of science (1967, 1972a, 1972b), attempted to avoid the difficulties apparent in attempting to inductively verify, or prove, a theory built up from a finite number of observations. Popper cleverly avoids the philosophical problems he associated with 'verificationism', in which scientists attempt to prove their theories, by proposing the alternative maxim of 'falsificationism'. As the term falsificationsim implies, Popper argued that scientists should attempt to refute, or disprove, their theories rather than prove them. At the risk of oversimplifying, what Popper proposes is that no theory can ever be proven by a finite number of observations. No matter how many confirmatory instances have been observed that support the theory, we can never be certain whether or not future observations might demonstrate the falsity of the theory. In other words he is questioning the viability of the right-hand, or inductive, side of Kolb's Learning Cycle, as a model for scientific practice, because we can never be certain that our experiences are exhaustive of all possible instances of the phenomena we are interested in. He is also posing significant issues for what we can claim from following the left-hand, or deductive, side of the Learning Cycle.

Let us use an illustrative example used by Popper – the statement that 'all swans are white'. In the past, to Europeans, this seemed self-evident as it seemed to have been confirmed (i.e. inductively verified) by countless observations that all swans had white feathers regardless of breed. This appeared to be a universally true statement to Europeans until they explored the Australian continent where they discovered black swans. A further example of the potential problems created by 'induction' is provided by the statement 'one plus one equals two'. Again this appears self-evident, something that has been verified or confirmed by so many observations it would be impossible to count them. But according to the maxim of Popperian falsificationism, despite these numerous (but finite) confirmatory observations, we cannot be sure that some future instance might demonstrate its falsity, or limit its applicability. Indeed, such a consideration is to some extent borne out by the observations made in subatomic physics, that when two subatomic particles collide, their resultant fusion creates a mass that is sometimes more, or less, than their combined masses (Capra, 1975).

So, to summarize, Popper argues that while theories can never be proven to be true, they can be falsified, since only one contradictory observation is required. For Popper, therefore, the defining features of scientific theories are that:

1 they must be capable of empirical testing;
2 scientists should not try to find confirming instances of their theories but, rather, should make rigorous attempts at falsifying them using deduction (this is called the hypothetico-deductive method);
3 science advances as falsified propositions and theories fall away leaving a core of theory which has not, as yet, been disproved and which can be taken to approximate the truth (Popper called this verisimilitude, or truth-like);
4 theories which have not been falsified can be used to guide practice but we have to be cautious because future observations might disprove them – therefore such theory-driven practice should only be undertaken carefully, on a small scale, and continuously evaluated in terms of its affects (Popper, 1957: 44–5).

So for Popper, knowledge grows through the above processes whereby error is detected and removed. It follows that a critical attitude is a fundamental distinguishing feature of both science and rationality. Indeed, for Popper (1967: 50)

> a dogmatic attitude is clearly related to the tendency to verify our laws and schemata by seeking to apply them and confirm them, even to the point of neglecting refutations, whereas the critical attitude is one of readiness to change them – to test them; to refute them; to falsify them, if possible.

What Popper calls the 'hypothetico-deductive' approach is summarized in Figure 3.5.

Stop and Think Exercise 3.4   To what extent do you think that Popper's critical attitude has penetrated actual management practice? What might be the barriers to its adoption by managers in practice?

The deductive tradition in the social sciences (although, as we shall show later, in Chapter 8, it is by no means unproblematic) clearly specifies what is involved in the development of 'scientific knowledge'. The 'hypothetico-deductive method' illustrated in Figure 3.5 emphasizes that what is important in 'science' is not the sources of the theories and hypotheses that the scientist starts out with, rather it is the process by which those ideas are tested that is crucial. Generally, the hypothetico-deductive approach to research is intimately bound up with what is often termed 'positivist' philosophy. Three of the main characteristics of positivism (there are others, which we shall consider later) are elaborated by Keat and Urry (1975: Ch. 4).

Figure 3.5 | The hypothetico-deductive method

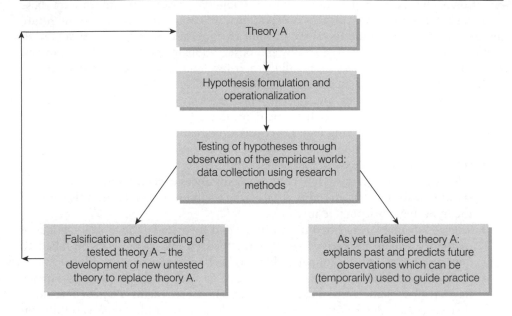

1 The view that, for the social sciences to advance, they must follow the
  hypothetico-deductive methodology used, with such evident success, by natural
  scientists (e.g. physicists) – in a nutshell, the experimental method and its
  derivatives;
2 The knowledge produced by, and the explanations used in, social science should
  be the same as those proffered by the natural sciences – e.g. that A causes B in
  specific circumstances;
3 The above entails social scientists treating their subject matter, the social world,
  as if it were the same as the natural world of the natural scientist.

Indeed, one could argue that the natural (or physical) sciences have to some
degree enabled the explanation and prediction of many aspects of our natural environments and thereby has allowed for human beings to exercise increasing control
over nature's vagaries – such as the occurrence of cholera. The advances in medicine,
engineering and agriculture, for example, can all be considered in this light. This has
led some social scientists, such as Hogan and Sinclair (1996), to argue that scientific
inquiry based upon the methods of the natural sciences are the proper means for examining what happens in organizations. These methods, they claim, enable replicable and
generalizable empirical validation to determine whether or not any theoretical description, explanation and prediction of members' organizational behaviour is accurate. The
findings are therefore pivotal in promoting organizational efficiency and effectiveness
through guiding management's interventions into organizations, affairs.

As Whitley (1984b: 369–71) has pointed out, the above belief that research methods derived from natural sciences can be applied to management in a straightforward
way is based upon three crucial assumptions:

- there is a single set of procedures which generates scientific knowledge in all circumstances – a universally applicable method;
- this universal method, although developed in the natural sciences, is directly applicable to the social world which can be studied in the same way as the natural world;
- the knowledge generated is directly useful to management and this is neither affected by the nature of the problems management might deal with nor by the power relations between managers and those whose behaviour they are trying to influence through their knowledge-guided interventions.

With regard to the third set of assumptions above, Whitley gives us a stark warning ...

... changing existing practices ... is premised upon the judgement that present patterns of social organization could be improved with respect to some general goal which is derived from a set of value judgements. The nature of such judgements affects the sort of situations which are seen as in need of improvement and the criteria by which solutions are evaluated as leading to desired improvements. In other words, what is seen as a problem and how knowledge about it is assessed are dependent upon the values adopted. (1984b: 373)

Thus, Whitley alludes to how the use of theory in management practice is not merely a technical issue of applying neutral scientific knowledge – rather it is also an issue of who defines what is a 'problem' and and who defines 'improvement'. This raises important ethical questions about whose values are at play here and whose are by default being excluded by the form and use of such partial definitions?

However, it is Whitley's first and second set of assumptions above, which we are going to be most concerned with below in our initial exploration of management research methods. This is because it is only too apparent that with management studies, we are concerned with the application of social science theory (see Lupton, 1971; Griseri, 2002) to understand and explain human conduct in organizational and/or business settings. But this raises a question, which has direct methodological relevance, regarding whether or not we can study the social world in the same way as the natural world (see Stop and Think Exercise 3.5).

Stop and Think Exercise 3.5

1 Given the incredible successes of the natural science (e.g. physics) in enabling us to both explain and exert control over the natural world, should the social sciences in general, and management science in particular, copy the research methods used by natural scientists and thereby hope to emulate their successes?

2 Is there a difference between the subject matter of the natural sciences (e.g. the behaviour of physical objects) and that of the social sciences (e.g. the behaviour of human beings) which means that for the latter to adopt the research methods used in the former would be therefore a mistake? If you see there to be differences between the subject matters, what are they?

As we shall see, disputes over questions 1 and 2, and different answers to these questions, have pervaded debates about research methodology and what is deemed appropriate in the social sciences.

Figure 3.6 | The inductive development of theory

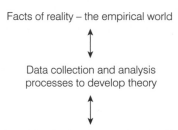

Facts of reality – the empirical world

Data collection and analysis
processes to develop theory

Theory developed that is already tested and verified because it
fits, and is grounded in, the observed facts

It is from objections to some of the implications and assumptions of such a positivist conception of social science that particular inductive approaches to management research arise. However, there is a need for some caution here for these objections, at first sight, seem to pose a significant break with positivism. However, as we shall see in later chapters, this is not necessarily the case because there are some further characteristics of positivism, which are underplayed by Keat and Urry's definition above, which are shared by some inductive approaches. So the break with positivism might not be so great as it first appears.

Induction

The logical ordering of induction is the reverse of deduction as it involves moving from the 'plane' of observation of the empirical world to the construction of explanations and theories about what has been observed. In this sense, induction relates to the right-hand side of Kolb's learning cycle (Figure 3.1): learning by reflecting upon particular past experiences and through the formulation of categories that class observed phenomena together and/or differentiate them; identifying patterns of association between those phenomena to produce theories and generalizations that explain past, and predict future, experience. In sharp contrast to the deductive tradition, in which a conceptual and theoretical structure is developed prior to empirical research, theory grounded in observation is the outcome of induction.

The debates and rivalry between supporters of induction and supporters of deduction, in both the natural and social sciences, have a long history (Ryan, 1970): debates which continue today amongst management researchers (see Johnson and Duberley, 2000; Johnson and Clark, 2006). However, contemporary justification for taking an inductive approach in the social sciences tends to revolve around two closely related arguments.

First, for many researchers working within the inductive tradition, explanations of social phenomena are relatively worthless unless they are grounded in observation and experience. Perhaps the most famous rendition of this view is provided by Glaser and Strauss (1967) in their much referenced book *The Discovery of Grounded Theory*. In this they argue that in contrast to the speculative and a priori nature of deductive theory, theory that inductively develops out of systematic empirical research is more likely to fit the data and thus is more likely to be useful, plausible and accessible especially to practising managers (see Tenbrunsel et al., 1996; Partington, 2000).

Key methodological concept

Grounded theory

'… theory that was derived from data systematically gathered and analysed through the research process' (Strauss and Corbin, 1998: 12).

As the above quotation implies, grounded theory is theory that is inductively generated out of the systematic analysis of data gathered by the researcher. Here the collected data is organized by the researcher (through what is often called coding) to conceptually categorize variations in the data in terms of observed patterns (i.e. similarities and differences) thereby creating indicators of particular phenomena the researcher in interested in. This involves the careful scrutinization of data to generate initial descriptive categories of the phenomena of interest that share particular distinguishing characteristics by constructing the uniformities and differences underlying and defining emergent categories. Successive categorical schemes are usually generated through a series of re-readings and re-codings of data where the properties of, the connections and differences between, emergent conceptual categories are reconfigured through elaboration, consolidation or division to further generate and develop those categories. Whilst these iterative processes inevitably entail some 'data reduction' since they involve 'selecting, focusing, simplifying, abstracting and transforming the raw data' (Miles and Huberman, 1994: 10) the overriding aim is to develop a scheme of 'saturated' categories that are exhaustive of all the data available in the sense that all variance identified in the data is eventually covered without any exceptions (see Glaser and Strauss, 1967: 106). Having conceptually categorized the data, the researcher then looks for patterns in the data that suggest causal relationships between different categories which enable the generation of hypothetical explanations regarding the phenomena of interest. Such hypotheses are revised and reformulated until all the collected data are explained by the emergent theory. Hence, data collection and analysis continue simultaneously throughout the research process until there are no observed exceptions to both the categorical scheme created to organize the observed data and their theoretical explanation – this involves numerous iterations between data collection and analysis which systematically refer to each other and should be mutually reinforcing.

The second, and related, rationale articulated in support of an inductive approach arises more overtly out of a critique of some of the philosophical assumptions embraced by positivism as initially, for our purposes here, defined above by Keat and Urry (1975). It is to this particular critique of positivism that we shall now turn. As we have seen, one of the main themes of positivism and of much of the deductive tradition in the social sciences is a conception of scientific method constructed from what is assumed to be the approach in the natural sciences, particularly physics. This positivist requirement is often called *methodological monism* (see Ross, 1991: 350). It involves the idea that only natural science methodology can provide certain knowledge and enable prediction and control. This necessarily entails the development of theory that successfully explains past and predicts future observations, through causal analysis and deductive-hypothesis testing. The format of this explanation and prediction is illustrated by Figure 3.7 below.

The use of methodological monism in the social sciences usually involves conceptualizing and explaining human behaviour deterministically: as necessary responses to the action of empirically observable, measurable and manipulable stimuli, causal variables or antecedent conditions. This form of explanation is often called *erklaren* (see Outhwaite, 1975). It is the various problems associated with using *erklaren* in

Figure 3.7 | Methodological monism

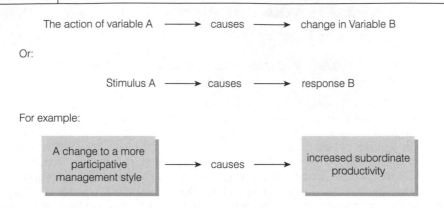

The action of variable A ⟶ causes ⟶ change in Variable B

Or:

Stimulus A ⟶ causes ⟶ response B

For example:

A change to a more participative management style ⟶ causes ⟶ increased subordinate productivity

the social sciences as an organizing frame of reference for research, that provide the initial point of departure for the second critique that justifies the use of induction in the social sciences.

Stop and Think Exercise 3.6   Lift a pen few centimetres in the air and drop it. You can understand the subsequent behaviour of the pen in terms of necessary responses to the action of external stimuli (e.g. the action of gravity, the friction of the pen against the air as it falls, the impact of atmospheric disturbances, and so on). You do not have to refer to the pen's subjective comprehension and evaluation of the situation in order to explain its choice of behaviour. This is because, as far as we know, the pen does not have any subjective apprehension of itself as an entity in particular social circumstances, etc. However, in contrast to the pen, human beings clearly do have subjective capacities, both emotional and cognitive, which influence how we consciously make choices about how to behave, where, and when. Hence, it may be argued that to ignore these subjective processes when explaining human behaviour is a mistake. It is precisely because the stimulus-response model of behaviour illustrated in Figure 3.7 ignores how human beings are agents who interpret and attach meaning to what is going on around them that leads to the model's rejection: active sense making that influences their generation, evaluation, selection and enactment of different courses of action. In other words, we are sentient beings not inanimate objects (like our pen) and therefore research methods originally developed to investigate the latter should not be used to investigate the former.

However, one tactic that is widely used to deal with the above issue is to assume that everyone subjectively apprehends the world in the same way and therefore there is no need to investigate it thereby preserving a stimulus-response model of behaviour because all stimuli will be interpreted by people in the same way. For instance, Game Theory in Economics homogenizes human subjectivity and presents a particularly pessimistic view of human 'rationality' that allows the theorist to model and predict human behaviour without further investigation of this subjective domain. In this, it assumes that all human interaction entails individuals attempting to 'rationally' calculate what behaviour best serves their own interests. Based on those calculations, individuals will always pursue courses of action that maximizes those interests even to the detriment of other people. Indeed, Game Theory assumes that individuals in seeking to maximize their personal advantage presume that other individuals are simultaneously undertaking the same kind of self-interested analyses to plot what they should also do. Essentially society is assumed by Game Theorists to be characterized by a war of all against all as it is constituted by the actions of self-serving individuals continuously strategizing about what they should do based upon their low-trust apprehension of other people. Of course what one could also argue is that perhaps the only people who believe that all people are like this are some economists and all psychopaths!

At the risk of oversimplifying, many supporters of induction in the social sciences reject the causal model illustrated in Figure 3.7 above because they consider that this kind of explanation is inappropriate. For instance, Guba and Lincoln (1994: 106) have argued that *erklaren*, with the quantitative measures of phenomena and the statistical reasoning it uses to investigate causation, imposes an external researcher-derived logic upon its subject matter which excludes, or at best distorts rather than accesses, actors' subjective sense making from the data that is collected. So although *erklaren* may be adequate for the subject matter of the natural sciences, it is not adequate for the social sciences. Hence, supporters of induction in the social sciences take a particular philosophical position regarding human behaviour which sees there to be fundamental differences between the subject matter of the social sciences (thinking, sentient, human beings) and the subject matter of the natural sciences (animals and physical objects). This differentiation directly leads to the use of what are generally labelled qualitative research methods which are primarily inductive.

This philosophical position is illustrated by Laing (1967: 53), who points out the error of blindly following the approach of the natural sciences in the study of the social world. 'The error fundamentally is the failure to realise that there is an ontological discontinuity between human beings and it-beings . . . Persons are distinguished from things in that persons experience the world, whereas things behave in the world.' By implication Laing is drawing our attention to the following issues:

1 Human action has an internal logic of its own which must be understood in order for researchers to be able to make that action intelligible and explicable. It is the rightful aim of social science to access and describe this internal logic through a methodological approach which is generally called *verstehen* (see Outhwaite, 1975) – a German word meaning 'to understand'. This has significant methodological implications for how researchers can and should investigate human activities.

2 The subject matter of the natural sciences does not have this subjective comprehension of its own behaviour – it does not have an internal logic which the scientist must tap in order to understand its behaviour. Therefore, the natural scientist can legitimately, and indeed has to, impose an external causal logic upon the behaviour of his or her subject matter in order to explain it. But such methodology is inappropriate and does not explain the actions of human beings, due to their subjectivity. For example, the behaviour of a pool or snooker ball might be adequately understood in terms of necessary responses caused by particular sets of stimuli in certain conditions: the amount of force delivered to the cue ball propelling it in a particular direction; the angle at which the cue ball strikes the object ball and the amount of momentum it delivers; the

friction of the balls in play against the cloth of the table and the friction of air of a specific humidity upon the moving balls, and so on. At no point do we have to refer to the subjective apprehension of the balls of what is going on around them in order to explain their behaviour. In comparison, to describe and explain the behaviour of the pool or snooker players in terms of stimulus-response would seem bizarre. For surely their behaviour can be only adequately explained through reference to their subjective motives and intentions, their strategic and tactical interpretation of the situation, their knowledge of the rules of the game, their expectations about the articulation, monitoring and enforcement of those rules by other people present during the playing of the game.

3   Therefore, the social world cannot be understood in terms of causal relationships that do not take account of the situation that human actions are based upon the actor's interpretation of events, his or her social meanings, intentions, motives, attitudes and beliefs; i.e. human action is only explainable only by understanding these subjective dimensions and their operation in specific social contexts. Therefore, human action is seen as purposive and becomes intelligible only when we gain access to that subjective dimension which is usually taken to be socially, or culturally, derived. In other words, the norms, beliefs and values that we deploy in making sense of our worlds, which play a crucial role in our construction of meaningful action, derive from our social interactions with other people during the course of our everyday lives, and therefore are to varying degrees shared with them in specific social contexts. Hence, it is more appropriate to talk about an *inter-subjective* dimension to human behaviour rather than a purely subjective.

4   It follows that research in the social sciences must entail what are called emic analyses, in which explanations of human action derive from the meanings and interpretations of those conscious actors who are being studied. This approach is usually generically called *interpretivism*. With an interpretivist approach the etic analyses embraced by deduction, in which an external frame of reference is imposed upon the behaviour of phenomena, are deemed to be inappropriate where the phenomena in question have subjective capabilities – it is this internal yet socially derived dimension that is the key to explanation in the social sciences. Moreover, one cannot make a priori assumptions about the nature of this subjective world – the researcher has to go out and discover it by observation and data collection, in other words through induction. This interpretive and inductive approach is therefore based upon a rejection of the stimulus-response model of human behaviour that is built into the methodological arguments of many positivists. 'Stimulus causes response' is rejected in favour of one of the two approaches represented in Figure 3.8 below.

As is evident from Figure 3.8, modes 1 and 2 are very closely related. Indeed, it may be a short step from initially accepting 1 to then accepting 2. In (1) above, the actor's subjectivity is taken to be an 'intervening variable' that mediates between the stimuli coming from the external world and subsequent human responses expressed as behaviour or action. In (2), however, the actor's subjectivity is accorded greater 'formative or creative' power in its own right. Here the interpretation of reality, upon which actions are based, is not a mere medium through which external stimuli act (as in (1)). Rather, interpretation has a projective quality in the sense that such inter-subjective processes create, or socially construct, the reality in which action arises

Figure 3.8 | Two modes of interpretive, or emic, analysis using *verstehen*

Mode (1)

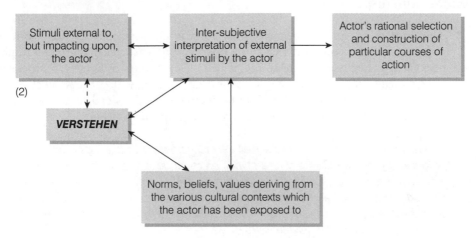

Mode (2)

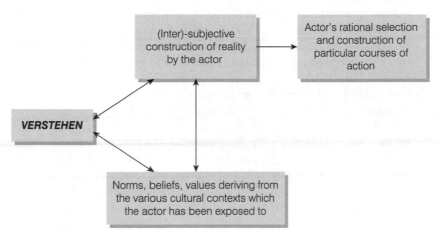

(see Berger and Luckmann, 1967; Burr, 1995), and hence the idea that (inter)-subjectivity mediates the action of external stimuli becomes rather meaningless: all that there is for us to research is human inter-subjective processes, through which their sense of reality is created, in order to explain behaviour.

Although these differences have resulted in somewhat different methodological approaches, both (1) and (2) above share a commitment to conceiving human action as arising out of actors' inter-subjectivity and hence the need in research methodology to undertake *verstehen*. Thus, both (1) and (2) entail the initial philosophical agreement that the possession by human beings of a mind has freed them from the stimulus-response relationships that dominate the behaviour of 'natural phenomena' (see Mead, 1934). As we have indicated, this perceived need drives particular methodological commitments but it also opens up some sources of debate and dispute within these more interpretive approaches as well as with mainstream positivism. These are summarized below.

Debates and disputes

1 The model of human behaviour underpinning *verstehen* creates serious objections to the contention of some positivists that social phenomena might be treated as being analogous to the 'it-beings' or 'things' of nature and thereby are amenable to a similar type of causal analysis in which the subjective or intentional dimension is ignored and effectively lost. Instead, it is postulated that the difference between the social and the natural world is ...

> *... that the latter does not constitute itself as 'meaningful': the meanings it has are produced by men (sic) in the course of their practical life, and as a consequence of their endeavours to explain it for themselves. Social life – of which these endeavours are part – on the one hand, is produced by its component actors, precisely in terms of their active constitution and reconstitution of frames of meaning whereby they organise their experience. (Giddens, 1976: 79)*

2 These considerations create the need for social scientists to explain human behaviour adequately, to develop a sympathetic understanding of the frames of reference and meaning out of which that behaviour arises. But of course this poses significant methodological questions around how this accessing of other's subjective interpretations of their experiences may be achieved. We will need to turn to this issue in much detail in later chapters. However, for the time being it is important to point out that these methods are generically called qualitative methods and they are usually recognized as having a direct concern with enabling *verstehen*. Through *verstehen*, qualitative methods are seen to be (see Van Maanen 1998; Alvesson and Deetz, 2000; Denzin and Lincoln, 2000) aimed at enabling a sympathetic understanding of others' experience by inductively accessing the actual meanings and interpretations they subjectively deploy in making sense of their worlds and which influence their ongoing social construction and accomplishment of meaningful action. Hence, explanation of behaviour is in terms of describing these cultural processes and elements. Thus, through 'fidelity to the phenomena under study' (Hammersley and Atkinson, 1995: 7) an array of qualitative methods have been developed in order to investigate how actors construct, sustain, articulate and transmit socially derived versions of reality in order to describe and explain their behaviour in specific social contexts.

3 Generally the methodological implications of *verstehen* usually entail the avoidance of the highly structured methodological approaches of deduction; these, it is usually argued, prevent and ignore the access to actors' subjectivity – or at best they distort our access to that subjective domain. This happens because the deductive researcher, prior to conducting empirical research, formulates a theoretical model of the behaviour of interest, which is then tested through data collection. Hence, they impose an external logic upon a phenomenon which has an internal logic of its own. It is precisely the discovery of this internal logic, through empirical research, that is the concern of many supporters of induction in the social sciences. To achieve

this, what is recommended are relatively less structured approaches usually using qualitative methods to research that ostensibly allow for access to human subjectivity, without creating distortion, in its natural or everyday settings. However, this claim to objectivity in exploring others' subjective worlds has become increasingly controversial amongst qualitative researchers and has led to considerable variability in how and why qualitative research is undertaken – something we shall return to in later chapters. Nevertheless, for the time being, the most important issue for us here is that an interpretivist view of human behaviour undermines methodological monism since a clear implication is that different methods are appropriate for investigating social and natural phenomena – not the same method.

4   Because interpretivism, in its various forms, undermines methodological monism this has provoked the response that if it was followed in the social sciences the latter would be unable to emulate the envied operational successes of the natural sciences. Moreover, the interpretive prescriptions described above have also encouraged the positivist counter-argument that because this kind of inductive research is relatively unstructured, it is unreliable since it is not easily replicable and therefore bias cannot be ruled out nor even investigated through the replication of research, by other social scientists, to cross check findings. This point is made forcefully by Behling (1980: 489) where he argues that research methods similar to those used in the natural sciences, whilst not immune to systematic bias do have built into them 'extensive means for protecting the researcher against personal biases' – unlike those qualitative methods which attempt to enable *verstehen*.

5   According to Giddens (1976: 19), many positivists regard the 'intuitive or empathic grasp of consciousness' as merely a possible source of hypotheses about human conduct and not a method for social science research in its own right. Moreover, some philosophers (e.g. Neurath, 1959) have argued that to attempt such grasping of others' culturally derived consciousness is inappropriate for science. This is because it is presumed that human subjectivity, and related inter-subjective processes, cannot be empirically observed in a direct, objective, manner. Therefore, social science theory based upon such attempts is inadmissible as genuinely scientific explanations. Indeed, trying to investigate actors' subjective processes, because they are considered to be unobservable in an objective fashion, might introduce into social science the very guess work and dogma (what Neurath calls 'the residues of theology' (1959: 295)) that science has been trying to eradicate since the Enlightenment. In other words, some positivists see that any genuine social science should limit itself to what they see as directly observable stimulus-response (or cause and effect) relationships preferably, and usually, using quantitative measures of such phenomena which are taken to be more objective and enable rigorous testing of hypotheses. Simultaneously, some interpretive researchers would reject such a dismissal by arguing that it is indeed possible to objectively access human subjective processes provided that the correct methodological steps are undertaken. However, such a claim to objectivity is simultaneously questioned by other interpretive researchers – another philosophical dispute, as we shall show in later chapters, that has led to an increasing diversity in how qualitative management research is undertaken.

Key methodological concept

Reliability

For many management researchers a key methodological requirement is to ensure distance between the researcher and the researched so that research processes and findings are not contaminated by the actions or idiosyncrasies of the researcher. Hence, a key way of evaluating the findings of research pertains to the reliability of findings in the sense that different researchers, or the same researcher on different occasions, would 'discover the same phenomena or generate the same constructs in the same or similar settings' (Lecompte and Goetz, 1982: 32). In other words, reliability refers to 'the extent to which studies can be replicated' (ibid.: 35). Therefore, the assessment of reliability requires the use of clear methodological procedures and protocols so that regulation by peers, through replication would be, in principle, possible. However, reliability becomes a contentious issue in qualitative research because the commitments to *verstehen* and induction usually mean that research design and fieldwork emerges out of, and is largely limited to and dependent upon, specific research settings. This lack of structure makes the possibility of replication problematic and hence makes the policing of findings by the wider scientific community difficult if not impossible.

Conclusions

In this chapter we have initially confronted some of the key philosophical debates that have a bearing upon the diverse ways in which management research is conducted in practice. As we shall see there are other philosophical issues relevant here which we have already hinted at and which we shall develop as we proceed in the book. A key point here is that research methods are not merely neutral tools or techniques that we can just take off the shelf and use to undertake management research. Rather different research methods come with considerable philosophical baggages which in part influence how you perceive and understand the management issue or problem that you hoping to investigate by using particular methodological approaches. This is an issue that we will repeatedly return to in the rest of the book.

For the time being, and as a way of summarizing much of that has been covered so far, it is possible to construct a continuum of research methods, as a heuristic device, that initially allows us to differentiate between different methods in terms of the various philosophical stances and logics they bring to bear in conducting research. That is, we can discriminate between different methods in terms of their relative emphasis upon deduction or induction, their degree of structure, the kinds of data they generate and the forms of explanation they create. At each extreme of the proposed continuum we can distinguish what are known as nomothetic and ideographic methodologies.

As Burrell and Morgan (1979: 6–7) note, nomothetic methodologies have an emphasis on the importance of basing management research upon the rigorous use of systematic protocols and technique. This is epitomized in the approach and methods employed in the natural sciences, which focus upon the process of testing hypotheses in accordance with particular standards of scientific rigour. Standardized research instruments of all kinds are prominent among these methodologies which articulate a set of rules that the researcher should follow. Emphasis is therefore placed upon covering-law explanations and deduction, using quantified operationalizations of concepts in which the element of motive/purpose/meaning is lost, partially because of the need for precise models and hypotheses for testing but also because of the particular philosophical assumptions about human behaviour that are being tacitly deployed that often render the subjective domain as non-researchable or even irrelevant.

On the other hand, according to Burrell and Morgan (1979: 6–7), ideographic methodologies emphasize the analysis of subjective accounts that one generates by 'getting inside' situations and involving oneself in, or accessing in various ways, the everyday flow of life without disrupting it. This usually involves the deployment of qualitative methods in management research. Here there is an emphasis upon theory inductively grounded in such empirical observations which takes account of subjects' meaning and interpretational systems in order to gain explanation by understanding (i.e. *verstehen*). However, it is important to note at this point that this shared commitment to *verstehen* does

Table 3.1 A comparison of nomothetic and ideographic research methods – a continuum

Nomothetic methods emphasize		Ideographic methods emphasize
1 Deductive testing of theory	vs	1 Inductive development of theory
2 Explanation via analysis of causal relationships and explanation by covering-laws (called etic or *erklaren*)	vs	2 Access to, and description of, subjective meaning systems and explanation of behaviour through understanding (called emic or *verstehen*)
3 Generation and use of quantitative data	vs	3 Generation and use of qualitative data
4 Use of various controls, physical or statistical, so as to allow the rigorous testing of hypotheses	vs	4 Commitment to research in, or access to, everyday settings, whilst minimizing the disruption caused by the research to those being investigated so as to preserve the natural context in which their behaviour arises
5 Highly structured research methodology to ensure replicability by other scientists and as a result of 1, 2, 3, and 4	vs	5 Minimum structure to ensure 2, 3 and 4 (and partially as a result of 1)

← **A methodological continuum** →

Laboratory experiments, quasi experiments, some action research, surveys,	Mixed methods, some action research, qualitative methods e.g. ethnography

(Cont'd)

not explain the considerable heterogeneity evident in qualitative management research. This heterogeneity suggests that considerable differences underlie the initial appearance of similarity usually invoked by the term 'qualitative' and it is something that we will turn to in much more detail when we come to consider qualitative management research.

For the time being, and as a heuristic device, it is useful as a way in to considering management research methods to propose that any method adopts a position on a continuum according to its relative emphasis upon the characteristics summarized by Table 3.1.

It is to the various different methods (e.g. laboratory experiments, quasi-experiments, surveys, various forms of action research and various forms of qualitative management research such as ethnography), their various commitments and characteristics, together with their use in management research, that we turn in the following chapters. It is important to remember that the above continuum is only an initial snapshot of some complex issues. Indeed, as we try to represent in Table 3.1 certain approaches, such as action research, do themselves vary in terms of our comparative criteria – something we shall consider in detail in Chapter 5. Notwithstanding this issue we shall begin this methodological journey with what many social scientists consider to be the gold standard of sciences: experimental research design.

Further reading

Lupton's (1971) classical work provides an interesting and important starting point for the consideration of the role and nature of theory in social science generally and with specific regard to management. For an interesting analysis of the interplay between management theory and practice the reader should see Tranfield and Starkey (1998). However, their account might be gainfully compared with an incisive critique of technicism in management education provided by Grey and Mitev (1995). Also useful for its focus on the world of the manager is Checkland (1981). Checkland, himself trained as a physical scientist, reviews the systems movement as a scientific endeavour to tackle the ill-structured problems of the managerial world. He comes to the conclusion that 'hard systems' engineering needs to be modified to something more appropriate which he calls 'soft systems' methodology. We have found the book to be particularly useful in helping students from a background in the physical or natural sciences to bridge the gap between deductive and inductive approaches to management research.

With regard to the issues around philosophy of science that have emerged in this chapter, Lessnoff (1974) provides a detailed survey of many of the philosophical issues important in social science research, with an interesting focus upon the relevance of a natural science 'model' for research in the social sciences. More recently Johnson and Duberley (2000) provide an overview of the key philosophical debates which influence management and organizational research. For an interesting and increasingly important perspective on the relationship between theory and data the reader could also turn to Ragin's (1994) discussion of how all social research constructs representations of social life through a dialogue between ideas (theory) and evidence (data).

Meanwhile, for those who wish to explore the assumptions that underpin differ-ent approaches to research and theory in further depth, they should turn to Slife and Williams (1995) who provide a thorough overview of psychoanalysis, behaviourism, humanism, cognitivism, eclecticism, structuralism and postmodernism. Assumptions specifically about human behaviour are investigated by Ashworth (2000) where he examines the major contributors to the development of our thinking about conscious-ness, selfhood, culture and the effects of the physical world on genetic inheritance.

For an important outline of the characteristics of positivist management research and its continuing relevance to managerial practice the reader should turn to Hogan and Sinclair (1996). Their argument is that scientific inquiry based upon the methods of the natural sciences is the proper means for examining what happens in organizations. These methods, they claim, enable replicable and generalizable empirical validation to determine whether or not any theoretical description, explanation and prediction of organizational behaviour is accurate. The resulting tested theory is directly helpful to management as it is pivotal in promoting organizational effectiveness through guiding their organizational interventions. Likewise Behling (1980) explores five major objec-tions to using research methods that derive from the natural sciences in the study of organizations – objections which he feels are not insurmountable. Whilst he concludes that using such methods does have its problems, and hence requires more thoughtful application, a key advantage of this approach, he argues, is that it has built in an exten-sive means for protecting the researcher against personal biases.

The ambiguous relationship between the concepts researchers might use to direct the focus of their fieldwork and the role theory is explored by Blumer (1954) in a famous article. Here the target of Blumer's attack is the use of what he calls 'defini-tive' concepts that are used in quantitative research and which once developed, and operationalized into sets of indicators, become fixed benchmarks which guide data collection. In contrast Blumer advises researchers to use what he calls 'sensitizing concepts' which suggest directions in which the research must look. This idea is of particular importance to researchers setting out to undertake inductive research because it clarifies the relationship between prior literature searches and subsequent inductive data collection. For Blumer sensitizing concepts taken from existing theory and literature are used in a way that only gives a sense of direction in which to look and can thereby act merely as a guide for uncovering the variety of ways in which a phenomena can empirically assume, rather than imposing prior conceptualized for-mat for engaging with, and recording variation in, phenomena of interest.

Morgan and Smircich (1980) take a very different approach to understanding qualitative research to that of Behling, or Hogan and Sinclair. They draw upon the concept of paradigm as previously used by Burrell and Morgan (1979). Here they directly relate the choices researchers make between quantitative and qualitative methods to varying philosophical assumptions about ontology, epistemology and human nature. In doing so they call for a more reflexive approach to understanding the nature of social research that admits how the choice of particular methodological techniques is contingent upon our philosophical assumptions about the nature of the phenomena under investigation.

However, the view put forward by the above writers of what natural science meth-odology entails, although widely accepted, is quite different to that presented by Whitley (1984b) who reviews a number of writers who claim that science is essentially a method of producing and validating knowledge that is directly useful to manage-ment. In his critique of this stance, Whitley exposes the tacit and uncritical adoption of positivistic philosophical assumptions that underpin such an approach and points to the substantial difficulties that render these assumptions, and their prescriptions for management research, as increasingly untenable. He proceeds to explore how management research can be understood as a practically orientated science in terms of its similarities to, and differences from, other social sciences as well as the natural sciences. Whilst Whitley feels that there are substantial differences between the subject matters of the natural and social sciences, he does not consider that these differences rule out the possibility of a social science that is broadly comparable with what he presents as a more sophisticated version of the natural sciences to that presented by Behling (1980) or Hogan and Sinclair (1996).

These journal articles are freely available on the companion website (www.sagepub.co.uk/gillandjohnson):

Hassard, J. (1991) Multiple paradigms and organizational analysis: a case study, *Organization Studies*, 12(2): 275–99.
Prasad, A. and Prasad, P. (2002) The coming age of interpretive organizational research, *Organizational Research Methods*, 5(1): 4–11.

Key methods in management research

Part II

Experimental research designs

4

Learning outcomes At the end of this chapter the reader should be able to:

● **outline deductive logic and define independent, dependent and extraneous variables;**

● **illustrate the translation of deductive logic into experimental methodological approaches;**

● **understand laboratory experimental research design;**

● **appreciate management research's example of laboratory experimental design;**

● **understand why experimental logic is often taken out of the laboratory;**

● **understand quasi-experimental design and demonstrate how it can be used to evaluate the impact of organizational changes and innovations;**

● **consider the strengths and weaknesses of laboratory and quasi-experimental research designs.**

This chapter begins by considering the methodological problems and issues that researchers using a hypothetico-deductive approach inevitably confront when undertaking empirical research: problems for which deductive research methods try to provide viable solutions. This chapter then focuses upon one particular set of solutions: the design and structuring of the 'laboratory' or 'true' experiment – often considered to be the gold standard in deductive research. We then critically examine some of the problems faced by those engaged in this form of experimental research including: manipulating independent variables (i.e. causes); observing and measuring change in dependent variables (effects); controlling for the influence of extraneous variables (i.e. rival hypotheses to the one(s) being tested) through matching experimental and control groups – the defining methodological feature of laboratory experiments. The chapter then proceeds to consider the problems which might arise from such experimental research designs, no matter how well they are undertaken, and investigates why and how experimental logic may be taken out of the laboratory in the form of the quasi-experiment or field experiment: an approach more common in management research than the laboratory experiment. The methodological advantages and disadvantages of quasi-experiments are then presented in relation to the laboratory experiment.

Deductive logic and the structuring of management research

... every branch of inquiry aimed at reliable general laws concerning empirical subject matter must employ a procedure that, if it is not strictly controlled experimentation, has the essential logical functions of experiment in inquiry. (Nagel, 1961: 452)

The design of empirical research at the deductive end of the continuum of research methods outlined in Chapter 3 attempts to provide a blueprint that enables the researcher to structure a research question or problem in such a way that the outcome is the production of valid, objective and replicable answers. Here it is important to remember that the researcher, through developing his/her research design, is usually trying to test hypotheses generated from a theory, through data collection, in order to see whether or not the theory survives those attempts at falsifying or disproving it. The point is that there are different ways of attempting to do this methodologically.

Nevertheless, all hypothetico-deductive research, regardless of the particular method being deployed by the researcher, involves an initial structuring process which can be seen as involving four basic steps.

1. The first step is to delineate carefully the questions or problems the research is attempting to tackle. In this it is important to identify the particular phenomenon or factor whose variation we are trying to explain or understand: that is, we must identify what is known as the 'theoretically dependent variable'.
2. The second step involves identifying the phenomena or factors whose variation, according to the theory or hypothesis we are testing, explains or causes changes in our dependent variable. These causal or explanatory variables are usually termed the 'theoretically independent variables', and are the phenomena whose influence upon the dependent variable we are specifically interested in investigating.
3. In order to monitor any variation in the dependent and independent variables it is also necessary to operationalize them. This not only allows for the observation and measurement of any variation in the dependent and independent variables but also sometimes involves the researcher purposively varying, or manipulating, the incidence of the latter in order to monitor its effect upon the dependent variable. As we shall see, the purposeful manipulation of the independent variable by the researcher is a key component of a particular type of experimental research design. Other hypothetico-deductive methods (e.g. the quasi-, or field, experiment) may instead just attempt to observe the effects of the 'natural' variation of the independent variable that occurs without the researcher's intervention.
4. The final step deals with the issue that any observed variation in the dependent variable might not necessarily be an outcome of the action of the independent variable(s). So it follows that the fourth step in research design is to try to neutralize, or control for, the effects upon the dependent variable of what are usually called 'extraneous variables'.

Figure 4.1 | The problems for research design in deductive research

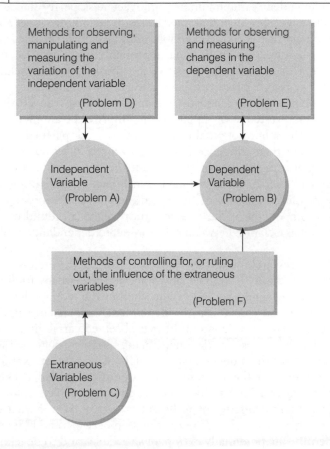

The term extraneous variable (see Figure 4.1) refers to any phenomenon that potentially might affect, or cause some of the variation in, the dependent variable but is not included in the research design as an independent variable. (Sometimes the term exogenous variable is also used here to describe this type of phenomenon.) In other words, extraneous variables are not specified by the hypothesis being tested as being of immediate interest as a cause of potential variation in the dependent variable. So whilst their potential effects upon the dependent variable are not being directly explored by the research, the research has to be simultaneously designed in a way that allows the researcher to control, or rule out, their potential influence. This is so that the researcher can then observe only the effects upon the dependent of the designated independent variable(s). This is a crucial issue in deductive research designs because if we fail to control for the potential influence of extraneous variables upon what we find, people could criticize our research because they could claim that what we putting forward as a viable (theoretical) explanation of observed variation in the dependent variable may instead be an outcome of the action of uncontrolled extraneous variables. Alternatively, we might be claiming that a hypothesis has failed our empirical testing when perhaps it hasn't due to the obscuring of its effects by the action of uncontrolled extraneous variables.

For instance, if we were interested in looking at the effects of improved training provision (independent variable) upon employees' task performance (dependent variable) we would have a problem that must be resolved in how we set about collecting data – this problem relates to the likelihood that task performance is an outcome of multiple causes amongst which training is probably just one. Other things that might affect task performance, either negatively or positively, will include variables such as the reward system in place, attitudes towards work, the nature of the work, relationships between employees and their manager, and so on. However, in this research we are just interested in the impact of the improved training provision upon task performance – the other potential influences upon task performance are not of immediate interest but their influence has to be minimized by our research design so that any subsequent statements we make about the influence of the new training actually refers only to its impact rather than the influence of these other, extraneous, variables. If the possible influence of these extraneous variables is not neutralized by some means in our design of the research, they might confound our interpretation of any observed association between the nominated dependent and independent variables.

So, if through our research design we fail to control for the effects of extraneous variables, the internal validity (Campbell and Stanley, 1963) of any findings is threatened. In other words, we could not be certain whether the independent variable did indeed cause the observed changes in the dependent variable. In sum, extraneous variables provide alternative explanations of that observed variability; that is, they in effect constitute rival hypotheses to the one(s) being tested through our specification and operationalization of the independent variable(s). If extraneous variables are not controlled, they can obscure (i.e. confound) our identification and assessment of the impact an independent variable has upon the dependent variable.

Therefore, it is vital in deductive hypothesis testing research, if we are to be able to make warranted statements about the relationship between the independent variables, both to identify any potentially extraneous variables and to develop a research design that neutralizes, rules out or controls for their confounding influence upon the dependent variable. Only when we have been successful in achieving this, and thereby have ruled out any rival hypotheses to those under test, can we claim internal validity for our research findings: only at that point can we make warranted statements about the association between independent and dependent variables.

Problems in deductive research design

These problems for research design at the deductive end of the continuum are represented in Figure 4.1. Although problems A to F in Figure 4.1 are all interrelated we can, for the sake of clarity, consider that problems A, B and C are concerned with identifying and defining the three types of variable and are essentially theoretical issues. Problems D, E and F are concerned with observing, manipulating, measuring and controlling variables and are essentially methodological issues. It is the different ways in which problems D, E and F may be dealt with that leads to different kinds of deductive research design. At this point it will be helpful to try to do Stop and Think Exercise 4.1.

Stop and Think Exercise 4.1   You are interested in the contention that the educational attainment of MBA students is improved by the addition of mineral supplements to their daily diets. Design a way of investigating this proposition by following stages 1 to 3 below:

1 Identify the dependent and independent variables by constructing a researchable proposition, or hypothesis, about the relationship between the consumption of mineral supplements and MBA students' educational attainments.
2 Identify any other (i.e. extraneous) factors that might influence any observed variation in your designated dependent variable.
3 Deal with problems D, E and F (see Figure 4.1) by developing an appropriate research design.

If you did try to follow steps 1 to 3 in Exercise 4.1 you will probably have attempted to construct a research design that used a deductive method. That is, you probably tried to vary the designated independent variable (the intake of mineral supplements) and monitor its effects upon the designated dependent variable (educational attainment), while trying to eliminate the effects of potential extraneous variables (e.g. age, IQ, prior management experience, motivation, application, etc.). How you might have designed these elements may have been use to experimental protocols for doing research – what these protocols are will be discussed below where we will proceed to consider experimental design in more detail by beginning with the 'true' or 'classical' experiment.

'True' or 'classical' experiments

Except for the situation in disciplinary areas such as work psychology (Schaubroeck and Kuehn, 1992) and information systems (Introna and Whitley, 2000), it appears that the true or classical experiment in management research is relatively unusual. Perhaps this is largely because in the true experiment the relevant behaviour of interest is not observed in its natural everyday setting. Rather, it is often only in 'laboratory conditions', where the researcher can exercise a great deal of control and manipulate the relevant variables, that the true experiment can take place. This creates not only numerous methodological strengths but also certain problems, particularly with regard to the artificiality of the research setting.

Despite the apparent rarity of the true experiment in management research, however, and despite its inherently problematic nature, it is important for any researcher to be conversant with the logic that forms the basis of the 'true' experiment for two reasons. First, elements of this logic are shared by the other deductive research methodologies commonly used in management research, some aspects of which are considered in later chapters and which in essence take the logic of experimentation out of laboratory conditions whilst providing different methodological solutions to problems D, E and F illustrated in Figure 4.1. Second, as we shall demonstrate later in this chapter, this logic as expressed in the quasi-experiment is very relevant to designing research that attempts to evaluate the impact of innovation and change in organizations – an important task for most practising managers.

The logic of the true experiment

The English philosopher, John Stuart Mill (1874), in his work A *System of Logic*, succinctly described the experiment as the 'method of difference'. Indeed, as we shall attempt to show, the processes of manipulating, comparing and looking for differences are at the heart of experimental logic, whether it is expressed in the form of the true experiment or in the form of quasi-experiments.

As in all deductive approaches to research design, the experimenter begins by developing a theoretical model of the phenomena of interest by identifying the independent, dependent and extraneous variables. Having operationalized those variables the model then enables the experimenter to produce hypothetical predictions which may then be tested by confronting them with 'reality' in a true experiment. For instance, the prediction that would have been tested in Exercise 4.1 would be that the intake of mineral supplements will cause an increase in educational attainment as measured by students' performance in some form of examination. However, to test such a prediction whilst ruling out rival hypotheses to the one under test, through the design of a true experiment the following conditions must be met:

1 The experimenter must be able to manipulate the occurrence and non-occurrence of the independent variable through his or her direct intervention (e.g. the intake of mineral supplements).
2 The experimenter must be able to identify and measure any subsequent changes in the dependent variable (e.g. variation in educational achievement).
3 The experimenter must be able to control the effects of any extraneous variables upon the dependent variable (e.g. age, IQ, etc.).

In accomplishing 1 and 3 above we can distinguish one of the best-known hallmarks of the true experiment: the creation of what are called 'control groups' and 'experimental groups'.

Key methodological concept

Control and experimental groups

An experimental group is composed of subjects who experience the effects of the independent variable (often called the 'experimental treatment'). Any changes in the designated dependent variable are then monitored and measured.

A control group is composed of subjects who have not undergone the experimental treatment (i.e. do not experience the effects of the designated independent variable) and who are to be compared with those who have been subjected to that independent variable. Any subsequent differences between the two groups, in terms of the dependent variable, are then identified and measured.

Therefore in our example, one (experimental) group of MBA students have mineral supplements and any changes in their educational attainment are then measured. Another (control) group of MBA students do not have any mineral supplements. Any changes in their educational attainment are also measured. The changes in each group's educational attainment during the course of the experiment is then compared and any differences identified.

The idea behind this procedure is that if the experimental and control groups have been matched so that they are exactly the same, save for the incidence of the independent variable, any subsequent differences between the two groups with regard to the dependent variable after the application of the experimental treatment must be due to the action of that treatment. Control and experimental groups are therefore used to ensure the elimination of the effects of as many extraneous variables as possible so that the only difference

Figure 4.2 | Experimental protocol and procedure

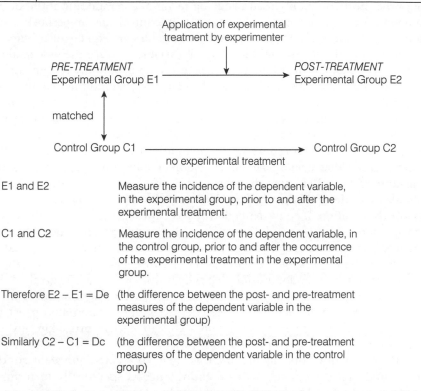

E1 and E2	Measure the incidence of the dependent variable, in the experimental group, prior to and after the experimental treatment.
C1 and C2	Measure the incidence of the dependent variable, in the control group, prior to and after the occurrence of the experimental treatment in the experimental group.
Therefore E2 – E1 = De	(the difference between the post- and pre-treatment measures of the dependent variable in the experimental group)
Similarly C2 – C1 = Dc	(the difference between the post- and pre-treatment measures of the dependent variable in the control group)

between them is the independent variable. It logically follows that any ensuing difference between them in respect of the dependent variable must be due to the effects of the independent variable. In this way it is possible to test the hypothetical predictions posed by the original theoretical model. This whole procedure is illustrated in Figure 4.2.

Any difference between De and Dc (as defined in Figure 4.2) must be due to the manipulation effects of the independent variable. The nature of this difference, or indeed lack of it, then casts light upon the accuracy of the original predictions from the theoretical model by enabling the testing of the original hypothesis.

The process of matching experimental and control groups

As is illustrated by Figure 4.2, the process of matching experimental and control groups prior to any 'treatment' is vital in the control of extraneous variables and allows for some confidence regarding the internal validity of any consequent findings.

Key methodological concept

Internal validity

Internal validity is a very important evaluation criteria for all deductive research – it refers to the extent to which we can be confident that the designated causes (independent variables) have actually produced the observed effects (changes in the dependent variable). In other words, it refers to the extent to which the research has been designed in such a way that allows for the control of rival hypotheses to the one(s) under test.

In the true experiment matching is usually achieved by one of two techniques. Perhaps the most commonly used matching technique is randomization, or random assignment. Subjects are randomly assigned to control and experimental groups, therefore leaving it to chance that extraneous variables are equally distributed among the groups. Indeed, the assumption is that all variables, except the independent variable, will be randomly distributed and hence the control and experimental groups will be equivalent and thus comparable. The reasoning behind this assumption is that if subjects are allocated on a random basis their individual differences, wherein lie many potential extraneous variables, will also be randomly distributed together with their potentially confounding influences upon the dependent variable(s).

In our example, the procedure would be to allocate the MBA students randomly between a group that would have mineral supplements and a group that would not. The assumption would be that the extraneous variables, such as age, IQ, and so on, would also be randomly distributed. However, although randomization appears to allow for the creation of equivalent control and experimental groups, there is always the chance, particularly when dealing with small groups, that some bias is accidentally introduced so that a particular type of person predominates in one group and not the other. Although this possibility reduces as the size of the groups increases, there is no absolute guarantee in randomization that the groups created are equivalent. Perhaps it is this concern, that some important extraneous variable might be unevenly distributed accidentally, that has led some researchers to adopt an alternative procedure for matching control and experimental groups. This alternative procedure involves the use of systematic controls over extraneous variables.

In using systematic controls the intent is again to create equivalent control and experimental groups, but in this case equivalence is specifically in terms of the extraneous variables that have been previously identified as potential sources of influence upon the independent variable. So an attempt is made to match subjects in the control and experimental groups on what appear to be characteristics and phenomena that might confound any results if they were not controlled for. Thus, in our example, a systematic attempt would be made to match the MBA students in the control and experimental groups according to characteristics that appear to have an influence on educational attainment (e.g. age). In identifying these characteristics, clearly the research would need to apply theory regarding educational attainment. Here a source of bias might creep in through a lack of knowledge about the influences upon educational attainment. A characteristic that influences educational attainment might be overlooked, not systematically controlled, and thus may inadvertently create non-equivalent experimental and control groups by not being evenly distributed.

Both randomization and systematic controls are physical controls (i.e. subjects are physically allocated to experimental and control groups through the use of either procedure) aimed at ruling out rival explanations to those being advanced in the experimental treatment. Nevertheless, they both entail threats to the internal validity of any subsequent findings: some deriving from chance and bad luck, others from a lack of knowledge about possible extraneous influences upon the dependent variable. In principle, however, if the control and experimental groups are exactly matched, and consequently the only difference between them is the action of the independent variable(s), the internal validity of the true experiment is potentially very strong. Yet the problematic nature of matching must always cast some degree of doubt on whether or not any observed changes in the dependent variable are actually attributable to the experimenter's manipulation of the dependent variable. This potential source of bias must be a constant concern in the design and implementation of experiments; as we shall see, however, it is not the only one.

So far we have discussed biases that might arise from the inadvertent selection of non-equivalent experimental and control groups. However, other biases might arise during the course of the experiment.

Biases arising during the course of a true experiment

At the risk of oversimplifying, it is possible to distinguish three potential sources of bias that can and do arise during the course of a true experiment – biases due to:

1 changes affecting the members of the experimental and control groups;
2 changes in the measurement processes;
3 the subjects' reaction to the processes and context of the experiment.

We shall now review each of these three problematic areas in turn.

1 Changes affecting group members
This first category of potential biases might threaten the validity of any experimental results. It refers to any unexpected and unintended changes, from the point of view of experimental design, that might affect members of the control and experimental groups during the course of the experiment and thereby influence or mediate the effects of the independent variable(s). In other words, such changes might create unforeseen extraneous variables. Any subsequent findings regarding the relationship between the dependent and independent variables must then be doubtful since they may be a result of the distorting influence of those uncontrolled extraneous variables. Unforeseen events and changes in the lives of subjects – varying, for example, from the psychological and physiological to the social, political and economic – may occur during the course of the experiment. These might affect how the subjects behave or perform and thus provide rival explanations to that proffered by the independent variable for any measured changes in the dependent variable. Essentially, the longer the time lapse between the pre-test and post-test measurements of the dependent variable the more likely it is that some of these events and changes may have occurred and their presence threaten the validity of any causal inference propounded by the unwitting experimenter.

So far, we have considered only changes in subjects created by processes happening outside the experimental context. Yet some inadvertent change might be created by the very procedures used by the researcher in his or her investigations. The processes of pre-testing and post-testing can themselves often cause a change in the dependent variable, thus obfuscating the experimenter's perception of the effects of independent variable(s) upon the dependent variable. Subjects may, for instance, become accustomed to, and more proficient at, the pre-test. Therefore, any changes in their scores when it comes to post-testing might be attributed to their greater experience of that procedure, rather than to the influence of the experimental treatment. Indeed, in our example, the MBA students might well become accustomed to the educational attainment tests used in pre- and post-testing.

Many of these sources of bias may be resolved through better experimental design, particularly through the matching of control and experimental groups. However, an even greater problem for experimenters arises from changes occurring in subjects during the course of the experiment, as a reaction to the artificiality of the context and processes of experimental research – a reaction which better experimental design might exacerbate rather than resolve. These problems will be considered more closely later in this chapter.

2 Changes in the measurement processes Generally, there are two main possible sources of change in the measurement process that can threaten the validity of any findings. The first is the withdrawal of subjects from either group during investigation, often called 'experimental mortality'. It becomes a significant problem when withdrawals are such that researchers are no longer measuring and comparing like with like at the pre- and post-test analyses of the dependent variable. Indeed, this problem will be exacerbated when the 'drop-outs', whether from the experimental or control group, share some characteristic that differentiates them from subjects who continue to participate in the research. The danger is that the researchers might draw conclusions from incomplete sets of data and hence the internal validity of those conclusions may be doubtful.

The second source of changes in the measurement process relates to intended or unintended changes in the instrumentation that enables pre-test and post-test measurement of the independent variable. If, for whatever reason, changes occur in the procedures used in measuring the dependent variable, any observed differences in that variable could be attributed to those changes rather than to any actual change in that variable. The different instrumentation may be inadvertently sampling and measuring different phenomena and thus the researcher is not observing the same things with his or her pre-test and post-test measurements and is no longer comparing like with like.

The implications of Type 1 and Type 2 biases The potential biases just discussed in the previous two sections can pose significant problems in experimental design. Moreover, they are important elements for consideration in evaluating the robustness of any experimental research findings particularly with regard to internal validity. But it is important to emphasize that they can be resolved largely through the careful design and maintenance of experimental procedures, particularly in the measurement of variables and the matching of control and experimental groups. In other words, the issues discussed above do not create inevitable or inherent biases in experimental design. Moreover, carefully designed and implemented experiments have several major strengths.

Experiments are highly structured and entail a priori delineation of the theory under test and the explicit construction and statement of the hypotheses that will be tested. In addition, since the methods for operationalizing, measuring and manipulating variables will be specified, other researchers can easily replicate experiments to check any findings. Furthermore, the use of control and experimental groups, together with the manipulation of one or more independent variables, enables researchers to control for, and rule out, the influence of extraneous variables. This high degree of (physical) control allows researchers to demonstrate and evaluate the independent variable(s)' causal effects upon the dependent variable through their manipulation of the conditions experienced by subjects. So the control afforded by the true experiment can provide some degree of certainty as to whether or not the independent variables did cause any observed changes in the dependent variable; that is the internal validity of the true experiment can be seen to be relatively strong.

However, while the high degree of structure and control provided by the true experiment confers significant strengths, those very strengths are seen to create particular problems that have led some researchers to question the utility of the true experiment in management and social science research. Many of these problems appertain to the reactions of subjects to the artificiality of the true experiment; an artificiality created by that same structure. So, as we address the issue of biases arising out of subjects' reactions to the processes and context of the true experiment, we confront weaknesses that stem from that very design which endows experimental research with particular strengths. Indeed, we confront what are perhaps irresolvable sources of bias inherent in the design of true experiments.

3 Subjects' reaction to the processes and context of the experiment   There are several complex and interrelated aspects to this issue of reactivity that need to be considered here. Some of these issues relate to the processes by which subjects comprehend, interpret and attach meaning to the stimuli that constitute the experimental treatment or independent variable(s). The problem is whether or not subjects, during these sense making activities, attach the same meanings to those stimuli as do fellow subjects and researchers. Do they experience the same phenomena or, because interpretation can vary, do they attach different meanings to those ostensibly shared events and thus experience different phenomena and stimuli? Obviously the internal validity of experiments depends upon the assumption that subjects experience the same stimuli that constitute the independent variable(s).

A second aspect of this problem relates to the social interaction that often occurs between an experimenter and subjects. As we try to illustrate, sometimes an experimenter might unintentionally influence events and thus distort or mediate the effects of the independent variable upon subjects' behaviour by his or her very presence in the research context, and by any subsequent interaction with subjects. Again, if this occurs, and if this is unavoidable in this type of experimental research, it creates a major threat to the internal validity of the experiment.

Finally, we must also consider the broader issue of the artificiality of the context in which a true experiment takes place. Since such research occurs only through the contrivance of a researcher by creating what amounts to a laboratory setting through intervening into everyday life by allocating subjects to control and experimental groups, its context is artificial, from the subjects' point of view. The situation in which a true experiment takes place is markedly different from and outside the normal, everyday situation in which subjects perform the acts that are the focus of the experimental design. This leads to the question whether or not it is possible for researchers to generalize or extrapolate their findings from the artificial social situation of a laboratory to the everyday and mundane situations in which people normally behave: in essence, are such findings limited to the laboratory context in which the research took place?

Stop and Think Exercise 4.2   Imagine a natural scientist conducting experiments upon the behaviour of plants in controlled conditions to test the effects of different kinds of fertiliser. For instance, the scientist would probably have a series of plots of separate land upon which are planted exactly the same plants. The plots of land are also exactly the same and close enough together so that weather conditions are consistent. However, the fertiliser applied is varied according to the hypotheses the scientist is trying to test. Measurements of the plants would occur before and after the application of the fertilisers in order to ascertain and compare its effects upon plant growth, etc. Now the point is that the plants are, as far as we know, completely unaware of the (artificial) contexts in which they have been placed in order for the scientist to conduct the experiment. They also don't have any comprehension of themselves and the behaviour of the scientist – they therefore cannot alter their behaviour based upon their subjective apprehension of the context in which they have been placed – they just automatically respond to the experimental treatments that the scientist administers. However, human beings are not like plants because we have subjective capabilities and are capable of purposively and self consciously changing our behaviour in the light of understanding of the social situations in which we have been placed.

What are the implications of the subjective dimension of human behaviour for the findings of experimental research using human beings?

The issues delineated above pose a potentially devastating critique of the use of the true experiment in social science and management research. In the natural or physical sciences these issues are not as significant since inanimate phenomena, such as molecules of water, plants, etc. are unaware of the context of the experimental research, the procedure in use or the behaviour of a chemist or physicist. But human beings patently would be aware of these aspects. Therefore, it is necessary to look at these matters more closely by considering an example of an influential experiment in management research. Here we include some of the problems confronted by the researchers and the ways in which they attempted to deal with them.

The Hawthorne studies

In 1924, at the Hawthorne Plant of the Western Electric Company in Chicago, there began a series of experiments aimed at investigating the relationship between different kinds of physical working conditions, such as illumination, temperature, humidity and the frequency of rest pauses, and the productivity of employees (Roethlisberger and Dickson, 1939). Underlying this approach was the assertion that, for instance, there would be an ideal level of illumination or temperature at which productivity would be maximized. Therefore, physical working conditions, such as the degree of brightness of illumination, were taken to be independent variables, which were experimentally manipulated and their effects upon the dependent variable, employee output, monitored.

Two groups of employees, matched in terms of their productivity, were selected and isolated from the rest of the workforce by placing them in what amounted to laboratory conditions in different parts of the plant. So, included in the initial research design was a control group of employees who were not subjected to the experimental treatments and whose output was also monitored. This experimental scenario is diagramatically illustrated in Figure 4.3.

The actual findings were rather unexpected and confusing. For example, output in the experimental group increased regardless of how illumination was manipulated. Even when lighting was dimmed to a flicker, output still increased! Output in the control group also steadily increased despite the absence of experimental manipulation of the physical working conditions.

The researchers then conducted a series of experiments in the relay assembly test room, to provide a more detailed investigation of the effects of different physical conditions upon employee productivity. These experiments again entailed segregating a group of employees (whose output had previously been secretly measured)

Figure 4.3 | The Hawthorne studies

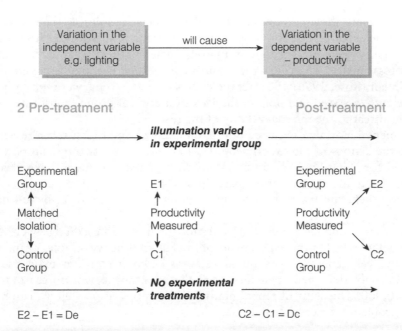

1 Studied relationship between:

Physical working conditions ⟶ and ⟶ Employee productivity

therefore it was predicted that:

| Variation in the independent variable e.g. lighting | ⟶ will cause ⟶ | Variation in the dependent variable – productivity |

2 Pre-treatment   **Post-treatment**

⟶ *illumination varied in experimental group* ⟶

Experimental Group   E1   Experimental Group   E2

Matched Isolation   Productivity Measured   Productivity Measured

Control Group   C1   Control Group   C2

⟶ *No experimental treatments* ⟶

E2 – E1 = De   C2 – C1 = Dc

Therefore, any difference between De and Dc must be due to the manipulation of the independent variable – the experimental treatment(s).

from other workers and manipulating their working conditions while monitoring their output. No matter what the researchers did – even lengthening the working day and reducing rest periods – there appeared to be little effect upon an upward trend in productivity.

These events caused the researchers to conclude that they were not investigating simply the effects of changing physical working conditions upon productivity. They were also inadvertently researching employee attitudes, values and norms, which were mediating the effects of the experimental treatments. These conclusions, and the later research which developed from such findings, have been credited with raising important issues regarding motivation and the role of the 'informal' organization (Schein, 1970). Methodologically, they are important here for demonstrating some of the problems associated with the true experiment, not the least of which has since become known as the 'Hawthorne effect'. Before turning to the 'Hawthorne effect' it is useful to consider some weaknesses evident in this research which could have been avoided through more careful design of the experiments:

1 Although the illumination experiments entailed the use of experimental and control groups, the researchers failed to match these groups by using randomization or systematic controls. It follows that the researchers were unlikely to be comparing like with like, and this was exacerbated by their failure to isolate the control and experimental groups under identical conditions. These particular threats to the internal validity of the experiments were heightened in their later research when, in the relay assembly test room experiments, the researchers inexplicably failed to use a control group to control extraneous variables.

2 External events affecting how subjects behaved occurred during the course of some of the experiments. For instance, the depression of the early 1930s caused the female subjects participating in the relay assembly test room experiments to express anxiety regarding their job security, and eventually halted that experiment (Rose, 1975: 108). Yet the effects of these events were not fully or competently assessed and, due to the lack of a control group, constituted yet another threat to the internal validity of the research.

3 Experimental mortality occurred during the relay assembly test room research due to the actions of the experimenters. At an early stage two operators were replaced for being 'unco-operative'. This characteristic seems to have clearly differentiated them from other participants and poses the danger that by replacing them the researchers began to draw conclusions from biased data sources.

4 This last issue implicitly raises the question of how representative were the personnel involved in the experiments of the Hawthorne workforce, or indeed of employees generally. The initial relay assembly test room experiments involved only six female personnel, yet the Hawthorne workforce totalled some 40,000. This issue of representativeness, or population validity, can be a major problem for experimental research.

True experiments by their very nature can only involve relatively small numbers of people. This poses the problem of how any findings can be generalized to the wider population when they are derived from such a small database. This matter might not appear to be a problem for experimental research in the natural and physical sciences, whose subject matter is assumed to be homogeneous (e.g. one molecule of water is considered to display the same characteristics and behaviour as any other molecule of water). Such an assumption is not possible, however, when research concerns human beings – who are so evidently heterogeneous.

In principle this problem of population validity can be partly resolved by the prior random sampling of people from a particular population (e.g. the Hawthorne workforce) and then assigning them to the experimental and control groups. Any results can then be extrapolated from the original population from which the sample of subjects was drawn. Thus, as with other problems so far discussed regarding the Hawthorne experiments, better design and maintenance of experimental procedures might have resolved them and allowed the researchers to avoid arriving at what seem to be spurious conclusions.

The Hawthorne effect

The behaviour of the subjects, in apparent response to the experimental treatments administered during the illumination and relay assembly investigations that so surprised the Hawthorne researchers, has since been explained by what has been termed the Hawthorne effect. This phenomenon refers to the way in which the novelty of experiencing a new situation, together with their sense of being a special group that had become the focus of attention, influenced the participants' response to their situation. It may therefore be argued that the observed increases in output, in the various control and experimental groups, were a product of the experimental situation itself. That is to say they were artefacts, created by these conditions, which in effect were mediating and obscuring the underlying relationship between the independent and dependent variables. Strangely, this phenomenon had been observed earlier and noted by Myers in a similar context. Myers (1924: 28, quoted in Rose, 1975: 96) claimed that 'sometimes the mere presence of the Institute's investigators and the interest they have shown in employees' work has served to send output up before any changes have been introduced'.

Generally, this phenomenon of the Hawthorne effect, is often associated with what are called 'experimental artifacts' (see Adair, 1984). The issue of experimental artifacts might usefully be subdivided into three related areas; indexicality, experimenter effects and subjects' mediation through interpretation. Below we elaborate each in turn and then consider their methodological implications.

1   *Indexicality* This refers to the way that people vary their behaviour according to the situation in which they find themselves. Our own everyday experience tells us that as we move from social context to social context we modify and try to control how we behave in terms of our understanding of the situation and our impressions of the people with whom we interact (Goffman, 1969; Douglas, 1976). For instance, it would be unlikely for someone to behave in the same way and use the same speech codes in a meeting at work as when drinking with friends at their 'local'. So it would appear that how we behave, and the impressions we 'give off' to others in a specific social context, are intimately bound to that context since it greatly influences their production.

Accordingly, a true experiment taking place in laboratory conditions is as much a social situation as drinking with friends in a pub or attending a lecture. However, it is obvious that how one behaves in either a lecture or in the pub with one's friends largely depends upon one's interpetation of the social context and what is presumed to be appropriate in that situation. Therefore, can any behaviours elicited during the course of a laboratory experiment be understood in isolation from the social context which has been contrived to produce it? Perhaps the Hawthorne experiments illustrate how such behaviour is indeed 'bounded' by, and intelligible only in terms of, that social context.

The problem this poses for the true experiment is whether or not the behaviour observed in an experimental situation will be repeated in a subject's natural or everyday surroundings. This raises the question whether or not the results of experiments are mere artifacts of the research procedures used and the social situation thereby contrived. This has led some commentators (e.g. Bryman, 1989: 90) to question whether the findings of laboratory experiments can be extrapolated to social contexts beyond that surrounding the experiment.

2   *Experimenter effects* This matter is closely linked to the problem of indexicality. It refers to the way in which a particular experimenter may inadvertently influence the behaviour of different subjects, or the varying effect that different experimenters may have upon the same subject. As we

have seen, the way people behave in a social situation is often influenced by how they perceive the other people present in that situation. In an experiment probably the most significant 'other' will be the experimenter. Therefore, the personal qualities attributed to the experimenter by subjects, together with any intended or unintended cues the experimenter gives about how subjects should behave, might all influence the way in which subjects conduct themselves in the experimental setting. Indeed, subjects' awareness that they are participating in an experiment might heighten their sensitivity to any cues deriving from the experimenter or the setting regarding appropriate expected behaviour (Rosenthal, 1966; Rosenthal and Rosnow, 1975). These predilections might be heightened by subjects' anxiety about how they will appear to the researchers to the extent that they will try to give the 'correct' responses to any stimuli (Rosenberg, 1968). All these factors add to the stimuli being administered in the experimental setting besides those constituted by the independent variable, thus making the interpretation of any subsequent data problematic.

3 *Subjects' mediation through interpretation* A further significant problem for experimental research derives from the situation that it is not necessarily possible to assume that a particular independent variable is experienced as the same thing or event by different subjects. Human beings are not passive creatures who automatically respond to the stimulus of any particular independent variable. Rather, people perceive and interpret and thereby attach meaning to the various stimuli they might experience in a particular environment. They then act in accordance with those understandings and meanings, which might vary from person to person and which may be related to the social context in which the stimuli are experienced. Therefore, independent variables, such as illumination in the Hawthorne experiments, cannot be considered as acting independently of the meanings and interpretations given to them by subjects; for it is those processes which form the basis of any subsequent behaviour. As Shotter (1975) has argued, much experimental research treats subjects as if they were analogous to an unthinking inanimate entity, such as an atom, at the mercy of stimuli administered by the experimenter. For Shotter this is a distorted image of a human being, who is in fact a free agent capable of making choices based upon his or her subjective interpretation of the situation. Indeed, these interpretative processes might be seen as rival explanations – to those constituted by the independent variable – of any subsequent behaviour observed in an experimental setting. As such they constitute a significant threat to the internal validity of any research findings.

The experimental artifacts analysed above and their threats to the internal validity of the true experiment are illustrated in Figure 4.4.

The problems created by experimental artifacts illustrate the paradox of the true experiment. By manipulating the independent variables while controlling extraneous variables, through the use of control and experimental groups, researchers appear to be able to conclude with some certainty that particular independent variables cause particular changes in particular independent variables. At first sight the internal valid-ity of the true experiment appears to be very strong. However, the need for structure and artificiality, so necessary for enabling manipulation and control, in itself creates a set of what might be seen as further extraneous variables. These in effect constitute rival hypotheses to the one(s) being tested by the original research design – rival

Figure 4.4 | Experimental artifacts: threats to the internal validity of the true experiment

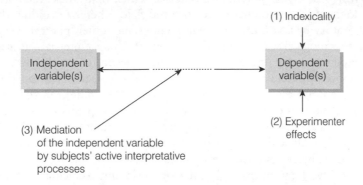

explanations for what is found in relation to the effects of the independent variable on the dependent variable.

These experimental artifacts, illustrated in Figure 4.4, are not a problem in the natural or physical sciences. The subject matter of those sciences does not have the subjective capacities that human beings so patently possess. It is the presence of subjectivity in human beings and their consequent variable reactivity to the artificiality and manipulation of the true experiment that casts doubt upon the internal validity of this type of research design (see Introna and Whitley, 2000). Furthermore, the artificiality of the experiment, since its context is divorced from the normal lives of subjects, makes it doubtful whether or not findings could be extrapolated to everyday behavioural situations: that is, the ecological validity of the true experiment appears to be low.

Key methodological concept

Ecological validity

Ecological validity is a criterion for evaluating research which leads us to consider the extent to which research findings may be generalized to social contexts other than those in which data has been collected. It raises questions about the extent to which the social context of research is typical of normal everyday life – how natural is the social context in which research takes place. As Cicourel points out, ecological validity refers to the extent 'our instruments capture the daily life conditions, opinions, values, attitudes, and knowledge base of those we study as expressed in their natural habitat' (1982: 15). For Argyle, experimental research requires working in research contexts which are 'simplified or stripped down, which may lack some essential features of the original situation, and *which may produce types of behaviour that would not normally occur*' (1969: 17, our emphasis).

Alternatives to the true experiment

The weaknesses of the true experiment that we have reviewed here have caused researchers in the various branches of the social sciences to try to develop alternative

research designs that avoid these problems yet maintain the logic of experimentation, in which lie many potential strengths. Thus, many researchers have tried to
take the logic of the experiment out 'into the field', thereby avoiding the artificiality
of the laboratory by investigating social phenomena in their natural everyday context.
The lack of ecological validity and the various threats to internal validity, inherent in
the true experiment are not, however, the only reason for this 'flight'.

For instance, in conducting an experiment the researcher is purposively induc-
ing changes among the subjects of the research. Depending on the nature of these
changes, and the moral code of the researcher, ethical problems may ensue. Indeed,
for many areas of research it is considered to be unethical to manipulate certain
kinds of variables since they might promote changes that might be detrimental to the
well-being of subjects. Alternatively, some research problems are quite simply not
amenable to investigation through a true experiment, particularly those concerning
macro-issues.

Thus, whatever the reason – pragmatic, ethical or methodological – many researchers have been concerned to try to preserve aspects of the logic of the true experiment
that might enable the control of extraneous variables, while undertaking research
outside the confines of laboratory conditions. It is to these endeavours, expressed as
quasi-experimentation, we now turn.

As we have attempted to demonstrate so far in this chapter the 'true' or 'classical'
experiment enables a researcher to test theories and hypotheses systematically since
it has the following characteristics:

1 The experimenter is able to allocate subjects to control and experimental groups
   in a systematic or random manner;
2 He or she is then able to manipulate the incidence of one or more independent
   variables and measure any consequent changes in the dependent variable(s);
3 Because of these characteristics a true experiment occurs through the direct
   intervention of the experimenter.

Although the ability to manipulate independent variables and to control extraneous
variables through this highly structured research design has many strengths, we have
pointed to the way these strengths also create severe problems mainly to the inevitable artificiality of the context in which the research takes place.

Many researchers have therefore sought to preserve much of the logic underpinning the true experiment while avoiding the difficulties that arise from the artificiality of the controlled laboratory context. In so doing they seem to be following
Nagel's (1961) injuction to follow the 'essentail logical functions of experimental
inquiry' which we quoted at the beginning of this chapter. They have attempted to
achieve this by taking this guiding logic and applying it to the investigation of an
environment that existed, or events that have occurred, without the investigator's
direct intervention (Campbell and Stanley, 1963; Campbell, 1969; Orpen, 1979;
Aguinis, 1993). By adopting this approach the researcher begins to lose some of the
attributes of the true experiment, particularly those deriving from the ability to control the incidence of the independent variable(s) and the ability to allocate subjects to
experimental and control groups either randomly or systematically. Meanwhile, the
attempt is made to avoid problems arising from the artificiality of the context and
processes of the true experiment.

In this sense the researcher is gaining naturalism or ecological validity as subjects
are investigated in their normal everyday environments. However, this strength is

acquired only at the expense of trading off control over extraneous variables – something that potentially reduces the internal validity of findings.

Such attempts at approximating the logic of the true experiment outside the confines of the laboratory controls, in a natural, or field, setting have generally been dubbed 'quasi-experiments'.

Quasi-experiments

As in the case of the true experiment, the prime aim of the quasi-experiment is to analyse causal relationships between independent and dependent variables. However, in a quasi-experiment, since it does not take place in laboratory conditions and since its focus is on real-life, naturally occurring events, subjects cannot be randomly or systematically allocated to experimental and control groups. This does not mean that control and experimental groups are not used; rather, control and experimental groups are identified in the field in terms of whether or not they have experienced the notional experimental treatment(s) or independent variable(s).

As such, the identified control and experimental groups are naturally occurring populations; and thus, many aspects of being able to match them exactly so as to compare like with like are not possible. Inevitably, some degree of control over extraneous variables, relative to that possible in the laboratory, is lost due to this lack of equivalence between groups. So instead of attempting to manipulate the incidence of the independent variable by selecting equivalent control and experimental groups and then administering an experimental treatment, the researcher attempts to identify people who have naturally experienced the notional experimental treatment. The attempt is then made to compare their consequent behaviour with as similar a group as possible who have not experienced that naturally occuring event or phenomenon. To summarize, a quasi-experimental approach is often adopted because it:

1 avoids the artificiality of the context in which a true experiment takes place;
2 allows research to be conducted in the actual settings to which any research findings must be extrapolated;
3 it is often adopted by researchers when they wish to investigate causal relationships in situations where manipulation of the independent variable and/ or the systematic assignation of subjects to control and experimental groups is not ethically or practically feasible.

Given these characteristics, quasi-experimentation seems to be a particularly useful approach to research designs aimed at evaluating various types of social policy innovations or reforms. This application has been considered by Campbell (1969) and it is useful to summarize one of his investigations that concisely illustrates the application of quasi-experimental logic.

Campbell and Ross (1968) discuss the application of quasi-experimental design to the investigation of the effects upon fatality rates of the 1955 'Connecticut crackdown on speeding'. In this they attempted to examine the effects of the police crackdown on speeding in Connecticut (the independent variable) upon the fatality rates on Connecticut roads (the dependent variable).

To determine the nature of this relationship Campbell and Ross needed to gather data pertaining to the rate of fatalities upon Connecticut roads prior to and after the crackdown. In essence they needed to measure the incidence of the dependent variable prior to and after the experimental treatment:

Data pertaining to fatality rates on Connecticut roads prior to 1955 ⟶
Crackdown ⟶ Data pertaining to fatality rates on Connecticut roads, 1955
and after.

But this simple 'interrupted time series design', in which any changes in fatality rates
before and after 1955 appear to provide evidence regarding the effects of the crackdown, fails to rule out other rival explanations. As Campbell and Ross (1968) point
out, the apparent fall in fatalities after the crackdown evident in the time series data
could have been caused by a host of extraneous variables. For example, there could
have been an improvement in the weather, making driving safer, or the fall in fatalities could have merely happened by chance.

So in order to rule out some of the potential rival explanations and thus improve
our understanding of the effects of the crackdown upon fatality rates, it was necessary to identify states which could serve as control groups and so provide comparative data regarding extraneous factors, as well as data pertaining to fatality rates.
Clearly, these states had not experienced a crackdown on speeding and although not
exactly equivalent to Connecticut in other respects could act analogously as control
groups. Thus, the research design adopted by Campbell and Ross entailed what is
often called a 'multiple time series' quasi-experimental design in which data were
collected from comparable, though not equivalent, 'subjects':

E1 (fatality rates on Connecticut roads prior to 1955) ⟶ 'Experimental
treatment' (police crackdown) ⟶ E2 (fatality rates on Connecticut roads,
1955 and after).
C1 (fatality rates in four comparable States prior to 1955) ⟶ No 'experimental treatment' ⟶ C2 (fatality rates in four comparable States, 1955 and
after).

Consequently, a comparison of the differences between C2 and C1 and between
E2 and E1 might better reveal the effects of the crackdown as compared with the
simple interrupted time series design. Therefore, in the case of the quasi-experiment
there is a lack of manipulative control over the independent variable(s) and a lack
of equivalence between experimental and control groups. This inevitably results in
some loss of control over extraneous variables. In so doing, quasi-experiments are
seen to confront problems arising from confounded extraneous variables which in
effect constitute rival hypotheses to the one(s) under test and thereby threaten the
internal validity of any findings by making cause and effect propositions tenuous.

Nevertheless, the quasi-experiment does attempt to follow the 'logic of difference'
by comparing the natural incidence and non-incidence of the notional experimental
treatment(s) in real-life situations. Indeed, it is this naturalism that not only confers
upon the quasi-experiment the ecological validity so lacking in the true experiment but
also allows for the experimental investigation of areas in which it would be ethically,
logically and politically problematic to conduct a true experiment. The possibilities
quasi-experimental designs offer for the evaluation of organizational change and innovation are only too evident and have not been lost on some management researchers.

For instance, the issues raised by the quasi-experiment's combination of naturalism and the logic of difference are vividly illustrated by the use of quasi-experimental
design to study the long-term effects of the implementation of autonomous workgroups in a greenfield manufacturing site (Wall et al., 1986). In this research Wall
and his colleagues set out to test the widely held assumption that this form of work

Figure 4.5 | Control series design comparing Connecticut fatalities with those in four comparable states (adapted from Campbell, 1969: 96)

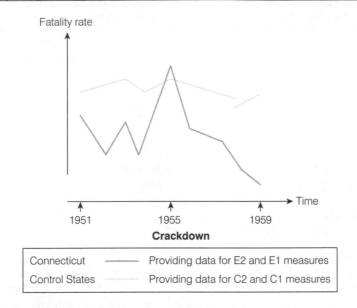

design enhanced work motivation and job satisfaction thereby improving group performance and reducing labour turnover. Moreover, the literature suggested to the researchers that a further effect of autonomous workgroups would be increased organizational commitment and improved mental health.

The empirical research was set within a large British confectionery company which was about to open a new factory where senior management had decided to try a new method of working with the day shift – autonomous workgroups. In terms of the researchers' quasi-experimental design, this day shift constituted a naturally occurring experimental group where the use of autonomous workgroups constituted the independent variable. Meanwhile the night shift at the same greenfield site, and day and night shifts in a factory elsewhere in the organization, because they used conventional work designs yet used similar technology to produce similar products under the same conditions of service, provided naturally occurring similar but non-equivalent control groups for the research.

It would seem that the original intention of the researchers was to use questionnaires to measure variance in the dependent variables (intrinsic job satisfaction, extrinsic job satisfaction, intrinsic job motivation, organizational commitment and mental health) three times in the greenfield site groups at 6, 18 and 30 months with simultaneous measures of the two control groups in the established factory at 6 and 18 months. However, because the researchers were working in a natural context without the level of control that laboratory experimenters enjoy, it proved impossible to measure the dependent variables in the evening shift at the established factory at 18 months because the shift was discontinued. Moreover, the control group at the greenfield site became in effect an experimental group after 12 months because management decided to extend autonomous working to the evening shift. While these changes must have been incredibly frustrating to the researchers they are all part of the risks quasi-experimenters have to deal with, particularly when undertaking long-term studies. The subsequent research design is summarized by Table 4.1.

Table 4.1　A quasi-experimental research design (adapted from Wall et al., 1986). ACADEMY OF MANAGEMENT JOURNAL by Wall et al. (1986). Copyright 1986 by ACADEMY OF MANAGEMENT (NY). Reproduced with permission of ACADEMY OF MANAGEMENT (NY) in the format Textbook via Copyright Clearance Center.

Measurement of five dependent variables	Experimental Group A: day shift/ greenfield site	Control/ experimental Group B: evening shift/ greenfield site	Control Group C: day shift/ established factory	Control Group D: evening shift/ established factory
@ 6 months	A1	B1 work subsequently redesigned in this shift	C1	D1 shift subsequently discontinued
@18 months	A2	B2	C2	
@30 months	A3	B3		

From this research design, if the hypotheses regarding the impact of autonomous workgroups upon intrinsic job satisfaction, extrinsic job satisfaction, intrinsic job motivation, organizational commitment and mental health were to survive this test, then employees in situations A1, A2, A3, B2 and B3 should record higher scores on each of the five dependent variables than employees in situations B1, C1, C2 , and D1. More precisely the research team made the predictions that measures of the dependent variables should display the following patterns: B1 < B2, B3; A1 > B1, C1, D1; A2, B2, >C2. Meanwhile measures of the five dependent variables in all A and C situations should remain constant but at higher levels.

Intriguingly, subsequent analysis of the data suggested that while autonomous work-groups enhanced intrinsic job satisfaction it did not seem to directly affect the other dependent variables. The symmetry of outcomes referred to in Chapter 1 is only too evident here in results of this research. Most significantly, the team could conclude that ...

the results show that autonomous group working is a viable proposition that is appreciated by those who experience it. Moreover it may have clear economic benefits. This is not, as the theory predicts, because groups enhance operators' motivation and effort; economic benefits stem instead from the logic of the groups themselves . . . indirect labour costs decrease and productivity benefits can accrue. (Wall et al., 1986: 299–300)

Conclusions

In this chapter we began by describing how all deductive researchers face particular problems in attempting to test hypotheses, derived from theory, through data collection. We then outlined how experimental research design provides a particular set of solutions to those methodological problems by structuring data collection through the use of matched control and experimental groups and the manipulation of experimental treatments or independent variables. These protocols enable researchers to control for the potential impacts of extraneous variables whilst measuring changes in the dependent variable(s). As we have demonstrated, such a structuring of research enables the experimental researcher to make observations of the effects of the independent variable(s) upon the dependent variable(s) whilst being able to rule out rival explanations, or rival hypotheses, regarding what has been observed. However, at the heart of the true, or laboratory, experiment lie significant methodological problems created by its reliance upon physical controls to deal with the threats deriving from potential extraneous variables. In particular the necessarily artificial context of the true experiment could actually create a new set of extraneous variables related to its lack of naturalism in practice. For this reason, and also because of the potential ethical problems that might arise from the experimenter's need to purposefully promote change in the subjects of research which could be detrimental to their well-being, often the logic of the true experiment is taken out of laboratory conditions and applied to naturally occurring events in the form of the quasi-experiment (sometimes alternatively called a 'field' experiment). Obviously the quasi-experiment avoids some of the potential ethical problems apparent in the true experiment because events would have happened anyway. Moreover, the increase in naturalism has significant benefits. However, because it entails the investigation of naturally occurring events there will be problems regarding the matching of control groups to experimental groups – therefore some degree of control over extraneous variables will be inevitably lost. In other words, ecological validity may increase but this is a trade off with some loss in internal validity. Nevertheless, as demonstrated by Wall et al. (1986) the potential utility for management researchers and practising managers of using quasi-experimental designs to evaluate organizational changes is only too evident.

Further reading

As we have already pointed out, the use of the true experiment in management research is relatively rare. So we suggest that accounts of where it has been used, such as Roethlisberger and Dickson's (1939) account of the Hawthorne studies, are particularly worthwhile (see also McAuley et al., 2007: Chapter 3 for a detailed consideration of the Hawthorne Studies and their philsophical and theoretical background). An outline of the nature of the experiment and the problems associated with this form of business and management research are provided by Adair (1984). The between-subjects experimental design, used by Wayne and Ferris (1990) to investigate the influence of subordinate's behaviour on work exchange quality, demonstrates how the laboratory experiment has been adapted (mainly by work psychologists) to facilitate manipulation of independent variables in a controlled environment, in keeping with classical experimental ideas. Both Orpen's (1979) and Wall et al.'s (1986) use of the field experiment illustrates how this logic is taken out of laboratory conditions to the quasi-experiment conditions that usually apply in management research. Much, but by no means all, research that attempts to evaluate the effects of change programmes, whether in organizations or elsewhere, takes a quasi-experimental approach in order to make its assessments. Those readers considering undertaking evaluation research in a management context should refer to the excellent guidance given by Rossi et al. (2003), Torres et al. (2005) and McDavid and Hawthorn (2005). For an alternative approach to evaluation that builds upon quasi-experimental designs that also examines the causal factors that might inhibit or engender change, the reader should turn to Pawson and Tilley (1997).

Meanwhile, there is a large body of literature and accounts of experimental research primarily orientated towards social psychology. However, much of this is relevant to management, particularly studies of decision-making. Good examples are Asch's (1951) investigation into the effects of group pressure upon our judgements and Milgram's (1963) study of obedience to authority figures.

Both Shotter (1975) and Gauld and Shotter (1977) provide reviews and evaluations of the philosophical assumptions regarding human beings that underpin experimentally based research in social science and proceed to consider alternative methodologies. For an insightful critique of the use of laboratory experiments in information systems research which argues that such research has neither external nor internal validity, and therefore should be actively discouraged while any findings must be treated with caution, see Introna and Whitley (2000).

These journal articles are freely available on the companion website (www.sagepub.co.uk/gillandjohnson):

Lee, A.S. (1989) Case studies as natural experiments, *Human Relations*, 42(2): 117–37.
Orpen, C. (1979) The effects of job enrichment on employee satisfaction, motivation, involvement and performance: a field experiment, *Human Relations*, 32(3): 189–217.

Action research

5

Learning outcomes At the end of this chapter the reader should be able to:

- **define action research with reference to Kurt Lewin's original approach;**

- **discuss the aims of action research to illustrate how they can be different from 'basic' research and consultancy;**

- **illustrate the key stages of the iterative cycles of activity usually associated with action research methodology;**

- **conceptualize how and why those methodological processes may vary in practice;**

- **identify the theoretical and practical outcomes of action research;**

- **understand the relationship of action research to experimental logic;**

- **appreciate some of the ethical issues that may arise in action research.**

We begin this chapter by considering how Kurt Lewin originally conceptualized action research as a means of contributing to the betterment of society by enabling the resolution of social problems. We then review how the aims of action research are somewhat different to both of the methodologies we have so far considered in previous chapters and consultancy, before moving on to outlining the various methodological stages of research that constitute what is called the action research cycle. Throughout we are concerned to indicate how what is generically called action research can vary considerably with regard to how these different stages are undertaken in practice. Finally, the appropriateness of action research to those undertaking research in business and management is considered together with its methodological and ethical justification.

Conceptualizing action research

Action research is the process of systematically collecting research data about an ongoing system relative to some objective, goal, or need of that system; feeding back these data back into the system; taking action by altering selected variables within the system based both on data and hypotheses; and evaluating the results of actions by collecting more data. (French and Bell, 1984: 99)

... action research is a participatory, democratic, process concerned with developing practical knowing in the pursuit of worthwhile human purposes, grounded in a participatory worldview .... It seeks to bring together action and reflection, theory and practice, in participation with others, in the pursuit of practical solutions to issues of pressing concern to people, and more generally the flourishing of individual persons and their communities. (Reason and Bradbury, 2006:1)

According to Uzzell (1995) action research has been variably used in the social sciences to investigate a broad range of issues and problems from community development and educational research through to organization and management research. Indeed, in recent years the term action research has become increasingly popular amongst management researchers to describe and account for a considerable range of their activities yet it continues to create much controversy regarding its rigour and viability as a research methodology (see Heller, 1993; Cassell and Johnson, 2006). This controversy is fuelled in part by the lack of an over-riding methodological definition of action research that is shared by all the researchers who use the label to define and justify their activities in organizations. Hence, when any management researcher turns to consider action research as a possible means of engaging with their subject of interest, they are immediately confronted by a bewildering array of apparently different methodological approaches. Thus, unlike the true experiment, or indeed the quasi-experiment, there is not an agreed set of methodological protocols, or rules, shared by all action researchers. Instead what we have is a variety of different yet related models, often informed by emerging and competing philosophical stances (see Cassell and Johnson, 2006) which legitimate much variation in actual research practices and which can thereby create much confusion for the uninitiated.

According to Chisholm and Eden (1993), this emerging variability is also expressed in terms of:

- the level of analysis at which the changes developed through action research initiatives take place which vary from the group through to the organizational, national and international;
- the extent of formal organization of the research setting which varies being highly organized to unorganized in terms of membership boundaries, shared cultural attributes; formalization of member relationships in terms of rules and procedures, etc.;
- the degree to which the research process itself is open-ended or pre-specified in relation to what will be studied, where, when and by whom;
- the different goals pursued by action research programmes, which can vary from attempts to improve organizational efficiency and effectiveness of specific aspects of an organization's operations through to fundamental cultural change aimed at empowering disenfranchised groups within society;
- the role of researchers in relation to that of participants with regard to the extent and degree of the latter's involvement in the planning and conducting of, and learning from, the research and their contribution to interpreting and disseminating research findings.

In summarizing this complicated situation, Reason and Bradbury have therefore described action research as a rich and diverse 'family of approaches' (2006: xxii). Nevertheless, despite the complexities that arise because of this diversity, action research as a guide for intervening and changing organizational arrangements and social relationships provides an important vehicle for conducting management research particularly for practising managers working within their own organizations (see Coghlan and Brannick, 2001).

In this chapter we are going to begin by trying to map some of the common methodological themes within this family whilst simultaneously illustrating how it varies in particular ways according to the perspective and approach of the action researcher. We will explore the philosophical underpinnings of this variability in Chapter 9. We shall begin this journey in this chapter by considering the work of Kurt Lewin who is usually seen to be one of the key founders of action research.

Stop and Think Exercise 5.1   Consider the two definitions of action research with which we began this chapter. Make a list of common themes embedded in these definitions and simultaneously identify how these definitions vary. Why do you think there are these differences given that both pairs of writers are using the same label for what they are describing?

Kurt Lewin and action research

Action research, in various forms, has been undertaken for decades. The first consciously self-directed use of the term is generally attributed to Kurt Lewin in the 1940s (see Lewin, 1946, 1948) even though it has also been traced back to the work of the American philosopher John Dewey and later to the work of John Collier, a commissioner of American Indian Affairs from 1933–1945 (see Passmore, 2006: 29). Lewin, a social psychologist, was concerned to apply social science knowledge to guide planned change to solve social problems, such as conflict between groups and the need to change eating habits during wartime. Others closely followed applying the approach, for example, to community relations issues, leadership training and resistance to change in manufacturing plants (see the Tavistock Institute management research example below). As we have already noted, whilst today's action research family is diverse, most action researchers still invoke Lewin's original model of action research to initially position themselves methodologically (see Burnes, 2004). However, this original model is somewhat sketchy since his premature death in 1947 prevented a comprehensive elaboration of what he saw as being precisely involved in the conduct of action research.

So whilst Lewin does not seem to have used any detailed or comprehensive definition of the term, he nevertheless refers to research programmes within organizations whose progress is guided by the needs of the organizations, and frequently uses the expression 'problem-centred research'. The main feature of action research, according to Lewin (1946), was that it should be focused on problems and their resolution: that analysis of the causes of problems should lead to some kind of intervention by the researcher, based on an understanding of the dynamic nature of change, followed by research on the effects of that intervention through studying and evaluating it as it actually took place. However, these practical concerns did not mean that Lewin was unconcerned with theory. By challenging the status quo and purposively changing things to solve or ameliorate problems, as an integral part of the research, Lewin thought that theory was pivotal to guiding how those problems were understood and acted upon by the action researcher. Moreover, by enabling intervention into everyday problems Lewin thought that action research also enabled hypothesis testing and that the action research process itself thereby enabled the refinement of theory and the evolution of new theory (see Marrow, 1969: 128).

Management research example The Tavistock Institute and early action research

At roughly the same time as Lewin's work, and virtually unconnected with these developments in North America, there was significant growth of action research in the UK. As in North America, the roots of this growth were to be found in the Second World War, during which psychologists, anthropologists and psychiatrists of a psychoanalytic orientation came together in multidisciplinary teams to work on a number of problems. During and just after the war a number of successful action research programmes were conducted in personnel selection and the treatment and rehabilitation of returning prisoners of war.

This work led to the formation of the Tavistock Institute of Human Relations, which was composed of people of various social science backgrounds but with the shared objective of attempting to find ways by which social science could contribute to finding solutions to some of the pressing social problems of the post-war period so as to 'improve both organizational effectiveness and dignity' (Passmore, 2006: 38). Although the term 'action research' was not specifically used by workers at the Tavistock Institute until the 1960s, almost all their work was problem-centred, entailed a

long-term involvement with clients with a focus upon their perceived needs and involved helping with the implementation and monitoring of changes.

In the management field probably the best-known early work in this tradition is by Jaques (1951), based on research in the Glacier Metal Company (discussed later in this chapter); Sofer (1961) in further education; Wilson (1961) in Unilever; and Trist et al. (1963), working in the Durham coalfield. Topics included planned organizational change, the analysis of tasks in organizations and the relationship of the organization to its environment, and the analysis of absenteeism, accidents and alienation as symptoms of organizational malfunction. In almost all cases the researchers included very full accounts of their fieldwork methods, especially the day-to-day interactions between researcher and client, and the contexts in which the work was carried out as being major influences on the change process. The work was guided throughout by a strong orientation towards the study of the research process and in particular to the relationships that developed between researcher and client and the extent to which these helped or inhibited utilization of findings. In more recent work, psychoanalytic ideas have become less prominent, although the analogy of the psychoanalytic situation, where the client is confronted with the researcher's perception of what in reality is occurring, is still a feature of much of the work in this tradition.

In contrast, some commentators have framed action research as 'appreciative inquiry'. This approach aims to investigate, and build upon, processes that successfully sustain and enhance organizational life in order to liberate creative and constructive potentials rather than attempting to solve or ameliorate organizational problems (e.g. Cooperrider and Srivastva, 1987; Ludema et al., 2006). Most action researchers, however, tend to follow Lewin by identifying what is distinctive about action research is an iterative cycle of problem identification, diagnosis, planning, intervention and evaluation of the results of action in order to learn from experience and as a prelude to further diagnostic activity and the planning of subsequent interventions (e.g. Checkland, 1991; Dickens and Watkins, 1999). This iterative cyclical process thus enables the development and improvement of research findings by allowing for the building upon evidence elicited during prior iterations of the action research cycle. Hence, action research, as originally formulated, uses theory to guide interventions into real-life situations and attempts to test that theory by evaluating the outcomes of those interventions in particular social contexts. From what has been learnt through the process of evaluation, new interventions into the social setting in question can then be made and a further iteration of the action research process may then begin.

In sum, Lewin's approach, when applied to management research, may generally be conceptualized as entailing the following stages:

- Through the involvement of various stakeholders, at all stages, it entails the identification and definition of the problems in client systems – such as work organizations.
- It entails the observation and analysis of the causes of those real-life problems in their everyday, natural, social context, and attempts to provide assistance to their resolution – in this sense there are sometimes, but not always, some close parallels to the methodological logics used in quasi-experimentation (see Chapter 4).
- The consideration of the causes of the problem(s) that has been identified inevitably involves the deployment of theory in order to make sense of, and explain, what is happening with regard to the problem of concern.
- The processes involved in diagnosis often entail the researcher helping organizational members to re-conceptualize the nature of the problem they initially thought they had.
- Based upon this diagnosis, action or interventions into the system are planned and agreed with participants aimed at the resolution or amelioration of the identified problem.
- Part of planning viable interventions is agreeing to a definition of what constitutes either the resolution of the problem or its amelioration; this provides answers to crucial questions regarding how we will know whether or not things have improved and what do we mean by improvement?
- Interventions are then implemented aimed at resolving the problem;
- The effects of those interventions are then monitored and evaluated not just in terms of the extent to which the problem has been resolved, etc. but also in terms of the implications for the relevant theory being deployed to guide the original diagnosis and intervention.
- Throughout what he called action research's 'spiral of steps' Lewin placed fact-finding in a pivotal position:

First it should evaluate the action. It shows whether what has been achieved is above or below expectation. Secondly, it gives the planner a chance to learn, that is, to gather new general insight . . . Thirdly, this fact finding should serve as the basis for correctly planning the next step. Finally it serves as a basis for modifying the 'overall plan'.
(Lewin, 1946: 38)

- Significant is that whilst the evaluation process focuses upon the effects of the implementation of remedial actions it should also lead to the identification of further issues that need to be resolved and indicate a further cycle of diagnosis so that remedial interventions can be identified, acted upon and evaluated ... and so on.
- Whilst the completion of one action research cycle may successfully deal with the initial problem, action research can involve an indeterminate number of cycles of diagnosis, planning, intervention and evaluation.
- A further important outcome of action research is the evaluation of the theories being deployed in making sense of and explaining the occurrence of the problem. This involves considering whether or not the theoretical diagnosis of a particular problem, in terms of specific causes that need to be acted upon through developing an intervention, has actually led to its amelioration. Such knowledge is usually seen as specific to a particular organizational context although some commentators do see this knowledge as being transferable to new contexts.
- A further important outcome of action research is a deeper understanding of a client's problem, in its organizational context, on the part of both the client and the researcher.

The generic stages, or steps, at the heart of action research cycles are illustrated by Figure 5.1 below.

In order to gain an initial understanding of action research, it is also useful to initially compare the stages of the action research cycle with those evident in both consultancy and 'basic' research in order to establish how action research is generically different from these approaches. Table 5.1 illustrates these differences but here we have added to the action research cycle entry and contracting stages: a complex social process whereby consultants, action researchers, and basic researchers all attempt to establish access to an organization through negotiations with the relevant 'gatekeepers' who control the organization's boundaries with the outside world.

Stop and Think Exercise 5.2   As illustrated in Table 5.1, action research, basic research and consultancy are quite different, especially with regard to the various stages of involvement with people in organizations. However, sometimes both action researchers and basic researchers, when working with or studying organization members, can get pushed into a consultancy role by powerful gatekeepers because of their need to justify, or legitimate, themselves and their research in order to get and maintain access to the organization. What kinds of problems can this create for both types of researcher?

The aims of action research

Throughout his work, Lewin emphasized how the most important aim of doing social science should be to practically contribute to the change and betterment of society and its institutions through resolving social problems. Of course, as we saw

Figure 5.1 | Stages or steps in action research cycles

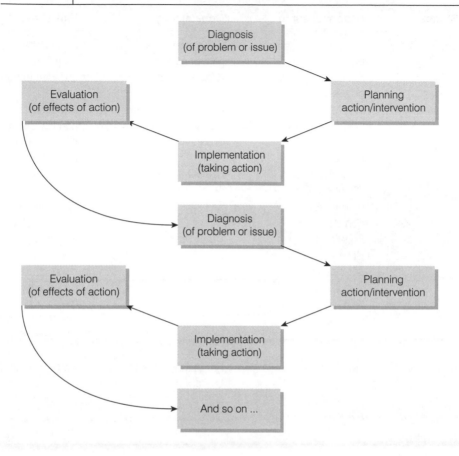

in Chapter 3, much 'basic' research undertaken in the social sciences does potentially have such practical implications as it contributes to our knowledge and understanding of the social world in diverse ways. Unfortunately, especially in the management area, aims such as betterment are always open to some dispute as they are open to retorts such as: Whose problem? Better for whom? What do we mean by 'better'? Moreover, as Lewin implies, how 'basic' research affects management practice, is usually through management practitioners applying the theories separately developed by management researchers to explain the occurrence or non-occurrence of various phenomena. In other words, there are two separate stages where conducting research is the sole prerogative of the researcher whilst the application of any findings, if it is undertaken at all, is the sole prerogative of the practitioner. Here there is always the lurking problem of whether of not the concerns of management researchers are actually relevant to the concerns of practising managers, or, indeed, the other people who have a significant stake in how the organization operates (e.g. different groups of employees, trade unions, customers, shareholders, the local community, etc.).

Of equal importance here is the possibility that the methodologies used by social scientists to conduct 'basic research' could exacerbate this problem of relevance. For instance, Susman and Evered (1978) who took much the same position as Argyris et al. (1985), believed that the principal symptom of what they describe as the crisis

Table 5.1   Action research, consultancy and 'basic' research

Stages	Action research	Consultancy	'Basic' research
Entry	Client or researcher presents problem. Mutually agreed goals	Client presents problems and defines goals	Researcher presents problems and defines goals
Contracting	Business and psychological contracting. Mutual control	Business contract. Consultant controls client	Researchers controls as expert. Keeps client happy. Minimal contracting
Diagnosis	Joint diagnosis. Client data/ researcher's concepts	Consultant diagnosis. Often minimal. Sells package	Researcher carries out expert diagnosis. Client provides data
Action	Feedback. Dissonance. Joint action plan. Client action with support. Published	Consultant prescribes action. Not published	Report often designed to impress client with how much researcher has learned and how competent he or she is. Published
Evaluation	New problems emerge. Recycles. Generalizations emerge	Rarely undertaken by neutrals	Rarely undertaken
Withdrawal	Client self-supporting	Client dependent	Client dependent

Source: Gill, 1986: 103

in the field of organizational science, to be that as research methods and techniques have become more sophisticated they have also become increasingly less useful for resolving the practical problems faced by members of organizations. Indeed, there is some research evidence for this point of view, in work undertaken by Van de Vall et al. (1976), who discovered that in more than 120 applied research projects surveyed in The Netherlands, of which 40 were in industry, deductive, positivist methodologies were less likely to be implemented. This seemed to be because rigorous deductive research designs in field settings were more likely to make managers defensive and to reject collaboration; solving the problem was the test of validity to practitioners rather than theories surviving the test through deductive research finding high correlations amongst variables arranged in elegant causal models (see Chapter 6 of this book). This apparent divorce between the concerns and methodologies of management researchers and those of practitioners appear to be still prevalent (see Tranfield and Starkey, 1998; Keleman and Bansal, 2002) because the former continue to be 'hemmed in by the methodological strictures that favour validation rather than usefulness' (Weick, 1989: 516).

In contrast, action research attempts to combine the processes of research and action based on what Schein (1987) describes as a key assumption of action research – that one can never really understand any human system without trying to change it. In other words, action research processes take place in everyday social contexts and their findings simultaneously emerge out of, and attempt to facilitate, changes in that social situation. Thus, a key aim of action research is often to increase both researchers' and practitioners' understanding of these complicated situations so that the latter can better practically cope by making their decisions more informed. Indeed as Dickens and Watkins (1999) note, Lewin tried to bridge the gap between theory building and research on practical problems where collaboration between researchers and practitioners is central. As they put it '[W]ithout collaboration, practitioners engaged in uninformed action; researchers developed theory without application; neither group produced consistently successful results' (ibid.: 128). In this vein, many influential commentators have emphasized how action research integrates theory and practice through 'systematic self-reflective scientific inquiry by practitioners to improve practice' (McKernan, 1996: 5); where tacit criteria of organizational 'health' have to be deployed in order to define and evaluate improvement (Schein, 1987, 1997); with the result that 'the pure applied distinction that has traditionally characterized management research' is dissolved (Coghlan and Brannick, 2001: 8).

For Lewin, to marshal social science behind the betterment of society and its institutions demanded some reorientation of social research so as to bridge the gap between what he called 'general laws' and the 'diagnosis' of specific social problems. The former dealt with

> ... the relation between possible conditions and possible results. They are expressed in 'if so' propositions ... and can serve as guidance under certain conditions. The knowledge of general laws can serve as guidance for the achievement of certain objectives in certain conditions. (Lewin, 1946: 38)

However, Lewin also saw such general laws as being context-free and it was not sufficient just to know them in order to act correctly, but also one must know the specific character of the situation at hand. In contrast, as we saw in Chapter 4, positivist methodological approaches, as for instance articulated by the 'true' or laboratory experiment, tend to regard the researcher as sole possessor of knowledge from which action (e.g. 'experimental treaments' achieved by researchers manipulating the incidence of the independent variable) will ensue and sole originator of action to be taken on an essentially passive world. By contrast, many scholars agree with Lewin that a human system can only be understood and changed if its members are involved in those processes. Hence, action research is usually undertaken through the involvement of external researchers 'with members over . . . a matter which is of genuine concern to them' (Eden and Huxham, 1996: 75) 'within a mutually acceptable ethical framework' (Rapoport, 1970: 499). Indeed, action research processes are usually seen as essentially collaborative, synthesizing the contributions that both the action researcher and the client, whose problems are being researched, make to solving problems. The action researcher with theoretical ideas and broad practical experience may help clients make more sense of, and reflect upon, their practical knowledge and experience in situations in which they are trying to solve their particular problems. In other words action research is not research that is done *upon* people, rather it is research *done with* those people.

Here it is important to point out that one of the key sources of variation in how action research is practically undertaken relates to how all-encompassing a definition of the 'client' is used in practice (e.g. is it just senior management or does it extend to all employees, and perhaps other identifiable stakeholders both inside and outside the organization) and how the clients' knowledge and understanding is accessed, developed and incorporated into the action research cycle. In other words this issue relates to questions about who participates, how do they participate and how do they influence the outcomes of various stages in the action research cycle? Simultaneously the issues that surround how members' participation is implemented directly influences the nature of the action researcher's field role. The latter can vary considerably in practice: e.g. from that of expert who unilaterally leads the research process to one of facilitator of members' design of the research process and their interpretation of findings (see Chisholm and Edem, 1993).

Who should participate in any action research activity is always problematic in management research because of the different coalitions of stakeholders who make up any organization and who have particular vested interests in how the organization operates. Thus, with action research centred on the resolution of a particular organizational problem it is usually taken to be important to identify stakeholders – individuals and groups, with varying amounts of power, who have an interest in the problem and who will be affected by any possible changes aimed at ameliorating that problem. How decisions are then made around who will actually participate in any action research project inevitably confronts issues around organizational politics and power. Whilst this is a complex issue for which there are no straightforward answers (see the Glacier Metal example below) it simultaneously raises the issue of how participation is accomplished in practice – as we shall see there are some very different approaches to these issues.

Regardless of these very important issues around participation, it is often argued that the effective resolution of clients' problems will come about because of the researcher's involvement in, not from a detachment from, the research process. This is quite different from some of the methodologies we have looked at so far in this book where researcher detachment and distance from what happens during data collection is valued so as to ensure their hard-won objectivity. In contrast, a key criterion for the success of the action research approach may lie in such behaviours as empathetic understanding, taking the role of the other and in specific means of data collection that are more collaborative, such as participant observation, non-directive interviewing, focus groups, etc. It follows that action research would not be granted the status of a valid science on the basis of the methodological standards of the true experiment. Indeed, for some commentators, it is inappropriate to apply such positivist standards to assess the contribution of action research and instead the ultimate criterion is the perceived likelihood of agreed innovations to produce desirable consequences for the organization (see Gustavsen, 2006; Park, 2006).

Of course, as we have noted already, key questions persist here as to who is involved in achieving this agreement, how is this agreement accomplished and whose desires are articulated in this? Different methodological answers to these questions again add to the diversity of action research in practice. Moreover, not all commentators would support the prescriptive views of action research articulated above which try to distance it from positivist methodology. For instance, Aguinis (1993) has been concerned to re-establish what he sees as action research's experimental credentials. Thus, he argues that what must be pivotal to the action research cycle is deductive causal analysis: a process of hypothesis building, testing and modification within organizational contexts so as to solve problems with reference to clearly defined goals and observable outcomes. Such an approach would considerably limit the form and extent of organizational stakeholders' participation in the action research process relative to that envisaged by either Gustavsen (ibid.) or Park (ibid.).

By following the action research cycle illustrated in Figure 5.1, it is to these inter-related processes, and their variability, we now turn.

The processes of action research

In the management area, action research usually begins with the establishment of initial contact between the action researcher and representatives, or 'gatekeepers' of a client organization. This early stage of research, often called the entry stage, entails:

1 Identification and discussion of perceived ongoing problems with the client, how these problems are being manifested, their effects upon stakeholders and the need for change.
2 A key issue here is actually establishing who the client is and who will participate in the research, how, where and when. Indeed here, especially in hierarchical organizations, there will be issues around how binding upon the organization any decisions made by participants are upon the different constituencies that make up the organization. Variations in the substantive elements of these nego-tiations have significant implications for the form that action research then takes.
3 The surfacing and sharing of the researcher's and the clients' pre-understanding of the problem, it's organizational context, it's symptoms and it's causes: accord-ing to Gummesson, 'pre-understanding refers to such things as people's knowl-edge, insights, and experience before they engage in a research programme' (2000: 57).
4 Initial establishment of a psychological contract between the action researcher and the client(s) that consists of the mutual expectations each party has regard-ing one another's behaviour and explores what the potential outcomes of any subsequent research may be.

As illustrated in Table 5.1, during the entry and contracting stages of the action research process, either the client or the researcher can take the initiative in present-ing the problem. In consultancy the client most usually presents the problem, and in 'basic' research the researcher generally asks for access to research a problem in which he or she is interested. The essential difference between the action research mode and the others lies in the former's close collaborative relationship, 'where there is mutual agreement at each stage of the action research sequence in order to contrib-ute both to the practical concerns of people in an immediate problematic situation and to the goals of social science' (Rapoport, 1970: 499).

Such a definition does, however, pose many questions – as Rapoport himself was well aware. The main difficulties arise from the inherent need for close collabo-ration between the parties. Close collaboration between the distinctive and very different cultures of the managerial and academic worlds gives rise to issues about whether the aims of the work will be concerned primarily with problem-solving for the particular organization, or with producing theoretical generalizations for the wider community (Gill, 1986). These ambiguities can take on a considerable degree of complexity in practice as illustrated by the example of the Glacier Metal Project conducted by Jaques and his colleagues at the Tavistock Institute of Human Relations.

Management research example Gaining entry to undertake action research and managing relation hips with stakeholders

This action research was undertaken in the Glacier Metal Company by a group from the Tavistock Institute of Human Relations led by Jaques, over three years from 1948 to 1950 (Jaques, 1951). Glacier, primarily concerned with precision engineering, had a wide reputation for its social policies and for its modern, progressive management methods. A relatively advanced company seemed to Jaques to be particularly appropriate for a deep study into the day-to-day problems experienced by the factory in its attempts to find more satisfying ways of working consistent with the demands of a competitive industrial environment. It was assumed such a company would be less likely to be concerned with mere procedural changes and more interested in the forces underlying them; and, being an innovator in its field, would be more likely to tolerate the stresses associated with unpredictable research activities. It was appreciated that work with one company, which was untypical, might make broad generalizations difficult on the basis of one idiosyncratic case. At the same time, however, it was believed that the problems under study – the psychological and social roots of stresses in group relations – in one factory would have common underlying features with similar problems elsewhere.

So Glacier was approached by Jaques and his colleagues, both for the reasons above, and also because an intermittent working contract over two years had already established that particularly favourable conditions already existed for adhering to a Tavistock principle that management, supervision and workforce should each independently agree to collaborate in any work undertaken.

Three months were taken up in reaching agreement with all the parties before access was gained. The managing director and his immediate subordinates were approached first. Although, unusually, the managing director was as interested in research into the company as managing it, preliminary agreement was not automatic partly because several members of senior management felt that the managing director was already spending too much of his time in social experiments and that production might be adversely affected by such 'diversions'. However, the fact that the managing director was particularly keen on the project and that the institute would not agree to the work being imposed from above, eventually resulted in agreement to start.

The works' council, for its part, was generally antipathetic and sceptical of industrial psychologists and psychiatrists but agreed to meet a member of the Institute to discuss the proposal. It suggested a senior member of the Institute but this suggestion was rejected on the grounds that persuasion of this kind would run counter to the principle of obtaining genuine co-operation from the factory. Accordingly the works' council, after hearing the leader of the research team, and in particular his stipulation that independent agreement would be required from the workers' side, referred the matter for independent consideration to the works' committee, a body composed entirely of elected representatives of the Glacier workforce.

At this meeting detailed questions were asked about, for example, who had initiated the project and who was paying for it. These questions were readily answered. Tavistock had made the approach, one of the research councils was paying for it and the Trades Union Congress was supportive. Other questions were more difficult to answer, such as the time scale for the work, how it would be accomplished and specifically what research methods would be employed. Underlying these questions lay employees' natural fears about speeding up their work and the rate cutting of bonus agreements. The answers to these questions were necessarily vague for there was by its very nature no clear specification for the research work and it was expected that topics for study would be chosen jointly as the work progressed. Nevertheless, despite this unavoidable vagueness, these explanations were accepted, particularly when it was realized that the Institute did not wish to work either for management or shop-floor but to define its client as the workforce as a whole.

The careful building up of the independence of the researcher role was justified on ethical and scientific grounds as avoiding becoming involved in conflict between groups in the factory and having conflicts projected on to the research team. Further, the research team wished to establish from the beginning that a part of the approach used would be the avoidance of capture of the team by any particular group.

Following the decision of the works' committee to go ahead, a project sub-committee of two management and three shop-floor representatives was established to work with the research team; its first task being to clarify issues concerning the control of the work. These discussions resulted in jointly agreed principles to include the reporting relationships of the research team and the ways in which research topics might be undertaken. It was agreed that the research team should be responsible to and report to the works' council and that any suggestions for the study of a topic should be effected only with the general approval of those likely to be affected by the results.

The attitude of the team was that it was not intending to solve all Glacier's problems, but hoped that it might find ways of achieving a smoother-running organization. Nothing would be done behind anyone's back and no matter would be discussed unless representatives of the group affected were present or agreed to the topic being raised.

In practice the team worked with any part of the factory at its request but would comment only on relationships within the immediate group and would not discuss matters relating to anyone not present. Indeed, so strictly did the team work in this respect that it limited relationships with members of the factory to formal contacts publicly sanctioned by the works' council. No personal relationships with Glacier employees either inside or outside working hours were entertained, except for the inevitable informal contacts occurring when, for example, eating in canteens. Even then care was taken to discuss only those aspects of the project which were public knowledge. Thus invitations to people's homes were refused as were invitations to play tennis on the factory's courts. The team regarded it as inconsistent to have informal relationships with members of one group and at the same time to hold a publicly independent attitude when debates took place between groups without being regarded as having been captured by one of them. After about a year the seriousness of the research team's intentions was appreciated and all such invitations gradually ceased.

Finally, care needed to be taken with an agreement regarding publication, a matter which may cause difficulty when undertaking research in organizations when the working lives of people are under scrutiny. Since individuals would be easily identifiable to anyone familiar with the company, steps were taken to agree a publications policy early in the course of the work. It was agreed that any public statements about the project would be governed by the same policy as other public statements about the company. For its part, the Tavistock Institute undertook to make public comments only in collaboration with the company, or after due consultation.

The research quickly got underway once the detailed, time-consuming preliminaries regarding independence had been negotiated and sufficient confidence had been developed in the research team; a confidence demonstrated by a number of sections of the factory offering collaboration on specific problems. Accordingly, projects began to be undertaken on, for example, relationships within the divisional managers' meetings; payment systems in mass-production assembly plants; and, at the request of the works' council, an extensive study of difficulties in the operation of channels of communication down the executive line. Studies generally followed the same pattern in that papers were written and then validated by submitting them for rigorous analysis by the groups concerned.

As illustrated by the Glacier Metal Case, contracting in action research is more than simply an issue concerned with regulating business relationships as is often the case with consultancy; or to maintain at least a sufficiently good relationship to preserve access to the organization, as is frequently the case with 'basic' research. Contracting in action research is generally described as 'psychological', as motives, goals and the locus of control, as well as business arrangements, are carefully discussed and agreed. However, as we indicated earlier, this immediately poses several questions – different answers to which configure action research in different ways and can express particular sets of philosophical commitments on the part of the action researcher themselves.

1 With whom are these agreements taking place in the organization?
2 With whom are the boundaries of participation/involvement in the action research project drawn, thereby including some organization members whilst excluding others?
3 What is the basis of the participation/involvement between researchers and those included in the design and conduct of the project?

In considering these questions it is also useful to differentiate two types of action research labelled by Brown (1993) as the Southern and the Northern traditions: 'the Southern tradition is committed to community transformation through empowering disenfranchised groups; the Northern tradition is concerned with reforming organizations through problem solving' (1993: 249). Now the difference between these traditions may well articulate philosophical disputes within the action research 'family' (see Cassell and Johnson, 2006), however how they articulate in practice largely pivots around the extent, degree and form of participation by various stakeholders in the action research process. For instance, there is a significant tradition within the action researcher family which sees that the relationship between researchers and organization members (note the organization member is being used in an inclusive sense and does not just refer to management) must be 'dialogical' (e.g. Sandberg, 1985) so as to open communicative space and bring *people together around shared topical concerns, problems and issues* ... in a way that will permit people to achieve mutual understanding and consensus about what to do' (Kemmis, 2001: 100, emphasis in the original).

Key methodological concept

Democratic dialogue

Obviously dialogue is a fairly abstract concept that requires some definition if it is to be effectively used in practice. Helpfully Gustavsen (2006: 19) provides a set of criteria for distinguishing what he calls 'democratic dialogue' that emerged out of the practical experience of undertaking highly participative forms of action research in Scandinavia.

- Dialogue is based on a principle of give and take, not one way communication.
- All concerned by the issue under discussion should have the possibility of participating.
- Participants are under an obligation to help other participants be active in the dialogue.
- All participants have the same status in the dialogue arenas.
- Work experience is the point of departure for participation.
- Some of the experience the participant has when entering the dialogue must be seen as relevant.
- It must be possible for all participants to gain an understanding of the topics under discussion.
- An argument can be rejected only after an investigation (and not, for instance, on the grounds that it emanates out of a source with limited legitimacy).
- All arguments that are to enter the dialogue must be represented by the actors present.
- All participants are obliged to accept that other participants may have arguments better than their own.
- Among the issues that can be made subject to discussion are the ordinary work roles of the participants – no one is exempt from such a discussion.
- The dialogue should be able to integrate a growing degree of disagreement.
- The dialogue should continuously generate decisions that provide a platform for joint action.

Stop and Think Exercise 5.3 Consider trying to promote dialogue, as defined above by Gustavsen, as a means of dealing with a problem in a hierarchical work organization with which you are familiar. What barriers do you think might be present in such an organization that might prevent dialogue taking place between the various stakeholders who have a direct concern with, and interest in, the problem?

The aim of dialogue is to 'promote a critical consciousness which exhibits itself in political as well as practical action to promote change' (Grundy, 1987: 154). Here there is often an overt commitment to democratizing action research cycles through the empowerment of often disenfranchised groups in organizations with the aim of 'emancipating themselves from the institutional and personal constraints that limit their power' (Kemmis and McTaggart, 1988: 23). Hence the possible challenge to the status quo of many organizations, where intra-organizational relations are embedded in hierarchy, goes well beyond a conventional concern to practically aid the resolution of particular problems for the betterment of organizations as it puts into the spotlight questions such as: whose problems take priority? Who should participate? Better for whom in the organization? What do we mean by better? Inevitably trying to implement such dialogue will confront issues around the unequal distribution of material and symbolic power in organizations – issues which may prevent genuine dialogue between stakeholders taking place (see Gaventa and Cornwall, 2006).

However, despite Lewin's own public commitment to democratic inquiry through the participation of actors (see Heller, 1976; Burnes, 2004), sometimes this is de-emphasized or redirected for what may appear to be ulterior purposes. For instance, as Schein observes (1995: 14), sometimes the direction and momentum for change within an action research project derives primarily from the scientist's agenda while the involvement of organizational members in the research process is principally about facilitating the implementation of pre-specified changes by reducing resistance to change.

Thus, such variable interpretations of what is meant by participation, who it involves and how it is facilitated in research processes obviously have important implications for how the various steps in action research are undertaken, as they impact upon who is involved and how they are involved in these steps and how decisions are made about the nature and direction of desired organizational change. With this variability in mind we shall now turn to the specific steps in action research illustrated earlier in this chapter by Figure 5.1.

Diagnosis

As we have indicated, the emphasis in action research is upon social scientists intervening in real-life social situations so as to ameliorate the practical problems of actors over a period of time in a manner which emphasizes gradual learning and incremental change. For Lewin the character of the specific situation being investigated by the action researcher is determined through what he termed 'a scientific fact-finding called diagnosis' (1946: 36). Heller (1986, 2004) also makes a distinction between what he calls 'research action' and 'action research'; a distinction depending on how much emphasis is placed on this fact finding or research phase. He defines work as action research when the fact finding phase plays a subsidiary role to the later implementation stage.

Nevertheless, diagnosis forms a pivotal stage in action research for it not only is about the researcher gaining an understanding of the organizational context of the practical problems facing people; it also entails an analysis of the causes of those problems and the production of ideas for how to change the organization in a manner that will ameliorate those problems. As Schein (1987) has observed, the notion that diagnosis precedes action by forming a discrete stage in the action research cycle can be somewhat misleading because change starts at the diagnostic stage stimulated by members' reaction to the very presence of the researcher and his/her fact-finding activities – activities which themselves start as soon as the researcher enters the organization.

For Lewin (1946) an initial holistic understanding of the social system is used by the action researcher for understanding its parts: knowledge is acquired by proceeding from the whole, to the parts, and back again. Whenever there are discrepancies between the parts and the whole a re-conceptualization takes place. This process emphasizes how researchers must access how different people, in different social contexts within the organization, may see things from different perspectives. The action researcher is thus forewarned that his or her own interpretation and understanding of the organization may never be exactly the same as that held by its members. This enables the researcher to understand better both his or her own preconceptions and those of the organizational members involved in the study. It also allows the researcher some detachment from the different ways in which members see their organization and may suggest problems and solutions not necessarily perceived by those organizational members.

So this diagnostic stage is ideally carried out jointly by action researcher and client(s) if the results of the investigation are to have the clients' commitment to the work and if outcomes are to have a chance of successful implementation.

Here researcher may introduce conceptual schemes and theories to organizational members that enable them to reinterpret and restructure how they understand their situation generally and the problems that they see as afflicting their organizational lives specifically. This joint endeavour generally can lead to the increased commitment of both parties to the ensuing diagnosis and will often include the client and researcher jointly devising instruments in order to collect further information on the nature of, and causes of, any perceived problem.

So action research is based upon at least respect for the client's knowledge of the organization in the sense that this knowledge is incorporated into any diagnosis of the problems subsequent interventions are aimed at resolving. Inevitably theory is deployed here in gaining an understanding of, and explaining the causes of, the problems experienced by the client(s). Here the theories of the researcher may be introduced through feedback to the client(s) so as to challenge their particular (and equally theory-dependent) interpretation of what is going on. The aim here is to purposively develop client(s) understandings in new ways and co-determine and plan possible interventions.

Key methodological concept

Action science

Argyris and colleagues (1985) distinguish 'action science' from action research on the grounds that they believe that action research has been regarded by social scientists as being primarily concerned with problem-solving for clients and not necessarily with testing theory. Second, they argue that many organizational researchers conduct their empirical work using rigorous deductive research methods which they believe to be unhelpful to utilization. As Friedman (2006: 133) observes, the aim of action science is to help members 'discover the tacit choices they have made about their perceptions of reality, about their goals and about their strategies for achieving them. The fundamental assumption of action science is that by gaining access to these choices, people can achieve greater control over their own fate'. By making the tacit explicit, by heightening members' awareness of the theoretical schemes they are using to guide their practices and construct versions of organizational reality, action science enables them to critically evaluate ongoing practices and consider alternative ways of working possibly based on alternative theories and associated definitions of reality.

Accordingly, in action science, the iterative cycles of problem identification, diagnosis, planning, intervention and evaluation, focus upon processual issues by developing an interpretative or emic understanding of members' tacit practical reasoning as 'theories-in-use'. By making these tacit theories explicit, action science enables members to critically examine and change the theories that guide their practical activities within the organization. However theories in-use often occupy organizational backstages and are hidden by the evasions constituted 'espoused theories' – what people say, or think, they do (Argyris and Schon, 1989; Argyris, 1993; Grubbs, 2001). As such these informal realities create organizational defences and can only be accessed by the researcher's deployment of what amount to ethnographic (Schein, 1987) or hermeneutic (Torbert, 1999; Gummesson, 2000) insights. Through the involvement of members, the aim is to engender single-loop and double-loop learning (Argyris and Schon, 1989). Single-loop learning is about the ability to detect and delete errors that might occur during members' practical activities aimed at achieving a particular goal. In contrast, double-loop learning is more about questioning the values and beliefs that underpin a particular way of working and justify the particular goals that members are ostensibly working towards. In this members 'surface and question their intuitive understandings ... undertake on-the-spot experiments ... [and] ... engage in reflective conversations with their situation' (Schon, 1983: 265).

Planning and intervening

As we indicate above, the feedback of the diagnosis itself to clients and stakeholders may form part of the intervention in its own right in that it can change how participants see themselves, their own organization and how they should do things. Moreover, the very process of coming to a diagnosis, as it usually involves clients themselves, can contribute to this challenging of their pre-understandings and the emergence of alternative ways of engaging with and conceptualizing these issues. So whilst the diagnostic process itself can form part of an intervention, it also enables the construction of plans regarding how any organizational change to resolve the diagnosed problem is to be accomplished and, most importantly, how the success or failure of any intervention will be known and evaluated.

The planning stage of action research further merges with diagnosis because it entails the consideration of, and selection from, the alternative possible actions that have been identified as possible means of ameliorating or resolving the problem(s) that have been defined and identified during diagnosis. As Kemmis and McTaggart have observed, these plans need to be flexible in order to allow changes to the plans as participants 'learn from their own experience' (1988: 8) and learn to cope with unpredictable demands or contingencies which may arise from the organizational context of the problem being researched. One way of understanding the complexities action researchers must cope with here is to realize that they are dealing with a complex and ever changing social context that 'answers back' with variable interpretations and responses to their activities: for example, as organizational members react to the issues raised by, or understood in new ways through, the action research process itself.

Here Lewin had also stressed the limitations of studying complex social events in a laboratory: especially the artificiality of isolating particular behavioural elements as dependent and independent variables in unnatural laboratory conditions. This critique was important to how he conceptualized the tensions between social science and practice, and the development of his still widely used notion of force-field analysis to guide interventions. Here any organizational situation is conceptualized as being in a quasi-stationary state maintained by a balance of equal but opposing driving and restraining forces: forces which in effect cancel each other out to create a situation held in equilibrium. A clue to a means of bringing about a desired change to state of equilibrium was then to intervene by choosing to unbalance these forces through intentionally reducing some of the restraining forces, rather than by increasing the driving forces (which Lewin thought would only result in a corresponding increase in resistance), so as to 'unfreeze' the situation. Once these sources of resistance were minimized the desired change could be implemented by moving the organization towards a new equilibrium. This general approach to organizational change is illustrated by Figure 5.2 below.

The approach illustrated by Figure 5.2 was developed during the famous Iowa studies (Lewin, 1948/1998) where Lewin and his associates attempted to promote change in the eating habits of American families. The aim was to get housewives to change their families' eating habits with regard to the type of meat they consumed. The agenda here was to promote types of meat the women considered to be inferior and hence would not normally purchase. The action research process entailed getting these participants to reflect upon their own resistance to eating those alternative types of meat and to try them out with their families.

Figure 5.2 | Lewin's force-field approach to organizational change

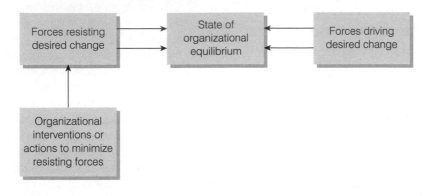

Stop and Think Exercise 5.4

1 Identify and describe a social problem or change issue that you have recently
   encountered either at work or in any social context with which you are familiar.
2 Describe the direction in which you would like change to occur – what do you want
   to happen or stop happening?
3 Identify and list the forces operating in your scenario that support, or could drive,
   the desired change.
4 Identify and list the forces operating in your scenario that resist, or oppose, the
   desired change.
5 Give a relative weighting to each of the forces identified in each of your above
   lists.
6 Consider only the forces resisting your desired change. Identify those forces which
   you can work on to reduce their power of restraint and formulate plans for practically accomplishing this reduction.

Part of the results of the Iowa research was Lewin's conceptualization of change by
action to minimize the restraining forces preventing change rather than increasing
the driving forces for change. It also led to his famous conceptualization of a successful change project as entailing three steps (see Burnes, 2004: 985–6):

1 *Unfreezing*: the need to destabilize the equilibrium state before old standards of
   behaviour can be discarded and new behavioural standards adopted;
2 *Moving*: the adoption of new standards of normative behaviour and the acceptance of their underlying values;
3 *Refreezing*: stabilizing the changes at a new state of quasi-equilibrium by taking
   steps to reinforce the new standards.

Such process generalizations were, he believed, applicable to any change problem and capable of being added to theory development in action research. Indeed
Lewin's approach is still a common frame of reference for those interested in
planned organizational change and has been highly influential upon management
fields of work such as Organizational Development (see, for example, Cummings
and Worley, 1993).

Management research example Action research, field role ambiguity and the problems of implementation: industrial relations at a refinery construction site

This project was undertaken in the late 1970s and had its origins in a research contract between the Stanlow refinery of Shell UK Ltd and Sheffield Polytechnic. It was designed to help management at BP's Stanlow refinery to resolve some industrial relations issues on the construction site and simultaneously to add to the general understanding of a number of industrial relations matters (Lumley, 1978).

BP had embarked on a major expansion programme on its petrochemicals complex on Merseyside involving a capital expenditure programme of £110 million over three years. This was expected to involve contractors on the production site with a peak labour force of more than 3,000.

The general experience from this and other large construction sites in the UK was of a high incidence of industrial relations unrest leading to expensive delays in completion times. BP was puzzled by the considerable differences between the behaviour of contractors' employees and that of its own more permanent refinery workforce on the same site. BP felt the need for some systematic research into the contractors' industrial relations behaviour as an aid to formulating policies to improve contractors' industrial relations and so reduce completion times. In particular, management were seeking predictors of contractors' industrial relations performance which would help them select contracting companies that would be relatively trouble free.

At the same time, the researcher intended to use the data for a parallel academic study he wished to present for publication and a doctorate, by making a specific substantive contribution not only to the nature of industrial relations on large construction sites but also to the resolution of some issues in the understanding of industrial relations as a field of study. He also wished to generalize about the practicability of a research strategy that had as its objective to satisfy simultaneously the needs of the client company and the academic community.

By definition most action research projects are pursued through the medium of a case study, and this was no exception, the work being confined to one large industrial construction site. This of course raised issues about the extent to which the findings were generalizable to other cases.

In all these respects, then, the project met the goals Rapoport defines for action research – but also raised many problematic issues. Three main pressures arose out of the dual role which is the lot of the action researcher.

One was the matter of independence and confidentiality of the work, for meaningful data could be collected only with the consent and support of contractors' managements, their employees and the trade unions. This in turn required the giving and acceptance of guarantees of anonymity, and in some cases confidentiality, of data. Furthermore, there was the matter of feedback of data and the uses to which this might be put. Accordingly, it was felt necessary to agree with the client, and a guarantee offered to other parties to the study, that the same written reports of findings would be made available to all the participants in the research. In addition, the client company as sponsor of the project would receive recommendations intended to be of help in reaching its objectives.

A second issue was that collaboration between researcher and client in defining the goals of the research might be at the expense of neutrality; while collaboration with contractors and unions, even if approved by the client, would doubtless be impracticable in a sensitive, often low trust, situation.

The third pressure was that of time. The temporary nature of construction activity was likely to inhibit the effective implementation of changes arising from the work. The client company was naturally keen to see that empirical findings were presented quickly, and this was accentuated by the client's unforeseen curtailment of its planned expansion, resulting in an earlier than expected rundown in the construction programme. This accentuated the practical problem of theoretical understanding and development and in consequence led to the work being achieved in two phases: first, by presenting the client with a specific report on the problems as defined within its timescale; and then subsequently developing theoretical and generalizable propositions.

In reviewing the outcomes from the work the theoretical objectives were reasonably well met: a substantial contribution was made to the understanding of workplace industrial relations, especially those on large construction sites.

On the matter of generalization of findings from a single case, it is clear that all findings needed to be qualified with the cautionary note that they applied only within the specific context; there was nevertheless clear evidence that they had wider applicability. Descriptive data from the site on, for example, the structural behaviours and characteristics of contracting firms led to the conclusion that they were fairly typical of those on large construction sites in the UK as a whole. Further, in the construction industry there is a large amount of intersite and interfirm mobility on the part of construction employees; so in general terms

the Merseyside site seemed not untypical of all highly unionized sites in the UK. Moreover, the methods used in the case study, of seeking multiple determining conditions, meant that the explanatory mechanisms underlying relationships put forward could be fairly specifically described and it seemed reasonable that they would apply to other, similar environments. Nevertheless, some issues clearly needed to be tested against data from other cases but a start had been made in an exploratory study on which others might build.

However, when we come to consider the extent to which the work was implemented, and the degree to which client needs were met, the evidence is less conclusive. The findings from an intensive study, in which the researcher absorbed himself in the culture of the site, led to recommendations at both long-range strategic planning and operational levels. Some were implemented directly by the client but others were of course dependent on the influence the client could bring to bear on the other parties on the site.

It was also clear that a major potential utility of the investigation was the provision of a large pool of information which could be of help in diagnosing situations that might arise and in predicting the likely industrial relations consequences of proposed actions. The extent to which these recommendations were accepted and implemented was clearly affected by the problems posed by the short timescale of construction projects in relation to a research activity requiring the collection of large amounts of data and long periods spent on the site. By the time reports were presented, work on the site was beginning to run down and the implementation of many recommendations had to await the commencement of a major new construction phase.

Other factors negatively affected implementation. The refinery manager who had initiated the project retired and the dispersion of industrial relations and construction personnel to other locations effectively eliminated the possibility of useful discussions on the site. In particular, for these reasons, meetings proposed by the researchers to bring together client, contractors and unions did not take place.

Clearly in work of this nature there is a tension between the need to remain independent, particularly from a client who, as in this case, was financing the work, in order to collect sensitive data from the other parties; and the danger that too little client involvement might lessen commitment to the conclusions. This was especially so in the phases of design, data collection, analysis and interpretation. Moreover, action research designs that attempt to involve clients with approaches

with which they are unfamiliar carry the risk that the researcher will be placed in the classic role of the detached academic, requiring him or her to work remotely, present findings and leave it to the client to decide whether or not the work will be implemented.

In this case a degree of independence was established at the cost of the client ascribing an expert role to the researcher and to a large extent withdrawing from close involvement in the conduct of the study. Although much of the work was utilized, closer involvement of the client in the research process, in the way this was achieved in the Glacier Metal case described above, may have greatly facilitated major changes based upon the study.

Evaluation

As both Marrow (1969) and Argyris et al. (1985) suggest, Lewin's greatest contribution was the idea of studying things through changing them and then seeing the effects of those changes so that the rigorous testing of hypotheses is not sacrificed, nor the relationship to practice lost. Thus, 'Lewin was led by both data and theory, each feeding off each other' (Marrow, 1969: 128) since actual practical outcomes can be evaluated and a modified hypothesis can be developed (Miller, 1995: 29). Thus, for Lewin evaluation was a critical stage in action research because it aimed to see 'whether what has been achieved is above or below expectation' (1946: 38). As Coghlan and Brannick point out (2001: 18) this evaluation process also raises questions about: whether or not the original diagnosis was correct; if the action or intervention taken was correct; if the action or intervention was taken in an appropriate manner; identifying what needs to be fed into a future cycle of diagnosis, planning and action. Moreover, evaluation also requires that the evaluators know what constitutes 'above or below expectations'. This raises the question of by what criteria will they know if improvement has or has not taken place?

This of course raises the issue of how such evaluation may be accomplished particularly since it may be important for enabling the testing of hypotheses as Lewin originally envisaged. This is where action research can run into methodological problems – especially when action research itself is evaluated from the positivist methodological stance encoded into experimental forms of research.

As we have illustrated action research involves a planned intervention by a researcher into some natural social setting, such as an organization, in order to ameliorate the effects of some perceived problem. The effects of that intervention are then monitored and evaluated with the aim of discerning whether or not that action has produced the expected consequences. In other words, the researcher acts upon his or her beliefs or theories in order to change the organization usually through the involvement or participation of organizational stakeholders at every stage of the project. From their intervention and subsequent evaluation action researchers intend not only to contribute to existing knowledge in the sense that their findings should 'help social scientists ... improve their understanding of the problem' (Warmington, 1980: 32) but also to help resolve some of the practical concerns of the people, or clients, who are trying to deal with a problematic situation. Therefore, as Argyris and Schon (1991: 86) point out,

> *It builds descriptions and theories within the practice context itself, and tests them through intervention experiments – that is, through experiments that bear the double burden of testing hypotheses and effecting some (putatively) desirable change in the situation.*

From this particular view of action research, the intervention may be perceived as analogous to the independent variable(s) of the true and quasi-experiment, with its consequences being treated as dependent variables whose change is monitored and evaluated in order to test hypotheses. Thus for some commentators (see also Aguinis, 1993), action research, in principle, can closely follow experimental logic and should entail the use of control groups so as to allow elucidation of cause and effect through the control of extraneous variables. As we saw in Chapter 4, the apparent strength of the 'true' experiment is its ability to methodologically create, or simulate, conditions of closure which allow the empirical testing of hypotheses and enable internal validity. As we have illustrated, for the experimenter, 'scientific' rigour amounts to: ensuring that every respondent had experienced the same experimental treatment within an experimental group; measuring variation in the dependent variable; and matching control and experimental groups so as to rule out the influence of extraneous variables through techniques like randomization.

However, Lewin's holistic and naturalistic concern with what Argyris and Schon (1989) call 'intervention experiments' in real-life situations militate against the full implementation of such 'true' experimental designs (Beer and Walton, 1987; Perry and Zuber-Skerritt, 1994): the practicalities of the situation being studied may preclude the identification of possible control groups. Moreover, given that the context is a 'live' management situation or problem, the possibility of matching control and experimental groups through the systematic or random allocation of subjects to enable the manipulation of experimental treatments is inevitably problematic. The tensions created by the desire to apply experimental logic in 'natural' organizational contexts has led Argyris and Schon (1989) to comment that the action researcher has a dilemma in that they must make the choice between rigour or relevance. For others this is a choice between 'science' or action research (for example, Stone, 1982; Brief and Dukerich, 1991) which, as Eden and Huxham (1996) have observed may mean that action research is rejected as 'unscientific'. A summary comparison of experiments, quasi-experiments and action research is given in Table 5.2.

Much, of course, depends upon what is tacitly being invoked as the benchmark for science when much of action research is rejected as 'unscientific'. Here it seems that a tacit positivist view is being deployed to distinguish science for non-science, something, as we shall see in Chapter 9, that is open to considerable challenge. Indeed the rigour-relevance dilemma noted above is only a dilemma if we are adopting a positivist stance that defines 'science' in terms of hypothetico-deductive concerns and objectives (see Cassell and Johnson, 2006). So whilst the natural, everyday context of action research may make

Table 5.2   A comparison of true experiments, quasi-experiments and action research

True experiments	Quasi-experiments	Action research
Entail the analysis of the direct intervention of the researcher	Entails the analysis of events that have naturally occurred without the intervention of the researcher, i.e. after the fact	Entails the analysis of the direct interventions of the researcher
Incidence of the independent variable due to the manipulations of the researcher	Incidence of the independent variable occurs naturally	Incidence of the independent variable is constituted by the actions of the researcher
Entails pre- and post-treatment, measurement and comparison of the dependent variable in both the experimental and the control groups	Entail pre- and post-treatment, measurement and comparison of the dependent variable in both the naturally occuring experimental and the control groups	Entails pre- and post-treatment, measurement and comparison of the dependent variable in the experimental group. Availability of an equivalent or non-equivalent control group problematic according to the context of the research
Entail physical control over extraneous variable through assignation of subjects to equivalent experimental and control groups	Since analysis entails naturally occurring events, prior assignation of subjects to control and experimental groups problematic. Instead, control and experimental groups are identified in terms of the incidence of the independent variable and cannot be exactly matched	As the incidence of the independent variable is constituted by the actions of the researcher prior identification of control and experimental groups is sometimes possible. However, their full equivalence problematic since such groups are usually naturally occurring
Strengths High internal validity	High ecological validity. Avoids problems associated with experimental artefacts; can have high population validity	Can be very high in ecological validity. Can avoid problems associated with experimental artefacts
Weaknesses Low ecological validity; often population validity is limited	Loss of control over extraneous variables	Population validity limited to those subjects involved; loss of control over extraneous variables

the use of control groups very difficult, some of the possible philosophical commitments of the action may make the use of control groups methodologically undesirable (see Chapter 8). For instance, even if it were possible to allocate subjects to equivalent groups for comparative purposes, some action researchers may see that the action researcher, by using such a methodology, would be in danger of destroying the very organizational situation s/he intends to study through the disruptions to everyday life it would create. Other action researchers would also play down the testing of hypotheses, as an aim of action research, in favour of evaluating whether or not what was hoped would happen has actually happened. If what was intended does happen then from this more pragmatic stance the action research is judged to be effective. Now this might merely sound like a re-articulation of the rigour relevance debate above – but coming down on the side of relevance. However, the underlying philosophical justification for such a view does exist in opposition to positivist views of science, but it is complex and therefore will be considered in more detail in Chapter 8.

So, for the time being, it is important just to note that some action researchers have argued that action research itself is a vehicle for judging the ideas in terms of their efficacy in actual application (see Gustavsen, 2006; Reason and Bradbury, 2006; Park, 2006). Moreover, throughout this chapter we have hinted at a more dialogical view of research-participant interactions. This is where researchers and organizational members are treated as equally knowing participants and where we see how action research may be geared to pursuing a different kind of science with a different philosophy which directly impacts upon how action research is undertaken. These commitments have led action researchers to try to produce a different kind of knowledge to that sanctioned by positivsm, in the course of which organizational members are developed, through engaging with dialogue, to solve their future problems in a democratic manner (see Grundy, 1987; Kemmis, 2001). Again our philosophical review in later chapters, especially in Chapter 8, may be regarded as offering further legitimization of such a dialogical view of action research.

Ethical dilemmas in action research

A particular set of ethical dilemmas can arise during action research because of how it aims to simultaneously contribute to the publicly available stock of knowledge about management and organizational issues and to resolving practical problems in specific organizational contexts.

First, there is the issue of the acceptability of the client to the researcher. Whether, for example, the action researcher should work for organizations such as tobacco companies, or for those known to be engaged in the manufacture of weapons was an issue posed in the pioneering work of the Tavistock Institute. Such difficulties were partly resolved by working in a values framework acceptable to both parties. So, for example, work between the Tavistock Institute and the Tobacco Research Council was made possible in this fashion. Tavistock was primarily interested in developing new mathematical models for multiple correlation analysis whereas the Tobacco Research Council wished to sell more tobacco. Both, however, shared an interest in individual responses to the stresses of life and the part played in it by tobacco, and this became a superordinate goal enabling the work to proceed. Another response to ethical dilemmas of this nature is to ensure sources of support from an array of stakeholders who have a vested interest in the outcomes of the proposed research e.g. trade unions, government agencies, local communities and so on.

Second, once work begins other ethical dilemmas may arise, for example confidentiality and the protection of participants and informants. This may be especially awkward in action research projects because of their specific, and so easily identifiable, character. Even though it might have been agreed that individuals or organizations would not be identifiable and that intra-organizational debates about issues should remain confidential, in practice this might prove very difficult to ensure, for anyone familiar with the identity of the researcher might soon become aware of the identity of both individuals and the organization, to their possible detriment. Moreover, the exposure of organizational processes, some of which might be usually surrounded by secrecy and even controversy, may be potentially harmful to the organization as a whole – particularly with regard to its relationships with wider society. Frequently, this issue may arise in the cases of student dissertations, for example those having a marketing content of possible advantage to competitors. In such cases the work may need to be protected for a period and made immediately available only to examiners, so depriving the research community of the findings for a while.

Third, because action research involves various interventions into normal everyday life so as to change things in particular directions, inevitably there will be direct and indirect affects upon people within the organization. Sometimes these affects could be detrimental to their well-being. Whilst some of the ethical problems that can arise here may be mitigated in some styles of action research, especially where there is a commitment to the informed participation of all stakeholders and dialogue to promote consensus about the nature of any change, not all the ramifications of any implemented change are usually foreseeable to those involved.

Finally, because action research usually involves outsiders working with organizational members to resolve problematic issues, usually reciprocal ethical obligations about the performance of each others' roles in the project have to be explicitly established and agreed early in the development of the project. However, expectations regarding such matters (as well as other aspects of participants' roles and responsibilities), are usually influenced by the different cultural and institutional backgrounds of participants in a tacit manner. The potential for a clash between academic norms of ethical behaviour and those of other participants is always present. The differences and the difficulties associated with trying to surface, articulate and agree all aspects of complex and often changing relationships add a further source of ethical tension in many action research projects.

Conclusions

Action research, then, is clearly an important approach to research in business and management, particularly given its declared aim of serving both the practical concerns of managers and other stakeholders whilst simultaneously generalizing and adding to theory. As we have seen, despite being characterized by a considerable diversity of approaches, in practice most action researchers agree that the best way to understand organizational processes must involve trying to change them and this involves a series of iterations of a cyclical step by step approach which involves, in varying ways, the participation of organizational members in investigating and changing their own behaviours.

Most researchers using this approach wish to do immediately useful work and at the same time to stand back from the specific so that their research may be more widely utilized. Indeed, this is the often stated requirement for student dissertations at master's level and beyond. These twin objectives may frequently be achieved by the resolution of a particular content problem in a specific case, and the investigation then widened to address more general issues, such as Lumley (1978) achieved in his research at the BP Stanlow refinery. Alongside the solution of a specific problem, generalizations may be made about the methods used to address the problem especially about the ways the relationship between client and action researcher developed during the course of the work, which of course is so crucial to smooth implementation. The interactions between client and researcher at each phase of the action research sequence may be a convenient way of structuring such an analysis especially if generalizations can be made about the contribution of the action research process to implementation, in the way described in Table 5.1.

Management students who approach their research work in this tradition will, even if working full time as a manager, probably be stereotyped as an academic – with all that may imply for the successful outcome of the work. Ethical and value dilemmas and problems of role ambiguity also arise from the very nature of action research. Implicit, too, in much of the literature on action research (for example, Reason and Bradbury, 2006) is its advocacy of alternatives to positivist social science and the consequent need to justify the approach in methodological terms – something which we shall return to later in this book especially in Chapter 8. Nevertheless, for the time being it is worth emphasizing here that an array of commentators have indeed dismissed action research as an approach which lacks scientific rigour – a vulnerability often exacerbated by the value action researchers often place upon their own critical reflection when reporting the outcomes of their own research project (see Somekh, 1995). Remarkably, in some management disciplines such as Information Systems Studies, this positivist-inspired dismissal occurred to the extent that it became very difficult to publish research findings based upon action research (see Lau, 1999). However we need to be careful here because what is meant by the term action research varies considerably and whilst some scholars vigorously defend an etic or hypothetico-deductive view of action research along with positivist criteria for assessing its appropriateness as a methodology (for example, Aguinis, 1993) others question the universal appropriateness of such positivist criteria due to the evident variation in philosophical stance taken by people who label themselves as action researchers (see for example, Cassell and Johnson, 2006; Johnson et al., 2006). Such divergence, dissensus and debate point to the variable set of practices and philosophical commitments that are embraced by action researchers. We will consider the contribution of those who clearly present an anti-positivist stance, and are inspired by philosophies as diverse as critical theory and postmodernism, in Chapter 8.

Further reading

There is a voluminous literature on action research. First, whilst Lewin's original work (1946) provides much insight into his thinking, it would be also informative to turn to carefully written considerations of his contribution to the development of action research which may be found in both Dickens and Watkins (1999) and Burnes (2004) – the latter's focus being more upon change-management in general. Next, McNiff and Whitehead (2005) provide an extremely useful introduction to action research that explores the key philosophical issues that underpin action research approaches and considers all aspects of undertaking an action research project. For those who need shorter introductions we have found the articles by Rapoport (1970), Susman and Evered (1978), and Chisholm and Eden (1993) particularly useful as they identify both the key characteristics of action research as well as how and why it can vary in practice. In addition, the paper by Warmington (1980) may be consulted for its focus on managerial issues in action research. More recently written with the manager in mind, an invaluable guide to undertaking action research that covers all stages of research from project selection to implementation and writing-up with useful practical examples and exercises, may be found in Coghlan and Brannick's book about doing action research, in your own organization (2001 or 2004). For an accessible overview of philosophical issues and the problematic relationships between consultancy, research, action science and action research, readers must turn to Gummesson's thoughtful book upon qualitative methods in management research (2000). Similarly, Cassell and Fitter (1992) provide an excellent contribution in which they describe the processes and implications of using an action research evaluation methodology within a participative framework and with interesting consideration of the nature of feedback in action research. Further insights into the important issue of participation in action research may be found in Whyte (1991), Reason (1994) and Gustavsen (2006).

Argyris et al. (1985) deal in some depth with philosophical and methodological matters, especially so in Part 1 and then proceed to develop some of the key characteristics of what they call action science. Special issues of the journals *Human Relations* (Volume 46, Number 1) and *Management Learning* (Volume 30, Number 2) focus exclusively upon action research and contain contributions from an array of scholars and practitioners upon different aspects of action research. Similarly Reason and Bradbury's edited volume (2001 or 2006) contains contributions from various action researchers operating from different philosophical perspectives including interpretative, participative, pragmatist and postmodernist orientations. In particular Reason and Bradbury's editorial introduction to either volume is very helpful as it provides an overview of current debates in action research and indicates how action research is becoming more and more diverse as practitioners draw upon an increasingly wide array of philosophical commitments which normatively influence their praxis. The implications of this increasing diversity for how action research may be evaluated are explored by Cassell and Johnson (2006). This can be contrasted with Aguinis (1993) where he demonstrates how and why action research does not meet key methodological demands of the hypothetico-deductive approach.

Finally a key text for any student considering undertaking an action research project as part of their studies for a higher degree, is Herr and Anderson (2005) who provide excellent advice upon how to do this covering all aspects of proposing the research, undertaking the research and writing it up, as well as the difficulties that can arise around the assessment of action research and ethical issues.

These journal articles are freely available on the companion website (www.sagepub.co.uk/gillandjohnson):

Cassell, C. and Johnson, P. (2006) Action research: explaining the diversity, *Human Relations*, 59(6): 783–814.
Guatavsen, B. (2008) Action research, practical challenges and the formulation of theory, *Action Research*, 6(4): 421–37.
Management Learning, 30(2) and *Human Relations*, 46(1) – special editions on action research.

Survey research design

6

Learning outcomes At the end of this chapter the reader should be able to:

- **appreciate the different practical stages in planning a survey;**

- **differentiate between descriptive surveys and analytical surveys and understand the logic of the time-series design;**

- **understand the different sampling strategies available to a researcher and the choices around administering a survey;**

- **appreciate how to design a questionnaire format and the role of piloting a survey.**

In this chapter we begin by outlining the main approaches to survey research methodology and their determinants; we then discuss examples drawn from business and management. Finally, we consider the essential practical steps entailed in undertaking surveys such as questionnaire format and issues in fieldwork.

Approaches to survey research

In terms of the methodological continuum developed at the end of Chapter 3, survey research occupies a variable, intermediate position somewhere between ethnography and experimental research. This is because the form a survey takes differs considerably depending on the intentions and dispositions of the researcher. For instance, on some occasions, by taking the logic of experimentation out of the laboratory and into the field so as to assess causal relationships, a deductive orientation is emphasized. Such analytical survey approaches acknowledge their intermediate position and their connection with the logic of deductive inquiry by their emphasis on reliability in data collection and the statistical control of variables in place of the physical controls of the laboratory. In their attempts to overcome a major perceived weakness of experiments, there is emphasis on the generalizability of results. Thus sample size, data collection procedures, analysis and measurement are major concerns of survey researchers; many texts deal with these matters and some of the most useful will be cited later. Alternatively, the use of surveys to explore a substantive area, often using open-ended questions to collect data in an inductive form, merges the survey approach with styles of research which are more ethnographic in orientation. Indeed, much survey research may begin with an unstructured and exploratory investigation using overtly ethnographic methods. Thus, theory is developed inductively to be tested later using a more structured questionnaire as part of the main study.

Other forms of survey are not necessarily concerned with the development and testing of theory, rather, the prime aim, just like a census, is to describe the characteristics of a specific population at a specific point in time, or at varying points in time for comparative purposes. It should of course also be noted at this preliminary stage that the point made succinctly by Bynner and Stribley (1978) and emphasized throughout this book, that qualitative and quantitative researchers have much to learn from one another, has force. On the one hand, those engaged in experimental research, as well as many survey researchers, may profitably use imaginative insights in the exploration of data as well as in the testing of hypotheses; and on the other ethnographers may need to be more aware of the analytical aspects of their research when inductively generated hypotheses may need to be rigorously tested and refined through a more structured methodology. This point is also made, for example, by Campbell and Fiske (1959) and Jick (1979a), and in practice is interestingly employed in Gladwin's (1989) method of ethnographic decision-tree modelling as a means of researching decision-making.

Planning survey research

How the researcher initially sets about conceptualizing and structuring a problem, so that it is amenable to investigation, is largely determined by the researcher's aims.

For instance, it is important first to be clear whether the intention is to test a theory deductively by elucidating cause and effect relationships among a set of phenomena, or whether the aim is to assess the attributes of a population of subjects. A consideration of these issues determines the type of survey research to be undertaken, whether analytic or descriptive. It thereby points to particular research design problems and issues that need to be addressed prior to any attempt at data collection (Figure 6.1).

Analytic surveys

As we have seen, analytic or explanatory surveys attempt to test a theory by taking the logic of the experiment out of the laboratory and into the field, for example to determine the relationship between accounting control systems and business strategy (Simons, 1987). Hence, in conceptualizing and structuring the research there needs to be an emphasis on specifying the independent, dependent and extraneous variables. This process must be undertaken with due attention to any existing research, theory and literature relevant to the problem as will be evident from the examples cited later in this chapter.

A thorough review of this literature is essential at this stage since it helps the researcher elaborate the various possible relationships that might exist between, and impinge upon, the phenomena whose empirical variation is of prime concern. Indeed, this prior review of the relevant literature is vital to a successful and internally valid analytical survey since it enables the researcher to identify any potentially extraneous variables whose influence must be controlled.

Figure 6.1 | Planning a survey – a summary

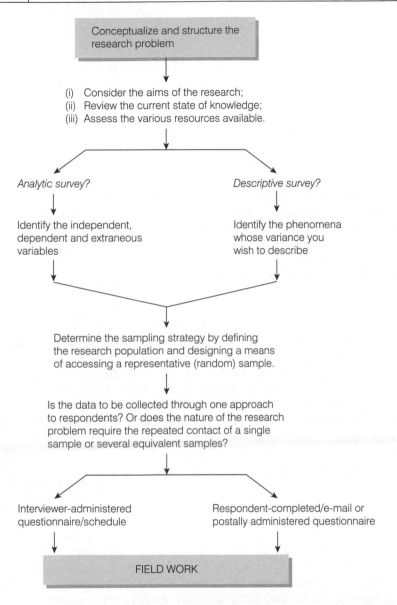

Conceptualize and structure the
research problem

(i)   Consider the aims of the research;
(ii) Review the current state of knowledge;
(iii) Assess the various resources available.

Analytic survey?

Identify the independent,
dependent and extraneous
variables

Descriptive survey?

Identify the phenomena
whose variance you
wish to describe

Determine the sampling strategy by defining
the research population and designing a means
of accessing a representative (random) sample.

Is the data to be collected through one approach
to respondents? Or does the nature of the research
problem require the repeated contact of a single
sample or several equivalent samples?

Interviewer-administered
questionnaire/schedule

Respondent-completed/e-mail or
postally administered questionnaire

FIELD WORK

The control of variables in analytic surveys is not achieved through the use of physical controls, by allocating subjects to control and experimental groups as is the case with experimental research. Rather, in analytic surveys the control of extraneous variables is achieved through the use of statistical techniques, such as multiple regression, during data analyses (Ahlgren and Walberg, 1979). This approach to the control of extraneous variables thus necessitates the prior measurement of all the pertinent variables through their inclusion in the questionnaire format. It follows that the failure to identify such extraneous variables, and so to neglect to anticipate the need to gather data on them so as to enable statistical control during analysis, will have unfortunate consequences for the internal validity of any subsequent findings. These issues thus make the prior conceptualization of the research problem, aided by a careful analysis of the existing literature, vital to the design of analytic surveys.

Descriptive surveys

In contrast to the analytic survey, a descriptive survey is concerned primarily with addressing the particular characteristics of a specific population of subjects, either at a fixed point in time or at varying times for comparative purposes. As such, they do not share the emphasis in analytic designs upon control but they do share a concern to secure a representative sample of the relevant population. This is to ensure that any subsequent assessments of the attributes of that population are accurate and the findings are generalizable – in other words, they have population validity. However, this is not to say that descriptive surveys are atheoretical and that prior reviews of the literature are not as important as in the case of an analytical survey. Rather, prior consideration of the relevant theory and literature may be vital in determining what kinds of questions need to be asked. For instance, if we were attempting to describe what it is that motivates employees in a particular context it would be vital to consider which theory of motivation should guide this task. If we were to adopt a Maslovian approach (Maslow, 1943) the types of questions we would ask would be very different from those deriving from the use of, for instance, expectancy theory (Lawler and Rhode, 1976). Moreover, it would be important to be able to defend from criticism the guiding theory employed. Hence, in order to justify the kinds of questions asked, even when the objective is to describe, prior consideration of the relevant literature and theory is vital.

In a business context, descriptive surveys may be used, for example, to ascertain attitudes to a company's products (Bearden et al., 1993) or the attitudes of an organization's workforce (Reeves and Harper, 1981; Hartley and Barling, 1998). In their useful book, Reeves and Harper (1981) consider at length most of the issues concerned with managements' use of attitude surveys to ascertain the views and opinions of employees. Such surveys may be undertaken, for example, to assess job satisfaction; motivation; morale and stress; employee grievances and the satisfactoriness of the means of dealing with them; and the reaction to possible changes in working arrangements. With regard to the latter, we saw in Chapter 4 how Wall et al. (1986) used repeated contact surveys to measure changes in several dependent variables as part of a quasi-experimental research strategy. Nevertheless, attitude research is a field where predominantly descriptive surveys are utilized and these, together with those used to ascertain some of the circumstances of management buyouts, will be used as examples later in this chapter. However, it must be remembered that employee surveys can be used for much more than a technical means of describing the status quo in an organization. For instance, Hartley (2001) notes how there has been an increasing use of employee surveys at a corporate level in both public and private sector organizations in the UK (see also O'Creevey, 1995). In an examination of why local authorities undertake employee surveys she found that they were increasingly used as an integral part of an HRM strategy as a means of bringing about or influencing organizational change. For Hartley, employee surveys often go beyond 'fact gathering' and may be used either as a diagnostic device prior to change or to facilitate changes through the feedback of findings and the monitoring of progress towards particular strategic goals. So it is worth emphasizing here that such surveys and the feedback of results can also form part of the action research programmes we discussed in Chapter 5.

Sampling

All surveys are concerned with identifying the 'research population' which will provide all the information necessary for answering the original research question. Often it is impractical to involve all members of this population – thus selecting who participates in a survey is a crucial issue. A key strategy entails random sampling – sometimes called probability sampling. The aim is to ensure that those who participate are a representative subset of the research population and thus any findings can be generalized or extrapolated to that target population with confidence. Properly taken samples enable an accurate portrayal of the research population while avoiding the prohibitive costs of surveying everyone.

The first step in this process is to select a sampling frame – a list of members of the research population from which a random sample may be drawn. Here problems may arise since any systematic discrepancy between the research population and the sampling frame is a key source of error because it means that the entire target population is not accurately represented – as we shall discuss this is a particular problem in internet research. Once a sampling frame has been selected it is necessary to decide upon the sampling method which will be used.

When a good sampling frame exists and the population is readily accessible, a good sampling method to use is simple random sampling – this involves the completely random selection of population members so that each member has an equal chance of being included in the sample.

An alternative sampling strategy is called stratified sampling. A prior knowledge of the make-up of the population from which a random sample is to be drawn will make the researcher aware that there may be particular population characteristics, or strata (e.g. ethnic minorities or age and gender distributions, etc.), that make random sampling from within specific subgroups necessary if the sample is to be representative and efficiently drawn. This is particularly important if there are known to be strata in the population which may have a systematic influence upon the dependent variable or other important variables. A search of the literature, or in the case of research into one organization employer databases should prove helpful, will of course aid the task of identifying the stratified characteristics of the research population. Once strata are identified the researcher organizes the sampling frame into those strata and uses simple random sampling within each stratum to select the appropriate proportion of people. Of course, any decisions regarding sample sizes and the sampling parameters for various subsections of the population must also take into account the time and finance at the researcher's disposal. Often where no lists of the research population are readily available, cluster sampling may be used. In a cluster the primary sampling unit is not the individual element in a population (e.g. employees) but a large cluster of elements (e.g. departments) which naturally occurs. Ideally, a cluster should be representative of the research population so that important characteristics are reproduced in the cluster and hence when a random sample is drawn from that cluster any findings can be extrapolated.

Calculating sample size

In order to generalize from a random sample and avoid sampling errors or biases, a random sample needs to be of adequate size. What is adequate depends on several issues which often confuse people doing surveys for the first time. This is because what is important here is not the proportion of the research population that gets sampled, but the absolute size of the sample selected relative to the complexity of the population, the aims of the researcher and the kinds of statistical manipulation that will be used in data analysis. For example, the greater the number of subdivisions or categories (for example, members' different organizational roles) the data might be subjected to in analysis, the larger the sample will need to be in order to have sufficient cases in each category. So while the larger the sample the lesser the likelihood that findings will be biased does hold, diminishing returns can quickly set in when samples get over a specific size which need to be balanced against the researcher's resources. To put it bluntly, larger sample sizes reduce sampling error but at a decreasing rate. Several statistical formulas are available for determining sample size.

Thus, one of the key questions for the survey researcher is how big should the sample be? The key concerns when determining sample size are; how to cater for sampling error, non-response bias and as discussed, in the previous paragraph, the extent to which subgroups in the sample will be analysed. Hence, the question that now needs addressing is, 'How large a sample is required for a researcher to be confident that the survey results are an accurate representation of the population of interest?'

There are numerous approaches, incorporating a number of different formulas, for calculating sample size. One of the most commonly used is Cochran's (1977) formula for calculating the sample size for categorical data.

$$n = \frac{P(100-P)Z^2}{E^2}$$

n = sample size required
P is the percentage occurrence of a state or condition
E is the percentage maximum error required
Z is the z value corresponding to level of confidence required

There are two key factors to this formula (Bartlett et al., 2001). First, there are considerations relating to the estimation of the levels of precision and risk that the researcher is willing to accept:

- E is the margin of error (the level of precision) or the risk the researcher is willing to accept (for example, the plus or minus figure reported in newspaper poll results). In most social research a 5% margin of error is acceptable. So, for example, if in a survey on job satisfaction 40% of respondents indicated they were dissatisfied with levels of pay, the true percentage of the entire population being dissatisfied would lie between 35% and 45%. The smaller the value of E the greater the sample size required as technically speaking sample error is inversely proportional to the square root of n, However, a large sample cannot 'guarantee precision' (Bryman and Bell, 2003: 194).
- Z concerns the level of confidence that the results revealed by the survey findings are accurate. What this means is the degree to which we can be sure the characteristics of the population have been accurately estimated by the sample survey. Z is the *statistical value* (based on the central limit theorem) corresponding to level of confidence required. The key idea behind this is that if a population were to be sampled repeatedly the average value of a variable or question obtained would be equal to the true population value. In management research the typical levels of confidence used are 95 per cent (0.05: a Z value equal to 1.96) or 99 per cent (0.01: Z = 2.57). A 95 per cent level of confidence implies that 95 out of 100 samples will have the true population value within the margin of error (E) specified.

The second key component of a sample size formula concerns the estimation of the variance or heterogeneity of the population (P). Management researchers are commonly concerned with determining sample size for issues involving the estimation of population percentages or proportions (Zikmund, 2002). In the formula, the variance of a proportion or the percentage occurrence of how a particular question, for example, will be answered is P (100 – P). Where, P = the percentage of a sample having a characteristic, for example, the 40% of the respondents who were dissatisfied with pay, and (100 – P) is the percentage (60%) who lack the characteristic or belief. The key issue is how to estimate the value of P before conducting the survey? Bartlett et al. (2001: 45) suggest that researchers should use 50% as an estimate of P, as this will result in the maximization of variance and produce the maximum sample size.

Stop and Think Exercise 6.1   *Sample size calculations*

An organization of 3,000 employees, is considering conducting an employee attitude survey to examine the degree to which employees are satisfied with the way the organization is managed. In the survey it is expected that 50% of the employees will agree with the statement *that they are satisfied with the recognition they get for good work.* The confidence level is to be at 95% and the margin of error that can be tolerated is 5%.

Calculate the minimum sample required.
(Z value for a 95% level of confidence is 1.96)

The formula for determining sample size, however, does not take into account the fraction of a population to be included in a sample (Fowler, 2002) and in situations where the calculated sample size exceeds 10% of population size, n has to be adjusted down by Cochran's (1977) sample correction factor (Bartlett et al., 2001).

$$n^1 = \frac{n}{1 + n/N}$$

N = size of target population
n = sample size
n¹ = new sample size

Notwithstanding this, the size of the population has virtually no effect on how well the sample is likely to describe the population and as Fowler (2002: 35) argues, 'it is most unusual for it [the population fraction] to be an important consideration when deciding on sample size.'

The use of formulas might seem a rather detailed and overly complicated process for the novice or part time survey methodologist. Given the required knowledge of the variance or proportion in the population and a determination as to the maximum desirable error, as well as the acceptable confidence levels, before appropriate sample sizes can be generated, the question might well be asked 'Why bother with the formulas?' Well, it is possible to use them to construct easy to read tables that can help researchers avoid the formulas altogether and that have been developed to calculate sample size while taking into account: the variance (or heterogeneity) of the population; the magnitude of acceptable error; the confidence level you need to have that the characteristics of the sample will represent the research population, and the kind of analysis to be undertaken (for example, Brewerton and Millward, 2001: 119).

Table 6.1 presents sample sizes that would be necessary for given combinations of precision, confidence levels, and a population percentage or variability of 50%

Table 6.1   Sample size based on desired accuracy

| Population Size | Variance of the population P = 50% | | | | | |
| | Confidence level = 95% Margin of error | | | Confidence level = 99% Margin of error | | |
	5	3	1	5	3	1
50	44	48	50	46	49	50
75	63	70	74	67	72	75
100	79	91	99	87	95	99
150	108	132	148	122	139	149
200	132	168	196	154	180	198
250	151	203	244	181	220	246
300	168	234	291	206	258	295
400	196	291	384	249	328	391
500	217	340	475	285	393	485
600	234	384	565	314	452	579
700	248	423	652	340	507	672
800	260	457	738	362	557	763
1,000	278	516	906	398	647	943
1,500	306	624	1,297	459	825	1,375
2,000	322	696	1,655	497	957	1,784
3,000	341	787	2,286	541	1,138	2,539
5,000	357	879	3,288	583	1,342	3,838
10,000	370	964	4,899	620	1,550	6,228
25,000	378	1,023	6,939	643	1,709	9,944
50,000	381	1,045	8,057	652	1,770	12,413
100,000	383	1,056	8,762	656	1,802	14,172
250,000	384	1,063	9,249	659	1,821	15,489
500,000	384	1,065	9,423	660	1,828	15,984
1,000,000	384	1,066	9,513	660	1,831	16,244

(the figure which many researchers suggest to maximize variance). The sample sizes reflect the number of obtained responses, and not necessarily the number of question-naires distributed (this number is often increased to compensate for non-response).

The sample size calculations described result in a figure for the minimum returned sample in order to be confident that the results are accurate. However, in most social and management surveys, the response rates for postal and e-mailed surveys are very rarely 100%. Probably the most common and time efficient way to ensure minimum samples are met is to increase the sample size by up to 50% in the first distribution of the survey (Bartlett et al., 2001). Researchers, however, often criticize this approach as it adds extra costs and the sample might not be representative of the population of interest, as the non-respondents may differ in important ways from those who do respond. If time and resources permit it, then effort might be best spent instead on making a second, and even third approach to the non-respondents, and doing relevant analysis on non-responds to see how they differ from respondents.

Although some form of random sampling is usually preferred, not all sampling entails random sampling. For instance, where a sampling frame is unavailable, or where research is exploratory, researchers may decide to strategically select a sample based upon his/her judgement about the population of interest, with a specific purpose in mind. Even though such a non-probability sample will not be fully representative, the rationale is that it will provide useful data from a sample judged to be typical of, or at least provide some interesting insight into, the wider population according to some characteristics thought to be prevalent amongst sample members. Because it is judgemental and purposive, it is essential that the researcher provides a clear rationale for his/her selection in the light of research objectives and questions.

Whatever the approach to sampling a researcher takes, it is essential that s/he provides a clear exposition of the rationale they have used and mount a defence of it that justifies their approach. A fuller treatment of sampling and statistical procedures is beyond the scope of this book, but those interested may consult a variety of useful texts (e.g. Kish, 1965; Oppenheim, 1966; Moser and Kalton, 1971; Sapsford and Jupp, 1996; Malim and Birch, 1997; Bryman and Cramer, 2004; Sapsford, 2006; Burns and Burns, 2008).

Contacting samples

The objectives of the research will determine whether or not data are to be collected by only one approach to the sample of the research population or whether information is to be repeatedly collected. In the case of collecting data at successive points in time, decisions need to be taken as to whether it is practicable to gain access to the same informants repeatedly and, if not, whether equivalent random sampling will suffice. Moser and Kalton (1971: Ch. 6) elaborate this point. Similarly, the size of the sample, together with its geographical dispersion, have a bearing on the researcher's decisions about how respondents are to be contacted and the requisite information to be elicited.

At its most basic this decision involves a choice between sending, probably by post or increasingly through e-mail, a questionnaire which the respondent self-administers, or the use of an interviewer to administer the questionnaire. The latter may either be administered face to face or in some cases may be economically conducted by telephone (Frey, 1989). Choices about such administration of questionnaires are influenced by a range of issues besides sample size and location. For instance, the complexity of the information required might necessitate the actual presence of an interviewer so that he or she can explain and elaborate the more problematic questions. Further, in considering these issues the researcher needs a prior understanding of the attributes of the target population, for example its degree of literacy and areas of technical competence, so that their ability to cope with questions might be predicted.

Overlaying this decision-making process are the inevitable limits of resources. E-mail is both quicker and cheaper than using the post. Postal questionnaires are generally less expensive and time consuming than those administered by an interviewer. However, the use of the latter does raise the problem of interviewer bias (Boyd and Westfall, 1970), while the former can exacerbate 'non-response' problems (Scott, 1961) – a key form of non-sampling error which can happen in survey research. If resources allow, it may be advantageous to undertake interviewing with another co-worker, especially if the investigation is particularly sensitive, as was the case with Braithwaite's investigation into corporate crime in the pharmaceutical industry (Braithwaite, 1985). There may of course be advantages other than corroboration in this approach, for co-workers may provide checks on memory, particularly when note-taking is difficult, and may also bring different perspectives and working hypotheses to the investigation (Bechhofer et al., 1984). Where the choice is made to have respondent self-administered questionnaires, a key strategy that has become increasingly popular in recent times has been the use of e-mail. Of course this option brings with it particular problems and opportunities which are worth considering.

E-mail administered surveys   The remorseless spread of e-mail since the introduction of the world wide web and the internet has provided new possibilities for data collection and has led to some debate amongst management researchers about the relative advantages and disadvantages of conducting this form of computerized self-administered survey (see Stanton, 1998; Tse, 1998; Simsek and Veiga, 2000; 2001; Stanton and Rogelberg, 2001). As we have already noted, relative to their postal equivalents, e-mail surveys entail major cost savings, are much quicker to conduct, non-responses are easier to identify and chase up, and responses are easier to analyse using SPSS because of their electronic form. Indeed, the possibility of accessing much larger research samples, and the ability to access previously difficult to contact research populations, present important opportunities for the management researcher. However, as Simsek and Veiga (2000, 2001) note, e-mail surveys can also bring with them particular sampling issues and non-sampling errors which require vigilance if we are going to have confidence in their research findings. Here we shall summarize the main points of Simsek and Veiga's discussion and we strongly recommend that any readers who are considering an e-mail strategy should read their original work.

With regard to sampling errors Simsek and Veiga are concerned primarily with representativeness. Whether one is trying to access members of a specific organization via its own intranet, or representatives of multiple organizations via the internet, they point out that such surveys can only access those who can and do use e-mail. Hence, depending on whom and what is being researched, concerns over representativeness and sample bias will vary widely. Obviously problems regarding representativeness can be exacerbated, whether research is into one organization or across a number of organizations. For instance, where e-mail use is not universal in the population and may systematically vary according to a range of factors – age, gender, organizational role are some of the more obvious ones. Where research focuses upon respondents in one organization it is usually possible to construct a useable sampling frame from which a representative sample may be selected because intranets typically serve known populations. However, this is rarely the case in internet research that involves respondents from multiple organizations where no comprehensive user lists are available. Obviously this causes problems since the population from which any respondents derive is unclear and hence it becomes difficult to generalize any subsequent findings. Moreover, unless the researcher has some way of verifying the identity of respondents, there is always the danger of respondents purposefully misrepresenting themselves to researchers or engaging in malicious multiple responses. Authenticating responses may be much easier in intranet surveys where employers have the ability to monitor and intercept employees' e-mail, but simultaneously such a facility may increase concerns over confidentiality and anonymity – which seem to be the key ethical challenges facing this kind of survey research (see Stanton and Rogelberg, 2001).

As the term implies, non-sampling errors are all errors except those that arise due to sampling method and size. As we mentioned earlier, a good example here is the bias that can arise when non-responses to the survey are patterned according to specific respondent characteristics which can range from personality variables, through to group norms and specific attitudes towards a survey's topic or even the use of e-mail surveys in their own right. Another example is where respondents systematically refuse to answer certain questions, or give incomplete answers, etc. Such measurement errors are according to Simsek and Veiga more likely when using intranet surveys because anonymity and confidentiality are compromised. As Simsek and Veiga (2001: 226) further observe 'with fear of retribution and reprisal heightened by a business environment of layoffs, downsizing, mergers and acquisitions, it is plausible to expect that as confidentiality decreases, candidness of survey responses will decrease.'

Because of the problems noted above Simsek and Veiga suggest a variety of strategies to increase the representativeness of samples, construct sampling frames, increase response rates and manage anonymity and confidentiality. To reduce sample bias they suggest the use of multiple survey modalities – that is using both an e-mail survey directly sent to respondents and using a web-based survey posted on a world wide web site. Furthermore, they suggest that internet surveys can be combined with other survey data collection techniques including postal surveys, telephone interviews and personal interviews which can be used to access respondents without access to e-mail, etc. However, such strategies are largely dependent upon having an accurate sampling frame in the first place. With intranet surveys of employees from a single organization constructing such a sample frame is possible using the employer's databases. However, this task is much more complicated with internet surveys and entails constructing a sampling frame either by solicitations through discussion groups, etc., or accessing relevant public directories, or recording e-mail addresses of participants in particular user environments.

To increase response rates, the tactics available are similar to those used with postal surveys. They include: advance notification to persuade respondents of the survey's social utility, emphasis upon respondents' importance to the project and its confidentiality; follow-up mailings to chase non-respondents; have sponsors or collaborators who respondents see as trustworthy; provide incentives for co-operation; have a good, clear and simple survey design.

Managing anonymity and confidentiality bedevil e-mail surveys because guaranteeing data security is quite simply usually not possible. With this in mind Simsek and Veiga suggest that anonymous remailers may be used so that recipients of completed surveys cannot identify the respondent – but they need to be third parties whom the recipients are likely to trust. Similarly, establishing trust with respondents is pivotal to allaying their fears about confidentiality. As with any form of survey it is essential that the researcher takes steps to establish his/her integrity. While there are no certain strategies here it is generally agreed that the researcher should: provide a clear explanation of the survey's purpose and how the respondent was selected; tell the respondent how the data will be used and by whom and the steps the researcher will take to assure confidentiality.

Generally most commentators seem to agree with Stanton and Rogelberg's (2001) call for more methodological research to understand how to design internet and intranet surveys and how to analyse the data collected and thereby ensure the appropriate use of this research medium. Indeed, it would seem such methodological research is lagging behind the research opportunities which the recent spread of networked personal computers in work organizations has provided and hence warrants guarded optimism about the utility of this medium for management research.

In sum, whether one is using e-mail, postal surveys or interviewer administered surveys the most appropriate choice of how to gain access to informants and how to collect information is ultimately dependent upon one's research questions and objectives formulated in the light of resource constraints. In essence, there is no best medium for surveys, each has its own distinct advantages and disadvantages. For instance, postal surveys may ensure greater confidentiality and anonymity in the eyes of respondents but trade off the speed and ease of e-mail. Meanwhile, if the management researcher has to retain control over question phrasing and be able to elaborate and probe then his/her presence at the administration of the questionnaire will be paramount. Whatever the eventual decision the result has significant implications for subsequent decisions the researcher must make regarding questionnaire format, which will be addressed in the concluding section of this chapter. At this stage we offer by way of illustration some examples of different types of survey designs.

Management research example An analytic survey

This study examined the relationship between top managements' entrepreneurial orientation and organizational performance (Covin and Slevin, 1988). It was designed to determine whether organization structure moderated the relationship between entrepreneurial style and organizational performance and, if so, to identify what type of moderating effect structure had on this relationship. A thorough review of the literature seemed to suggest that the use of an entrepreneurial management style and company performance were contingent upon the state of the organization's structure. The following hypothesis was constructed:

1 In organically structured companies, increases in top managements' entrepreneurial orientation will positively influence performance; in mechanistically structured companies, such increases will negatively influence performance.

When organization structure was divided into organic and mechanistic, and management style into entrepreneurial and conservative, it enabled a theoretical framework to be constructed of four 'pure' styles:

(a) effective entrepreneurial companies with entrepreneurial top management styles and organic structures;

(b) 'pseudo' entrepreneurial companies with entrepreneurial top management styles and mechanistic structures;

(c) efficient bureaucratic companies with conservative top management styles and mechanistic structures; and

(d) unstructured, unadventurous, companies with conservative top management styles and organic structures.

This classification then gave rise to a second hypothesis:

2 Companies in which the organization structure is congruent with the management style, i.e. cases (a) and (c) above, will perform significantly better than companies in which these variables are incongruent, i.e. cases (b) and (d) above.

Methodologically, data were gathered from business companies throughout the continental USA, randomly selected from a publicly available mailing list. In view of the size of the population, questionnaires were mailed to the most senior executives in 507 firms, roughly equally divided between the manufacturing and service sectors. Eighty usable questionnaires were returned, for a response rate of 15.8 per cent. The low response rate was explicable, it was suggested, as the mailing list was widely used and the respondents were all senior executives. Examination of response bias revealed no significant difference between the responding and non-responding firms in terms of the two key characteristics.

Measures of the variables used in the research, namely, entrepreneurial style, organization structure and organizational performance, were reviewed by a panel of four academicians and pretested with a sample of six managers.

A six-item Likert-type scale was used to measure elements of entrepreneurial style characterizing the collective management style of their business unit's top managers. Items such as risk-taking, innovation and proactiveness were derived from the literature and instruments used elsewhere. The ratings on these items were averaged to arrive at a single entrepreneurial style for each business. This seemed warranted when the items were factor analysed to assess their dimensionality or factorial validity. In-detail scaling is beyond the scope of this book but the interested reader may consult Kidder and Judd (1986: Ch. 9) on scaling generally and the widely employed Likert scales in particular.

Similarly, organization structure was measured by using a five-item Likert-type scale to determine the extent to which organizations were structured in organic or mechanistic ways.

Performance was measured by asking respondents to indicate on a five-point, Likert-type scale how their top managers would rate the performance of their businesses over the previous three years on each of the following financial performance criteria: operating profits, profit to sales ratio; cash flow from operations; and return on investment (see Table 6.2).

As a check on the validity of these perceptual performance measures secondary performance data, such as sales growth rate, were collected on 20 of the sampled firms. The zero-order correlation coefficient between these figures and the firm's subjective performance scores was very high, indicating evidence of construct validity for the performance measure. It also confirmed that respondents' perceptions of how well their businesses were performing constituted an acceptable basis for an organizational performance variable.

The first hypothesis was then tested using moderated regression analysis which was considered to be an appropriate technique for testing hypothesized contingency relationships. In moderated regression analysis the statistical significance of interaction effects is tested by regressing the dependent variable on two or more main variables, one being the independent variable and the other the hypothesized moderator variable, and the cross-product of those main variables.

The second hypothesis was tested by dividing the sample into congruent companies, i.e. entrepreneurial style and organic structure; conservative style and mechanistic structure – and incongruent companies, i.e. those with entrepreneurial styles and mechanistic structures; conservative styles and organic structures. Then a t-test was used to compare the subgroup performance means.

The result of these analyses suggested that organizational performance was jointly determined by the interaction of organizational style and organicity. Since the interaction term had a positive

Table 6.2 Extracts from Covin and Slevin's (1988) questionnaire on the relationship between entrepreneurial orientation and organizational performance

The following statements are meant to identity the collective management style of your business unit's key decision-makers rather than any one individual's management style or philosophy. Please indicate, by circling the appropriate number, the extend to which the following statements characterize the management style of your business unit's top managers.

The entrepreneurial style scale

The operating management philosophy of the top management of my business is ...

1	2	3	4	5	6	7
Strong emphasis on the marketing of true and tried products or services and the avoidance of heavy research and development costs				Strong emphasis on research and development, technological leadership and innovation		

How many new lines of products or services has your business unit marketed in the past five years? Please exclude minor variations.

1	2	3	4	5	6	7
No new lines of products or services in the past five years				Very many new lines of products or services in the past five years		

In dealing with competitors my business unit ...

1	2	3	4	5	6	7
Typically responds to actions which competitors initiate				Typically initiates actions which competitors respond to		

The operating management philosophy of the top management of my business unit is ...

1	2	3	4	5	6	7
Tight formal control of most operations by means of sophisticated control				Loose informal control: heavy dependence on informal relations and norm of co-operation for getting work done		

regression coefficient it was suggested that an entrepreneurial top management style made a greater contribution to performance in organically structured firms than in those mechanistically structured.

As regards to hypothesis two, the results of a one-way analysis of variance across the four firm types as well as t-tests between them revealed no significant differences between these firms in terms of numbers of employees. It was therefore concluded that firms in which the structure fitted the management style outperformed those in which the fit was poor.

Despite this the authors note some limitations of the study. The reliability of the entrepreneurial style and organization structure data is based on the perceptions of one organizational member; clearly data collected from multiple respondents would have had more validity.

Further, the data are cross-sectional so causal links among the variables could not be firmly established. Firm performance is a function of prior, not contemporary, management practices and organizational forms. Accordingly, longitudinal data would be required, rather than data at one point in time, to establish causal relationships and control for time-lag effects such as was suggested in the previous chapter.

Because the principal direction of the causal relationships between firm performance, entrepreneurial style and organization structure is unknown, alternative theoretical frameworks may provide equally plausible explanations of the data: for example, that top management's entrepreneurial orientation moderates the relationship between organization structure and firm performance. This is evident, as in moderated regression analysis the labelling of one of the independent variables as the predictor and the other as the moderator is arbitrary.

Thus, while this study raised the strong possibility that organization structure may exist in a causal relationship with entrepreneurial style and company performance, a potentially fruitful area for research still remained to discover the determinants and consequences of such orientations.

Management research example A descriptive survey

There follows an example of research based on evidence from a survey of management buy-outs in the UK.

Exploratory research was conducted by Wright (1986) to determine some aspects of management buy-outs, a field about which little was known. Management buy-outs were defined as occasions when the management purchase the company for which they work from the previous owners. Buy-outs may occur on the retirement of the previous owners, from an independent or parent company in receivership or from a parent still trading that wishes to dispose of a subsidiary.

An attempt was made to answer issues raised in a preliminary theoretical discussion through a mailed questionnaire survey, and by case studies of a subsample of the companies surveyed, both carried out in 1983. The research was designed to find answers to the following questions:

1 What is the extent of management buy-outs involving trading relationships with the former parent?
2 What is the strength of the trading relationship and hence the implied level of dependency of the bought-out company on the former parent?
3 Does continued dependence after the buy-out improve or worsen trading relationships?
4 Are attempts made to reduce dependency on the former parent?

From telephone surveys of the financial institutions and searches of the financial press it had been estimated that up to the time that the sample for the survey was drawn, 580 buy-outs had been completed. Since it had been estimated that the current failure rate was one in ten, the surviving population from which the sample was drawn was approximately 520.

Access was an issue in this research; relatively few buy-outs are reported in the press as the data are often somewhat sensitive, and financing institutions were apparently the only source of the names and addresses of target companies. All institutions agreed to contact their clients to find out whether

Table 6.3   Extracts from Wright's (1986) questionnaire on management buy-outs

Company details

1   Location of head office and name before buy-out, it changed.
2   How many companies (subsidiaries, etc.) were bought out?
3   Have any employees outside the buy-out team contributed any funds for the purchase of
    the company?
4   Who provided the finance for the buy-out?

Management

5   How many were in the buy-out team?
6   Have there been managerial changes since the buy-out?
7   Where no changes have taken place, are any planned?

The company

8   From how many sites does the company operate?
9   What is/are your principal product(s)/service(s)?
10   Did you lose any customers as a direct effect of the buy-out?
11   What changes do you expect in profits before interest and tax in the next financial year?
12   Have you experienced any cash flow problems since the buy-out? If so, what were they?

they wished to participate, some providing names and addresses, and others preferring to mail questionnaires direct to maintain confidentiality.

In this way, from a distribution of 191 questionnaires, usable replies were received from 111 buy-outs, producing a response rate of 58.1 per cent without a reminder being sent. In assessing the reliability of the results it needs of course to be borne in mind that data were available from only a minority of buy-outs which had taken place. This was because earlier buy-outs were not termed as such, or they had already received much press publicity, or because they were in a precarious position and did not wish attention to be drawn to the fact (Table 6.3).

The second stage of the survey involved writing case studies on 20 companies to discuss issues arising from the buy-out in more detail, to ascertain the kinds of changes and problems that had occurred.

Analysis of the questionnaire survey, which (as can be seen) was concerned throughout with largely factual information, provided evidence that transfers of ownership existed where there were transactional relationships between parent and subsidiary, but that for the most part the level of dependence was likely to be low. The need for independence was also stressed when, in two cases where transactional relationships existed, the parent subsequently went into liquidation after the buy-out. Attempts to reduce dependency apparently began soon after the buy-out but with informal relationships continuing to be maintained.

Management research example A time series survey

The primary objective of a study by Allen and her colleagues (2001) was to examine changes in work attitudes after organizational downsizing. A problem in studies that investigate post-event phenomena is that researchers frequently fail to test whether or not their post-event relationships hold over time. Seven job variables thought to be especially susceptible to change following organizational downsizing were selected for investigation: role overload, role clarity, job involvement, satisfaction with top management, satisfaction with job security, organizational commitment, and intent to turnover. The research was designed to examine how organizational downsizing affects a number of common survivor attitudes as measured over three distinct periods of time. The following hypotheses were proposed:

1 Employee attitudes will be impacted by organizational downsizing and these changes in attitudes will vary across time.
2 Changes in role overload, role clarity, satisfaction with top management, and satisfaction with job security will be related to changes in organizational commitment and turnover intentions.
3 Job involvement will moderate the relationship in role overload, role clarity, satisfaction with top management and satisfaction with job security with organizational commitment and turnover intentions.

The research was conducted in a large consumer packaged goods organization in which 106 middle and upper level marketing related managers participated in all three phases of the study. Surveys were mailed directly to the entire population of middle and upper level managers who remained with the firm following the downsizing. All participants were assured confidentiality and were surveyed at three different points in time.

- *Time 1* Managers were initially surveyed approximately one month after the internally imposed downsizing. They were asked to respond to the survey regarding their attitudes to the organization prior to the restructuring.
- *Time 2* Managers were surveyed a second time approximately four months after the downsizing.
- *Time 3* Managers were surveyed a third time approximately 16 months after the downsizing.

The choice of the Time 2 measurement point was chosen to be representative of an early point in the transition process. The Time 3 measure was believed to be a point when attitudes would have stabilized.

Potential response bias was investigated by examining the demographic characteristics of all correspondents compared with the 106 managers who responded to all three surveys. Examination of the data suggested that the characteristics of the total population initially surveyed were similar to the 106 individuals who responded to all three surveys.

Each of the attitudinal variables was measured using five-point Likert scales.

The results were that hypothesis 1 predicted that the impact of the organizational downsizing on survivors' attitudes would vary across time. This hypothesis was tested by conducting a repeated measures multivariate analysis of variance examining the main effect of time on each of the attitudinal variables. The overall means, standard deviations, F tests, and the results of the planned comparisons for each of the attitudinal variables were as predicted in that time had a significant overall effect on each of the dependent variables except role clarity. Hypothesis 2 predicted that changes in role overload, role clarity, satisfaction with top management, and satisfaction with job security would be related to changes in organizational commitment and turnover intentions. Considerable support for hypothesis 2 was found. Changes in the independent variables were able to predict changes in both organizational commitment and turnover intentions four months after the Time 1 measurement and one year after the Time 1 measurement. Hypothesis 3 asserted that changes in role overload, role clarity, satisfaction with top management, and satisfaction with job security on changes in organizational commitment and turnover intentions would be moderated by job involvement. In each case, as predicted, there was a stronger relationship between the environmental variable and the outcome variable when job involvement was higher than when job involvement was lower.

The research established that the most negative impact on attitude occurs during the immediate post-downsizing period. After a longer period of time attitudes generally reached more favourable levels. Downsizing seems to have an effect on work attitudes, this effect varies over time, and the initial impact is generally negative. Furthermore, preliminary evidence suggests that after a longer period of time attitudes may begin returning to their pre-downsizing level.

Finally, the researchers acknowledge some limitations of the research. The research was conducted in one organization and respondents were primarily employed in one broad functional area, that of marketing managers. Thus, the generalizability of the findings may be limited, especially given that the sample consisted primarily of Caucasian men holding college degrees. It is therefore suggested that future research might explore the attitudes of non-management personnel within different organizational settings. It is finally argued that the study extends past research by revealing that the nature of the effects vary across time and differ for individual variables. The findings highlight the importance of longitudinal research to understand post-event phenomena.

The choice of questionnaire format

A vital skill in undertaking a survey is the ability to structure, focus, phrase and ask sets of questions in a manner that is intelligible to respondents. Such questions also need to minimize bias, and provide data that can be statistically analysed. To achieve these objectives it is important to consider four inter-related issues in questionnaire design: questionnaire focus, question phraseology, the form of response, and question sequencing and overall presentation (see Figure 6.2).

Questionnaire focus

By focus we mean the extent to which the questions intended to be asked cover the various aspects of the research problem adequately and in sufficient detail. For instance, in analytic survey research it is particularly important that there is provision in the questionnaire for eliciting data on all the important variables. This enables statistical analysis of the relationship between the independent and dependent variables, as well as statistical control over extraneous variables, to allow the theory to be tested.

Figure 6.2 | The questionnaire format

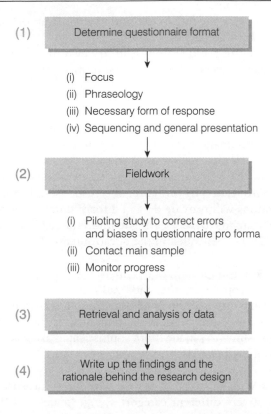

(1) Determine questionnaire format

    (i)   Focus
    (ii) Phraseology
    (iii) Necessary form of response
    (iv) Sequencing and general presentation

(2) Fieldwork

    (i)   Piloting study to correct errors
        and biases in questionnaire pro forma
    (ii) Contact main sample
    (iii) Monitor progress

(3) Retrieval and analysis of data

(4) Write up the findings and the
rationale behind the research design

Conversely, it is also important to ascertain whether or not all the questions to be asked are really relevant to the research problem. It is incumbent upon the question-naire designer continually to assess whether a question is really necessary and to exclude any questions that do not clearly serve the objectives of the investigation. The more incisive a questionnaire the more costs are reduced and, particularly in the case of postal questionnaires or e-mail, the better will be the response rate.

Questionnaire phraseology

Phraseology is the term used to describe whether or not the ways in which questions are asked are intelligible to respondents, and on these matters generally it will be useful to consult Payne (1951). An important aid in judging these problems will be provided by feedback from the pilot study, a matter which will be considered later. At this early stage in questionnaire design, however, the following considerations should be reviewed by researchers with reference to the characteristics of the population from which the sample is to be drawn:

1 Are the purposes of the research revealed to respondents in a way that will promote the likelihood of their co-operation without biasing subsequent responses?
2 Are any instructions to respondents clear and unambiguous?
3 Can the questions be understood; are they free from jargon, esoteric terminology, inappropriate assumptions and ambiguity?

4 Are the respondents likely to possess the requisite information and knowledge to answer the questions?

5 Is it possible that respondents might find the wording of questions offensive, insensitive or embarrassing?

6 Might the wording of the questions lead to bias through 'leading' the respondent to particular answers or imposing assumptions that may be unwarranted?

The form of response

As we have emphasized, the data provided must be elicited in a form that permits subsequent analysis. This analysis usually entails computer-aided, statistical manipulation. It is therefore vital that measures of the variables important to the research problem are built into the questionnaire by asking questions in an appropriate way and providing an appropriate pro forma for the responses. The key to success is to ensure that the questions will provide data in a form suitable for the statistical techniques the researcher intends to use, bearing in mind the reliability and validity of the measurement scales actually encoded in the questionnaire design.

Scaling   At the outset it is important to be sure to use the type of scale for measuring any variable that is appropriate to the statistical techniques to be used during data analysis. In considering this issue it is helpful to follow Kidder and Judd (1986: 59–62), who differentiate four types of measurement scale: nominal, ordinal, interval and ratio. For those wishing to pursue more sophisticated aspects of scaling it may be helpful to consult Maranell (1974).

1 *Nominal scales* With this type of scale a variable is measured in terms of two or more qualitatively different categories, e.g. 'male' and 'female'. The scale indicates differences of category but these have no arithmetical value.

2 *Ordinal scales* As with nominal scales, an ordinal scale contains two or more categories that allow differentiation of variables in terms of those categories. As the name implies, however, some degree of ordering is involved as different points on the scale indicate the quantity being measured. For example, Kidder and Judd (1986) illustrate this by the example of how much autonomy workers might have in their jobs: 1 = little autonomy (e.g. assembly line workers), 2 = moderate autonomy (e.g. construction workers) and 3 = much autonomy (e.g. doctors). Different points on the scale indicate greater or lesser amounts of the phenomena being measured relative to other points on the scale. But it does not imply anything other than establishing an order, since an ordinal scale says nothing about the distances between the points on the scale.

3 *Interval scales* These have all the characteristics of an ordinal scale except that the distances between the points on the scale (i.e. the intervals) represent equal quantities of the measure variable (e.g. degrees Fahrenheit on a thermometer). However, interval scales do not have a true zero; rather, zero is arbitrary. So although we can add or subtract the numbers on an interval scale they cannot be multiplied or divided. The lack of a true zero makes the multiplication and division of points on an interval scale meaningless. An interval scale is used in Table 6.2.

4 *Ratio scales* These have all the characteristics of an interval scale except that they have a true zero and it therefore becomes possible to say that, for example, a score of ten represents twice as much of the construct as a score of five. So multiplication and division of points on a ratio scale become meaningful.

In Chapter 3 we discussed the issue of operationalizing abstract concepts into indicators. How does this process relate to the measurement processes and asking questions in an appropriate fashion in survey design?

In the analysis of survey data it is important to use the statistical methods appropriate for the types of measurement scales that have previously been encoded into the questionnaire format. For example, statistical techniques, such as multiple regression, which depend on the distances between quantitative points on a scale being equivalent, cannot be used on, for instance, nominal or ordinal data. So how variables are operationalized and measured, and how this is encoded in the questionnaire design, must fit the statistical techniques the researcher intends to use. This latter choice depends upon the purposes and aims of the research.

The problems surrounding the use of the correct type of measurement scale also raise the issues of validity and reliability. Validity refers to the extent to which a scale encoded into a set of questions actually measures the variable it is supposed to measure. We may assume, for instance, that an examination is a means of measuring the variation in candidates' knowledge of a particular substantive area. However, such an assumption may be invalid in that it may not only measure knowledge of the substantive area, but other variables influencing candidates' performances may be inadvertently measured, such as the ability to cope with stress and the speed of writing.

The only way to assess the validity of such measurement devices is to evaluate the results against some other measures, or criteria, which have already demonstrated its validity. Although this is not without difficulty, a thorough knowledge of previous research literature will aid this calibration process by providing possible criteria (H. W. Smith, 1975; Cronbach and Meehl, 1978). For instance, in our example of analytic research cited above, Covin and Slevin (1988) checked the validity of their measures of managerial perceptions of company performance with secondary performance data such as sales growth rate.

Validity refers to the accuracy of the measurement process while the reliability of measurement refers to its consistency; that is, the extent to which a measuring device will produce the same results when applied more than once to the same person under similar conditions. The most straightforward way of testing reliability is to replicate; either by administering the same questions to the same respondents at different times and assessing the degree of correlation, or by asking the same question in different ways at different points in the questionnaire. More sophisticated versions of these processes are succinctly reviewed by Moser and Kalton (1971: 353–7) and in more detail by Summers (1970). Finally, it is important to note that questionnaire designers need to be aware that, although they may have a highly reliable measure, it may not necessarily be measuring what it is intended to measure: reliability does not necessarily imply validity, whereas if the measure is valid it will be reliable.

By building measurement scales into a questionnaire a researcher necessarily limits subjects' replies to a fixed set of responses which have encoded the requisite measures and thus are readily compared and computed. This form of question is usually called a 'closed' question, and allows comparison and statistical manipulation. Generally questionnaires are most suited to closed, specific, questions rather than open questions, because the latter are notoriously difficult to analyse across large samples (see Robson, 1993). However, closed questions have the disadvantage of limiting, and perhaps distorting, responses to a fixed schedule, so preventing respondents answering in their own way. In many respects closed questions prevent a lot of data being collected – something which is both a strength and a weakness depending on the objectives of the researcher.

By contrast, 'open-ended' questions do not impose such artificial limitations, and leave respondents free to answer in their own terms. Data might thus be elicited with greater depth and meaning, revealing insights into pertinent issues. The disadvantage is that, due to the lack of structure, information is not readily code-able and comput-able, nor is comparison across respondents easy. Thus, while open-ended questions provide richer data, analysis becomes much more difficult. Again, the nature of the problem being investigated, as well as the aims of the research, has a bearing on all these issues.

Question sequencing and overall presentation

Finally, in designing the format of a questionnaire it is important to consider the sequence of the questions to be asked. This is particularly necessary (as is the over-all presentation) where a postal self-completion questionnaire is to be used. With regard to question sequencing it is helpful to both respondents and interviewers if the designer ensures that the questions have a natural and logical order. For instance, it assists both rapport and respondents' understanding of what is required if more general and factual questions precede narrow, detailed questions and questions of opinion.

The quality of the overall presentation of the questionnaire, its conciseness and the attractiveness of the design are also of importance in ensuring a high completion rate, as is a suitable covering letter and a stamped, addressed envelope for its return. Low completion rates are often a feature of surveys by questionnaire, especially if admin-istered by post; the key issue being whether respondents differ in a significant way from non-respondents. Two methods are often used to answer this question: first, to compare the two groups on available characteristics, as was done, for example, in the case of the research reported above by Covin and Slevin (1988); second, to compare the original respondents with those produced by follow-up letters – which, incidentally, can be an effective means of increasing response rates. Factors affect-ing response rates to mailed questionnaires are covered in detail by Herbelein and Baumgarter (1978).

Fieldwork

Whether it is intended to use a postal questionnaire, e-mail or an interviewer-administered schedule it is always important to begin fieldwork by conducting a pilot study. In essence, pilot research is a trial run-through to test the research design with a subsample of respondents who have characteristics similar to those identifiable in the main sample to be surveyed. Piloting is necessary as it is very difficult to predict how respondents will interpret and react to questions. Conducting a pilot before the main survey allows any potential problems in the pro forma of the questionnaire to be identified and corrected. Moreover, where an interviewer-administered question-naire is to be used piloting provides the opportunity to refine and develop the inter-viewing and social skills of the researchers and helps to highlight any possible sources of interviewer bias. When the pilot study is completed it is then possible to conclude the design of the questionnaire and finalize any arrangements for its administration.

During the main study it is important to assess its progress by monitoring the postal returns or maintaining contact with the interviewers in the field. In the case of questionnaires administered by post, failure to respond by particular subgroups may be a feature, and in this case it is important to discover any pattern to this.

Data analysis and the presentation of findings

Although this book does not deal in any depth with quantitative data analysis and presentation, it is important to remind the reader that a vital aspect of planning a survey is to secure access to any computing facilities necessary for the analysis of data. Similarly, it is important to allow sufficient time for the transfer of data from completed questionnaires and schedules to computer software as well as for the subsequent writing up and critical evaluation of any findings. All these issues are succinctly dealt with by Moser and Kalton (1971: 410–88) and more recently by Sapsford (2006), Burns and Burns (2008) and by Bryman and Cramer (2004).

Ethics and survey research

The ethical issues, which will be briefly discussed in the case of the ethnographic approach, also apply when researchers derive data from surveys. This is particularly the case when data is derived from one organization, and especially so in respect of surveys that are commissioned by one interested party, such as management. This special case is considered at some length by Reeves and Harper (1981: Ch. 11), who make the following points:

1 the results may lead to decisions that affect the respondents;
2 as a consequence, interested parties will wish to be consulted about the purpose of the survey and the manner in which it is conducted;
3 choice of questions may need to be governed not only by survey, but also by organizational considerations;
4 providing opportunities for employees to have their say may be an important consideration in the survey design.

In a discussion of the need for a code of practice governing survey research, such as is contained in the British Sociological Association's 'Statement of Ethical Principles' or the Market Research Society's code of conduct, Reeves and Harper (1981) consider there are four minimum requirements for any code of practice governing survey research within an organization.

1 The researcher should consult with all interested parties before undertaking fieldwork and should proceed only by consent and agreement. This will probably require free access to employee representatives including representatives of the trade unions.

There may, however, be some difficulties in practice in this regard in the case of analytic surveys designed to test hypotheses where the researcher may not wish to reveal details of the hypotheses to be tested. To state in advance what hypotheses the researcher hopes to falsify or confirm is to invite subjects to respond less according to their own feelings but, rather, according to what they believe the researcher wants or does not want to hear. In a full discussion of this dilemma, Barnes (1979) believes that the solution is for the researcher to demonstrate that, as far as possible, anyone interested can find out as much as he or she wishes to about the inquiry, its aims and methods, and that the only restrictions are those entailed by the process of data collection itself. He suggests that in this way researchers may hope to gain the confidence of the people they work with.

2 Agreement needs to be reached with all interested parties as early as possible over the dissemination of results before too great an investment of time is made in an inquiry which will lead nowhere.

3 The purposes of an employee survey and most types of survey research should not be concealed, as this prevents any judgement by respondents as to whether their participation may adversely affect them.

4 Any special circumstance that might affect the interpretation of the results should be clearly reported.

Further reading

There are many basic texts on survey research design, for example, Moser and Kalton's (1971) is a classical text. However, for a more contemporary guide to survey research that deals with most issues from sampling design to constructing measurement scales and analysing quantitative data we would recommend Sapsford (2006). For detailed guidance regarding the use of SPSS to analyse statistical data the reader should turn to Burns and Burns (2008) who also provide good advice regarding how to collect, input, interpret and present statistical data in a business and management context. Reeves and Harper's (1981) guide to undertaking surveys at work is still a particularly useful book for students of business and management, which is also available as a student project manual. It is chiefly concerned with the technology of carrying out employee surveys but in doing so also considers in some detail phases of the research process, such as entry to the organization and drawing conclusions from the data. Meanwhile, excellent advice on using e-mail surveys can be found in Simsek and Veiga (2000, 2001) whilst Stanton and Rogelberg (2001) provide sensible tips on using internet/intranet web pages to collect organizational research data. Data analysis is covered to some extent in the texts already mentioned above, but a very good alternative is Bryman and Cramer (2004). This book covers its subject in an interesting and highly accessible manner and provides excellent guidance upon using the Statistical Package for the Social Sciences (SPSS) throughout. Also Sirkin (1994) provides an accessible coverage of statistical techniques which directly relates them to processes of interpretation and analysis. For those who require detailed help on using statistics to test theories and hypotheses, Bobko (2001) provides a comprehensive guide with lots of good examples related to industrial psychology and management.

These journal articles are freely available on the companion website (www.sagepub.co.uk/gillandjohnson):

Baggaley, A.R. (1981) Multivariate analysis: an introduction for consumers of behavioral research, *Evaluation Review*, 5: 123–31.
Simsek, Z. and Viega, J.F. (2001) A primer on internet organizational surveys, *Organization Research Methods*, 4(3): 218–35.

Qualitative methodology:
the case of ethnography

Ethnographic research is a form of qualitative research and as such is fundamentally different from some of the approaches to management research we have considered so far in this book. Recently there has been a growing interest in the use of qualitative methodology by management researchers (see Boje, 2001; Smith, 2001) – an interest that also constitutes a philosophical challenge to quantitative methodologies (e.g. experimental and survey research) that have tended to dominate the various sub-disciplines that make up management research (e.g. marketing, strategy, organization behaviour, accounting, finance, human resource management, etc.). So whilst qualitative research may be gaining some acceptance as a means of undertaking management research (see Van Maanen, 1998; Symon et al., 2000; Goulding, 2002) this development has also been fraught with controversy. For instance, Denzin and Lincoln (1998: 7) claim that the work of qualitative researchers generally has been called '... unscientific, or only exploratory, or entirely personal and full of bias ...'. So immediately we are confronted by the question: why has qualitative research been the target of these accusations? In part we can see why this is so through trying to define qualitative research before moving on to explore ethnography as a distinctive form of qualitative methodology, in terms of a set of methodological commitments. Here we will explore its practice through consideration of examples from management research. We then turn our attention to some recurring themes in ethnographic research practice. These include the matter of gaining access to organizational sites in order to undertake ethnography and the various field roles which might be adopted by the ethnographer. Next we consider some ethical issues which might arise from the ethnographic approach before finally moving on to one of the critical issues for all forms of qualitative research, including ethnography: the analysis of data and the inductive development of theory through the use of analytic induction and grounded theory.

Defining qualitative research

Various commentators have argued that qualitative research is very difficult to define. This is because of what is often seen as its variable, 'flexible and emergent' (Van Maanen, 1998: xi) nature which results from it being 'designed at the same time as it is being done' (Gephart, 2004: 455). Nevertheless, often qualitative research is defined as an approach in which quantitative data are not used. For example, Strauss and Corbin (1998: 11) describe it as 'any type of research that produces findings not arrived at by statistical procedures or other means of quantification'. Whilst it is important to note that qualitative research does not involve the use of statistical procedures to either describe the characteristics of phenomena, or to test hypothetical predictions about those phenomena, defining qualitative research in this way can rather miss a key point of all qualitative research – how it embraces a very different philosophical view of how human behaviour arises. This alternative view of human behaviour is pivotal for it leads to a very different way of explaining why people do the things that they do in various social contexts. This view in turn explains and justifies the requirement to collect certain forms of data in a particular way, which is illustrated by a very important type of qualitative research: ethnography. However, for the time being, this philosophical issue returns to the differences between *erklaren* and *verstehen* initially covered in Chapter 3 of this book.

In Chapter 3 we discussed how much of social science has methodologically attempted to copy how research has been done in the natural sciences. This mimicry has usually been labeled methodological *monism* (see Ross, 1991: 350) and entails the assumption that human behaviour may be studied in a manner similar to the way in which physical phenomena are studied in the natural sciences. As we saw, this leads to human behaviour being understood and explained in a deterministic fashion often called *erklaren*: that human behaviour can be explained as necessary responses to empirically observable, measurable, and manipulable, causal variables without any need to investigate human subjective processes (see Outhwaite, 1975 and Figure 7.1 below). As we illustrated in Chapter 3, this stimulus-response model of human behaviour enables the investigation of human behaviour through the use of Popper's (1959) hypothetico-deductive method.

Popper's hypothetico-deductive method is most clearly expressed in the use of laboratory experimental methodology – the logic of which is exported out of laboratory settings through the use of quasi-experimental methods, analytical survey research, and some (but definitely not all) forms of action research. All these approaches to management research entail the deductive testing of theoretical predictions, in the form of hypotheses, by collecting data in different ways. All deductive methods necessarily involve the researcher conceptualizing and operationalizing key dimensions of respondents' behaviour prior to data collection by, for example, causally modelling that behaviour by defining different aspects as dependent, independent and extraneous variables. This is done in order to be able to statistically measure variation in that behaviour and thereby test hypotheses through data collection, rather than beginning data collection with how people subjectively interpret and make sense of their worlds.

Indeed, as we discussed in Chapter 3, human subjectivity is often excluded from such explanations of behaviour because those subjective elements are sometimes seen to be empirically unobservable in an objective fashion and hence supposedly inadmissible as scientific explanations. To some extent this deductive stance might explain the condemnations of qualitative research reported by Denzin and Linoln (1998: 7) as 'unscientific' because it articulates a particular of view of what science should be – one that actually excludes the methodological concerns of qualitative researchers with *verstehen*.

So despite the diverse nature of qualitative research (see Patton, 1990; Snape and Spencer, 2003) it is usually recognized as having an underlying unity derived from a methodological commitment to *verstehen* (see Outhwaite, ibid.). In Chapter 3 we defined *verstehen* as the assumption that all human action, or behaviour, has an internal logic of its own which must be understood and described in order for researchers to be able to explain that behaviour. But, as Guba and Lincoln (1994: 106) note, quantitative measures of phenomena and statistical reasoning are seen to impose an external researcher-derived logic which excludes, or at best distorts rather than accesses for inspection, actors' subjective interpretation of their worlds – something which must be understood by the researcher in order to explain the behaviour of those actors. Hence, qualitative management research has been seen as arising in response to these perceived limitations in conventional quantitative management research (see also Prasad and Prasad, 2002).

A methodological commitment to *verstehen* is therefore based upon the idea that to follow the approach of the natural sciences in the study of the social world is an error because human action, unlike the behaviour of non-sentient (e.g. physical) objects in the natural sciences, has an internal subjective logic which is also intersubjective in the sense that it is created and reproduced through everyday human social interaction. It follows from these philosophical assumptions that the legitimate aim of social science must be to access and describe these internal logics through the deployment of what are generally construed as qualitative, as opposed to quantitative, research methods. In other words, many researchers who use qualitative methods think that the social and natural sciences should not share the same methodology because how the behaviour of their different subject matters arises is quite different and therefore how each type of behaviour may be explained and investigated by researchers should also be quite different. This philosophical stance, with its perception of difference based upon a particular view of human behaviour, rejects methodological monism and simultaneously justifies the use of qualitative methods in the social sciences. Indeed, all qualitative methods of data collection aim to access and describe the culturally derived meanings and interpretations any actor is thought to subjectively deploy in making sense of his/her social world: interpretations which have a pivotal influence upon their intentional construction of meaningful behaviour.

In sum, qualitative researchers use research methods, such as ethnography, in order to describe and explain people's behaviour for a specific reason: they think that it enables the investigation of how the actors, whose behaviour they are attempting to describe and explain, experience, sustain, articulate and share with

Figure 7.1 | *Erklaren* and *verstehen* compared

1 *Erklaren and quantitative methodologies*

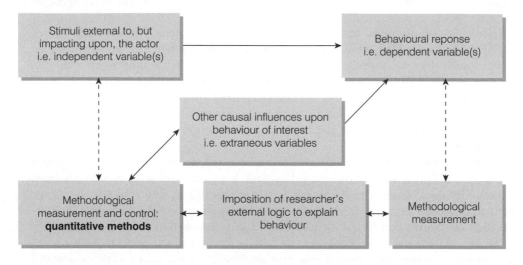

2 *Verstehen and qualitative methodologies*

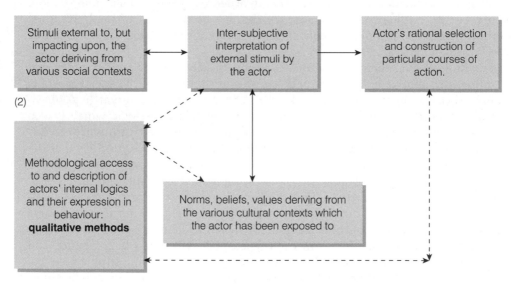

others socially constructed everyday realities that lead them to behave in particular ways (see Van Maanen, 1998; Schwandt, 1999; Alvesson and Deetz, 2000; Denzin and Lincoln, 2000). This commitment, in relation to the approach of quantitative methodologies based upon *erklaren*, is illustrated by Figure 7.1. In order to illustrate the methodological implications of *verstehen* in qualitative management research we now turn to one of the most influential approaches in management research: ethnography.

Ethnography and its development

Ethnography is the art and science of describing a group or culture. The description may be of a small tribal group in some exotic land or a classroom in middle-class suburbia ... the ethnographer writes about the routine, daily lives of people. The more predictable patterns of human thought and behaviour are the focus of inquiry. (Fetterman, 1989: 11)

Ethnography is ... the study of people in naturally occurring settings or 'fields' by means of methods which capture their social meanings and ordinary activities, involving the researcher participating directly in the setting, if not the activities, in order for them to collect data in a systematic manner but without meaning being imposed on them externally. (Brewer, 2004: 312).

Ethnographic research has a long history in the social sciences generally (see Wax, 1971) and has equally played, and continues to play, a significant part in the development of many areas of management research. Ethnography derives from traditions in social anthropology where the researcher would spend long periods of time out in the field, living amongst what appeared to them, people of alien or exotic cultures. This allowed the researcher to collect information about the lives of the people they were investigating through social interaction and observation enabled by trying to share aspects of their experience through participating in their everyday activities. As the famous social anthropologist Bronsilaw Malinowski put it, the aim was to grasp 'the native's point of view, his relation to life, to realize his vision of his world (sic)' (1922: 25). In developing this understanding, anthropologists usually took the view that the aim was to become able to think and feel like a member of the culture being studied. Simultaneously they had to avoid 'going native' and being captured by that culture by actually becoming a member and thereby forgetting their research role as a trained social anthropologist from another culture. Interesting examples of such research, and the problems encountered in the field, are provided by Mead's account of adolescence in Samoa (1943/1928) and Berreman's account of the caste system in a Paharis village in North India (1962).

However, social anthropological research methods were not just used to investigate situations which were ostensibly completely 'foreign' to the researcher. For instance, an interesting early example of using a social anthropological approach to study industry is provided by a famous author of books for children – Beatrix Potter. During the late nineteenth century Potter was working with Charles Booth to investigate various aspects of the lives of British industrial workers. In this project, Potter, the daughter of an industrial magnate, wished to study working people in their homes as well as in their workplaces. In order to do this she enlisted the help of her maternal grandmother, who had been the daughter of a powerloom weaver, to arrange an introduction to a working-class community. However, so that they would not be inhibited by her 'grand' status, a 'pious fraud' was carried out, and she was introduced as a farmer's daughter. Potter proceeded to carry out participant observation studies in a London sweat shop where she was employed as a seamstress and later, with her husband Sydney Webb, published one of the earliest texts on research methodology (Webb and Webb, 1932/75).

Stop and Think Exercise 7.1 What do you think are the possible methodological justifications for Potter's 'pious fraud'? What ethical problems may arise by undertaking such 'covert' ethnographic research?

Much later, especially in the USA, there were developments in social anthropology using participant observation techniques in the tradition of ethnographic fieldwork. In the University of Chicago this came to be known as the Chicago School, and was to be chiefly concerned with the study of ethnic groups in the city. Whyte (1984), for example, describes these influences upon his first industrial study in the Phillips Petroleum Company in 1943. During the 1950s and 1960s a few, now classical, ethnographic studies were carried out, for example by Dalton (1959) into managerial practices in four companies in North America (see below) and by Sayles (1964) into the nature of managerial tasks in one division of a large American manufacturing organization. This interest in the nature of managerial work has continued with, for example, the famous ethnographies of Mintzberg (1973), Jackall (1988) and Watson (1994). Other famous research includes that of Sayles (1958) and Gouldner (1954a, 1954b) who turned their attention to shopfloor matters in ethnographic studies of industrial work groups, a wildcat strike, and aspects of bureaucracy in action, respectively. A similar focus was also the concern of Lupton (1963), who built upon the participant observation studies of Roy (1960) by studying the work organization and culture of the shopfloor in two manufacturing plants in order to explain the occurrence of restriction of output by employees. This concern with the impact of organizational control and employee resistance has more recently been extended to the ethnographic investigation of how managers attempt to manage culture in organizational settings (Kunda, 1992; Willmott and Knights, 1995), the everyday experience of work (Rosen, 1985; Kondo, 1990; Van Maanen, 1991; Giroux, 1992; Meyerson, 1994) and issues such as gender and identity at work (Pollert, 1981; Ely, 1995; Parker, 2000).

In sum, there is a long history of using ethnographic methods in the broad area of management research. Of course this begs the question, what is ethnography?

Management research example Dalton's ethnographic work

Dalton was concerned to immerse himself in the cultures of three manufacturing firms and one department store to investigate problems arising from the gap between unofficial and official ways of doing things. These studies are described in *Men Who Manage* (Dalton, 1959) which contains a useful appendix on methods, later expanded with much insight (Dalton, 1964), and which serves as a useful guide to ethnographic practice.

Dalton started with some preconceptions. He believed that natural science methods were inappropriate to the study of social situations. For example, no hypotheses were formulated at the outset as it was considered that what was relevant in forming an hypothesis was unclear until the situation was well known and, further, that a precisely formulated hypothesis would prove restrictive. Rather, Dalton proceeded by hunches, some of which were dropped and others followed as his knowledge increased. Second, he had a preference for what is described as 'idea over number' (Dalton, 1964: 56), by which he meant the avoidance of quantification of data for its own sake; finally, he took a pragmatic view of ethical questions arising from 'insider' research, a matter we consider later.

Dalton was employed as a member of staff at a factory he called Milo when the idea of undertaking an investigation of its managerial culture occurred to him, largely because he was puzzled by many incidents at the plant. He continued his studies when he left the organization and Milo became the focus of his work, which continued for a decade. Interpretations from Milo were checked at other locations, at some of which he had been employed and at all of which he had 'intimates'. Data were gathered directly by formal interviewing, his own work diaries and participant observation in the course of his normal work as an employee, which he says was uncompromised. This activity was either fitted into his usual duties as an organizational member, or, more often, interviewing was done after working hours both in the plant and at employees' homes. Much of Dalton's work was covert in that he did not seek entry to his target organizations through official channels – believing formal interviews would reveal only official expectations.

Dalton also relied upon key informants as a source of data – whom he called intimates. These were people who Dalton selected over a period of several years on the basis of mutual trust and the freedom with which they were prepared to speak about their problems and be unlikely to jeopardize his research; they showed acceptance of what Dalton could reveal to them and did not pry into data he was obtaining from others; they also gave him guidance and hints which 'if known would have endangered their careers' (Dalton, 1964: 65). Dalton found female secretaries and clerks particularly helpful in this respect, as acute observers of differences in status and influence as well as having access to records and important events. As he remarks, where 'female secretaries are treated as intellectual menials they are disposed to be communicative with those who show awareness of their insights and knowledge of affairs' (Dalton, 1964: 275). In one notable case Dalton tacitly

exchanged some counselling help with a female secretary's interest in dating an employee in return for the supply of confidential data on managerial salaries to which she had access. There was clearly danger to the secretary in supplying this information but the bargain was struck and the data flowed while the dating continued. Dalton notes with satisfaction that, despite his crude attempts at counselling, the secretary married the employee within a year!

Of the specific techniques used by Dalton to collect data the least significant was formal interviewing, as it was considered inadequate in providing information about unofficial activities. Where formal interviews were used, for example in gathering data on managers' careers from senior officers, questions were prepared but quietly dropped to pursue interesting leads as these emerged. Notes were not taken except at the request of the interviewee, as Dalton considered them to inhibit subjects and to divert him from close observation. Interviews, including notes of non-verbal expressions, were reconstructed as soon after the event as possible. Dalton used loose-leaf notebooks to record events, gossip, initial hunches and leads which might be followed. His work diaries were increasingly of use as a guide to the research and a source of insight to him through reflection on the data.

The most used method was participant observation. This has its disadvantages; its closeness to unique events, for example, limits attempts to classify and generalize from the data; 'intimates' may be an unrepresentative sample; and the presence of the researcher may distort the data. Friendliness with respondents may provoke leading questions, and unusual events may be mistaken for the typical, particularly if the researcher is new to the situation. In other words, personal observation can have low internal and external validity (see Chapter 9), but Dalton believed that, especially when combined with other methods, these defects were outweighed by its flexibility, particularly in exploratory research. Its advantages are that the researcher is not bound by rigid research plans and interviewing can also be conducted more flexibly and pointless questions avoided. There is time to build greater intimacy, allowing access to covert information and to the motives of informants; and uniquely equipped informants can be treated differently and access to confidential data enabled by a selective and informal process. In other words, Dalton believed that his methodology allowed access to what is called the informal organization – an area of organizational life often surrounded by secrecy and controversy and hence usually inaccessible to outsiders (see Figure 7.2).

Stop and Think Exercise 7.2 As illustrated above, Dalton undertook ethnographic research in an organization in which he was already working as a manager. Whilst such access provides significant opportunities for any practising manager for undertaking research, consider the possible problems which may arise if you were to try and undertake ethnography in the organization where you already work.

Defining ethnography

Ethnography literally means the study, or writing about, or description of, people – or more specifically their cultures. As Schwartzman puts it, one of the defining characteristics of ethnographic research is that 'ethnographers go into the field to learn about a culture from the inside out' (1993: 4). Ethnography is about the researcher trying to discover the shared systems of meanings and interpretations deployed by a specific group of people, which leads them to perceive themselves and reality in particular ways, and leads them to interact and behave in regular but distinctive ways. This is achieved by the researcher gaining access to the group's everyday social worlds by sharing and experiencing the routine and normal from the point of view of the member (see Hammersley and Atkinson, 1995; Brewer, 2000). However, in describing what ethnography actually entails we are immediately confronted by a problem. Unlike in experimental or survey research, which both have fairly clear, agreed, working protocols which guide the design, undertaking and reporting of research, which may even be followed in principle by a novice, ethnography lacks a codified specification of what should be done and how it should be reported – as we noted earlier, like much other qualitative research it is flexible and emergent.

In very general terms, ethnographic management research usually has a focus upon the manner in which people interact and collaborate in observable and regular ways – usually in organizational settings. Typically such work has taken long periods of intensive study and immersion in a well-defined locality involving direct participation with some of the members of the organization in their activities. So, while a wide portfolio of data collection methods may be used, ethnographers usually place more emphasis on some form of participant observation and semi-structured interviewing than on documentary and (descriptive) survey data, although both have frequently been used in ethnographic studies generally as supplementary material. Nevertheless, it is very difficult to talk about research design in ethnography as we have done with regard to approaches like the experiment, quasi-experiments or surveys. In part, this is because what ethnographers do largely depends upon the nature of the social situation they are trying to investigate and hence it contingently varies often in unpredictable ways according to the demands placed upon the researcher in coping with the pressures deriving from that context. Therefore, there is no ideal to which ethnography should conform. However, it is possible to try and define ethnographic research in terms of a set of methodological commitments which strongly influence the methodological decisions that ethnographers make during the course of fieldwork.

Ethnographic methodological commitments

1 *Verstehen*

We have already introduced the reader to one key methodological commitment in ethnographic research that it shares with other qualitative approaches. This has been called *verstehen*: that human behaviour is grounded in actors' interpretations of the social situation in which they are located and therefore it is crucial that in order to explain any behaviour the management researcher must gain access to how those people are making sense of what is going on around them and, very often, consider the social influences that impact upon that sense making and the ongoing social construction of meaningful action. To a degree this commitment drives other interlinked commitments which we now turn to below.

2 Avoid ethnocentrism

Ethnography's general commitment to *verstehen* means that the researcher needs to develop a comprehension of actors' behaviour based upon those actors' own terms of reference, or perspective. In other words, the ethnographer must gain access to the culturally derived rationality, or internal logic, that underpins the behaviour of the actors being investigated which makes that behaviour sensible, logical, reasonable and rational. The assumption is that different people deploy different, but equally rational, logics in constructing their behaviour. The danger is that if the ethnographer does not get access to that rationality, various behaviours may be discounted as bizarre or irrational because he or she is judging things from the stance of what is 'normal' according to what are merely different, socially relative, cultural standards and norms of behaviour. But ethnographers themselves, like any other human being, have been previously socialized into a particular set of cultural norms, beliefs and values that influence their own behaviours and the judgements they make about the behaviour of others. So what the ethnographer must simultaneously do, in order to accomplish an adequate level of understanding, is avoid inadvertently imposing his/her own culturally derived logic or rationality upon the behaviour of the people being investigated.

In Malinowski's terms (1922) accessing the 'native's point of view' means that the ethnographer has to keep his/her own equally cultural point of view out of any description or account: otherwise there is a danger of ethnocentricity – that the ethnographer imposes his/her own culturally driven values, etc. upon the behaviour of the others being investigated and thereby fails to gain the 'native's point of view' – their equally rational but different point of view. Whilst it is today fairly obvious that there are all kinds of dangers if one tries to consider and judge the behaviour of people who are from societies very different to your own, by imposing your own social mores upon that behaviour, as Goffman illustrates this equally applies to organizational research within one's own society (see below).

Key methodological concept

Ethnocentricity and Organizational Research

Erving Goffman: *Asylums: Essays on the Social Situation of Mental Patients and Other Inmates* (1961)

> It ... is ... my belief that any group of persons – prisoners, primitives, pilots, or patients – develop a life of their own that becomes meaningful, reasonable, and normal once you get close to it, and that a good way to learn about any of these worlds is to submit oneself in the company of members to the daily round of petty contingencies to which they are subject (Goffman,1961: 7)

In his account of 'total institutions', organizations where individuals are cut off from wider society and incarcerated in places of residence and work where their lives are formally controlled by others, Goffman undertook ethnographic research into the 'social world of the mental hospital inmate, as this world is subjectively experienced by him (sic)' (ibid.: 7). This wide ranging, and at the time controversial, work tried to interpret the experience of patients rather than justify the organizational processes that surrounded them. Obviously, from the point of view of the outsider, many of the behaviours engaged in by the inmates may at first sight seem bizarre. However, because Goffman was committed to attempting to describe what was going on from the patient's point of view he had to try and seek out the underlying rationality of the patient that motivated their behaviour rather than accepting clinical definitions of such behaviour as abnormal or even psychotic.

For instance, he observed how very often patients would horde a vast array of everyday items, sometimes in secret 'stashes', at other times on their person, wherever they went. Often this would result in inmates carrying around various bulky containers, or adapting clothing, to accommodate 'books, writing materials, washcloths, fruit, small valuables, scarves, playing cards, soap, shaving equipment (in the case of men), containers of salt, pepper, and sugar, bottles of milk' (ibid.: 223).

According to Goffman this behaviour may well seem odd to an outsider. Indeed, the hospital authorities saw it as evidence of psychosis and in many cases as evidence of further deterioration in the patient's condition since admission into the hospital. However, as Goffman implies, such an interpretation of this behaviour fails to understand the subjective rationality being deployed that explains what is going on. In other words, such an 'official' interpretation is ethnocentric because it does not begin with the patient's point of view. For Goffman, once we access the patient's experience of the hospital such behaviour is in fact eminently rational.

As Goffman argues, when patients entered the hospital, especially if they were excited or depressed, they were denied any secure personal storage space for things: 'valuables or breakables, such as false teeth, eyeglasses, wrist watches, often an integral part of body image might be locked up out of their owners' reach ... . Cosmetics, needed to present oneself properly to others, were collectivized, being made accessible to patients only at certain times' (ibid.: 222). Even on convalescent wards, boxes were made available but these were unlockable and hence the contents vulnerable to theft and often kept in rooms inaccessible to patients during the day. Given this experience, Goffman argues that there were good reasons for these 'bulky carrys-ons ... Many of the amenities of life, such as soap, toilet paper, or cards, which are ordinarily available in many depots of comfort in civil society, are thus not available to patients, so the day's needs had to be partly provided for at the beginning of the day' (ibid.: 224).

Later Goffman noted a further very important explanation of this behaviour that demonstrates its rationality, that many of the items secreted on the person were 'talismanic-like possessions that inmates use as symbolic devices for separating themselves from the position they are supposed to be in' (ibid.: 269). Now what Goffman is referring to here is how very often we define ourselves as individuals through the unique collection of possessions we have – our clothing for instance. However, patients had been incarcerated in a system where personal items were purposively kept to a minimum, where often even clothing was taken away by the staff at night – so attempting to hoard or stash personal possessions is not only a way of preserving one's individuality in a 'total' institution – it also is a means by which 'someone ... is attempting to stand apart from the place accorded to him' (ibid.: 270) by the institution. Interestingly, from the relevant literature Goffman also identifies similar forms of behaviour in other 'total institutions', such as prisons, something which implies a move in Goffman's work from substantive to formal theory (see Figures 7.7 and 7.8 later in this chapter).

The opposite of ethnocentricity is called 'going native'. This happens when the ethnographer forgets his/her research role and actually becomes a member of the culture or social group being investigated. This can occur when the ethnographer becomes socialized and begins to accept the cultural beliefs, values, and norms of those being studied as his/her own. This can be a significant risk in ethnographic research because often ethnography exploits the ability of anyone to learn a new culture through members of that culture attempting to socialize the ethnographer into their way of seeing the world. Whilst these processes are an important source of data to the ethnographer, they simultaneously can undermine their ability to undertake research. For instance, the result can be over-identification with the culture and the loss of the researcher's perspective with consequent loss of sight of the research aims being supposedly pursued.

Consequently, ethnographers have to negotiate, whilst in the field, an often precarious balance between insider and outsider. This balance involves being able to participate in the activities of the people being studied in order to get the insider's point of view, perhaps to the extent of seeming to be a member of their culture, yet simultaneously retaining a degree of detachment to enable the fulfilment of his/her research aims whilst avoiding an ethnocentric interpretation. These issues have significant implications for how fieldwork is conducted which we shall discuss later in this chapter.

Stop and Think Exercise 7.3   Goffman's work provides us with useful organizational examples of ethnocentric explanations of behaviour. They are ethnocentric because they fail to access the experience and interpretations of people which lend rationality to their behaviour – no matter how strange it might initially seem to the outsider. In contrast going native entails being absorbed by the culture under investigation and becoming a member cognitively and emotionally.

Imagine that you decided to undertake ethnographic research in your own organization. Now think about the following issues.

1   What are the potential sources of ethnocentricity and going native which could affect your own account of what you experience, or observe, regarding the behaviour of the various social groups who make up your organization?
2   How are ethnocentricity and going native related to one another in this research situation?
3   What steps could you take to ameliorate such potential problems regarding how you interpret what you see to be going on?

3 Induction

As is evident in Goffman's work, ethnographers assume that how people behave largely depends upon how they interpret the social situation in which they find themselves. Simultaneously how they make those interpretations is something that has to be discovered by the ethnographer by going into the field and examining the native's point of view – hence ethnography has to be inductive in its approach to theory otherwise the accusation of ethnocentricity looms large (see also Chapter 3). In other words, in ethnographic work, you cannot start collecting data with a description or potential theoretical explanation already formulated because this would prejudge issues yet to be identified and result in an ethnocentric imposition of the researcher's own common sense assumptions upon the issues he or she intends to investigate in the field. Now this is a point which we shall return to later in this chapter both immediately below and also when we turn to looking at the analysis of qualitative data and its relationship to the inductive development of theory. This commitment to induction is further reinforced by our next methodological commitment.

4 Behaviour varies according to the social situation in which it takes place

According to ethnographers our behaviour varies according to the social situations in which we find ourselves: it is generated through social interaction and hence varies from social context to social context. It follows that if management researchers place people in an artificial social context (for example, a laboratory experiment – see Chapter 4) in order to collect data about their behaviour, that information will be influenced by that specific social situation as respondents try to make sense of what is going on and what is happening to them. In other words, ethnographers are committed to the idea that the social world cannot be understood by studying artificial simulations of it created by, for instance, experimental conditions. The use of such methods only shows how people behave in those specific social situations created to enable data collection. Therefore, because people have subjective capacities, which lead to their meaningful social construction of behaviour, it is important to study that behaviour in the normal everyday situations in which it takes place. Therefore, in ethnography there is a commitment to what is called 'naturalism' (see also Chapter 3), that the

> social world should be studied in its 'natural 'state, undisturbed by the researcher. Hence natural not artificial settings … should be the primary source of data. The primary aim should be to describe what happens in the setting, how people see their own actions and those of others, and the context in which action takes place. (Hammersley and Atkinson, 1995: 6)

In his thinly veiled attack upon methodological monism, Denzin (1971: 166) describes what he calls the logic of naturalistic inquiry. This is where the researcher actively enters 'the worlds of native people … to render those worlds understandable from the standpoint of a theory that is grounded in the behaviours, languages, definitions, attitudes, and feelings of those studied' and tries to theoretically explain what shapes and influences their behaviour. In doing so, Denzin discusses the implications of naturalism for the researchers' field role, how data is collected and analysed, the processes by which theory is inductively developed whilst reducing 'the distance between [the researcher's] outsider imposed concepts and those employed by the native person' (ibid.: 168). Throughout this programmatic statement for naturalism, Denzin preserves a commitment to what he calls sophisticated rigour so that theories are 'brought in closer touch with the empirical social world' (ibid.: 167) whilst 'resisting schemes or models which over-simplify the complexity of everyday life' (ibid.: 168).

Naturalism has devastating implications for organizational research. Besides the need to collect data in natural settings so as to inductively generate theory that explains what has been observed, it also requires ethnographers seek to minimize and simultaneously monitor their own impact upon any research setting so as to observe social processes as they naturally occur. Hence, there is the need to minimize what is called reactivity (members' reactions to the presence of the researcher) whilst the ethnographer attempts to remain internally reflexive (able to monitor any reactions to his/her presence). Therefore, far from seeking to manipulate events they seek to minimize any disturbance to the setting created by their very presence. For instance, Hammersley (1992) argues that the commitment to naturalism means that ethnographers have to continuously monitor and reflect upon the impact of their role in the field, through which they have collected data, upon the research setting so as to reduce potential sources of disruption to what goes on. The idea is to enhance what is called ecological validity (see below) by minimizing potential sources of contamination created by people's reaction to (i.e. reactivity to) the very presence of the ethnographer and his/her methods of data collection. Obviously these issues have significant implications for how ethnographic research may be undertaken in the field.

Key methodological concept

Ecological Validity

Ecological validity is one important means by which the quality of ethnographic research, and indeed any qualitative research, may be assessed. As we shall see in Chapter 9 there are also others. Ecological validity refers to the extent the ethnographer has been able to gain access to and observe social processes as they naturally occur. It thus relates to questions such as: 'Do our instruments capture the daily life conditions, opinions, values, attitudes, and knowledge base of those we study as expressed in their natural habitat?' (Cicourel, 1982: 15).

For many ethnographers, how experimental and survey researchers collect data actually creates specific social situations in which data is collected about actors' behaviour through some form of contrived social interaction with the researcher. But these occasions are not the normal, natural, everyday contexts in which the behaviour being investigated usually takes place – they are specifically constructed occasions created by the researcher to enable data collection and are simultaneously interpreted by the 'subjects' of the research as they try to make sense of what is going on. Therefore, there is always the question – will the behaviour accessed and displayed in these contrived situations be also displayed in other social contexts? Can one extrapolate, or generalize, what has been observed in an artificial setting to natural, normal, everyday behavioural situations?

Stop and Think Exercise 7.4   What are the implications of a commitment to ecological validity for how ethnographers must manage their field roles when undertaking management research, firstly in the organization in which they normally work and secondly in an organization where they have not previously been a member?

Undertaking ethnographic research: methodological decisions and choices in the field

As we have argued, it is not possible to define ethnography as a single mode of collecting information since it usually entails the varying application of a battery of techniques so as to elucidate the subjective basis of the behaviour of people. Nevertheless, it is still possible to broadly review the practice and design of ethnographic research in terms of the various choices available to an ethnographer in undertaking a piece of research. Many of these decisions appertain to the way the ethnographer is to observe the phenomena of interest in a systematic fashion and are contingent upon various factors, including the purposes of the research, the setting in which the research will take place, the resources available to the researcher and the aims of the study. As we have indicated, these various choices are usually taken in the context of an ethnographer's philosophical commitment to comprehending the behaviour of people in their natural and everyday settings through an inductive development of an empathetic understanding of their rationalities.

Smircich (1983) considers there to be three main available approaches: observation, participation in the setting and gathering reports from key informants. Regardless of the approach or combination of approaches used to collect data each entails the researcher using the capacity that any social actor possesses for learning new cultures. Whilst in everyday circumstances this capacity is deployed often without us thinking much about it, ethnographers have to go about this task in a much more systematic fashion.

According to Fetterman (1989: 42–4) all ethnographers work under variable sets of constraints deriving from the kind of access they have to social settings and the resources they have available to conduct their work. Despite the resultant variation in the nature of ethnographic research in practice, all ethnographers have to initially make decisions about several key interrelated issues. These issues refer to *what* to study, *where* and *when* to study it, *who* to investigate, and *how* to undertake the research. So first they have to decide upon the research questions they wish to explore in the field. These questions influence the selection of both the site of subsequent work and the initial selection, or sampling, of people in that site whose behaviour will be investigated. Who is included in this sample will probably change as the research progresses and more is learnt about the site, the people in question and the phenomena under investigation. One key constraint the ethnographer is working under at this stage is his/her ability to gain access to a suitable site. Here a balance has to be often struck between what is possible and what is desirable – where perseverance, luck and good fortune can all play significant roles (see Van Maanen and Kolb, 1985). We will return to the issue of access later in this chapter since it is highly affected by the nature of the field role adopted by the researcher.

Once access is gained, even where the ethnographer is researching a familiar social setting, s/he is required to treat it as anthropologically 'strange' in an effort to make explicit the assumptions that people take for granted as a culture member. In this way the culture is turned into an object for study (Hammersley and Atkinson, 1995: 9). However, which of the approaches indicated by Smircich are available to the researcher, and how they are to be used to collect information, are largely governed by decisions about the type of 'field' or 'social' role to be adopted (Junker, 1960; Adler and Adler, 1987). It is to these issues that we now turn.

Field roles in ethnography

As we have seen, there are numerous aspects to the field role which an ethnographer may adopt, and perhaps the most important relate to the extent to which the researcher decides to 'participate' in the natural setting of members' behaviour, and the extent to which the identity and purposes of the ethnographer are revealed to those members.

Participant and non-participant observation

In essence these choices may be conceptualized as varying from the observer's complete immersion in a social setting, by adopting a role of full participant in the everyday lives of ordinary members, to that of spectator in which the ethnographer only observes events and processes and thereby avoids becoming involved in interactions with members. In the former the researcher attempts to participate fully in the lives and activities of members and thus becomes a member of their group, organization or community. This enables the researcher to share their experiences by not merely observing what is happening but also feeling it emotionally. Although this form of observation was first developed by anthropologists investigating 'exotic' tribal cultures, it has been successfully applied to the study of people in organizations, including managers.

As illustrated by Figure 7.2, participant observation usually enables a great deal of depth in research since it allows the researcher to get very close to the phenomena of interest by ostensibly 'catching reality in flight' by experiencing the often hidden experience (Madge, 1953) of members. For Douglas (1976), participant observation can enable the researcher to penetrate the various complex forms of 'misinformation, fronts, evasions and lies' that he thinks are endemic in most social settings,

Figure 7.2 | Participant observation and organizations

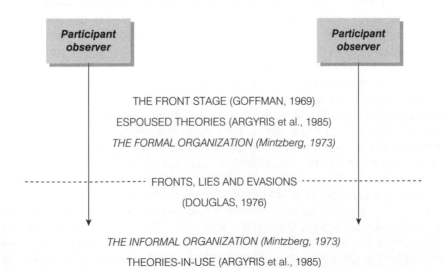

including organizations. So in management research, Mintzberg (1973) discovered it can enable access to what people actually do (the informal organization), as opposed to what they might claim they do and which official sanctions notionally impel them to do (the formal organization) (see also Prasad and Prasad, 2002). In Goffman's terms, a key methodological strength is that participant observation facilitates access to uncensored organizational 'backstages' (Goffman, 1969) which constitute an alternative to organizational realities hidden behind organizational frontstages. Argyris et al. (1985) call these 'backstages' 'theories-in-use' as opposed to officially sanctioned 'espoused theories', and are characterized by multiple perspectives and practices often in opposition to those specified and demanded by the formal organization (see also Pettigrew, 1985b). As Goffman notes there is always the danger that researchers may become an audience for impression management where organizational members ...

> ... cooperate to present an audience a given definition of the situation ... We often find a division into a back region, where the performance of a routine is prepared, and a front region, where the performance is presented. Access to these regions is controlled in order to prevent the audience from seeing the backstage and to prevent outsiders from coming into a performance that is not addressed to them. Among members of the team we find that familiarity prevails, solidarity is likely to develop, and that secrets that could give the show away are shared and kept. (1969: 231)

Particularly where the phenomenon of interest is rather controversial or surrounded in secrecy (e.g. Roy, 1960; Lupton, 1963; Golding, 1979), participant observation may be the only viable means of discovering what is actually happening by getting past the fronts created by impression management.

This dual purpose of empathetically experiencing hidden data and thereby penetrating secrecy is illustrated in Douglas's (ibid.) articulation of 'depth-probe' research. In this the researcher surrenders to the everyday experience while in the natural setting but, instead of going native, remains latently committed to being a researcher, and comes back to reflect and report upon the experience as a member. Depth-probes are vital in getting at the more secret aspects of social life, those about which members would not talk or possibly even think about. For Douglas, depth-probes involve 'defocusing', that is, immersion in and saturation by the setting through allowing oneself to experience that setting as much as is possible, in the same way as any other organizational member. At the same time the researcher retains a commitment to being a researcher and later moving to more systematic observations and analyses of that setting. However, without such direct or 'lived' experience of the setting the researcher might be forced to 'rely upon the members to communicate it to him, which makes him dependent upon their honesty and their abilities to symbolize their experience' (Douglas, 1976: 111). Douglas would find the truthfulness of such accounts exceedingly problematic for they would remain uncheckable, and as such the researcher might be unable to avoid 'being taken in, duped, deceived, used, put on, fooled, suckered, made the patsy, left holding the bag, fronted out and so on' (Douglas, 1976: 57). Moreover, such intimate knowledge of members' frames of reference is taken to be essential for deciphering their everyday behaviour and thereby avoiding misunderstanding (Adler and Adler, 1994).

Management research example Participant Observation

A more recent addition to ethnographic research on managers is provided by Watson's fascinating *In Search of Management* (1994). Here Watson follows the tradition of Gouldner (1954a and 1954b) and Dalton (1959) when he spent a seconded year working as a participant observer in a company based in Nottinghamshire employing some 3,000 people developing, making and selling telecommunications products. He wrote his book as an attempt to appeal to both academic and industrial audiences.

The company was mainly chosen because its management had engaged in a series of change initiatives of the type associated with the key managerial text *In Search of Excellence* (Peters and Waterman, 1982) – so being particularly useful to Watson as he could turn to published work to discover the principles on which some of the company's key policies were based. It also meant that the study could contribute to a wider understanding of corporate strategic issues. In Watson's words he was in search of management in both an intellectual and practical sense to tackle the question of how could one best understand management as a form of occupational activity and also help those who wished to become more effective managers.

This concern about how managers see their jobs was shared by the personnel director and organizational development executive in the company with whom Watson negotiated taking a managerial role, as a participant as well as an observer, as part of his one year secondment from his university. They were keen to have help in identifying

ways of encouraging all their managers to see themselves as 'business managers' rather than solely as departmental managers. One of Watson's main tasks as a participant for the company was to develop a scheme identifying the management competencies which the company might use in selecting and developing managers for the future; this scheme is included in his book as an appendix.

As well as being in search of management Watson was also interested in many sub-questions such as how managers generally think about their work and how they relate their personal lives, values and priorities to the work they do. How do they manage themselves at the same time as managing their jobs? What part is played by the theoretical understandings which lie beneath the surface of their everyday pragmatic behaviour? Why is it, Watson asks, that people in the managerial world often seem so bad at putting to use what they already know?

In order to understand matters like these it is necessary to look closely at the thoughts and ideas of managers in the context of the specificities of the organization. This requires getting close to managers as individuals and becoming involved with their organizational context. All of this suggested an ethnographic or participant observation research method. Watson sees ethnography as a coming together of the 'everyday' thinking of the subjects of the research and the body of academic knowledge to which the researcher has access. And there is attention to meanings through which the members of particular worlds make those worlds meaningful to themselves and others. Watson believes his study can in part be read as a critique of contemporary managerial practice but he makes clear that it is a critique which emerges from his dialogue with organizational managers rather than one imposed by a critical sociologist. He also makes clear that like any other social researcher he was influencing those he was researching and that he was endeavouring to be honest about this reflexivity.

Watson finally makes clear that ethnographic research involves 'feeling one's way in confusing circumstances, struggling to make sense of ambiguousness, reading signals, looking around, listening all the time, coping with conflicts and struggling to achieve tasks through establishing and maintaining a network of relationships' (1994: 8). As Watson makes clear this is what managers do in their more formalized managerial roles and in conducting his research he has come to see the research craft as very similar to the craft of the manager. 'It is through speaking to each other that all of us make sense of the worlds we move in whether we are trying to make sense of things as managers, as researcher or as part of our ordinary daily lives' (1994: 8).

WATSON'S IN SEARCH OF MANAGEMENT (1994)

Whilst participant observation does allow for significant strengths in research, there is also the imminent danger that, by becoming embroiled in the everyday lives of members, the researcher internalizes member's culture and becomes unable to take a dispassionate view of events and unintentionally discards the researcher elements of the field role. That is, they actually become a member of the organization, or 'go native' by internalizing or assimilating the culturally derived frames of reference of those being studied. As we have already noted, ethnographers are usually alert to this potential problem hence there is usually an emphasis upon avoiding 'overrapport' and over-'identification' with members by retaining 'social and intellectual distance' and 'analytical space' (Hammersley and Atkinson, 1995:115). Often to illustrate how they have maintained this precarious balance between being involved yet not being over-involved during fieldwork ethnographers provide detailed accounts of the research processes they have engaged in. Indeed, through 'confessional tales' that reveal aspects of themselves and the research process the ethnographer tries to persuade the reader that s/he 'can rely on the writer's hard won objectivity' (Seale, 1999a: 161). Such an account is a vital part of what is called an audit trail – something we shall further discuss when we come to the analysis of qualitative data.

Nevertheless, ethnographers argue that over-maintenance of social distance between themselves and the members they are investigating can lead to other problems. For instance, although using different data collection methods to participant observation, Gouldner argued that 'deep rapport has its perils, but to treat the norm of impersonality as sacred, even if it impairs the informant's cooperation, would seem to be an inexcusable form of scientific ritualism' (1954b: 247). So where the field role is limited to that of a non-participating spectator, the consequent lack of interaction with subjects can raise the opposite problem of ethnocentricity: that is, the observer fails to gain access to and to understand the cultural underpinnings of subjects' overt behaviours and actions. Indeed, the observer may inadvertently analyse and evaluate those events and processes from the perspectives and rationality of his or her own culture. Such distortions may be compounded by an inability to penetrate the 'fronts and evasions' alluded to by Douglas (1976). It might, however, be claimed that since the role of the spectator entails no interaction with subjects it is less likely that the observer's presence will affect the situation and cause some change in their usual behaviour; particularly where such observation is being undertaken secretly, for example by means of a two-way mirror. This last point involves consideration of the next important aspect of field role choices, namely, overt or covert observation.

Overt and covert observation

This aspect of the field role refers to whether the actors who are being investigated know about, or are aware of, the presence of a researcher. There are usually two main rationales behind the use of covert observation.

First, it is often argued that people may behave quite differently when aware that they are under observation. Thus, the degree of naturalism or ecological validity is reduced if observation is not employed covertly. So in many versions of ethnography there is an obsession, similar to that in deductive methodologies, to eliminate the effects of the researcher upon the data (although a very different set of strategies is adopted in attempting to achieve this goal). This objective has two important dimensions: first to eliminate reactivity amongst those being researched to the researcher's presence, personal qualities and research techniques; and, second to eschew the idiosyncratic imposition of the researcher's own frame of reference upon the data. Here we shall concern ourselves only with the former since the latter is reviewed in Chapter 8 when we consider the issues surrounding the contentious possibility of a theory-neutral observation language for social science in general.

As we have already suggested, often the most vaunted advantage claimed for ethnography over other research procedures is its greater ecological validity because it entails studying social phenomena in their natural contexts. To preserve this naturalism, ethnographers have sometimes adopted covert field roles (e.g. Roy, 1960). This, it is argued, reduces subjects' reactivity to the researcher and his or her data collection procedures. However, where participant observation is being used, even where the ethnographer's presence is covert, he or she is present and involved as a member and inevitably must affect the phenomena under investigation in some way. It seems certain that members must react to the various qualities and attributes 'given off' by the covert researcher and, as such, their everyday lives are being disturbed to some degree. This problem has important implications for the practice of ethnography, in that 'instead of treating reactivity merely as a source of bias, we can exploit it. How people react to the presence of the researcher may be as informative as how they react to other situations' (Hammersley and Atkinson, 1995: 18).

Hence, there is a still a need for the researcher to be 'reflexive' – even in covert research. Rather than to attempt to eliminate the effects of the researcher on the phenomenon under investigation, the researcher should attempt to understand his or her effect upon, and role in, the research setting and utilize this knowledge to elicit data. Therefore, the social and interactive nature of ethnographic research becomes clear:

once we abandon the idea that the social character of research can be standardised out, or avoided by becoming a 'fly on the wall' or a 'full participant', the role of the researcher as an active participant in the research process becomes clear. He or she is the research instrument par excellence. The fact that behaviour and attitudes are often not stable across contexts, and that the researcher may play an important part in shaping the context becomes central to the analysis. Indeed it is exploited for all it is worth. (Hammersley and Atkinson, 1995: 19)

As Hammersley and Atkinson go on to observe, rather than seeking by one means or another to eliminate reactivity, its effects should be monitored, and as far as possible brought under control. By systematically modifying one's role in the field, different kinds of data may be collected whose comparisons may greatly enhance interpretations of the social processes under study. The 'problem' of reactivity is thus converted into a research tool: the researcher attempts to shape aspects of the social context in which interaction takes place by manipulating dimensions of the role to promote controlled types of reactivity.

So the kind of reflexivity proposed here entails scrutinizing the impact upon the research setting and findings of the researcher and his/her research strategy (Hammersley, 1992a: 64). This might include the effects of the various field roles adopted during data collection so as to ensure a 'necessary' balance: between 'outsider' and 'insider' (Horowitz, 1986); between 'distance' and 'inclusion' (Pollner and Emerson, 1983); between 'detachment' and 'involvement' (Shalin, 1986) while avoiding the problems of 'overrapport' considered earlier in this chapter. However, if one is trying to pass oneself off as an ordinary member in order to remain covert, purposefully varying one's relationship with members in order to collect data may be impossible – especially if it involves violating their expectations regarding the behaviour of a 'normal' colleague. Hence, covert research may well be too restrictive.

So it would appear then that one of the notional advantages of covert over overt participation might be pragmatically mistaken in many circumstances – regardless of the potential ethical problems that may arise when adopting a covert field role. Indeed, an overt role may enable the researcher to manipulate dimensions of the field role more effectively since the overt researcher may be allowed by members to behave strangely or variably; behaviours which if entered into by a presumed member would result in sanctions being applied if group norms were broken. Such limitations may not only restrict the ability to shape aspects of the social context reflexively but also affect the freedom to sample different social settings by moving around the organization unhindered. Hence, covert research might allow some access to the phenomena of interest but it might be severely limited, particularly by the norms that govern members' interactions and freedom of movement: because the covert researcher is publicly perceived as an 'ordinary' member, inevitably his or her freedom of action may be curtailed by the expectations of others with regard to how an ordinary member should behave. In other words, in many circumstances, being overt may enhance the ethnographer's freedom of action during research rather than limit it. Clearly, many of these advantages and limitations of covert and overt participant observation apply equally to circumstances in which the field role is limited to that of spectator.

A second reason for using covert research is often because it would be impossible to obtain access to do the research if the subjects knew one was a researcher. Certainly in such circumstances some degree of deception may be pragmatically defensible but may still be regarded by many as ethically dubious. Sometimes when attempting to gain access some researchers may mask the actual aims of the research from organizational members – that is people are aware of the presence of the researcher but are to some degree uninformed or even misled about their intentions. Obviously this may be a pragmatically useful tactic and may enable some of the advantages of overt research by avoiding the compromisation of findings through members constructing fronts and evasions around the specific focus of the research. Douglas has called this ploy the 'principle of indirection' (1985: 137). However, this too may be considered unethical, especially with contemporary demands for fully informed consent on the part of participants in any management research.

Figure 7.3 | A taxonomy of field roles

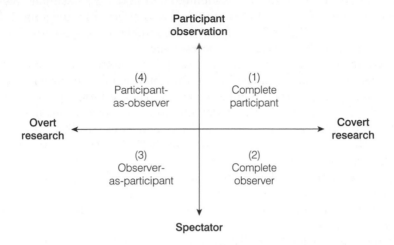

In sum, two of the most significant choices the researcher must make on starting fieldwork are the extent to which the work is covert and the extent to which the researcher interacts with members by performing an existing role within the organization. A useful conceptualization of these choices is provided by Gold (1958), later modified by Junker (1960), whose taxonomy of four field roles might be represented by Figure 7.3.

> ## Stop and Think Exercise 7.5   Use Gold's taxonomy of field roles to classify
> Watson's research *In Search of Management* summarized earlier in this chapter.
>   What are the advantages and disadvantages of Watson's field role in comparison to
> the three alternatives illustrated by Gold's model?

Whilst Gold usefully summarizes the various advantages and disadvantages attached to each role, we wish to emphasize that these choices are largely contingent upon the aims of the research, the skills and experience of the researcher and the nature of the social setting to be investigated. In many respects the difficulties surrounding access are highly influenced by the researcher's choice of role, which we next consider.

Access

The problems associated with the negotiation of access for ethnographers largely stem from the very nature of ethnography, for in most cases the researcher initiates a process of inquiry which at the outset is necessarily vague in its aims. Its methods too are difficult to describe, particularly to organizational gatekeepers (senior organizational figures who control admittance to the organization) whose expectations about research may derive from very different research traditions. Therefore, ethnographers often have to be highly opportunistic in the sense that they have to grasp opportunities that present themselves and simultaneously balance what is desirable, given their research aims, against what is possible, in a pragmatic fashion. In so doing, very often they may have to make compromises and simultaneously may have to strike bargains with gatekeepers regarding their role in, and contribution to, the organization in order to be able to be admitted and in order to maintain their ongoing access (see Johnson et al., 1999). Access is also affected by the approach to the study. The typology in Figure 7.3 of four possible modes of observational research is useful in clarifying some aspects of the access issue.

In the complete participant role the researcher's activities are concealed and the investigator joins the organization as a normal member in order to carry out research covertly. There are a number of examples of ethnographers undertaking covert work of this nature in the wider literature but few in business and management; by definition, in this role access clearly presents little problem for a researcher. Alternatively, as in the case of Dalton (1959) referred to earlier in this chapter, he was already a member of the organization when they decided to study it. At the other extreme is the complete observer, who has no contact at all with those being observed and is also in a relatively unusual role in ethnographic studies in management, but access again of course presents less of a problem because of its covert nature.

Mostly the researcher roles described earlier fall into the categories of participant-as-observer and observer-as-participant. In the former the primary role is that of participant but both fieldworker and informants are aware that there is an ongoing research relationship. This is probably best exemplified by Lupton (1963) who overtly played the part of industrial worker for several months in two shopfloor pieceworking groups, which he termed 'open participant observation' (see also Delbridge, 1998). It is, however, likely to be the role played by part-time management students engaged in dissertations and project work who, if working in their own organizations, will take various positions within the broad participant-as-observer role. What is more common is where researchers have primarily been observers who have not been members of the organization but have at times taken part in its activities as a member in order to maintain access. Usually this field role involves much more data collection through the use of structured observation where the researcher observes members doing particular activities of interest to the research but minimizes any other social interaction with the members (e.g. Prasad, 1993). This field role also probably relies upon the greater use of interviewing of members using semi-structured schedules so as to explore particular elements of organizational life of specific relevance to the research. For this group access has generally been difficult and since the activity has been completely open has had to be negotiated with the organization.

Issues that generally arise when access is overtly negotiated include the benefit which might be afforded to the organization such as feedback on some aspects of the study; the amount of organizational time likely to be taken up; and particularly the extent to which the work is to become public through publication. In most of the cases we have instanced eventual publications have been agreed provided the identity of the organization was disguised and the anonymity of individuals preserved. Some form of feedback may also be negotiated and even specific organizational help offered in order to gain access. While negotiations may be protracted, initial reactions at this stage generally provide crucially important insights into the organization's culture (Alderfer, 1968). Clearly, particular care needs to be taken if the issues to be investigated are matters of conflict and involve more than one party, such as trade unions and middle or senior management, otherwise, at the very least, problems may emerge later.

Access, then, is time consuming and often difficult, especially when the researcher lacks powerful support or a prestigious academic base. The use of all possible sources of help, such as friends and business contacts, has frequently been found to be useful in successful entry strategies (Glidewell, 1959) – as well as 'dumb luck' (Van Maanen and Kolb, 1985: 11).

Direct and indirect observation

So far we have focused upon the use of direct observation in ethnography, where the researcher observes by directly watching and listening to the behaviour of subjects. The ethnographer may, however, choose to gain access to data through indirect observation of an event not personally witnessed but which may be reported by an informant either orally or in writing.

Although all four of the field roles shown in Figure 7.3 will involve some degree of indirect observation, the observer-as-participant role may rely particularly upon interviewing informants about events the researcher has been unable to observe. Similarly, the complete observer may rely particularly on the use of various organizational documents, or 'secondary data', to supplement the primary data gathered through observation. In the case of the former, as with any interview, whether it is directive and structured or non-directive and unstructured, there is the problem of interpreting and verifying the informant's statements. Nevertheless, it has the advantage of allowing some access to events to which, for whatever reason, the researcher was unable to gain access directly.

Management research example Ethnography using documents

Ashworth's ethnography relies solely upon documentary sources, including participants' memoirs, diaries, and letters as well as battalion histories and the papers of military elites, to develop what he calls *The Sociology of Trench Warfare*. He uses these sources to develop a vivid description of how an informal military organization arose amongst the British, Irish, French, German and Bulgarian armies involved in trench warfare during the First World War (1914–1918), which was in direct opposition to the norms and demands of the formal military organization.

According to Ashworth the formal British military organization required that, in all circumstances, interaction between the soldier and the enemy had to be governed by the norm of offensiveness. Here '[T]he object of war was to eliminate the enemy both physically and morally ... the 'offensive' or 'fighting' spirit ... limited only by fatigue, orders to the contrary or the shortage of weapons and ammunition' (1968: 409). Military elites systematically tried to instill this norm into combatant officers and troops during training, through propaganda, and in formal face-to-face situations. Ashworth's documentary evidence is presented through a series of direct quotations from combatants' letters, diaries, etc. which contain an important insight into this rarely considered aspect of life in the trenches. This account gives the reader a glimpse of another side of military life during this period which is very different to the picture of carnage that arises during large scale offensives such as the Battle of the Somme.

Ashworth suggests that in many sectors of the front line, for long periods of time, warfare was not governed by the official offensive norm. He summarizes his analysis of this secondary data by presenting a description of how an informal 'live and let live principle' operated

> ... a collective agreement between front-line soldiers of opposing armies to inhibit offensive activity to a level mutually defined as tolerable. This understanding was tacit and covert; it was expressed in activity or non-activity rather than in verbal terms. This norm was supported by a system of sanctions. In the positive sense it constituted a system of mutual service, each side rewarded by the other by refraining from offensive activity

on the condition, of course, that this non-activity was reciprocated. Negatively, violations to the norm were sanctioned. (ibid.: 411)

Even within respective armies, sanctions also operated in the form of 'group disapproval ... against those individuals whose activities were defined as too offensive' (ibid.: 415). The result was a ritualized and routinized structure of often perfunctory, and mutually acceptable, offensive activity well below that prescribed by military elites as appropriate – yet sufficient to give the appearance of animosity to the uninitiated. Front-line officers colluded in maintaining this co-operation, and secrecy, because it was equally in their interests to do so: just as with their subordinates, the informal norm also increased their chances of survival.

ASHWORTH (1968) THE SOCIOLOGY OF TRENCH WARFARE

Stop and Think Exercise 7.6   What steps do you think Ashworth may have taken to corroborate his account of the secret 'informal' organization amongst the military?

However, it needs to be borne in mind that interviews are an outcome of the social interaction of the participants. Similarly, the secondary data provided by various types of organizational documents such as correspondence, memos and personal files can provide useful insights into organizational events and processes, though of course great care needs to be taken in interpreting their meaning and significance. It is particularly important to avoid taking such documents at face value and to make some allowance for the audience for whom they were originally intended and the possible motives the author(s) might have in saying what they said. Although such data might be gathered in an unobtrusive manner the dangers of misinterpretation and ethnocentricity must be checked out against other ethnographic procedures. Clarification of some of the key issues in ethnographic fieldwork, and particularly those concerned with fieldworker roles, may be assisted by Stop and Think Exercise 7.4.

Stop and Think Exercise 7.7

Tasks:

1   To observe and describe the social norms that regulate employees' (e.g. cleaners, library staff, secretaries) behaviour during breaks.
2   To observe and describe the social norms that regulate fellow students' behaviour during breaks.

Discussion:

a Compare and evaluate the different types of field role and their particular difficulties used for each of the above tasks.
b Reflexively consider the different sources of bias that may have influenced what you observed.
c From (a) and (b) devices a checklist of the issues ethnographers need to be aware of before, during and after ethnographic fieldwork.

Ethics and ethnography

Ethical issues in ethnography arise from the nature of the relationship between researcher and host organization and between the researcher and the subjects he or she studies, both of which may block other researchers if hostility is aroused.

The findings of ethnographic investigations are often eventually published and this may bring with it a number of ethical problems. These are mentioned, for example, by Morgan (1972), who discusses a case in which he gave a paper on a piece of research in a factory which was distorted by some sections of the press, who also discovered the identity of the company; this caused him embarrassment, particularly with his informants on the shopfloor. Nevertheless, in apologizing for the affair Morgan was incidentally enabled to add considerably to his understanding of the plant.

More commonly, researchers who have agreed to have work checked for accuracy by host organizations are sometimes requested to delete passages found to be offensive perhaps because they are perceived to suggest a negative public image. Whyte (1984), for example, presents several amusing cases of this sort, one of which explains why his classic study, *Human Relations in the Restaurant Industry* (1948), has two appendices, one of which – on 'job attitudes' – is seemingly superfluous. This evidently occurred as the outcome of a negotiation to allow the publication of his work.

Clearly, it is crucially important to contract unambiguously with organizations in such matters and to fulfil the researcher's side of the bargain, including offers to make presentations and provide reports to the host organization. Another key matter that arises is whether or not to use deception in research, and the answer should perhaps be clear cut: that producing a more comprehensive study is never justified by putting the job of an informant at risk. While the risks were probably very small, Dalton (1959) might have put employees' jobs in danger. In the final analysis, 'ethical fieldwork turns on the moral sense and integrity of the researcher negotiating the social contract which leads his subjects to expose their lives' (Dingwall, 1980: 885) and at the heart of the contract lies the matter of trust between the parties. In the case of student research work the need for confidentiality frequently arises, particularly when the work is being undertaken in the student's own organization. Although often an inadequate solution to the problem, most academic institutions recognize these difficulties by offering protection of dissertations and theses by restricting their publication for a period. It is, of course, also possible to protect the identity of individuals and context through the use of fictitious names, although this may frequently prove to be difficult.

The analysis of qualitative data: theory building through induction

As we indicated at the beginning of this chapter, ethnography is one particular approach to collecting qualitative data. There is a vast range of other ways of collecting qualitative data varying from different forms of interview through to critical incident techniques, repertory grids, research diaries, case studies, and so on (see Cassell and Symon (2004) for a comprehensive exposition of these different methods). Regardless of the methods by which qualitative data has been collected, the analysis of qualitative data is a complex and difficult task; one which is often, in our experience, done the least satisfactorily by students undertaking qualitative management research. Even professional researchers may sometimes just present findings without an account of how they came to those findings through revealing the processes of analysis via what is called an 'audit trail'. This is also the case in some published qualitative research, often because the word limits imposed upon journal articles by editors prevent a full exposition of the process of analysis. As we shall demonstrate, there is a need for qualitative researchers to meticulously present how they have analysed data for these processes are pivotal to enabling a full justification of their findings and are an essential aid to the evaluation of those findings.

Much qualitative research, such as ethnography, may not be explicitly concerned with the collection of data so as to enable the inductive development of theory. Rather, it may often be concerned primarily with the 'thick' description of members' cultures so as to gain 'access to the conceptual world in which our subjects live so that we can, in some extended sense of the term, converse with them' (Geertz, 1973: 24). Although rigour regarding sampling both within and among settings is evident in much of such descriptive ethnography, theory largely remains implicit and underdeveloped. In this kind of qualitative research, the explanation of human behaviour is left at the description of key elements of actors' subjective cultural worlds. Whilst many qualitative researchers may not wish to go beyond such description, this level of analysis is not enough for others. For instance, Loftland (1970) accused this descriptive approach of suffering from 'analytic interruptus': where researchers fail to fully identify variations in the cultural phenomena under investigation and fail to explore how those categories of cultural phenomena relate to one another. Moreover, they are often seen to fail to take the crucial further step of developing theory that explains why any observed variation in those observed categories happens (see Denzin, 1978). Indeed, as Hartley (1994) has observed with regard to organizational case study research, without a theoretical framework the researcher is in danger of providing description without wider meaning.

However, where ethnographers, for example, adopt a more 'behaviouristic' approach (Sanday, 1979) they are overtly concerned with the development of 'grounded theory' (Glaser and Strauss, 1967; Strauss and Corbin, 1990; Goulding, 2002) so as to explain variations in phenomena observed in the field by observing it across different settings in order to identify and explain 'patterns and processes, commonalities and differences' (Miles and Huberman, 1994: 9). These differences between qualitative approaches are illustrated by Figure 7.4 below.

By building different types of description and explanation, all the qualitative research approaches illustrated in Figure 7.4 entail the use of induction in slightly different ways (see Cresswell, 1998, for an alternative model of qualitative research traditions). As we argued in Chapter 3, although the debate between rival proponents of induction and deduction is complex (see Lessnoff, 1974), the justification for induction usually revolves around two related claims which we shall revisit briefly here.

First, it is argued that in contrast to the speculative and a priori nature of deductively tested theory, explanations of social phenomena which are inductively grounded in systematic empirical research are more likely to fit the data because theory building and data collection are closely interlinked (Wiseman, 1978) and therefore are more

Figure 7.4 | Different qualitative research aims and the role of theory

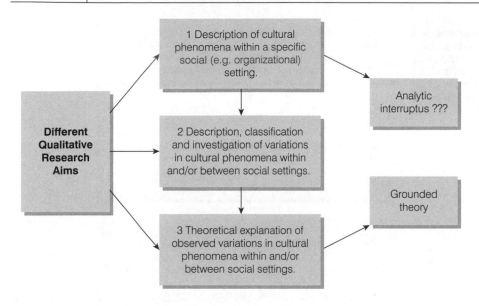

plausible and accessible (Glaser and Strauss, 1967) especially to organizational members. Hence, where the feedback of findings is provided in order to facilitate members' reflection upon events and/or promote organizational change, the inductive grounding of findings may make this process easier (see Locke, 2001). A related point is also made by Miles and Huberman (1994: 10) that qualitative research focuses upon naturally occurring events and therefore has 'a strong handle on what "real life" is like'.

Second, there is the argument that deduction's etic analyses, in which an a priori external frame of reference, created by the researcher, is imposed upon the behaviour of phenomena in order to explain them, are inappropriate where the phenomena in question have subjective capabilities (see Shotter, 1975; Giddens, 1976; Denzin and Lincoln, 2000). It follows that social science research must entail emic analyses, in which explanations of human action are generated inductively during data collection in order to develop an understanding of the interpretations deployed by the actors who are being studied. The three approaches illustrated in Figure 7.4 all share this particular commitment to *verstehen*. However, they differ in the extent to which they produce theory that explains what has been observed and organized into a descriptive account of the phenomena of interest.

Below we shall mainly concentrate on the forms of qualitative analysis primarily associated with types 2 and 3 illustrated in Figure 7.4 since the latter (3), which formally develops theory, is usually dependent upon the successful completion of the former (2) which in turn subsumes type 1. In doing so we shall combine specific key features of two closely related approaches to analysing qualitative data that result in the inductive development of theory: analytic induction and grounded theory.

Methods for inductively developing theory

As noted above, there are two approaches to inductively generating theory out of observations of the empirical world – one is called analytic induction, the other

Figure 7.5 │ Phases of inductive analysis – a combined approach

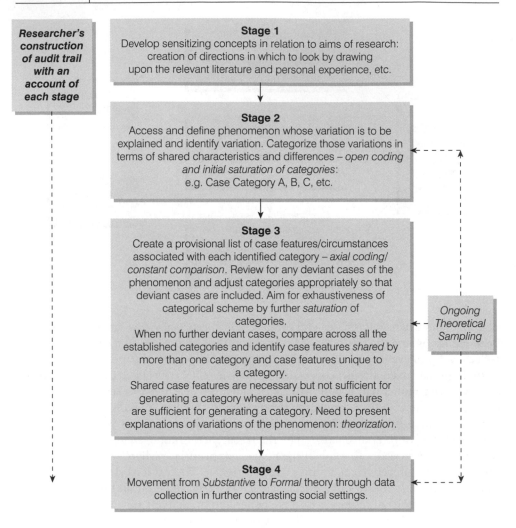

grounded theory. Both sharply contrast with deductive methodologies in which a conceptual and theoretical structure is constructed prior to observation and then is ostensibly tested through confrontation with the 'facts' of a cognitively accessible empirical world. Analytic induction is the much older approach but is rarely explicitly used today in management research despite some notable exceptions (e.g. Bansal and Roth, 2000). However, both are closely related methodologically and each can be seen as contributing to the other especially in terms of overcoming each other's deficiencies. For instance, analytic induction is very helpful in aiding the causal analysis of qualitative data in order to explain variation in phenomena whilst grounded theory is very helpful in aiding the detailed identification of variation in those phenomena in the first place – the basic building blocks of the emergent theory.

So here we are going to develop a combined approach using elements of both grounded theory and analytic induction – as illustrated and summarized by Figure 7.5.

Stage 1

Here the researcher usually begins by deploying what are called sensitizing concepts prior to data collection. Blumer (1954) developed the notion of sensitizing concepts in his discussion of what he calls 'definitive' concepts. The latter are used in quantitative research and when once developed, and operationalized into sets of indicators, become fixed benchmarks which guide data collection (see Chapter 3). In contrast Blumer advises researchers to use what he calls 'sensitizing concepts' which give 'the user a general sense of reference and guidelines in approaching empirical instances ... [and] ... merely suggest directions in which to look' (ibid.: 7). This idea is of particular importance to researchers setting out to undertake inductive analysis research. This is because it clarifies the relationship between prior conceptualization and subsequent data collection. Whilst personal experience may provide a key source of sensitizing concepts, one important source of sensitizing concepts may well be what has already been written on whatever the researcher is interested in. Hence, a literature review is important here which is initially driven by the overall aims of the researcher regarding fieldwork, but how it is done is quite different to how a researcher using a deductive approach would use the literature to formulate hypotheses and operationalize concepts prior to data collection (see Chapter 3). Instead, for Blumer, sensitizing concepts must be used in a way that merely guides the researcher initially by suggesting the variety of ways in which a phenomena may possibly empirically vary, rather than imposing previously conceptualized prescriptions of what to see and how to record through the process of operationalization used by deductive researchers. In other words, there should be no 'preconceived theory that dictates, prior to research, "relevancies" in concepts and hypotheses' (Glaser and Strauss, 1967: 215).

Stage 2

Both analytic induction and grounded theory emphasize how data analysis and data collection should occur simultaneously each recursively referring back to each other in order to establish concepts and categories which, during early stages, are in a constant state of flux as the researcher revises them as new data are collected and analysed. So using sensitizing concepts to direct initial data collection, researchers then begin to organize their observations by examining, breaking down, comparing, grouping, classifying and labelling their data according to perceived similarities and differences (see Miles and Huberman, 1994: 9). Here the process is one of identifying particular repeated events, behaviours, ideas, statements, actions, etc. observed in the field to be indicators of specific related phenomena. These related observations are grouped together so as to formulate what Glaser and Strauss call *conceptual properties* (1967: 35–6). Here what the researcher is trying to do is to initially identify patterns in the data that may form the basis of what are usually called *conceptual categories* which group together related conceptual properties and differentiate one grouping from another. Different categories refer to specific variations in the phenomena of interest identified by the observer and are adjusted as new data are collected so that the scheme of categories embraces all the researcher's observations without any exceptions. Here the relationship with what Blumer called sensitizing concepts is implicitly elaborated by Glaser and Strauss ...

Although categories can be borrowed from existing theory, provided that the data are continually studied to make certain that categories fit, generating theory does put a premium on emergent conceptualizations. There are a number of reasons for this. Merely selecting data for a category that has been established by another theory tends to hinder the generation of new categories, because the major effort is not generation, but data selection. Also, emergent categories prove to be the most relevant and best fitted to the data. Also they are emerging, their fullest possible generality and meaning are continually being developed and checked for relevance. (1967: 36–7)

Strauss and Corbin (1990: 181) call this initial stage of analysis 'open coding' where the aim is 'to discover, name and categorize phenomena; also to develop categories in terms of their properties and dimensions'. At this stage the researcher should be careful to review his/her data (e.g. field notes, interview recordings, life histories, etc.) in order to identify patterns and maintain a link between the data and the emergent concepts that form the basis of the desired categories. Here computer programmes, such as Nvivo, can be of great help in sorting the data – but only where the data is easy to transcribe. Regardless of the method used to collect the data, qualitative research will usually produce a vast amount of data which will have to be transcribed if analysis using Nvivo software is to be applied. This is time-consuming and often expensive, so an alternative is to do this analysis manually – it can be quicker depending upon the scale and complexity of the research (see Fielding, 2002). Regardless of the aids used the aim of this stage is to synthesize the data (Morse, 1994) by constructing the uniformities and differences underlying and defining emergent categories. Usually successive categorical schemes are generated through a series of re-readings and re-codings where the properties of, the connections and differences between, emergent categories were reconfigured through elaboration, consolidation or division to further generate and develop agreed observer-identified categories (Loftland, 1970). Here the researcher is also simultaneously seeking to 'theoretically saturate' the categories by continuing to collect data until 'no additional data are being found whereby the sociologist can develop properties of the category' (Glaser and Strauss, 1967: 61). This entails the use of what is called 'theoretical sampling' – an ongoing process throughout data collection whereby the researcher firstly aims to 'discover categories and their properties' (ibid.: 62), but then seeks to develop the emergent theory by identifying 'what data to collect next and where to find them, ... [a] process ... controlled by the emergent theory' (ibid.: 45).

Key methodological concept

The audit trail

It is usually regarded as good practice for the researcher to develop an audit trail which is composed of 'records stemming from the inquiry' (Lincoln and Guba, 1985: 319) which enable a future reader to follow the process of analysis and evaluate the reasoning behind the key decisions the researcher has made in developing his/her analysis. As Seale notes (1999a: 30) ' ... acceptance of the researcher's case can ... partially depend on the capacity of the researcher to expose to the reader judgements and methodological decisions made in the course of ... research ... '. This record of decisions and judgements can therefore cover all aspects of the research including choice of site(s) for the research, the development of initial sensitizing concepts, the choice of data collection methods, sampling within and between sites, the process of data analysis, theory development, etc. With regard to data analysis, such a record can help answer some important questions relevant to the evaluation of findings: How did the researcher come to these particular findings and conclusions with regard to what was observed? Why were other possible interpretations of the data discounted?

Figure 7.6 | Progressive focusing and qualitative data analysis

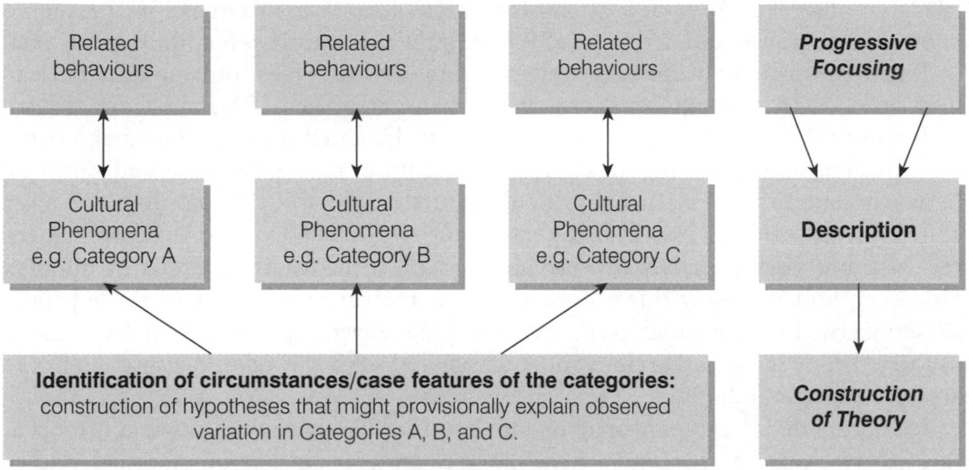

Related behaviours	Related behaviours	Related behaviours	**_Progressive Focusing_**
Cultural Phenomena e.g. Category A	Cultural Phenomena e.g. Category B	Cultural Phenomena e.g. Category C	**Description**
Identification of circumstances/case features of the categories: construction of hypotheses that might provisionally explain observed variation in Categories A, B, and C.			**_Construction of Theory_**

Stage 3

The primary aim so far has been to inductively develop an initial taxonomy, or set of categories, which describe variation in particular phenomenon, or phenomena, of interest to the researcher. Very often grounded theory might cease at this point – the findings being presented as a set of categories that describe variation in those phenomena – and hence, to a degree, provides a picture of the cultural processes that lead to different behaviours in the research setting(s) (see Figure 7.4). However, many grounded theorists may wish to further develop a theoretical model that explains the variation in the phenomena that has been observed. This process involves moving down what Hammersley and Atkinson (1995: 206) call the 'funnel structure' of 'progressive focusing' with a shift in concern from description to the development of theory regarding the now increasingly saturated categories by analysis of their 'involvement in a complex of inter-connected variables that the observer constructs as a theoretical model ... which best explains the data ... assembled' (Becker, 1970: 196) (see Figure 7.6).

Usually this stage entails continuing to develop and elaborate categories in relation to the data being assembled but simultaneously attempting to develop connections between categories by linking them to the social contexts of their occurrence in order: to provisionally identify what are often called circumstantial case features; explore their relationship to other identified categories; investigate what might be causing their occurrence through the construction of hypotheses. This also involves what Glaser and Strauss called the 'constant comparative method', where the researcher ...

> ... starts thinking in terms of the full range of types of the category, its dimensions, the conditions under which it is pronounced or minimized, its major consequences, its relation to other categories, and its other properties. (1967:106)

The question here is how does the researcher construct a theoretical model that explains variations in the categories that have been developed?

The answer to this question involves a significant move down the funnel structure of progressive focusing towards explicitly developing explanations of what has been observed. As such it attempts to provide answers to questions presented above. For Strauss and Corbin (1990: 96) the answer is what they term axial coding – this usually occurs after open coding and involves 'putting data back in new ways ... by making connections between categories'. The aim here is both to further refine the categories and, significantly, generate hypotheses about the relationships between categories and what might be causing the observed variation between categories. This usually involves further theoretical sampling and data collection in order to establish the emergent hypotheses and to develop a theoretical framework that causally explains variation in the phenomena of interest. However, how precisely this is done is rather unclear in the work of those primarily concerned with grounded theory. Where a clearer exposition may be found is in the work of those researchers more associated with the related approach noted above – analytic induction.

Both grounded theory and analytic induction enable theory development to occur through two related processes – first, the hypothesis itself may be modified, and/or second, the categories of the phenomena of interest being explained may be redefined. With either process, the range of application of the hypothesis is limited to exclude, or extended to embrace, new observations that initially defy explanation. The result should be the creation of causally homogeneous categories with no negative or deviant cases (i.e. exceptions) to the proposed hypothesis (Kidder, 1981). For Fielding and Fielding 'the result of this procedure is that statistical tests are actually unnecessary' (1986: 89). In this manner a theory is slowly developed which is applicable to a number of cases and constitutes a generalization specific to particular social contexts.

Mitchell (1983: 197), for instance, argues for the exhaustive strategic selection of new cases through the articulation of a formal model that forces the researcher to formulate and state his or her hypotheses in such a way so as to indicate crucial tests of the emergent theory and permit the explicit search for negative cases. In the language of grounded theory this entails further theoretical sampling in new social contexts. So, having developed a theory to explain observations of a particular case of the phenomenon, a researcher can decide on theoretical grounds to choose to examine new cases that will provide good contrasts and comparisons and thereby confront the theory with the patterning of social events under different circumstances.

However, here can lie dangers. For instance, in his critique of Znaniecki (1934) and Cressey (1950), Robinson (1951: 192–208) argued that in their version of analytic induction the procedures used were inadequate because their approach failed to analyse circumstances in which the phenomenon being explained did not occur. By only looking at situations in which the phenomenon already occurred, they could only identify 'the necessary, and not the sufficient conditions for the phenomenon to be explained' (ibid.). In order to identify sufficient conditions, Robinson argued that cases have to be studied where the circumstances specified by the hypothesis hold – in other words the articulation of predictions that indicate where the phenomenon should occur and hence enable subsequent analysis aimed at appraising whether or not the phenomenon always occurs in those circumstances, and if not, why not. This further round of data collection, specified by Robinson, would entail a move towards deductive testing of hypotheses in new circumstances.

It is to deal with this problem that Bloor (1976, 1978) develops a set of procedures for analytic induction that allows for the differentiation of necessary and sufficient conditions yet would simultaneously avoid deductive testing. With regard to both Lindesmith (1947) and Cressey (1950), Bloor (1978: 547) argues that the problem with both studies was that the researchers were unable to distinguish between 'the necessary and sufficient causes of addiction or embezzlement ... [since] ... they lacked control groups in which necessary but not sufficient cases could be located'. Bloor avoids this problem by developing an approach which categorizes, in terms of similarity and difference, variations in the phenomenon to be explained so that 'cases in other categories could stand as a control group for those cases in the category being analysed' (ibid.).

Bloor's approach emphasizes the need to compare across categories looking for case features (i.e. circumstances) which are shared by more than one category and for those which are unique to a particular category. Bloor judges shared case features as necessary rather than sufficient for the occurrence of a particular category of the phenomenon; whereas unique features are sufficient to generate, or cause, the category. We can develop Bloor's ideas here by arguing that:

1 *randomly* distributed circumstances/case features can be ruled out as systematic influences upon the observed variation in categories of the phenomenon of interest;
2 circumstances/case features *shared by all* categories are necessary but not sufficient for generating a category;
3 circumstance/case features *shared by two or more categories* might explain differences between those two sharing categories and other non-sharing categories;
4 circumstances/case features *unique to a category* are sufficient for generating or causing the category.

Bloor's scheme for inductively analysing qualitative data seems to follow on from Mill's (1874) original methods of inductive analysis (see Johnson and Duberley, 2000: 22). For example, Mill's 'Method of Difference' states that if an instance in which the phenomenon occurs is compared to an instance in which it does not and it is evident that each instance is the same, save for one circumstantial element that only occurs in the former instance, then that unique circumstantial element, or case feature, is part of the cause or effect of the phenomenon:

Instance	Circumstances/case features/conditions	category x:
1	@bcd	occurs
2	bcd	absent

In other words, circumstance or case feature @ is unique to the occurrence of category x, where as bcd are held in common with other occurrence of categories. Thus, we could propose the hypothesis that circumstance @ is sufficient for causing the category whereas bcd are merely necessary but not sufficient circumstances or conditions. It is on the basis of these necessary and sufficient conditions associated with each category of the phenomenon that it is possible to postulate theoretical explanations (i.e. causes) of variance in the phenomenon that in essence have already been tested through induction and observation.

Figure 7.7 | (Substantive) inductive theory – categories and behaviour

Category: Social loss of dying patients. Properties: Nurses calculating social loss on the basis of learned and apparent characteristics of the patient.	Hypotheses: The higher the social loss of a dying patient, (1) the better his/her care, and (2) the more nurses develop loss rationales to explain away patient death.

However, our confidence in these explanations could be improved by paying attention to Robinson's critiques of analytic induction noted above. This could be implemented by reversing the data collection processes outlined in Figure 7.6. This process begins by elucidating the various circumstantial case features of new potential cases of the phenomenon, in new situations, where variation in the phenomenon under investigation may occur. By analysing that data it is then possible to predict which category each new case should be in, and then collect further data in order to elucidate the accuracy of those expectations. This enables the investigation of cases where circumstantial conditions specified by the hypothesis vary and, as Hammersley points out (1989: 196–7), if the predicted categories of the phenomenon do occur, analysis may then stop.

Of course the outcome of induction may not be solely about what factors lead to the development of particular cultural dispositions as we have discussed above. It might also be concerned with explaining the occurrence of behaviours observed and associated with different cultural categories. Glaser and Strauss (1967: 42) provide a useful example of this with regard to how the nurses they observed, treated and reacted towards patients who were dying. This theoretical focus upon the effects of a category, rather than what causes the category to occur, is illustrated by Figure 7.7.

Management research example   Analytic induction to develop theory

Unfortunately there are few examples of AI in management research. A recent exception here is provided by Lennon and Wollin (2001). Here they report research in progress in four Australian organizations attempting to become learning organizations. The heart of their methodology is how multiple studies were linked through Analytic Induction. Here they use a test-adjust-theory-test iteration performed sequentially as each study is conducted. Evidence from the first study, combined with prior understanding, is used to form an expanded explanation of the phenomena. A subsequent study is then carried out and findings from it are fitted to the explanations generated by the first study. The researcher uses the discrepancies between explanation and each study's findings together with other explanations from the literature to modify the theory for better fit to all studies. Each subsequent study iteratively modifies the explanation until a robust theory is generated. Further cases are added until further cases produce little further useful explanation. At the completion of analysis the resulting theory represents the findings common to all case studies while accounting for exceptions.

Stage 4

As we have tried to illustrate inductive theory-building approaches ostensibly seek to capture aspects of the social world from the perspective of actors and allow the revision of hypotheses and conceptual structures through the analysis and elimination of negative cases. In doing so they attempt to maintain a faithfulness to empirical data gathered from a relatively small number of cases. However, as Eisenhardt (1989) argues, whilst there is a possibility that theory generated inductively is likely to be testable, novel and empirically valid it lacks the sweep of 'grand theory' and remains at a modest, idiosyncratic level. Thus, this small number of cases can be seen as a critical weakness because the method can rarely make claims about the representativeness of its samples and therefore any attempt at generalizing is tenuous.

For Mitchell (1983) such a criticism would show a confusion between the procedures appropriate to making inferences from statistical data and those appropriate to induction. He argues that analytical thinking based upon quantitative procedures is based upon both statistical and logical (i.e. causal) inference and how there is a tendency to elide the former with the latter in that 'the postulated causal connection among features in a sample may be assumed to exist in some parent population simply because the features may be inferred to co-exist in that population (Mitchell, 1983: 200). For Mitchell inductive research derives its validity from the thoroughness of its analysis achieved by eliminating exceptions and revising hypotheses. Thus, in induction extrapolation is derived from logical inference based upon the demonstrated power of the inductively generated and tested theoretical model rather than the statistical representativeness of the events in relation to some identifiable population (Mitchell, 1983: 190). In other words, inductive research enables us to specify the processes that lead to certain behaviours in particular conditions or contexts. This helps us to generalize by specifying the circumstances in which the behaviour would be expected to reoccur.

Whilst we shall return to the issue of generalization in Chapter 9 when we consider how the finding of management research may be evaluated, it is important here to differentiate between what Glaser and Strauss call substantive and formal theory. Figure 7.7 illustrates a substantive theory about particular empirical occurrences of a phenomenon in a specific organizational setting. According to Glaser and Strauss, formal theory is much more general and following their example through is illustrated by Figure 7.8.

The point is that formal theory subsumes substantive theory. Substantive theory is usually the outcome of inductive management research i.e. the findings are specific to events in a particular organization or type of organization. In order to establish formal theory out of substantive theory the management researcher may have to engage in further rounds of theoretical sampling in order to refine the theory in new organizational contexts and social settings.

Figure 7.8 | Formal inductive theory – categories and behaviour

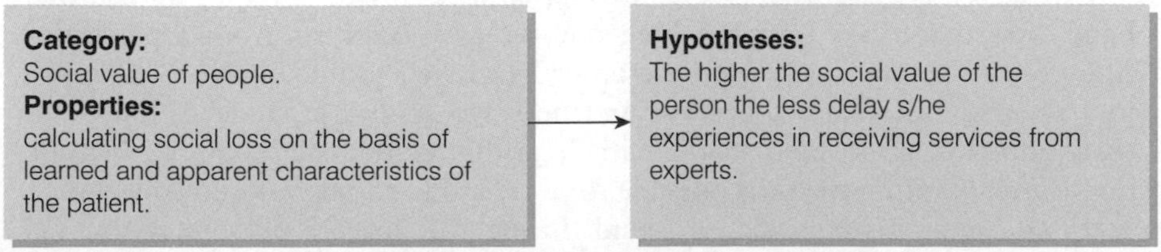

Category:	Hypotheses:
Social value of people.	The higher the social value of the person the less delay s/he experiences in receiving services from experts.
Properties:	
calculating social loss on the basis of learned and apparent characteristics of the patient.	

Conclusions

We began this chapter by outlining ethnographic approaches to management research before moving onto considering how to analyse qualitative data. So while there are a number of divergent trends in the practice of ethnography, practitioners would probably agree that extended participant observation is a central feature of most studies. As participant observers an attempt is made to learn about the culture under study and so interpret it in the way its members do. This approach is based upon the belief that the social world cannot be understood by studying artificial simulations of it in experiments or interviews, for the use of such methods only shows how people behave in those artificial experimental and interview situations. Ethnographers' commitment to naturalism thus leads them to argue that, in order to explain the actions of people working in organizations, it is necessary to arrive at an understanding of the various cultures and subcultures operating in particular organizational settings, for it is out of these systems of meanings, beliefs, values and mores that rational action arises.

Here it is important to emphasize that ethnography is just one means of collecting qualitative data but it shares the commitments we outlined with other qualitative methods of data collection – particularly *verstehen*. We then turned to analysing qualitative data. Here we presented what amounts to a composite approach which blended elements of both grounded theory and Analytical Induction (AI). Here we tried to map how qualitative data analysis entails the movement from the thick description and categorization of subjects' phenomenological worlds to propounding theoretical explanations of those categories and their impact upon members' behaviours. This entails an initial (re)presentation of subjects' internal logics grounded in *verstehen* in order to formulate categories, but to avoid analytic interruptus AI requires the researcher to shift to a form of analysis that entails his or her imposition of an external causal logic which exists independently of, and explains, the subjects' internal logics. Some qualitative researchers may be very reluctant to take such a step and therefore may limit their analyses to description of the cultural phenomena at play.

In conclusion there remains a basic question regarding the extent to which 'pure' induction is possible. For instance, Glaser and Strauss are highly normative when they argue that although any researcher will study a particular area with a particular

> … perspective, and with a focus, a general question, or a problem in mind. But the researcher can (and we believe should) also study an area without any preconceived theory that dictates prior to the research, 'relevancies' in concepts and hypotheses. (1967: 33)

This statement seems rather confusing as it seems to say that on the one hand we cannot avoid approaching our research interests from a particular (theoretical) perspective yet on the other hand we should somehow minimize its impact upon what we observe and how we analyse it. Indeed, the claim that induction is possible shares with hypothetico-deductive approaches the implicit assumption that it is possible for a researcher to access and collect data without contaminating what is found during the process of observation – a key assumption of all forms of empiricism (see Chapter 3). In philosophical terms this assumption refers to the possibility of what is called a theory-neutral observational language. When one adopts that assumption the suitably trained researcher is assumed to be a neutral conduit who can objectively elucidate and present the 'facts' of a cognitively accessible empirical world (see Johnson and Duberley, 2000). For many people, to ground any methodology in such a philosophical assumption ignores the processes by which any observer inevitably projects background preconceptions embedded in his or her own cultural background – something we cannot discard prior to undertaking research in order to be 'objective' (see for example Spinelli, 1989). For ethnographers like Hammersley (1992) and Van Maanen (1995b), such issues are especially problematic for any approach which is committed to accessing and describing how people subjectively interpret the world, through *verstehen*. It creates a contradiction between an objectivist, or empiricist, impulse that emphasizes how such accounts can and should correspond with members' subjective interpretations and a subjectivist impulse that suggests that all people interpret the world to produce socially constructed versions of reality – culturally derived processes to which researchers surely cannot be immune. These philosophical disputes, and their methodological implications, will be further explored in the next chapter and their implications for how we evaluate research will be considered in the final chapter of this book.

Further reading

There are numerous ethnographic studies of organizational life. One of the most useful accounts of ethnography which provides a description of the methods employed remains Dalton's (1959) classical work. More recent ethnographies relevant to management research include both Watson (1994) and Jackall (1988). Substantively, both provide remarkable insights into how managers make sense of their organizational lives and outline readable accounts of doing ethnography in organizations. Meanwhile Kunda's ethnography (1992) provides a superb analysis of management's attempts in a 'high tech' corporation to shape corporate culture and its effects upon employees. Simultaneously Kunda's work provides many insights into undertaking ethnographic research in organizations and the pressures the ethnographer can experience in the field.

Hammersley and Atkinson (1995) is a useful text written for the beginner and covering most aspects of ethnography from its philosophical basis to writing ethnographic accounts. It is not written with the business and management reader particularly in mind but is nevertheless an excellent introductory text to ethnography. We would recommend that where possible readers get access to the second edition. Also helpful are Fetterman (1989), a readable, practical guide to ethnography by an anthropologist, and Schein (1987) which clarifies ethnography by comparing it with the clinical perspective which is more associated with action research. For a very helpful book that focuses upon qualitative research design, and is especially helpful to researchers putting forward qualitative research proposals, the reader should turn to Maxwell (2005). For a book on the issues that inform qualitative research generally and with an important section covering issues relating to reflexivity the reader should turn to May (2002). Cassell and Symon (2004) provide a comprehensive and highly accessible account of different techniques for collecting qualitative data in organizational contexts which is useful to the ethnographer and important for anyone conducting qualitative management research. Methods covered include case studies, life histories, interviewing, participant observation, research diaries, critical incident techniques, soft systems analysis, repertory grids and intervention techniques. Different approaches to the analysis of qualitative data are also covered in detail.

Meanwhile, Hammersley (1992) critically explores the methodological rationale for ethnography and its policy and political implications. Of particular importance is Hammersley's discussion of the tensions between objectivism and relativism in ethnography and his insightful critique of the common distinction between quantitative and qualitative methods. Those interested in aspects of the historical development of certain traditions in ethnography should also read Hammersley (1989). For an important text which explores the literary and rhetorical conventions deployed by ethnographers the reader should see Atkinson (1990). For a good discussion of some of the ethical dilemmas ethnographers might encounter, see Chapter 6 of Glesne and Peshkin (1992). On the politics and ethics of fieldwork, see also Punch (1986) or Gubrium and Silverman (1989).

Locke (2000), Charmaz (2006) and especially Goulding (2002), who has a focus upon management research, are key texts for anyone considering undertaking the inductive analysis of qualitative data, whilst Bryant and Charmaz (2006) provide excellent coverage of the evolution of grounded theory, its practice and practicalities as well as its integration with approaches such as critical theory. Meanwhile, Dey (1993), Miles and Huberman (1994) and Strauss and Corbin (1998) provide detailed consideration of the processes of analysing qualitative data and cover the increasing use of computer packages. For a comprehensive guide to using the qualitative data analysis software Nvivo we recommend Bazeley and Richards (2000). For more general texts that give excellent advice upon analysing qualitative data which include the use of computer software see Richards (2005) and/or Denzin and Lincoln (2003).

These journal articles are freely available on the companion website (www.sagepub.co.uk/gillandjohnson):

Locke, K. (1996) Rewriting the discovery of grounded theory after 25 years?, *Journal of Management Inquiry*, 5(3): 239–45.

Putnam, L., Brantz, C., Deetz, S., Mumby, D. and Van Maanen, J. (1993) Ethnography versus critical theory, *Journal of Management Inquiry*, 2(3): 221–35.

Philosophical issues and developments in management research

Part III

Philosophical disputes and management research

8

Learning outcomes At the end of this chapter the reader should be able to:

● understand the different types of philosophical commitment available to the management researcher with regard to nature of human behaviour, epistemology and ontology;

● understand how these different philosophical commitments impact upon how management research is conceived and conducted;

● differentiate between mainstream positivism, qualitative positivism (sometimes called neo-empiricism); critical theory, pragmatism and postmodernism in terms of varying philosophical and methodological commitments;

● understand how shifts in philosophical stance impact upon methodologies such as ethnography and action research.

In the earlier chapters of this book we have tried to provide the aspiring researcher with an overview of several methodological approaches, or research strategies, widely used by management researchers. In undertaking a piece of research, inevitably any researcher must choose between a wide array of different approaches in making an area of interest researchable. The nature and content of the 'problem' or question to be investigated, as well as the extent of the available resources, clearly influence this choice. However, these decisions are much more complex than merely choosing a methodology that is thought to be practically viable in relation to a specific research context with its apparent constraints and opportunities. Inevitably when we try to conceptualize what it is we are trying to investigate, and most significantly here, how we are going to investigate it, we tacitly deploy philosophical assumptions that lead us to comprehend and construct these issues in particular ways.

In many respects any research method articulates, and is constituted by, philosophical commitments which are often sublimated if those methods are presented as mere tools for enabling us to collect particular types of data and to deal with particular research questions. As we have already suggested in earlier chapters, how different methodologies are variably constituted inevitably expresses the appropriation of often competing philosophical commitments. So far, our discussion of these issues has been purposefully limited to the choice between *erklaren* and *verstehen* by research-ers. However, let's take the decision to use hypothetico-deductive research meth-ods that are designed to test, and indeed try to falsify, previously formulated theory through confronting its predictions with empirical data, or facts, objectively gathered through observation of the social world. Clearly this decision draws upon an array of philosophical assumptions and commitments beyond the disputes between those who favour *erklaren* over *verstehen*. To many contemporary management researchers, these commitments are highly contestable yet so often remain uninterrogated by those using them. Indeed, the above sentence, that describes hypothetico-deductive research methodology, has embedded in it two particularly significant philosophical assumptions:

1   that it is possible to neutrally gather data without contaminating them through the very act of observation;
2   that there exists an independent social reality, out there, awaiting our inspec-tion, through the deployment of a suitable methodology;

However, whilst we cannot avoid making philosophical commitments in undertak-ing any research, any philosophical commitment can be simultaneously contested. This is because the philosophical commitments which are inevitably made in under-taking research always entail varying stances with regard to knowledge constituting assumptions about: the nature of truth; the nature of human behaviour; the pos-sibility of neutral representation of the facts; and the independent existence of the social reality we are supposed to be investigating. In other words, tacit answers to questions about *ontology* (what are we studying?) and *epistemology* (what is the basis of warranted knowledge about our chosen domains?) impact upon any methodologi-cal engagement.

The philosophical assumptions we make in dealing with these questions implic-itly present different normative definitions of management research along with particular justificatory logics which support the selection of particular methodolog-ical approaches. Moreover, as we shall explore in Chapter 9, these philosophical assumptions influence the criteria that are used to normatively evaluate the find-ings of management research. Even a cursory inspection of the management field would show that such methodological choices are common place yet, by default, also involve the decision not to engage through alternative means: alternatives that themselves articulate different philosophical commitments to varying degrees. For example, as we have already discussed in this book, philosophical assumptions about 'human nature' (that is the nature of the processes that influence human behaviour) impact upon to decision to build theory inductively out of observation of the empirical world using qualitative methods that enable *verstehen*, rather than deductively testing previously formulated theory by deploying quantitative meth-ods that enable *erklaren*.

Because methodological choices always entail taking a position upon the philo-sophical issues noted above, there is a need for any researcher to be aware of these often hidden and unnoticed aspects of management research so that they make their philosophical commitments not by default but through their conscious interrogation of the assumptions inevitably at play in undertaking any research. Such an orienta-tion to methodology supports some recent developments in management research. For instance, although initially inspired by Burrell and Morgan's work (Burrell and Morgan, 1979; Morgan, 1983, 1986, 1993) it is largely since the early 1990s that there has been much discussion of the notion that in order to understand ourselves as social science researchers we must reflexively engage with ourselves through thinking about our own beliefs and how those beliefs have repercussions for our engagements with our areas of interest. Although this 'new sensibility' (Willmott, 1998) has many implications for management research, several commentators have emphasized how it entails noticing, and being suspicious of, the relationship between the researcher and the substantive focus of his/her research. This involves reflecting upon how those often tacit, unacknowledged, pre-understandings impact upon: how those 'objects' of research are conceptually constituted by the researcher; what kinds of research question are then asked by the researcher; and how the results of research are arrived at, justified and presented to audiences for consumption (e.g. Chia, 1995; Holland, 1999; Alvesson and Deetz, 2000; Johnson and Duberley, 2003). Simultaneously, such increased vigilance might serve to broaden the philosophical repertoire available to management researchers so that alternatives to the current Positivist mainstream are also understood and not merely dismissed as bizarre, or even perverse, aberrations not worthy of serious consideration.

Thus, this chapter largely involves elucidation of the overarching structures of thought within management research so as to explore how divergent philosophical conventions inform different methodologies: the often subliminal a priori knowledge constituting assumptions which tacitly organize theoretical and methodological variation. It is thus about the choices management researchers always have to make in doing research and we hope that it will enable the reader to engage with a fuller consideration of the ever present alternatives rather than inadvertently limiting the focus of their decisions, by default, to that which is often presented as the 'normal' way of doing research in particular management disciplines.

So as Morgan (1983) has pointed out, decisions on methodological matters are largely determined by the philosophical assumptions researchers implicitly and explicitly make by adopting what he terms a 'mode of engagement' (see also Johnson and Duberley, 2000). We have deliberately used Morgan's terminology at this point since his use of this term is intended to indicate how empirical research is not simply a choice of method; rather, as he points out, research as a mode of engagement is part of a wider process ...

> ... that constitutes and renders a subject amenable to study in a distinctive way. The selection of method implies some view of the situation being studied, for any decision on how to study a phenomenon carries with it certain assumptions, or explicit answers to the question 'what is being studied?' (Morgan, 1983: 19)

It is to these wider, essentially philosophical questions and choices that we now turn. This will be facilitated by a discussion of some of the problems associated with the dominant philosophical position in management research: positivism. Here we will build upon the philosophical issues we first raised in Chapter 3 and subsequently developed in Chapter 7. In particular we will focus upon three key philosophical questions and debates – to which there are competing answers which directly impact upon our methodological choices:

1 What is the nature of human behaviour?
2 Epistemology – is it possible to neutrally observe social reality?
3 Ontology – does social reality exist independently of the cognitive processes through which we apprehend what we take to be "out-there"?

The nature of human behaviour

We argued, particularly in Chapters 3 and 7, that interpretative qualitative approaches to research, such as ethnography, arise out of a critique of positivism's tendency to reduce human action to the status of automatic responses excited by external stimuli (i.e. *erklaren*). Essentially we argued that this reduction was achieved by Positivists ignoring the subjective dimensions of human action, that is, the internal logic and interpretative processes by which action is created. Many Positivists (e.g. Neurath, 1959: 295) justify such an approach by being concerned to prevent a divorce of the social sciences from the natural sciences; attempts at such a severance being perceived as a result of the 'residues of theology' (Neurath, 1959: 295). Other Positivists, as Smart (1975) indicates, have justified their concern to follow what is assumed to be the approach of the natural sciences by expressing a desire to achieve in the social sciences the evident operational successes of the former. The result of the positivist's concern to emulate natural science methodology thus necessitates a denial of the importance of human subjective, or interpretive processes, because the physical objects that constitute the subject matter of natural science do not display such processes – their behaviours are merely responses elicited by causal stimuli. This denial of the relevance of the subjective in the explanation of human behaviour is usually supported by further methodological criteria. As Giddens points out,

> the specific unreliability of the interpretation of consciousness, indeed whether by self or by an observer, has always been the principal rationale for the rejection of verstehen by such schools. The intuitive or empathetic grasp of consciousness is regarded by them merely as a possible source of hypotheses of human conduct. (1976: 19)

On the other hand, interpretative approaches such as ethnography reject what they perceive as the Positivist's over-deterministic orientation towards an understanding of human action and behaviour. Instead they argue that, unlike animals or physical objects, human beings are able to attach meaning to the events and phenomena that surround them, and from these interpretations and perceptions select courses of meaningful action which they are able to reflect upon and monitor. It is these subjective processes that provide the sources of explanation of human action and thereby constitute the rightful focus for social science research enabled through the deployment of qualitative research methodologies such as ethnography. Thus, the aim of such interpretative approaches is to understand (*verstehen*) how people make sense of their worlds, with human action being conceived as purposive and meaningful rather than externally determined by social structures, innate drives, the environment or economic stimuli and so on.

We are therefore confronted with a philosophical choice regarding the nature of human action and its explanation which has direct methodological implications. Which set of philosophical assumptions we implicitly or explicitly adopt regarding what Burrell and Morgan (1979: 6) have termed 'human nature' influences our subsequent choice of particular 'modes of engagement' and what we see as warranted in research. If we accept the philosophical assumptions of positivism and its consequent epistemological prescriptions, we are invariably drawn towards the exclusive utilization of deductive (i.e. nomothetic) methodologies. Conversely, if our philosophical orientation is interpretative the ensuing epistemological mandate impels us towards a more inductive (i.e. ideographic) methodology such as ethnography as it enables *verstehen* (see Burrell and Morgan, 1979: 1–37).

However, lurking here there are other important philosophical commitments which seem to moderate the apparent differences between the deductive and inductive methodologies we have considered so far in this book. For instance, most of the methodological approaches we have considered so far share the assumption that it is possible for researchers to neutrally research, through the observation and collection of data, without contaminating that data through the very process of researching. Thus, the dispute between many positivists who limit themselves to undertaking deductive research and many qualitative researchers, referred to above, is largely about whether or not human subjective processes are observable in a neutral, objective, fashion. Clearly many ethnographers think that it is possible to do this whereas the former reject ethnography and its basis in *verstehen* as being too subjective (see the quote from Giddens above) and hence not proper science. But ironically one can discern in this dispute a shared epistemological and ontological commitment expressed in terms of assumptions about being able to neutrally observe the world out there provided that the correct methodology is used by the researcher. It is this very commitment to objectivity that has been recently challenged by many management researchers: particularly those working in what we have broadly defined as qualitative management research and who have thereby added to the heterogeneity of management research (see Johnson et al., 2006). We shall now turn to this particular set of philosophical disputes, which have been articulated by a range of important alternatives to positivism, including postmodernism and critical theory.

Epistemology

The philosophical term epistemology ...

> *derives from two Greek words: 'episteme' which means 'knowledge' or 'science'; and 'logos' which means 'knowledge', 'information', 'theory' or 'account'. ... epistemology is usually understood as being concerned with knowledge about knowledge. In other words, epistemology is the study of the criteria by which we can know what does and does not constitute warranted, or scientific, knowledge. (Johnson and Duberley, 2000: 3)*

Epistemology is a pivotal issue in any form of research for it is about *how we know* whether or not any claim, including our own, made about the phenomena we are interested in, is warranted. That is, what do we mean by the concept 'truth' and how do we know whether or not some claim is true or false? In other words, what is our theory of truth? These are major epistemological issues and we can only introduce the reader to some of these debates and thereafter direct those interested to further reading.

Very often people think that such processes of justifying knowledge claims are in principle straightforward: in judging the truth or falsity of any such claim surely 'the facts speak for themselves'? All we need to do is look for the relevant evidence whose content will either support or refute any claim. Thus, it is often thought that what is true is something that corresponds with the given facts: the empirical evidence that we have collected by undertaking some form of empirical research. Whilst such a view of truth arose out of various attacks upon what was construed as religious dogma (see Johnson and Duberley, 2000: 12–13), today these views of warranted knowledge, at first sight seem apparently harmless and uncontentious. However, recently they have been subject to much dispute in both the natural and social sciences: a dispute which is now of direct concern to management researchers, and has had a direct influence on the evolution of an increasing philosophical diversity in management research wherein the positivist mainstream has come under considerable further attack.

Key methodological concept

Positivist epistemology

According to many commentators (for example, Keat and Urry, 1975; Giddens, 1979) two of the most significant characteristics of positivist epistemology contain the claims that warranted science is concerned with:

1 only directly observable phenomena, with any reference to the intangible or subjective being excluded as being meaningless; and
2 the testing of theories, in a hypothetico-deductive fashion, by their confrontation with the facts neutrally gathered from a readily observable external world.

However, as we imply above, even those who reject key aspects of positivist epistemology around the use of hypothetico-deductive methodology, and the exclusion of the subjective as meaningless, will sometimes retain a commitment to being able to inductively investigate human intersubjective cultural processes by gathering the facts from a readily observable external world. In a sense the result is a kind of 'qualitative positivism' (see Knights, 1992; Van Maanen, 1995b; Schwandt, 1996; Prasad and Prasad, 2002), which although different from mainstream Positivism shares its commitment to what is called a theory-neutral observational language (see Figure 9.1).

Stop and Think Exercise 8.1   How and to what extent do the qualitative methodologies illustrated in Chapter 7 involve a break with positivist philosophical commitments?

This attack has largely been driven by the view that it is not possible to neutrally apprehend the facts 'out there', regardless of the methodology used, in order to test the veracity of knowledge claims. Thus, the positivist philosophical commitment, that it is possible to objectively, or neutrally, observe the social world and thereby gather 'positively given' data in order to test theoretical predictions, has been considerably undermined by those who think that in observing the world we inevitably influence what we see. Indeed, as Willmott (1998) explains, there has been some erosion of the positivist consensus by scholars who have dismissed the possibility of what is called a neutral observational language and who argue that notions of truth and objectivity are merely the outcomes of prestigious discursive practices which mask rather than eliminate the researcher's partiality. For Willmott a key implication of this 'new sensibility' is the potential demise of managerialism. This is because any claim that management is founded upon a technical imperative to improve efficiency, justified and enabled by objective analyses of how things really are, epistemologically crumbles and along with it some elements of managerial authority. The latter become highly problematic because the idea that managers may govern because they have superior knowledge and expertise is simultaneously undermined. Below we shall trace in much more detail how this attack upon positivist epistemology has developed and where the alternative philosophical stance leads us in terms of management research.

Positivist epistemology limits its conception of valid or warranted knowledge (i.e. science) to what is taken to be unproblematically observable 'sense-data'. If a theory corresponds with a researcher's observations of these facts its truthfulness is taken to be established. If it fails to correspond, it is discarded as mistaken or false. Thus, the theory of truth that is proposed, implicitly and explicitly, is a correspondence theory of truth. Such a view of truth is made viable only through the prior assumption that it is possible to observe the facts of the external world neutrally and objectively by the application of rigorous methodological procedures and protocols aimed at testing the theory. This latter assumption is often called the assumption of a theory-neutral observational language. As Hindess (1977: 18) points out,

> it makes possible a very precise conception of the testing of theory against observation. The testing of theory against irreducible statements of observation is equivalent to a direct comparison between theory and the real world. If they fail to correspond then the theory is false and therefore may be rejected.

In this way doxa (what we believe to be true) becomes transformed into episteme (that which we know to be true), hence epistemology. At first sight, particularly from a standpoint imbued with Western cultural norms, this positivistic epistemology appears as eminently rational – indeed commonsensical. However, there seem to be major problems with this view of scientific endeavour:

1 it seems self-contradictory;
2 the possibility of directly and objectively observing phenomena, and thereby accumulating the 'facts' of the world so as to test the truthfulness of a theory, seems dubious.

We shall now proceed to discuss each of these problems in turn.

1 Positivist epistemological self-contradiction   In order to observe directly, and objectively, the phenomena in which they are interested, positivists must assume what is called a dualism between 'subject' and 'object'; that it is possible to separate the 'subject' (the knower, the observer, the researcher) from the 'object' (the known, the observed, what are taken to be the 'facts' of the world) by the application of scientific methodology. Therefore, by using rigorous methodology it is possible to have knowledge that is independent of the observer and uncontaminated by the very act of observation. As we noted previously, this idea is central to positivism. Indeed, it is embedded in the term 'positivism': for as Comte (1853) originally proposed, science could only progress by ridding itself of (e.g. religious) dogma through the examination of the 'positively given': those empirical data or objective facts which were cognitively accessible through sensory perception. Thus, explanations of the world which relied upon the claim that they were caused by God's will, or by the actions of supernatural beings such as demons etc., were dismissed from the realm of scientific explanation. This limitation of the scientific to phenomena that were empirically observable was the culmination of the social and philosophical upheaval called the Enlightenment (see Johnson and Duberley, 2000: 12–19).

In order to be pursue their research agenda, positivists have to assume the possibility of generating and/or testing theory by direct comparison to the real through

Figure 8.1 | Positivist dualism

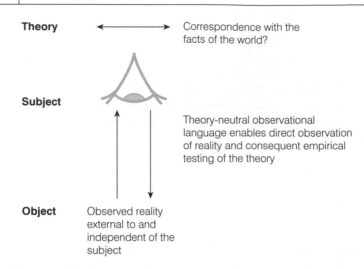

the deployment of a theory-neutral observational language. Thus, it is only through the prior assumption that a dualism between subject and object is possible, and consequently that a theory-neutral observational language is available, that the correspondence criteria of the positivist (i.e. his or her epistemology) becomes viable. This is illustrated by Figure 8.1.

According to both Hindess (1977) and Gorman (1977), however, the contention above about the nature of subject/object relations (i.e. a dualism) demonstrates the contradictory nature of positivism. As we have tried to show, many (but not all) positivists exclude from what is taken to be warranted knowledge, the metaphysical – that is to say the intangible, the subjective or abstract. These domains are ruled out because it is thought we cannot empirically observe them. Indeed, operationalization processes, so central to positivist methodology and discussed in Chapter 3, are about making the abstract observable in a valid and reliable manner. Whilst there are disputes about kinds of information, etc. this commitment excludes from scientific processes the problem of self-contradiction lies at the heart of this stance. This is because by rejecting the metaphysical it rejects as meaningless our knowledge of subject/object relationships (i.e. our own relationship as researchers to the phenomena we are trying to observe as illustrated in Figure 9.1) upon which any epistemology, including positivism's own, is ultimately grounded. There is therefore a potential contradiction since positivism seems to exclude from its conceptualization of warranted knowledge its own philosophical grounds for warranted knowledge (see Hindess, 1977: 135). Thus, it would appear that since positivism cannot account for itself on its own terms, it becomes indefensible in its own terms, and is thereby lapses into epistemological incoherence. Obviously such a contradiction applies less to what we have termed 'qualitative positivists' since they do not exclude human subjective processes from what they take to be a legitimate area for scientific inquiry. However, most of the contemporary attacks upon positivism tend to focus more upon our second problematic issue.

2 Is positivism's theory-neutral observational language possible? As we have shown, positivism, with its articulation of a subject-object dualism, assumes that there

Figure 8.2 | Science as a neutral endeavour

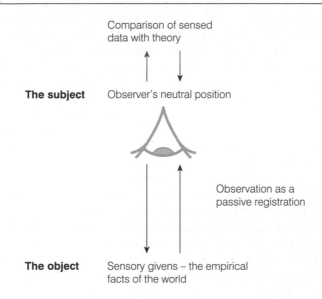

is some neutral point from which the observer can stand back and observe the world objectively. That is, the observations that are registered are independent of the very process of the observer observing and thus 'truth' is to be found in the observer's passive registration of the 'sensory givens' (Mattick, 1986), or facts, that constitute reality. This philosophical commitment to objectivity and neutrality is illustrated by Figure 8.2.

As we have already suggested, and following Van Maanen (1995b), it is important to note here that some interpretive management researchers share this commitment to a theory-neutral observational language – save that this would be construed as a subject-subject dualism where the observer can stand back and neutrally apprehend what other knowers subjectively know. For instance, here it would be assumed that it is possible for organizational ethnographers to neutrally describe members' cultural attributes and how these subjective elements impel particular modes of organizational behaviour (see also Hammersley, 1992; Knights, 1992; Alvesson and Skoldberg, 2000; Prasad and Prasad, 2002).

Figure 8.2 illustrates the empiricist maxim that science should be, and can be, a neutral, value-free and disinterested endeavour. So as Rorty (1979: 46) argues, a correspondence theory of truth relies upon the received wisdom that the veracity of competing theories may be adjudicated through an appeal to their correspondence with the facts of an external objective reality that is 'mirrored' in the 'Glassy Essence' of the observer.

This is often labelled as an *objectivist epistemology* as it presupposes the possibility of a theory-neutral observational language where our sensory experience of the 'given' 'facts' of reality provides the only secure foundation for social scientific knowledge (e.g. Ayer, 1971). Located in this dualism, observers can 'picture' (Wittgenstein, 1922) the external world objectively and thereby deductively test, or inductively generate, theory in an objective fashion. Thus truth, as correspondence, is to be found through the observer's passive registration of the facts that constitute reality. Here we have indicated that two approaches to management research are evident – positivism and qualitative positivism: the latter is more commonly called neo-empiricism (see Alvesson and Deetz, 2000). Both share the empiricist commitment that our sensory experience provides the only secure foundation for management research. As we have argued, where they part company is over what they understand to be observable as opposed to metaphysical (see Lessnoff, 1974). Unlike the positivists, neo-empiricists argue that in order to understand human behaviour in organizations we must access their cultures through *verstehen* and the deployment of qualitative methods of data collection. So as to legitimate this interpretive methodological imperative, neo-empiricism questions the methodological unity of the sciences, grounded in *erklaren*, as proposed by positivists. Positivists have reciprocated by denying both the possibility and desirability of *verstehen* thereby restoring the methodological unity of natural and social sciences (e.g. Abel, 1958).

Because each of the dualisms noted above rest on a putative epistemic objectivity, which privileges the consciousness of the management researcher as capable of discovering the 'truth' about the world in a correspondence sense, regardless of the methodology used there is a constant concern with maintaining the objectivity of the researcher by ensuring the 'right' methodological moves: a critique and evaluation of the 'technical' aspects of the particular methodology deployed, rather than the underlying philosophical assumptions that justify that methodology in the first place, in order to nurture and sustain objective inquiry.

However, in assuming the possibility for an observer to register passively the facts of reality, this epistemological position ignores the possibility that the observer's perceptual apparatus does not provide mere reflections of what is out there, but is proactive and creative in influencing what we apprehend. As Habermas (1974b: 199), a famous Critical Theorist, contends,

> even the simplest perception is not only performed pre-categorically by physiological apparatus – it is just as determined by previous experience through what has been handed down and through what has been learned as by what is anticipated through the horizons of expectations.

Factors that might influence observation

It is now important to turn to considering how various factors might influence observation/sensory experience and thereby consider their implications for the possibility of a theory-neutral observational language. Once one rejects the possibility of a neutral observational language there occurs a move towards a much more *subjectivist epistemological* stance. Such a stance assumes that what we perceive is, at least in part, an outcome of how we engage with the world and the conceptual baggage that we bring to bear in order to make sense of what we experience. The origins of this baggage are usually assumed to be social in origin hence are encapsulated in the idea that we *socially construct* either versions of reality or indeed reality itself (see Burr, 1995). Thus, in order to explain this subjectivist stance we shall review the processes of perception and how many scholars argue that far from being theory-neutral, observation is inevitably 'theory-laden' and thereby pursue what amounts to a devastating critique of the objectivist epistemology shared by positivists and neo-empiricists and the assumption that observation can be a neutral, objective and unbiased endeavour.

The process of perception   As we have illustrated, for both positivists and neo-empiricists (i.e qualitative positivists), warranted knowledge about the world

Figure 8.3

emanates from social reality, that is an external world directly and objectively accessible through human sensory experience provided that the correct methodology is used to, in effect, polish Rorty's 'mirror in the mind': a possibility that Rorty disputes (1979). As such, warranted knowledge is that which has a correspondence with the world that has been established through our neutral and passive registration of various sensory inputs.

Stop and Think Exercise 8.2   What do you see?

Often the same event or identical set of sensations is perceived and experienced by people in different ways.

For instance, consider the two objects in Figures 8.3 and 8.4. How many women do you see in Figure 8.3? Do you see the object in Figure 8.4 in three dimensions? If so, how many cubes do you see? Can you also see it as one dimensional and composed of squares, triangles and parallelograms, etc.? People outside Western cultures may perceive this figure in only one dimension.

If the sensory process of perceiving even relatively simple objects was indeed merely a matter of the passive reception and registration of their evident characteristics, how is it that the same object can be apprehended so differently by people? This must surely imply that we are not passive receivers of external stimuli and data but rather that we apply various inferences and assumptions which mediate what we 'see'. Perhaps there is more to seeing than meets the eye-ball?

What are the implications of this for the claim that we can possess a neutral observation language as put forward by positivists and neo-empiricists?

It would seem from Exercise 8.2 that our interpretation of the relatively simple figures illustrated can vary considerably. This has led people to argue that whilst we

Figure 8.4 |

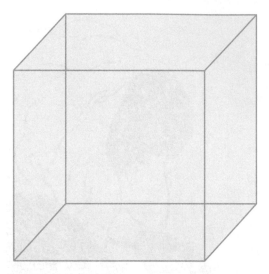

are continually bombarded by sensations and stimuli, we project on to those inputs a form and substance that derives from within, from our own 'cognitive processing mechanisms' (Unwin, 1986: 300). Such projection entails selection, as we choose what we sense by giving attention to particular stimuli while de-emphasizing, filtering out or ignoring others. The selected sensory stimulations are simultaneously organized and interpreted by being put into a coherent and meaningful whole. This organization, interpretation and consequent imposition of order may be highly influenced by the schemas built up from our previous experience, or received as stocks of knowledge, or *discourses*, through our social interaction in various cultural milieu. We usually do these things rapidly and automatically and often unconsciously. Although the result may appear objective and separate from ourselves – as 'out there' – in many respects perhaps we are actively creating, or at least influencing through interpretation, what we apprehend. So far from being a process that involves the *passive* registration of sensory 'givens' emanating from a reality separate from us, 'perception allows us to impose a logic and order on the chaos of the thousands of sensations that bombard our senses … perception allows us to make sense out of all these sensations' (Spinelli, 1989: 38). In other words, it would seem that we are active participants in the process of perception as we experience an interpreted world and not one that is directly accessible through passive sensory capacities imprinting on our minds mere reflections of what is 'out there'. So what we perceive as being external to and separate from us is just as much an expression of our subjective processes as what is actually going on 'out there'.

The theory-laden nature of observation   The ways in which we make sense of the various sensations that bombard our senses also direct attention to the issue that has usually been termed the 'theory-laden' nature of observation. This term refers to the way in which prior theories influence what we take to be factual, given, observations. Hanson (1958) contends that, rather than a theory and the data accumulated to test that theory being separate elements, they are actually intimately linked.

To illustrate this point, Hanson asks the reader to imagine two famous sixteenth century astronomers, Tycho Brahe and Johannes Kepler observing the sun at dawn. He poses the question; what do they see? According to Hanson (ibid.: 23–24) Brahe, because he adheres to the (then) Catholic Church's officially sanctioned, geocentric Aristotlean cosmology, or theory of the universe, sees this apparently simple everyday event, quite differently from Kepler who adheres to Copernicus's alternative, and at the time heretical, cosmology. Brahe has previously imprinted on his mind the Church's Aristotlean theory that tells him that a static Earth is at the centre of the universe, around which all the planets and the stars, including the Sun, orbit. In contrast Kepler adheres the heliocentric theory that proposes that the planets, including the spinning Earth, orbit the Sun. The operation of rival theses theories lead Brahe and Kepler to interpret the same mundane event (dawn) in very different ways. According to Hanson (ibid.: 23–24) Brahe would 'see the sun beginning its journey from horizon to horizon. He sees that from some celestial vantage point the sun ... could be watched circling our fixed earth'. However, Kepler, due to his heliocentric theory, 'will see the horizon dipping, or turning, away from our local fixed star. The shift from sunrise to horizon ... turn is occasioned by *differences between what Tycho and Kepler think they know*' (our emphasis).

In other words, Hanson claims that observation is theory-laden in that our theories influence what we see, and hence there is no actual separation between theory, interpretation and data. If Hanson is correct, then there are devastating implications for positivism's epistemological claim to theory-neutrality in observation.

Implications

Our brief discussion of the various processes involved in perception and the theory-laden nature of observation casts doubt upon the possibility of there being a theory-neutral observational language that would enable theory to be tested directly against empirical reality. Thus, the assumption of a subject–object dualism, so necessary for epistemology based on a correspondence theory of truth, appears implausible. Advocates of such correspondence criteria fail to acknowledge what is known as the 'hermeneutic circle', that no 'pure' description of data free from interpretation based upon presuppositions is possible. As Spinelli (1989: 58) comments, 'the assumed separation between the data being analysed and the person who analyses them ... becomes questionable'. It seems that the possession of a theory-neutral observational language is impossible. Further, it implies that what we take to be warranted knowledge is not objective and independent but is imbued with the partiality and theoretical dispositions of the observer, through the action of our 'cognitive processing mechanisms' (Unwin, 1986: 300).

Thus, for a long time, many scholars have argued that any observer, explicitly or implicitly, projects a priori beliefs and sentiments upon sense-data and thereby moulds them through this imposition of common sense or theoretical (Hanson, 1958; Quine, 1960; Habermas, 1974a) or paradigmatic (Kuhn, 1970) or unconscious (Hunt, 1979) assumptions and background expectancies (Giddens, 1976). It may of course also be moulded by cognitive schemes to which researchers may be emotionally committed (Mitroff, 1974) and whose nature is highly influenced by social factors (D. Bloor, 1976; Barnes, 1974, 1977; Law and Lodge, 1984). Indeed, as Gadamer (1975) in his critique of Dilthey argues, the notion of a neutral, detached observer is a myth. Interpretations cannot escape background preconceptions embedded in the language and life of their authors. In other words, social intersubjective processes, to which we have been exposed, are at the heart of how we make sense of what we think is 'out there'.

The result is a subjectivist epistemological stance which implies that:

1 scientific claims cannot be seen as true descriptions, in a correspondence sense, of some external reality but are socially constructed creations of the scientist;
2 the acceptability of a scientific claim is not the outcome of the application of some universally valid evaluation criteria (see Chapter 9), rather, the product of the value-laden subjectivity of an individual scientist or a community of scientists;
3 the truth or falsity of statements is 'underdetermined' by empirical data in that observation cannot provide objective control over scientific claims.

So from the above philosophical stance, the notion of interpretation is not just applied to the meaningful behaviour of the organizational members we happen to be investigating; it equally must apply to the researcher him/herself. Hence, as we indicated earlier, while some ethnographers clearly attack positivism on the grounds that human action is interpretive and therefore, cannot be investigated using methods that derive from the investigation of non-sentient physical phenomena, simultaneously they may often tacitly share positivism's commitment to an epistemology that preserves a neutral observational language in the form of a subject–subject dualism (see Marcus, 1994). Obviously a key debate in social science generally, and increasingly in the management disciplines, is how the rejection of positivist notions of neutrality then impact upon our research and the methods we use.

So it follows that the processes described in the previous sections are not merely interesting curiosities that we should try to sublimate or ignore in considering the status of our research findings. Rather, their implications demand that we should attempt to develop epistemologies capable of coping with their burgeoning critique and which by implication have devastating consequences for how we undertake management research. It is precisely this issue which Willmott (1998) is referring to in his call for an increasing sensitivity in management research.

It is now therefore imperative to consider some of the methodological implications of this alternative epistemological stance, albeit briefly. However, before doing so we need to attend to one further area of philosophical controversy that has plagued management research. This is to do with what is called ontology.

Ontology – status of social reality

As we have tried to show, once we reject the possibility of neutral observation, we have to admit to dealing with a socially constructed reality. But this philosophical shift can, but not necessarily, entail a questioning of whether or not what we take to be reality actually exists 'out there' at all? This leads us to the philosophical issue that revolves around our ontological assumptions.

Like the term epistemology, the term ontology also is a combination of two Greek works – but in this case they are ontos and logos. The former refers to 'being' whilst the latter refers to theory or knowledge, etc. Ontology is a branch of philosophy dealing with the essence of phenomena and the nature of their existence. Hence, to ask about the ontological existence of something is often to ask whether or not it is real or illusory. Here ontological questions raise questions regarding whether or not some phenomenon that we are interested in actually exists independently of our knowing and perceiving it – or is what we see and usually take to be real, instead, an outcome, or creation, of these acts of knowing and perceiving? So we are primarily concerned with what is called the ontological status of social reality and the phenomena we take to constitute aspects of that reality. Importantly it is useful to differentiate between realist and subjectivist assumptions about the status of social reality.

- *Realist assumptions* about the ontological status of the phenomena we assume to constitute social reality entails the view that they exist, 'out there', independently of our perceptual or cognitive structures. We might not already know its characteristics, indeed it may be impossible for us to ever know those characteristics in a correspondence sense, but this reality exists, it is real, and it is there potentially awaiting inspection and discovery by us.
- *Subjectivist assumptions* about the ontological status of the social phenomena we deal with which, philosophically, entail the view that what we take to be social reality is a creation, or projection, of our consciousness and cognition. What we usually assume to be 'out there', has no real, independent, status separate from the act of knowing. In perceiving, or knowing, the social world we create it – we just probably are not usually aware of our role in these creative processes.

By combining the above ontological assumptions with the competing assumptions regarding epistemology we have already discussed, we can see three different philosophical positions which impact upon management research. These are illustrated in Figure 8.5. These philosophical assumptions about ontology and epistemology are always contentious and debatable, because that is all they are – assumptions. Indeed, we cannot operate without adopting some epistemological and ontological position: but we should be aware of them, be prepared to defend them, and consider their implications. The trouble may be that we don't always subject our particular philosophical choices to critical inspection and often make them by default. Major differences over these issues pervade areas like management research and in part account for the diversity illustrated by Figure 8.5.

Figure 8.5 | Epistemological and ontological assumptions: the constitution of different approaches to management research

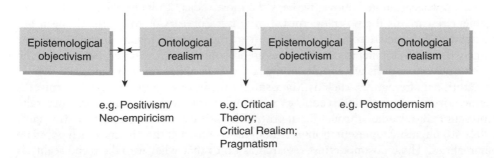

Methodological implications: alternatives to positivism and neo-empiricism

One response to the philosophical issues raised here appears to involve their suppression in undertaking research through the maintenance of what many management researchers would now consider to be a naive and unreflective empiricism that makes various research methods used appear as philosophically expurgated techniques and protocols. Obviously, this is a strategy with which we have little sympathy. We would particularly concur with Giddens's (1984: xviii) warning that 'the social sciences are lost if they are not directly related to philosophical problems by those who practise them'.

However, such attacks upon correspondence theory can have far more radical implications. Indeed, as Sayer (1981: 6) observed over 20 years ago, the 'shattering of innocence' that has arisen through the radical undermining of positivism by the rejection of the doctrine of the theory neutrality of observation has often produced much more critical approaches to management research. Whilst these approaches vary considerably, but are often given the umbrella label Critical Management Studies (see Forester et al., 2000; Fournier and Grey, 2000), they share Willmott's (1998) 'new sensibility' in part due to the subjectivist epistemological stance they articulate. Below we shall trace the development of some of these alternatives before moving on to how particular methodologies have been reconfigured in response to the shift in philosophical assumptions that drives these alternatives.

For instance, the positivist basis of a variety of management disciplines has increasingly been subject to various critiques – for example, accountancy (Tinker, 1985; Lehman, 1992; Johnson, 1995); corporate strategy (Knights and Morgan, 1991; Barry and Elmes, 1997; Darwin et al., 2002); human resource management (Townley, 1994; DuGay, 1996); and organization theory (Reed and Hughes, 1992; Hassard and Parker, 1993; Burrell, 1997; Hancock and Tyler, 2001; McAuley et al. 2007). Although substantively varied, epistemologically these critiques tend to share a desire to demystify those disciplines through a rebuttal of what is seen as the positivist, tendency to present those disciplines as objective, value-free and technical enterprises; to point to how such a perspective is grounded in an epistemological objectivism expressed in terms of the unreflexive application of a theory-neutral observational language; to reject the objectivist view that the essentials of the world are to be discovered through the exercise of managers' privileged reason (i.e. rationality); and to replace it with a social constructivist view of management knowledge which exposes and disrupts the partial taken-for-granted assumptions that underpin ostensibly neutral management practices.

Postmodernism

Of the approaches noted above, perhaps the most radical in its implications for management research is the postmodernist. In the last 20 years or so postmodernism has emerged and attracted considerable interest in most of the management disciplines. Largely these developments can be seen as an outcome of a growing disillusion with the positivistic assumptions which still dominate those disciplines and the apparent demise of traditional alternatives, such as Marxism. As we have suggested, postmodernism is characterized by a profound scepticism regarding the idea that language can neutrally represent reality. Rather, through what postmodernists call the 'linguistic turn' (Lyotard, 1984: 40) linguistic representations are thought to construct the objects which populate our realities. Thus, postmodernist research assumes that what we take to be reality is itself created and determined by our acts of cognition. Here the social world isn't there waiting for us to discover it, rather that act of knowing creates what we find. Whilst this philosophical stance also argues against the possibility of an objective empirical science of management, it is also a relativistic stance. For the postmodernist, efforts to develop theories that reveal causal relationships through accumulating objective empirical data are a forlorn hope. This is not just because knowledge is contaminated by the discourse of the social scientist, rather their theoretical stance, their norms, beliefs and values, etc. encoded into their academic disciplines act to constitute, or create, what we take to be social reality. The result is that what we take to be reality becomes a self-referential and arbitrary output of linguistic or discursive practices – which are potentially always open to revision. For Baudrillard (1983, 1993) such hyper-realities have no independent ontological status as they are divorced from extra-linguistic reference points, in which there is nothing to see save simulations which appear to be real. The result is 'you can never really go back to the source, you can never interrogate an event, a character, a discourse about its degree of original reality' (1993: 146).

Here the concept of discourse is pivotal. Discourses are subjective, linguistically formed, ways of experiencing and acting and constituting phenomena which we take to be 'out there'. As such they are expressed in all that can be thought, written or said about a particular phenomena which through creating the phenomena influence our behaviour. Therefore a discourse, for the postmodernist, stabilizes our subjectivity into a particular gaze by which we come to normally construe ourselves, others, and what we take to be social reality. A dominant discourse, which is taken for granted by people and hence is not challenged, thereby limits our knowledge and practices by dictating what is legitimate. Inevitably a dominant discourse excludes alternative ways of knowing and behaving – alternative discourses and their associated practices are always possible, they are just being suppressed. So here, social reality (which post-modernists often call hyper-reality) becomes a self-referential and arbitrary output of the researcher's, and other actors', discursive practices. However, there is a tendency to externalize, objectify and then forget built into how we are the source of what we assume to be 'out there'. The result is that discursively produced hyper-realities are mistaken for an independent external reality: a 'false concreteness' is accorded to these subjective linguistic outcomes which appear as being natural and out-there independent of us. Hence, the epistemological fulcrum provided by a commitment to reality as an independently existing reference point is erased since 'the world is not already there, waiting for us to reflect it' (Cooper and Burrell, 1988: 100). For Chia (1995, 1996) it follows that knowledge or truth has no secure vantage point outside, and is always relative to, socio-linguistic, or discursive, processes.

From this philosophical stance, the interrelated methodological tasks of the post-modernist are:

1 to describe these discursive forms often through a distinctive form of discourse analysis (e.g. Ball and Wilson, 2000);
2 to explore how they have developed and impact upon people, through gene-alogy and by examining discursive truth effects (e.g. Knights and Morgan, 1991);
3 to examining how discourses adapt and change by, for instance, deploying narrative theory (e.g. Barry and Elmes, 1997);
4 to destabilize dominant discourses so that alternative discourses, which are always possible, might then develop through the use of deconstruction (e.g. Calas and Smircich, 1991; Kilduff, 1993; Linstead, 1993b) or through a distinctive form of action research (e.g. Barry, 1997; Treleaven, 2001).

Key methodological concept

Postmodern action research (Treleaven, 2001)

An example of postmodern action research is provided by Treleaven's account of a 'collaborative inquiry' that deconstructed the gender narratives at play in an Australian university. By integrating 'the turn to action with the linguistic turn' (ibid.: 261) Treleaven used a collaborative inquiry group to facilitate 11 female co-participants' deconstruction of critical incidents within their organizational experiences. This involved these co-participants reflecting upon the patterns of meanings they deployed in making sense of their various organizational experiences and reconstructing those meanings through the use of discourse analysis to foreground and inspect the taken-for-granted factors that shaped these processes of sense making. This served to unsettle the dominant discourses which were usually at play in their sense making and enabled the surfacing of alternatives which allowed for the production of new subjective interpretations of their experiences and the construction of alternative subjective identities for the participants themselves. This reinterpretation of experience opened up the possibility of change within and beyond their university workplace. For Treleaven, the various discourses surfaced and at play, offered the formation of new subjectivities based upon the liberation of multiple new understandings of their social experience by participants. However, these discourses were often contradictory and hence could provide sites for both ambivalence and resistance. So an outcome of this postmodernist deconstructive intervention through action research was not just to destabilize the hegemonic patriarchal discourse of gender but to 'highlight unsettling actions and points of contradiction as strategic opportunities for change in the workplace' (ibid., 266). Thus, through Treleaven's postmodern form of action research, participants became empowered to manipulate signifiers to create new discursive means of apprehension of themselves and their workplace thereby engendering discursive diversity rather than the discursive closure that the operation of dominant discourses can create.

However, while postmodernism poses an important challenge to positivist orthodoxy, it also has its own contradictions located in its apparent sanctioning of relativism.

First, relativism is riddled with fundamental contradictions. As Mannheim (1952: 130) has observed, 'the assertion of relativity itself claims absolute validity and hence its very form presupposes a principle which its manifest content rejects'. In other words, the emergent relativism of postmodernist views of management is incoherent in that it is unable to cope with its own critique of itself and thereby cannot justify its approach on its own grounds. If we take Townley's Foucauldian analysis (1994) as an example, she portrays human resources management as involving the social constitution of knowledge and order – a process of representation in which organizational worlds are rendered known, visible and potentially manageable (ibid., 144). Power is made invisible by the presentation of information as objective facts ostensibly independent of the interests of those who produce it (ibid., 145). But if we accept this postmodernist claim that all knowledge is the outcome of such partial and arbitrary linguistic processes, what therefore is the epistemological status of Townley's, and other postmodernists', own accounts? Is there a danger that they construct discourses about discourses that inadvertently assert an implicit claim to privilege for their own accounts through some epistemological backdoor?

Alternatively, if the above contradiction is avoided, postmodernism must adopt a relativistic argument that concludes that since all knowledge is discursively produced, there are no good reasons for any discursive closure: that is preferring one discursive representation over another – including their own. Indeed, it would seem that pivotal for many postmodernists is the preference-less toleration and promotion of the polyphonic (many voices) since any discursive closure must mean the arbitrary dominance of a particular discourse which merely serves to silence alternative voices and hence must be disrupted (see Gergen, 1992; Rosenau, 1992; Chia, 1995; Barry, 1997).

So despite the optimistic assertions of Bauman (1995) that relativism can provide a liberating potential it is also evident that it undermines the basis of critique. Indeed, relativism can also promote a disinterestedness that tacitly supports the status quo by engendering a conservative silence about current practices (see, for example, Neimark, 1990: 106). Thus, the naiveté of positivisms objectivism gives way to possibly more dangerous and contradictory views which promote the idea that knowledge is not subject to any extra-discursive checks.

However, perhaps some of the above criticism is unfair for, as illustrated by Treleaven's action research, the possibility of intervention is evident within a postmodern stance. However, this intervention is primarily about destabilising hegemonic discourses without being able to, as a researcher, put forward any alternative because of the perceived dangers of arbitrary discursive closure.

Critical realism and pragmatism

Sayer (1992) presents a Critical Realist stance which overtly attempts to avoid what he sees as the epistemological quagmires of both objectivism and relativism. In this he draws indirectly upon American pragmatism, and more directly upon Marxist traditions, by developing an alternative approach to truth which he calls practical adequacy.

> To be practically adequate knowledge must generate expectations about the world and about the results of our actions that are actually realised ... These expectations in turn are realised because of the nature of the associated material interventions ... and of their material contents. In other words, although the nature of objects and processes (including human behaviour) does not uniquely determine the content of human knowledge, it does determine their cognitive and practical possibilities for us. (Sayer, 1992: 69–70)

Here Sayer is in many respects following Kolakowski in differentiating between 'thought objects' and 'real objects'. Kolakowski (1969: 75) believes there is an external reality independent of and resistant to human activity; but this is a 'thing in itself' which remains unknowable. Such 'things in themselves' do not have conceptual counterparts; rather, our objects of knowledge – 'things for us' – are constituted by 'active contact with the resistance of nature [that] ... creates knowing man and nature as his object at one and the same time'. So as Kolakowski claims, while reality does exist, we can never ultimately know it because of our lack of a theory-neutral observational language; but this is not to say that our engagements with the external world are completely determined by us.

The implications of this combination of epistemological subjectivism and ontological realism are further elaborated by Arbib and Hesse (1986). As implied by Kolakowski (1969), they argue that the constraints and tolerance of spatio-temporal reality provide a feedback procedure that enables evaluation of the pragmatic success of our 'cognitive systems' and 'networks of schemata'. This pragmatic criterion prevents 'science' becoming purely an intersubjective representation of, and consensus about, social realities. These schemata allow people to make sense of the world – a world so complex that it is amenable to many interpretations.

For Arbib and Hesse (1986), while such schemata are not individualistic but socially shaped and constructed, they are not socially determined. Rather, since such schemata are guides for action, the pragmatic criterion operates consciously and unconsciously as people adjust and reject schemata when the expectations they support are violated (see also Barnes, 1977). Thus, schemata are ideological, pragmatic and interest laden in the sense that they are enmeshed with our knowledge of how to interact with the world, and such knowledge of 'how to' is 'intertwined with our knowledge (not necessarily conscious) of our goals and what we wish to achieve through our actions' (Arbib and Hesse, 1986: 129).

Law and Lodge (1984: 125) attempt to investigate further these social processes through the notion of 'workability', that is, truthfulness in a pragmatic sense. In this they argue that if a theory/network allows people to interact satisfactorily with their environment it is then reinforced, but if, from the stance of theory, their environments become unpredictable and uncontrollable the theory is undermined and is likely to change. Therefore, they argue that the workability of a theory is a function of the purposes for which it is used.

The importance of these issues lends force to Morgan's (1983: 393) consideration that since the pursuit of knowledge is a particular form of human action that has an essentially social nature, 'it must be understood as being an ethical, moral, ideological and political activity as it is an epistemological one'.

If, therefore, there are any criteria available for evaluating knowledge they do not relate to some quest for absolute knowledge; rather, they relate to 'the way knowledge serves to guide and shape ourselves as human beings – to the consequences of knowledge, in the sense of what knowledge does to and for humans' (Morgan, 1983: 393).

It follows that research embracing practical adequacy maintains the necessity for reflexivity on the part of the researcher. Knowledge, as such, is evaluated in terms of how successfully it may guide action towards the realization of particular objectives which are the expressions of particular interests or needs. This necessarily leads the researcher to reflect upon the partisan nature of his or her research with regard to its human consequences. As Carchedi (1983) argues, this inevitably involves questions such as: for whom and for what does the resultant construction of reality proffer aid? Management researchers should therefore accept their (albeit fallible) role as that of partisan participant in interest-laden dispute and divest themselves of allusions to the role of detached observer (Chubin and Restivo, 1983) occupying a neutral position.

Hence, according to the 'pragmatist' position, the 'truthfulness' of any methodologically corroborated explanation or account would be ultimately available, or testable, only through practice. This makes it incumbent upon the researcher to provide a clear guide to the practical ramifications of the theory and the subsequent practices that would pragmatically test that theory. Therefore, as Fay (1975: 94–5) comments, there would be an explicit recognition that social theory is interconnected with social practice such that what is to count as truth is partially determined by the specific ways in which scientific theory is supposed to relate to practical action. Thus, the theories of such a science will necessarily be composed of, among other things, an account of how such theories are translatable into action.

The processes by which our methodologically produced and corroborated accounts, or 'cognitive systems', might then be tested by these practical concerns are illustrated in Figure 8.6.

Figure 8.6 | The pragmatist position

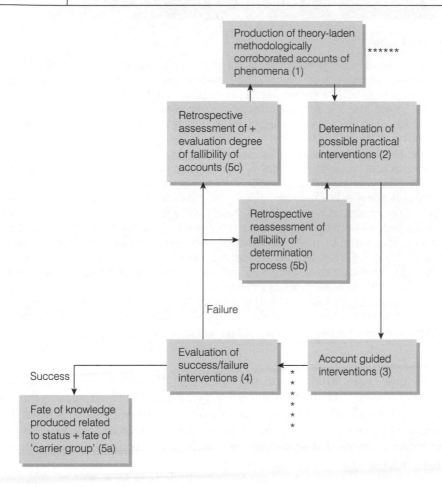

So, all these considerations regarding the 'truth' imply that research should not stop at the presentation of an account that has been produced and corroborated by the methodologies reviewed and evaluated in this text. Rather, research should proceed at least to identify the practical ramifications of that account and, ideally, should also proceed to test that account through practical interventions into our world so as to get feedback from that external reality. Indeed, inspired primarily by Critical Theory, some action researchers have integrated similar epistemological commitments into their work in a distinctive manner to produce coherent methodologies. As we shall illustrate, a key difference is how these action researchers produce its stage 1 in the first place.

Critical theory: reconfiguring action research and ethnography

Critical theorists (for example, Habermas, 1974a; Beck, 1992, 1996) deny the possibility of a theory-neutral observational language – what counts as warranted knowledge or truth is always conditioned by the operation inescapable socially established and linguistically based modes of engagement. The key epistemological question is how have these modes of engagement been socially established? Six key implications arise here for the critical theorist are illustrated below.

Key methodological concept

Critical theory

1 Any claim that management research may be morally founded upon a technical imperative to improve the efficiency, effectiveness or health of an organization through the analysis of how things really are must be questioned.

2 If all knowledge is a discursive, social product, why should the culturally relative products of some organizational groups acquire greater epistemological and social standing at the expense of alternative ways of knowing and acting?

3 Because all knowledge is socially constructed, the only moral legitimization for knowledge can be the *unforced consensus* established through argument and analysis embedded in democratic social relationships and without resort to coercion, distortion or duplicity (see Alvesson and Willmott, 1992: 13–14). This is Critical Theory's epistemological standard for all legitimate knowledge.

4 The extent to which actual communication deviates from this democratic ideal (and hence from the truth in a consensual as opposed to a correspondence sense), depends upon the degree of repression in society.

5 Because most discursive forms have not been produced under genuinely democratic consensual conditions they are the product of power plays and thus carry with them distortions that reflect the partial interests of powerful groups within society.

6 Critical theory therefore aims to empower and emancipate people who are disadvantaged and disenfranchised in organizations and wider society.

Given the above agenda, which is driven by Critical Theory's argument for a democratic epistemological standard for all knowledge, Critical Theorists seek to show the practical, moral and political significance of particular communicative actions. They also investigate how a particular social structure may produce and reinforce distorted communicative actions that practically and subtly shape its members' lives. Because they have not been developed in the democratic conditions of what Habermas calls the 'ideal speech act' (1974a, b), actors' culturally derived subjective apprehensions must in some sense be the outcome of asymmetrical power relations and hence are ideologically distorted.

Therefore, as Forrester argues, Critical Theory entails structural phenomenology which investigates the social construction of intersubjective meanings in a particular social and historical context – 'the objective social structure in which those actors work and live' (1983: 235). In order to accomplish structural phenomenologies Critical Theorists usually undertake a modified form of *verstehen* often called 'critical ethnography' (see Forrester, 1992, 2003; Putnam et al., 1993; Thomas, 1993; Morrow and Brown, 1994). The aim here is to investigate the nature of contemporary cultural forces and how these hegemonic regimes of truth impact upon the subjectivities and behaviour of the disempowered in contemporary organizational contexts. According to Thomas (1993: 2), what makes this ethnographic work *critical* is the attempt to 'describe, analyze and open to scrutiny otherwise hidden agendas, power centres and assumptions that inhibit, repress and constrain'. As Jermier observes (1998: 242), there is therefore a controversial commitment to attempting to access actors' culturally derived world views while revealing the socio-economic conditions which create and maintain asymmetrical power relations by ' ... the blending of informants' words, impressions and activities with an analysis of the historical and structural forces that shape the social world under investigation' (1998: 242).

Hence, the form that ethnography takes here moves beyond the description of actors' subjective worlds to considering the structural forces that have led to the development of these subjectivities and considers how these subjectivities entrap people in particular ways of understanding themselves and their worlds that serve particular interests at play in society. In other words, because those culturally derived views have most likely not been established under dialogical conditions, the subjective situation of the actors under investigation through conducting a critical ethnography is inevitably ideologically forced and distorted. Therefore, to this research agenda many critical theorists add (e.g. Freire, 1972a, b; Dryzek, 1995) a further important element. This involves both enabling the disempowered to become aware of the forces that have contributed to their oppression and through the establishment of a democratically grounded critical consciousness enable them to overcome these forces through promoting, for instance, organizational change through a distinctive form of action research often called critical-emancipatory action research.

For critical theorists, due to the problematic status of any epistemic authority not grounded in democratic relations, the role of the action researcher is fundamentally reconstructed to one of facilitating democratic agreement. For Freire, to avoid 'introjection by the dominated of the cultural myths of the dominator' (1972a: 59), action researchers must facilitate the development of a 'critical consciousness' (1972a: 46). He argues that the necessary prerequisites for the development of a critical consciousness, that dismantles the current hegemony, are not only the recognition by actors of their present oppression through that hegemony, but also the understanding that a critical consciousness is only constitutable through an authentic dialogue with the educator/action researcher where both are 'equally knowing subjects' (Freire, 1972b: 31).

By examining how particular interest-laden discursive practices sustain, for instance, particular strategic or operational preferences and change manoeuvres, Freire would see such a programme as an educative and therapeutic catalyst because the intent is to engender, through reflection, new (theory-laden) self-understandings. People should thereby begin to: understand those practices as social constructions; become aware of their own role in production and reproduction of those practices; construe those practices as mutable; identify how they might intervene in the evolution of their organizations and society. The result would be a challenge to traditional management prerogatives and the negotiation of alternative renditions of reality which create novel questions, inaugurate new problems and make new forms of organizational practice sensible and therefore possible (see, for example, Gaventa and Cornwall, 2006; Park, 2006).

Thus, a direct consequence of the epistemological ontological position taken by critical theory is a concern with organizational change – not just in the form of a distinctive analysis and critique of current management theory and practice but also in the form of a moral imperative to engender democratic social relations and thereby shift the balance of power to currently marginalized groups. For management researchers who ally themselves with critical theory, those individuals and groups whose perspectives are ordinarily silenced in organizations must be given voice. The demand is for members' conscious self-determination of social values and practices through participation and dialogue (e.g. Greenwood and Levin, 1998; Kemmis and McTaggart, 2000; Gustavsen, 2006; Kemmis, 2006). The epistemological demand is to mobilize and emancipate stakeholders usually silenced or duped by the status quo, through, for instance, 'co-operative inquiry' (Heron, 1996; Reason, 1999). Reason (1999) suggests that those who advocate co-operative inquiry focus on two

Figure 8.7 | Critical-emancipatory action research processes

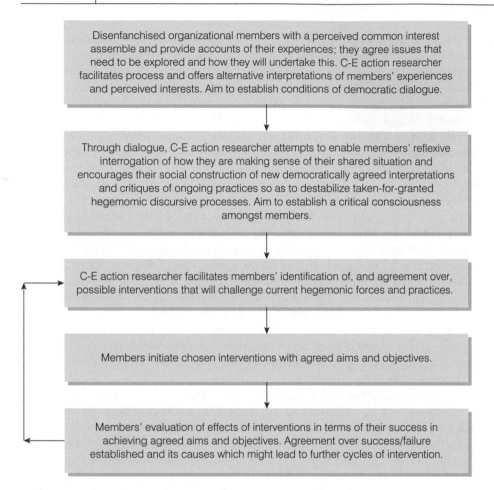

important purposes. The first is to 'articulate and offer democratic and emancipatory approaches to inquiry' (ibid.: 207). This suggests that in line with critical theory, those traditionally silenced in the academic research process are provided with some kind of voice in all aspects of the research endeavour, ranging from designing the research questions, to planning eventual action strategies. The second (ibid.: 208) purpose has a deliberate aim of critiquing the epistemology underlying the positivist view of the action researcher as a detached expert who exercises a legitimate role as architect of change as this is seen to be a process that disenfranchises the less powerful who have as much claim to epistemic authority as any other putative change-agent. Key elements in this critical-emancipatory action research process are illustrated by Figure 8.7.

Here it is important to note that pragmatist action researchers see themselves as complementing and extending the perspective and praxis of critical theorists. While admitting to the significance of social construction, pragmatists develop extra-discursive criteria of truth that complement and supplement the critical theorists' demand for democratic agreement (see Levin and Greenwood, 2001).

In Sayer's terms, these extra-discursive criteria are (1992: 69) in the form of the 'actual realization of expectations' through interventions which enable contact with the tolerance of reality. This epistemology has led some action researchers to argue that action research itself becomes a vehicle for judging ideas in terms of their efficacy in actual application (see Gustavsen, 2006; Park, 2006) while retaining democratic consensus as pivotal to generating the ideas in the first place (Levin and Greenwood, 2001).

In sum, the epistemological commitments of critical theory and pragmatism reconstitute action research. The intent is to engender new (socially constituted) self-understandings and simultaneously expose the interests which produce and disseminate knowledge which was taken to be authoritative and hence unchallangeable. In doing so, members democratically reclaim alternative accounts of phenomena – 'transformative' redefinitions which thereby become available to transformative interventions which can themselves be judged by the pragmatic criterion of 'what works' in terms of the pursuit of particular goals and interests.

Conclusions

In this chapter we have attempted to review several key philosophical disputes which influence how management research is both conceived and undertaken. Largely we have presented these disputes as revolving around different assumptions about the nature of human behaviour (i.e. *erklaren* vs *verstehen*); and different assumptions about whether or not we can neutrally engage with the social world as researchers (i.e. epistemology); and different assumptions about whether or not the social world exists independently of our cognitions (i.e. ontology). Often these contentious philosophical issues are ignored, or even suppressed, in management research leading, by default, to the preservation of what amounts to a positivist status quo – a point we shall take up further in the final chapter of this book. However, increasingly this status quo has been questioned by an array of management researchers who deploy philosophical assumptions that contest those embedded in the Positivist approach(es). As we have tried to illustrate these shifts in assumptions about epistemology and ontology drive various methodological reconfigurations in particular critical theory, postmodernism, critical realism and pragmatism. Although diverse, these alternatives to the positivist mainstream seem to shared an increasing commitment to philosophical introspection in that they require management researchers to be able to interrogate and contest the philosophical assumptions they inevitably make when engaging with research. One of the outcomes of this increasing sensitivity is that management researchers should be able to articulate, explain and defend the philosophical baggage they inevitably bring with them in and through their modes of engagement. The role this baggage plays in how we plan and undertake research is illustrated by Figure 8.8.

However, there is one further key implication of the various philosophical shifts we have described in this chapter. This is to do with how management research may be evaluated – a key concern for anyone undertaking management research and a further area that expresses philosophical disputes and differences. We turn to this area called Criteriology in our next and final chapter.

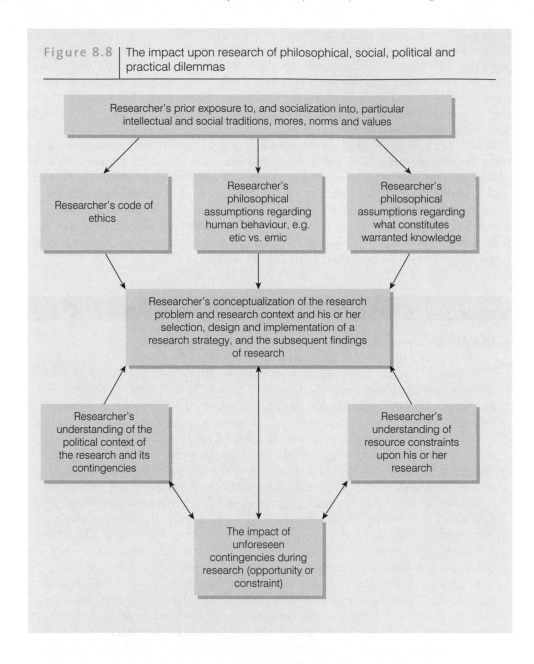

Figure 8.8 | The impact upon research of philosophical, social, political and practical dilemmas

Further reading

For an overview of the principal epistemological debates in management research we obviously recommend Johnson and Duberley (2000). This covers positivism, conventionalism, postmodernism, critical theory and critical realism and calls for more reflexive approaches to management research. Also Alvesson and Skoldberg (2000) provide an accessible guide to undertaking reflexive research which reviews how different epistemological commitments are expressed in various qualitative approaches including grounded theory, ethnography, critical theory, postmodernism and feminism. Meanwhile, Alvesson and Deetz (2000) contain a detailed discussion of how critical theory can inform organizational research and interventions. Postmodernist theory and research is incisively discussed and carefully evaluated in Hancock and Tyler (2001). We also recommend Law's (2004) fascinating critique of positivism and empiricism in social science methodology. His argument is that the research methods we use in social science do not merely describe social realities but actually help create them.

As we have indicated in this chapter postmodernists attempt to describe and deconstruct discursive forms, explore how they have developed and impact upon people, identify how they might change and then ultimately to destabilize them so that alternative discourses, which are always possible, might then develop. Interesting examples of the use of deconstruction are provided by Kilduff (1993) and Linstead (1993b) and discourse analysis by Ball and Wilson (2000). The examination of how discourses develop through using genealogy is provided by Knights and Morgan (1991) and how they adapt and change is provided by Barry and Elmes (1997). The use of a distinctive form of postmodern action research in order to destabilize the hegemonic patriarchal discourses of gender is provided by Treleaven (2001). The methodological implications of critical theory for ethnographic research, and the tensions it creates, are illustrated by Putnam et al. (1993). Critical theory's concern with forms of research aim to be both participative and emancipatory are also evident in feminist methodology. Here we recommend Mies' (1993) highly influential critique of positivism. With regard to critical theory's reconfiguration of ethnography and action research we recommend for the former Thomas (1993) and Jermier (1998) along with Kemmis (2006) and Gaventa and Cornwall (2006) for the latter. critical realism has significant implications for how both quantitative and qualitative methods are deployed and how the results of research are used and understood. These aspects are discussed by Mingers (2000) whilst critical realism's reconfiguration of ethnography may be found in Porter (1993).

These journal articles are freely available on the companion website (www.sagepub.co.uk/gillandjohnson):

Cooper, R. and Burrell, G. (1988) Modernism, postmodernism and organizational analysis: an introduction, *Organization Studies*, 9: 91–112.
Holland, R. (1999) Reflexivity, *Human Relations*, 52(4): 23–48.

Conclusions: Evaluating management research

9

Learning outcomes At the end of this chapter the reader should be able to:

- define the different evaluation criteria available for assessing management research;

- understand how many of the methods used in management research have distinctive strengths and weaknesses when evaluated using evaluation criteria such as validity and reliability;

- appreciate how case study research is an expression of methodological pluralism by combining different methods of data collection in a single piece of research;

- understand how the different types of evaluation criteria that may be used to evaluate management research articulate varying philosophical commitments regarding ontology and epistemology;

- distinguish between the various criteria used to assess research inspired by positivism, neo-empiricism, critical theory, and affirmative forms of postmodernism as examples of very different kinds of management research inspired by varying philosophical commitments;

- understand why there is no one best way of evaluating management research and appreciate that what is appropriate depends upon the philosophical assumptions at play in any given piece of research.

In this final chapter we turn to considering the complex issues that surround the evaluation of the quality of any findings when we complete a piece of management research. Inevitably, when we try to undertake any evaluation of research we have to deploy evaluation criteria that allow us to assess whether or not the research meets particular benchmarks, which are deemed important, and thus come to some judgement about whether or not the research is any 'good' or not. Clearly such processes of evaluation are very important for all management researchers, whether they are students undertaking various kinds of dissertation or experienced researchers submitting work for publication in prestigious academic journals: all are subject to such assessments undertaken by other people which directly affect their careers. Simultaneously management researchers regularly have to assess the work of others either informally when we read and try to make sense of others' published research or when we get involved in more formal peer review and student examination processes. However, as we shall try to show in this chapter, such evaluation is not a straightforward process – even though it may often be presented as such. This is because considerable confusion seems to permeate this area especially because, very often, the evaluation criteria that express particular underlying philosophical assumptions may be unintentionally applied as if they are the only means of assessing all research rather than being specific to only particular sets of philosophical commitments which we discussed in Chapter 8 of this book. Therefore, as Bochner forcefully observes (2000: 267), there is a danger of the widespread misappropriation of evaluation criteria and hence the unfair assessment of research findings. As he argues, this is because evaluation criteria constituted by particular philosophical conventions may be universally applied, as if they were 'culture-free' and hence indisputable, to what is a heterogeneous field inspired by a number of different epistemological and ontological dispositions which thereby justify a range of competing possible means of evaluation.

For example, this evaluation problem is sometimes fuelled by rather philosophically parochial reviews of evaluation criteria and policy statements in prestigious management journals (e.g. Behling, 1980; Mitchell, 1985; Scandura and Williams, 2000) which present specific criteria, that tacitly articulate positivistic philosophical assumptions, as if they were indeed universally applicable and thereby serve to exclude and undermine research inspired by the alternative philosophical stances discussed in Chapter 8. Given that the field of management research has been getting more philosophically diverse in recent years this issue of misappropriation has taken on an even greater importance as it may have created significant barriers to the use and publication of research outside the positivist mainstream (see Symon et al., 2000). Hence, one of the aims of this chapter is to demonstrate that there is no one universally applicable way of undertaking the evaluation of research: rather, what is appropriate depends upon the nature of the philosophical assumptions embedded in the research that is being assessed. The investigation of the varying ways in which research evaluation can, and indeed should, be undertaken is often called *criteriology*. We shall begin this investigation of these criteriological issues by looking at the most commonly used assessment criteria which operationalize positivist philosophical assumptions before moving onto the alternatives using neo-empiricism, critical theory, and affirmative forms of postmodernism as examples of criteriological diversity.

Positivist evaluation criteria

Here we shall first consider some of the most important criteria that are widely used to assess the quality of management research. However as we shall show, these criteria emerge out of positivist philosophical commitments and therefore are inappropriate to the evaluation of other types of management research. Nevertheless, they provide important insights into the inherent strengths and weaknesses embedded into some of the methodological research designs we have considered in this book. We shall therefore also consider these strengths and weaknesses in the light of these criteria. Whilst we have already touched upon some of these criteria in previous chapters it is worth elaborating them here by listing the most prominent criteria together.

1 *Internal validity* This criterion refers to whether or not what is identified as the 'cause(s)' or 'stimuli' actually produce what have been interpreted as the 'effects' or 'responses'. In other words, it refers to the issue of whether of not what has been defined as the independent variable actually is responsible for any identified variation in what has been defined as the dependent variable. It thus refers to the extent to which any research design allows the researcher to rule out alternative explanations, deriving from what we have defined as extraneous variables, of any observed variance in the dependent variable. Ideally the research design should also involve the use of procedures to gather data that allow the researcher to demonstrate that the action of the independent variable temporally precedes identified changes in the dependent variable. In other words, the research design should enable the researcher to tell if variation of the independent variable precedes that of the dependent variable thereby allowing him/her to elucidate the direction of causation between those variables.

2 *External validity* Generally, this criterion refers to the extent to which any research findings can be generalized, or extrapolated, beyond the immediate sample of people from whom data has been collected and/or the social setting in which the research took place. Therefore, the matter of external validity is often subdivided into the following two criteria.

(a) Population validity – this criterion concerns the extent to which it is possible to generalize from the sample of people involved in the research to a wider population. In other words, it refers to how representative those people, from whom data has been collected in a piece of research, are of a defined larger population to which research findings are intended to be generalized.

(b) Ecological validity – this criterion is concerned with the extent to which it is possible to generalize from the actual social context in which the research has taken place, and data thereby gathered, to other social contexts and settings. This is also related to the issue of how artificial or atypical the research setting is relative to 'natural' contexts typical of normal, everyday life.

3 *Measurement validity* This criterion refers to the operationalization processes discussed in Chapter 3 whereby abstract concepts are translated into a series of measures which tell the researcher whether of not instances of the abstract concept have empirically occurred and to what extent they have occurred. In other words, it is to do with whether or not the measures of independent, dependent and extraneous variables used in a research design faithfully measure those variables they claim to measure through the operationalization process.

4 *Reliability* This criterion basically refers to the consistency of results obtained in research. To satisfy this criterion it should be possible for another researcher to replicate the original research using the same, or equivalent, people and the same research design under the same, or equivalent, conditions in order to see whether of not the same results are then found. Hence, the assessment of reliability requires the use of clear methodological protocols so that regulation by

peers in the scientific community, through replication, would be possible in principle. For Merton (1938: 259) such processes are a vital aspect of scientific work as they involve a key aspect of what he called the 'scientific ethos': an 'organized scepticism' regarding any research findings and therefore the need for any findings to be checked by peers in the wider scientific community in order to guard against fraudulent, or mistaken, contributions.

It is important to emphasize here that the role of the above criteria, and their formulation, derive largely from positivist philosophical commitments. As we have seen in previous chapters, all positivist methodology emphasizes objective data collection in management research so as to test hypotheses by having built in 'extensive means for protecting against personal biases' (Behling, 1980: 489) which thereby afford some protection against 'fanciful theorizing' (Donaldson, 1996: 164). Here progress in management research entails a 'pursuit of "truth" that is a closer and closer fitting of our theories to the one objective reality we presume exists' (Mitroff and Pondy, 1978: 146). In order to preserve a theory-neutral observational language during data collection so as to enable this pursuit of a correspondence theory of truth, positivists try to methodologically ensure distance between the researcher and the researched so that research processes and findings are not contaminated by the actions of the researcher. Here positivists try to ensure this view of scientific rigour by deploying these particular conceptions of validity and reliability – evaluative criteria which assume that findings can be independent of the researcher, and the methodology used, provided that the 'correct' procedures are followed. Moreover, these criteria, especially reliability, express an important ontological commitment: that there is a "real" social world "out there", which is stable thereby allowing replication tests.

As Scandura and Williams (2000) argue with regard to management research, the deployment of the above criteria are seen to be pivotal to enabling progress through the assessment of the various methods used by management researchers. However, ecological validity is not usually considered in this specification of validities which researchers should pursue. This apparent oversight seems to largely derive from the implicit emphasis upon *erklaren* rather than *verstehen* in these list of criteria. Instead greater emphasis is given to the other types of validity and to the reliability of findings. Even some qualitative researchers have maintained this emphasis. For instance, Lecomte and Goetz have just slightly modified these positivist criteria and retained reliability in the sense that different researchers, or the same researcher on different occasions, would 'discover the same phenomena or generate the same constructs in the same or similar settings' (1982: 32) – something, as we shall see, some qualitative methodologies may have great difficulty in ensuring.

Stop and Think Exercise 9.1   The aim of this exercise is to evaluate the inherent strengths and weaknesses of some of the research methodologies we have discussed in this book when they are designed and used in the most appropriate manner according to the various methodological protocols and rules devised by researchers.

   With these issues in mind, evaluate the six methods listed below in the table with reference to how potentially strong or weak they are, relative to one another, in terms of the evaluation criteria discussed above.

   You should be able to discern a pattern in the relative strengths and weaknesses of these methods – as you gain something under these criteria something else is lost: what are these trade-offs?

	Internal Validity	Population Validity	Measurement Validity	Ecological Validity	Reliability
1 Laboratory experiment					
2 Quasi-experiment					
3 Positivist action research					
4 Analytical survey					
5 Ethnography					

Now read below where, armed with these criteria, we use them to evaluate each of the methodologies listed above to elucidate their potential strengths and weaknesses.

The application of positivist criteria to evaluating research methodologies

Ideal or laboratory experiments

As we demonstrated in Chapter 4, the highly structured nature of experimental research designs, with their identification and manipulation of independent and dependent variables with assignation of subjects to control and experimental groups, endows this approach with significant strengths of internal validity and reliability. Being highly structured, with clear protocols to follow, it is comparatively easy to replicate many aspects of an experimental research design. Moreover, its utilization of matched control and experimental groups enables observation of the effects of manipulating an independent variable while providing a high degree of confidence that the effects of any potential extraneous variables have been ruled out, or controlled, thus allowing the establishment of causal connections. This issue of internal validity may be further enhanced because the temporal ordering of cause and effect should be discernible through the manipulation of the independent variable, through experimental treatments, by the researcher. Simultaneously, experimental researchers can use a battery of measures to monitor changes in the dependent variable to, in principle, ensure measurement validity.

However, the ideal experiment, in gaining these strengths through its high degree of structure, loses or 'trades off' naturalism: experiments are low in ecological validity because of the artificial nature of the research process and context created by their very structure. Such weaknesses raise the issue of the extent to which any conclusions from ideal experiments are mere artefacts of the research process and context and thus inapplicable to social contexts outside those in which data have been collected (see Introna and Whitley, 2000). A further significant weakness in much experimental research is that it is often low in population validity since it may involve small numbers of subjects, who may often be unrepresentative volunteers. Researchers using experiments can, however, increase population validity by giving greater attention to the random sampling of subjects.

Quasi-experiments and positivistic forms of action research

Quasi-experiments and positivistic forms of action research attempt to take the research design of the ideal experiment out of the laboratory and into the field (see Chapters 4 and 5). As in the ideal experiment there is a concentration on measuring changes in the dependent variable often using a battery of measures so as to enhance measurement validity. By attempting to undertake research in relatively natural, non-artificial settings both are seen to gain naturalism and therefore are relatively higher in ecological validity. But here we confront the paradoxical relationship which exists between control and naturalism in research design. Through venturing into the field, naturalism may be gained, but only at the expense of losing the ability to manipulate the incidence of independent variables and control the incidence of extraneous variables. Except on rare occasions, in positivistic action research it is usually much more difficult for a researcher to manipulate the independent variable and assign subjects to matched and experimental groups. Indeed, to attempt to create such groups often disturbs the normal lives of subjects and so reduces naturalism. For quasi-experimental research it is very difficult to match naturally occurring control and experimental groups – that lack of match inevitably reduces internal validity. So, by increasing ecological validity quasi-experiments and action research trade off internal validity when compared with the ideal experiment. With regard to reliability, the socially specific context in which action research is undertaken, will frequently result in a relative decline in reliability as it becomes more difficult to replicate. In the case of quasi-experimentation, with its precise protocols and methods of measuring change in the dependent variable, replication in principle becomes much easier.

As with the ideal experiment, it is often the case that researchers using either a quasi-experimental design or action research fail to give sufficient attention to sampling. This causes problems regarding population validity. While this may be understandable given the difficulties of gaining access in the field, it is not necessarily an intrinsic weakness of these research approaches as methodological steps can be taken to improve it.

Analytical surveys

It should now be apparent that the qualities displayed in analytical survey research give it much strength in population validity and reliability (see Chapter 6). Such surveys usually entail the careful random selection of samples that enable results to be generalized to wider populations with a high degree of confidence. Concurrently, by using highly structured questionnaires to gather data in a form that is quantitatively analysable survey-based research is usually regarded as easily replicable and hence potentially reliable. In principle the questions on the questionnaire attempt to operationalize independent, dependent, and extraneous variables and measure their variation in a valid manner. However, the resultant high degree of structure, although conferring strengths, appears to create a relative lack of naturalism. For instance, the context in which data collection takes place will not usually be as artificial as the context of the ideal experiment. Nevertheless, respondents might often be constrained or impelled by the prompts of an interviewer or the rubric of a self-completion questionnaire. This may lead them to make statements which, although fitting into the conceptual and theoretical pro forma of the research, give little opportunity for the respondent to articulate the ways in which he or she personally conceptualizes and understands the matters of interest. It is usually for these reasons that survey research is often considered to be relatively low in ecological validity.

Analytical surveys are also considered to be relatively weak in internal validity as compared with experiments; that is, they have certain difficulties with regard to their control of rival hypotheses. For instance, analytic surveys rely on the use of the statistical controls of multivariate analysis to control extraneous variables, and this potentially weakens any causal conclusions arrived at. This is because correlation does not necessarily signify the presence of a causal relationship. Rather the presence of a correlation is taken to be necessary but not sufficient proof of a causal relationship whilst conversely its absence enables falsification of the hypothesis under test. Moreover, the presence of a correlation gives little indication of the direction of causation between independent and dependent variables unless some temporal ordering is simultaneously evident – something which very often is difficult to discern.

Ethnography

As we have attempted to make clear in earlier chapters, the more research is structured the more easily it can be replicated. Ethnography, with its commitment to induction and relatively unstructured qualitative methods of data collection, creates severe problems regarding replicability, and consequently reliability also appears problematic. Moreover, as we have seen in Chapter 7, since ethnography usually entails the intensive study of a small number of cases, its claims to population validity are usually considered to be limited to the actual phenomena in a specific social context under investigation during fieldwork. Although this apparent limitation regarding population validity has been thoroughly disputed by Mitchell (1983) (see also Bloor, 1976, 1978) in his discussion of the use of analytic induction and grounded theory, the main strength of ethnography is generally considered to be ecological validity.

It is often considered that ethnography has inherent advantages over other research methodologies (e.g. laboratory experiments and surveys) that suffer from deficiencies in ecological validity (Brunswick, 1956; Bracht and Glass, 1968). That is, ethnographic research (unlike many other research methodologies) takes place in the natural setting of the everyday activities of the subjects under investigation. This, and the research procedures used, ostensibly reduce contamination of the subject's behaviour by the researchers themselves and the methods they use for collecting data. However, few ethnographers would claim that it is possible completely to eliminate subjects' reactivity to the researchers' personal qualities or techniques of data collection. As we have already discussed, the ethnographer instead attempts to use a particular form of reflexivity; that is to say, an attempt is made by the researcher to understand his or her own effect upon, and role in, the research setting and to utilize this knowledge to elicit data.

Where ethnographers are concerned with inductively generating grounded theory, their commitment to naturalism may often obstruct their establishment of control and experimental groups and hinder their ability to manipulate independent variables. As such, ethnography is often considered to have difficulties regarding the clear establishment of cause-and-effect relationships and consequently is taken to be low in internal validity. This claim is, however, problematic for several reasons.

Because ethnographers can produce large amounts of qualitative data in an inductive fashion it is perhaps the most likely of all the methodologies indicated above to identify and include all the relevant variables in any subsequent theoretical analysis. In contrast, the experimental and survey approaches entail the formulation of theory prior to data collection through operationalization and instrumentation. At each stage of this process the deductive researcher is, in effect, excluding variables from consideration and limiting the extent and form that data take in an a priori fashion. To put it crudely, the researcher's deductive research strategy leads them to throw information away! – or at least not collect it in the first place.

Despite the ethnographer's inevitable selection of relevant aspects to study, he or she is more likely than deductive researchers to become aware of important factors that did not form part of his or her preconceived notion of the situation. This is particularly so when this process is combined with forms of analytic induction and grounded theory, which can enable the establishment of what are in effect control and experimental groups. In this way the criticism that ethnography is inevitably low in internal validity is open to question. Moreover, since ethnographers usually have a commitment to naturalism, they have the scope to rule out some of the threats to internal validity that stem from the artificiality of the research context and procedures; something to which the more structured research styles are evidently victims. Thus, it seems that the internal validity of ethnography can be problematic in some circumstances as it depends largely upon rigorousness and the specific concerns of the ethnographer. When those concerns entail analytic induction, and/or grounded theory, as well as reflexivity, the internal validity of the ethnographer's theoretical conclusions may well be very high in comparison to many of the deductive approaches.

However, the point is, that save for ecological validity it is probably inappropriate to use positivistic versions of reliability and validity to assess ethnographic research which has key philosophical differences in that the emphasis is upon *verstehen* rather than *erklaren*. This is a point which we shall return to when we discuss the evaluation criteria associated with what is called neo-empiricism.

Multi-methods: the criteriological justification

We are really like blind men led into an arena and asked to identify an entity (say an elephant) by touching one part of that entity (say a leg). Certainly we might make better guesses if we could pool the information of all the blind men, each of whom has touched a different part of the elephant. (Smith, 1975: 273)

The perceived need for what is often called methodological triangulation is illustrated by the above quotation from Smith (1975). Here he tried to metaphorically capture the idea that different kinds of complementary data about a 'problem' may be acquired by using different research techniques in the same empirical study. Such 'methodological triangulation' is thought to overcome the bias inherent in any single-method approach by advocating the use of multiple methods to address the same problems and research questions, on the basis that in this way different methodological strengths will be enhanced, and inherent weaknesses will be cancelled out, to produce more convincing findings.

Indeed, from the previous evaluation of some of the different methodologies we have considered in this book, it would seem that each approach has distinctive strengths and weaknesses. Hence, it would seem to make sense to combine the different methodologies in the same study to enhance the findings in terms of the evaluation criteria put forward earlier. This suggestion has long been discussed by methodologists who often have put forward the idea that we should combine quantitative and qualitative methods as it will provide opportunities for methodological triangulation.

For example, Denzin (1970: 297) defined triangulation, a term derived from surveying, as 'the combination of methodologies in the study of the same phenomenon'. Multiple and independent methods, especially if undertaken by different research

workers investigating the same problem, should (he argued), if reaching the same conclusions, have greater validity and reliability than a single methodological approach
to a problem. Elsewhere such triangulation is also described as the multimethod/
multitrait approach (Campbell and Fiske, 1959), and for the most part presents the
idea that complementary qualitative and quantitative methodologies can complement
one another rather than constituting competing approaches (Jick, 1979a; Fielding and
Fielding, 1986). This is illustrated by Jick's work summarized in the case study below.

Case Study 9.1   Methodological triangulation in action

Jick (1979a) describes his doctoral project (Jick, 1979b) to study the effects of a merger
of hospitals on their employees as an example of triangulation. As is usual in merger
cases there was high employee anxiety and one of the main purposes of the research
was to discover the sources and symptoms of this stress and its impact on the operation of the newly created organization.

On the basis of a review of research methods, especially those designed to collect data on the complex topic of employee stress, Jick decided that there was no
ideal, sole method of collecting such data. There were a number of possibilities. He
decided he might interview employees; use some indirect form of projective test; ask
those interacting with the focal person; systematically observe the person's behaviour;
measure physiological symptoms, and so on. Clearly all these strategies had strengths
and weaknesses which suggested some form of triangulation, and a design accordingly
emerged using a combination of methods. Methods eventually used in practice were
surveys distributed to a random sample of the population, followed by semi-structured,
probing interviews; interviews were also conducted with supervisors and co-workers to
ascertain their observation of particular employees.

In addition, and particularly fruitful, were data based upon unobtrusive measures (Webb
et al., 1969) and non-participant observation as well as archival materials. For example,
what is described as an 'anxiety thermometer' was developed from an observation by
the archivist in one of the organizations that employees frequently used comprehensive
newspaper files to compare recent reports of the organization's future with those in the
past. Employees were evidently seeking information to relieve their anxieties, and it was
hypothesized that the more people visited the archives the higher their level of anxiety.
Such data were compared with those derived from other data sources such as interviews
and surveys and the hypothesis for the most part confirmed.

Quantitative data sources were used largely to supplement qualitative data but, as
Jick observes, 'it is a delicate exercise to decide whether or not results have converged
… should all components of a multimethod approach be weighted equally? … there are
no formal tests to discriminate methods to judge their applicability' (Jick, 1979a: 607).

Nevertheless, in Jick's judgement the various methods taken together produced convergent findings. There were some discrepant findings, but data sources (whether divergent or discrepant) may of course be equally valuable, and discrepant findings are likely
to enrich explanations. In this particular case, for example, some employees, known to
be highly stressed on the basis of surveys of self-reports, were apparently least likely to
visit the archive files. The discrepancy was investigated by conducting further interviews
and observations, which helped to reconcile the apparently conflicting data by suggesting that poorly educated employees tended to rely more on oral communications than
written documents.

Methodological pluralism

The advocation of the use of multiple methods in the same study, in order to enable methodological triangulation suggests that these advocates do not perceive there to be any fundamental irreconcilable conflicts between quantitative and qualitative methods and thereby justifies what is seen as the adoption of what may be termed a *'methodologically pluralist'* position (see McLennan, 1995).

This position implies the possibility of rapprochement between quantitative and qualitative research methodologies, as articulated, for example, by McCall and Simmons (1969), McCall and Bobko (1990) and Cresswell (1994). From this stance the difference between the methods of the social scientist are perceived as being ones of trade-off around reliability, internal and external validity, etc. A slightly different argument is put forward by Currall et al. (1999) where they support pluralism on the grounds that qualitative ethnographic data can be used to discover or develop theory whilst quantification of that data using content analysis and statistical techniques enables theory testing and evaluation. Other methodologists have tended to emphasize instead that it is their appropriateness to the research topic that should decide which methodologies to use. One of the first to put forward this idea was Trow (1957: 33) when he proposed that 'different kinds of information about man (sic) and society are gathered most fully and economically in different ways, and the problem under investigation properly dictates the methods of investigation ... the methods and techniques most useful to the problems at hand'.

However, any pluralistic *rapprochement* is usually only tenable within philosophical assumptions which recognize the importance of actors' intersubjectivity and the consequent need for, and possibility of, *verstehen* whilst simultaneously recognizing the influence of external causal variables upon behaviour (see McLennan, 1995). For example, many pluralists would perceive qualitative methods as the most appropriate for fulfilling a commitment to an exploration of actors' intersubjective worlds whilst quantitative methods are deployed in order to explore the external causal forces that are presumed to impact upon actors' and are mediated by their intersubjective (that is, culturally derived) interpretations.

Moreover, it appears that such 'pluralism' is founded upon 'realist' assumptions about the ontological status of social reality, 'which postulate that the world is a real world made up of hard, tangible and relatively immutable structures' (Burrell and Morgan, 1979: 4). As we have seen in Chapter 8, this assumption considers that social reality has a concrete existence independent of human consciousness and cognition, which is, within this pluralist stance, empirically identifiable and presumably measurable in some way. Therefore, experimental or analytical survey researchers may legitimately impose their operationalizations of social reality upon their subjects, which become measured stimuli to which subjects' responses are also measured in some valid manner. Indeed, operationalization and measurement of social reality (stimuli) and action (responses) become the key activity in scientific inquiry and are clearly underpinned by the assumption that we all live in the same independent and external social world which we can neutrally access provided that the 'right' methodology is used in an appropriate fashion. In other words, positivist ontological and epistemological assumptions remain largely unchallenged. However, such methodological pluralists would also follow Laing (1967) in attacking the contention that social phenomena are analogous to the 'it-beings' or 'things' of nature and are thereby amenable to a type of causal analysis in which human beings are reduced to entities that automatically react to external stimuli in the same fashion as inanimate phenomena behave.

In the methodological pluralist position outlined here, human action is assumed to have an internal logic, for human beings have been freed from the 'reflexive arc' (Mead, 1934). It therefore creates a perceived necessity to explore the meanings people attach to that all-embracing, identifiable, concrete social reality – meanings integral to the construction of responses, i.e. action. Qualitative methods that enable *verstehen*, such as ethnography, are for the pluralist the methods appropriate for fulfilling their commitment to exploration of actors' phenomenological worlds. Therefore, as we have indicated above, in the methodological pluralist's web of what are essentially philosophical choices, ethnography takes its place within a version of 'variable analysis' (Blumer, 1967). This position is often promulgated through attempts at providing what Fay (1975: 84) has termed 'quasi-causal' accounts. In clarifying what he means by this term, Fay states that, 'in these sorts of conditionship relations, consciousness functions as a mediator between the determining antecedent factors and the subsequent actions, in other words, men act in terms of their external conditions, rather than being governed directly by them (sic)' (Fay, 1975: 84–5). In this, stimuli (social reality as measured and defined by the social scientist) and responses (human actions as measured and defined by the social scientist) are mediated by the actors' subjective processes of attaching meaning to and interpreting stimuli.

For example, within this epistemological stance, the experimental and survey researchers can legitimately follow their 'crafts' by imposing operationalizations of their versions of social reality upon subjects and subsequent data, through highly structured research strategies. The relationship between stimuli and responses may often be investigated while taking into account (or controlling for) the creative processes of interpretation and meaning construction by subjects with some kind of qualitative analysis aimed at ruling out competing hypotheses. In other words, pluralists would attempt to increase the internal and ecological validity of their findings by attempting to 'control' for the indexicality of their experiment or survey by using the research methods most suitable for that purpose. However, as we have tried to show, within this pluralist position qualitative methodology is not used purely within a hypothetico-deductive framework to control extraneous variables deriving from indexicality. Alternatively, methodological pluralism may arise from a commitment to linking micro-analyses of individual or group action(s) with a macro-structural analysis of society.

So in summary, the methodological pluralist position suggests that not only are different quantitative and qualitative methodologies suitable for different kinds of problem (e.g. Trow, 1957) but they also complement one another in a variety of ways that add to the credibility of a study by providing an internal cross-checking or monitoring device during the research process (e.g. McCall and Simmons, 1969; Denzin, 1970; H. W. Smith, 1975), as well as constituting aids for spanning the micro–macro divide (Godsland and Fielding, 1985; Fielding, 1988). It is now appropriate to turn looking at methodological pluralism in action and the most common vehicle for this in management research: the case study.

Mixing methods: case study research

There is a growing importance in the management field of what is often termed a mixed methods approach: research that may integrate quantitative and qualitative methods of data collection within a single project. As we have seen above, the use of different methods of data collection in the same study is presumed to have considerable benefits since any method has distinctive strengths and weaknesses and therefore research designs may benefit from counter-balancing strengths of one method with the weakness of others and vice versa. Within the area of management the most significant means of doing this is the case study. Now we need to be careful here since one could argue that much ethnographic research and action research could, for instance, also be categorized as case study research, and in many respects they are. However, here, following Yin (2003), we are only looking at case studies that purposefully mix quantitative and qualitative methods in data collection for the pluralistic epistemological reasons outlined previously in this chapter (see also case study 9.1). Based upon the concerns about triangulation referred to earlier in this chapter, case studies usually use a variety of methods to access different sources of evidence, amongst which the most commonly used are interviews, direct and participant observation, documentation and archival records. For Yin (2003), no single source has a complete advantage over the other sources, and that as the sources may be seen as complementary, a good case study will use as many different sources as possible collected via different appropriate means.

Despite some ambiguity concerning its status as either being a method in its own right or a research strategy that combines methods, the case study is being increasingly employed in organizational research and in the field of social sciences in general (Hartley, 2004). Indeed, the use of case studies has grown in importance over the past two decades and is often the preferred label for exploratory and evaluative research that is conducted by many research students in the management disciplines, often in organizations where they are employed. But we must be careful about using this catch-all phrase.

Whilst different writers define the case study in different ways, most seem to agree that a case study entails empirical research that focuses on understanding and investigating particular phenomena and their dynamics, within the context of a naturally occurring real life single setting, that uses multiple sources of evidence, usually using an array of quantitative and qualitative methods to collect that data (e.g. Eisenhardt, 1989; Yin, 2003; Hartley, 2004). In other words, a case study can be an intensive study of an individual, a group, an organization or a specific process. Basically the unit of analysis varies according to the interests and aims of the researcher: hence what constitutes a 'case' inevitably varies. Rather than following a fixed research design (as in the case of experiments and surveys) to examine a limited number of variables, the case study involves an in-depth examination of a single instance. The case is the situation, which is the focus of interest. So, with regard to management research, a case study can involve a detailed investigation, of one or more organizations, groups within an organization, or individuals therein, with the aim of providing some type of analysis of the context and processes involved in affecting the incidence and form taken by the phenomena of interest. Hence, case studies are a very flexible approach to research in the sense that the form they take, the methods used, and what they try to do, varies considerably according to the aims of the researcher.

For instance, a case study can be used to either inductively generate, or deductively test, theory. Alternatively they might be used to conduct merely exploratory pilot studies or descriptive research (see Yin, 2003). However, what is important here is that the purposes to which the case study is being put has an important bearing upon how the case study is, or the case studies are, selected by the researcher at the outset of the research, and in particular, how far the researcher wants to be able to generalize, if at all, any findings beyond the case(s) investigated. In other words, whilst case studies through various forms of triangulation may enhance our understanding of what is going on in a particular case, is there any means of being able to theorize from that case to other cases not investigated by the research? Within the pluralist epistemological stance there appears to be several strategies which may be viable for enabling such types of generalization.

One of the key weaknesses in much case study research is sometimes the lack of a coherent rationale for case study selection. Now often this may be because of the difficulty of getting access to organizational sites in management research. The practicalities of the situation may go against developing a thorough reasoning beyond some attempt at after the fact justification. Nevertheless it is always worth considering some of the strategies for selection available to researchers. For instance, as Flyvbjerg (2006) notes, there are a variety of possible rationales that might be used, in principle, in the selection of cases for investigation. Unlike with the random sampling strategies used in survey design, where generalization is based on the representativeness of the sample with regard to a specified population, case study selection should attempt to maximize the utility and richness of the information content provided by a small sample and single cases.

For instance the researcher may select what is called a 'critical case' where the phenomenon of interest is most likely or least likely to occur (Flyvbjerg, 2006: 231) because the information then gathered from that case is more likely to either support or falsify more general propositions and hypotheses, the rationale being: 'If this is (not) valid for this case then it applies to all (no) cases'. The example that Flyvbjerg uses is particularly apposite Robert Michel's work on oligarchy. As Flyvbjerg notes 'By choosing a horizontally structured grass roots organization with strong democratic ideals – that is a type of organization with an especially low probability of being oligarchical – Michels could test the universality of the oligarchy thesis; that is, "If this organization is oligarchical, so are most others"' (ibid.). An alternative strategy for selecting cases is termed 'maximum variation' (ibid.: 230–2). This is where the cases selected vary in terms of particular chosen dimensions so as to provide specific comparisons and contrasts. For instance, one might wish to investigate the impact of different forms of organizational governance structure upon feelings of job satisfaction by choosing several organizations that varied in terms of how bureaucratic or mechanistic they were in terms of organization structure and then measure variations in job satisfaction in each organization to provide important comparisons. This strategy of maximum variation could lend itself either to the falsification of a priori hypotheses, or could be part of theoretical sampling during the inductive development of grounded theory through the constant comparative method (see Chapter 7 of this book).

In sum, case study design involves the same attempt at answering the following interrelated questions usually prior to fieldwork:

- What are the aims and objectives of this research?
- Which processes and phenomena are to be investigated in their everyday social context?
- How are cases going to be conceptualized, in other words, what is the unit of analysis?
- What is the conceptual framework (this covers the main features aspects, dimensions, issues, variables) of a case study and their presumed relationship?
- What are the initial research questions (what, how, why, where, when)?
- Is the approach going to be inductive or deductive?
- What is the sampling strategy both within any case (who, where, when, what is going to be investigated) and what is the rationale for selecting these particular cases given the aims of the research?

- What are the key sources of primary and secondary data necessary to access during fieldwork?
- How is secondary data going to be accessed?
- Which different methods of primary data collection are to be used and for what purposes and why?
- How is primary and secondary data going to be analysed?

In sum, a case study is an example of the use of multiple methods of data collection to investigate specific phenomena in their natural settings. Sometimes the case study can almost reflect aspects of quasi-experimental research through attempts at identifying critical contrasts and comparisons that enable theory testing through the selection of specific cases. Alternatively the logic of grounded theory may be used in the selection of cases in order to develop theory across and within cases. Within cases, multiple sources of primary and secondary data are used with both quantitative and qualitative methods being used to collect that data where appropriate to ensure triangulation. Thus, methodological pluralism, in the form of the case study, considers that combining quantitative and qualitative methods is not only viable, it actually would significantly improve management research in terms of mainstream positivist criteria. However, such a stance can only be maintained by accepting the relevance of both *verstehen* and *erklaren* to social science and by assuming that there are no significant philosophical differences at play – something which not all researchers are prepared to agree with. It should be remembered that within the above ensemble of philosophical assumptions, once the role of human intersubjectivity (for whatever reason) is understood as irrelevant to the explanation of social phenomena, increasingly qualitative methods will be dismissed as irrelevant to management research. This, implicitly or explicitly, re-establishes a dichotomy between the quantitative and the qualitative by dismissing the latter as irrelevant to social science research. Conversely, other researchers may dismiss quantitative approaches as overly deterministic and as undermining their commitment to what we have called naturalism (see Chapters 3 and 7) and hence limit their work to the deployment of qualitative methods. This has led some of these researchers to overtly re-evaluate positivistic evaluation criteria and develop alternatives. It is to these alternative forms of evaluation that we now turn.

Re-evaluating evaluation criteria

In Chapter 7 we reviewed certain ethnographic research practices as examples of management research which were influenced by the epistemological assumption that it is possible to collect qualitative empirical data in an unbiased and objective fashion and simultaneously reject hypothetico-deductive falsificationism in favour of induction. This type of management research is an example of has been more generally called 'qualitative positivism' (see Prasad and Prasad, 2002: 6) or neo-empiricism (see Alvesson and Deetz, 2000: 60–74) because researchers use non-quantitative methods within largely positivistic assumptions (see also Chapter 8). For example, within an interpretive agenda, these researchers deploy what Schwandt (1996: 62) calls a 'third-person point of view' that privileges the consciousness of the management researcher (see also Knights, 1992; Van Maanen, 1995b) by retaining the key positivist assumption that there is a social world out there, awaiting to be discovered and explored in an objective manner provided that the correct methods are used to collect data.

In doing so, neo-empiricists rely upon an array of qualitative methods to inductively develop thick descriptions of the patterns in the intersubjective meanings that
actors use to make sense of their everyday worlds and investigate the implications
of those interpretations for social interaction usually in organizational settings (see
Prasad and Prasad, 2002). Often these data are used to generate grounded theory that
can explain and predict behaviour through the deployment of Glaser and Strauss'
(1967; see also Strauss and Corbin, 1990; Locke, 2000; Partington, 2000) constant
comparative method (see Chapter 7). Thus, the key differences with mainstream positivism, and its largely quantitative methodologies, are primarily about what is open to
direct, neutral, observation through sensory experience and the continuing relevance of
induction in the social sciences.

For some people these apparent philosophical differences with mainstream positivism are not very significant and therefore they argue that it is legitimate to directly
apply the positivist evaluation criteria (e.g. Lecompte and Goetz, 1982; Kirk and
Miller, 1986), illustrated earlier in this chapter, in the assessment of all qualitative
research. According to others these differences with quantitative research are philosophically significant and it is therefore inappropriate to attempt to evaluate qualitative research by applying unreconstructed criteria such as reliability and validity.
Therefore, they have attempted to revise those positivist evaluation criteria to both
reflect their inductive agenda and attempt to devise alternative ways of demonstrating the qualitative researcher's objectivity and rigour.

For instance, in some early work, Lincoln and Guba (1985: 290) argued that 'conventional' (i.e. mainstream positivist) evaluation criteria have evolved in response to
some important questions regarding the determination of any findings' truth, applicability, consistency and neutrality. In doing so they argue that these conventional
criteria need to be revised for what they call naturalist inquirers. In doing so they
emphasized the need for qualitative researchers to provide various audit trails, in a
self-critical fashion, that allow audiences to make judgements for themselves as to its
rigour. In specifying the need for an audit trail they also suggested the following four
general principles for assessing the quality of qualitative research, which combine to
enable the assessment of what they call the *trustworthiness* of the research. Each of
these criteria, they argued, should replace an equivalent criterion deriving from the
assessment of quantitative research.

1 Internal validity is replaced by *credibility*: the provision of authentic representations of the cultural worlds of the people who are being investigated. This is
   primarily established by what they call 'member checks' (1985: 314): feeding
   back to those members the researcher's account of their worlds so as to assess
   the extent to which they recognize and give assent to those representations.
   This allows evaluation of the extent to which an account is corroborated by
   accurately representing members' subjective dispositions.
2 External validity is replaced by *transferability*: the extent of applicability of
   the findings both within the social context situation under investigation and
   to other social contexts. With regard to the former, this is established by sampling different aspects of the social setting under investigation. By producing
   in-depth accounts of that setting and cultural phenomena Lincoln and Guba
   (ibid.: 316) argue that the researcher provides other researchers with a database
   which allows them to judge the extent to which the findings are transferable
   to other social settings with which they are familiar. Here, there has to be '...
   enough "thick description" ... available about both "sending" and "receiving"

contexts to make a reasoned judgement about the degree of transferability possible' (ibid.: 247).

3 Reliability is replaced with *dependability*: the minimization of researcher idio-syncrasies. This criterion is mainly met through the provision of the audit trails mentioned above. An audit trail involves documentation of all stages of the research, and the choices made by the researcher, from inception to comple-tion: detailed evidence that would enable other researchers to reconstruct the processes by which the researcher came to any findings. In particular it should provide information upon the conceptual development of the research so that the theoretical inferences made by the researcher are justified and thereby open up those processes to critical scrutiny and assessment.

4 Objectivity is replaced by *confirmability*: researcher self-criticism and the demonstration that the researcher's analysis is 'grounded in the data' (ibid.: 323). This too is largely established by the provision of an audit trail where the researcher provides a self-critical account of key research processes and the methodological decisions they have made.

In contrast to Lincoln and Guba's approach, Morse (1994) focuses more specifi-cally upon the inductive analysis of qualitative data in establishing not so much evalu-ation criteria *per se* but conventions, or guidelines, which make explicit the processes of theory construction and which researchers ought to follow. In this respect she adds to and complements key aspects of Lincoln and Guba's approach.

1 Morse begins with what she calls *comprehending* and learning about a setting prior to any fieldwork. Here she argues that it is important for researchers to be familiar with any relevant literature but they simultaneously need to distance themselves from it to avoid the contamination of the setting by any precon-ceptions deriving from that literature. Thus, her stance is similar to that of Blumer (1954), which we discussed in Chapter 7, where sensitizing concepts are derived from the literature in order to give directions in which to look, rather than theoretical preconceptions.

2 This first stage is followed by *synthesizing* where the researcher sifts the data collected during their fieldwork to identify different themes and concepts in order to construct patterns in the data and produce categories and initial explanations.

3 This is closely related to the next stage that involves *theorizing* to produce explanations that fit the data in the most coherent and parsimonious manner. Here data are confronted with various possible theoretical schemes which pro-vide alternative explanations. The sources of these theoretical schemes entail both the use of those deriving from other settings and the use of induction to construct theory from the data collected in the setting. The causal linkages sug-gested by different theoretical schemes are tested upon different informants to enable corroboration of the explanation that best fits the data.

4 The final stage involves *recontextualizing* – the development of the emerging theory so that it is applicable to new settings. This involves abstracting the emerging theory to new settings and populations as well as by relating it to established knowledge to assess its contribution.

Throughout, a significant issue for Morse is that the qualitative researcher must provide an account of how the inductive analysis of the organizational settings under investigation was accomplished by demonstrating how concepts were derived and applied as well as showing how and why alternative theoretical explanations have been considered but rejected (see also Adler and Adler, 1994; Miles and Huberman, 1994; Locke, 1996). Morse's approach therefore further reinforces the importance of the audit trail in the evaluation of qualitative research.

As Seale (1999a: 45) notes, auditing 'is an exercise in reflexivity, which provides a self-sustaining critical account of how the research was done, and can also involve the use of triangulation exercises'. Here Seale is referring to a particular form of triangulation rather unlike those referred to earlier in this chapter. It entails the contingent use of multiple researchers and/or multiple data sources, sometimes accessed by using different qualitative methods, to cross reference and compare data pertaining to the same phenomenon to substantiate the objectivity of findings by demonstrating their convergence and consistency of meaning (see Leininger, 1994; Miles and Huberman, 1994; Lowe et al., 2000).

For other commentators, usually with reference primarily to ethnographic research (see Chapter 7), an important aspect of the audit trail's reflexivity is the researcher's critical scrutinization of the impact of their field roles upon the research setting and findings, so as to reduce and evaluate sources of contamination and disturbance, thereby enhancing naturalism or ecological validity whilst demonstrating how the researcher has avoided 'over rapport' with those members and 'going native' (see Brunswick, 1956; Bracht and Glass, 1968; Cicourel, 1982; Pollner and Emerson, 1983; Hammersley, 1989, 1990, 1992). Here the ethnographer has to maintain a balance, and demonstrate this balance in the audit trail, that involves trying

> to be both insider and outsider, staying on the margins of the group both socially and intellectually ... For this reason it is sometimes emphasised that, besides seeking to 'understand', the ethnographer must also try to see settings as 'anthropologically strange', as they would be seen from another society, adopting what we might call the Martian perspective. (Hammersley, 1990: 16)

Hence, a further key aspect of the audit trail is for the researcher to demonstrate how they have also maintained 'social and intellectual distance' and preserved 'analytical space' for themselves (Hammersley and Atkinson, 1995: 115) whilst simultaneously gaining access to what is going on. So, as Seale notes (1999a: 161), through revealing aspects of themselves and the research process, again as a crucial aspect of a traceable audit trail, these concerns stress how researchers must demonstrate their 'hard won objectivity' thereby establishing the credibility, dependability and confirmability of findings: key aspects of Lincoln and Guba's trustworthiness criterion (1985) illustrated previously.

In sum, neo-empiricist evaluation criteria express an interpretive stance that has an interest in building theories out of accessing organizational actor's subjective, cultural, meanings in order to explain their actions in varying organizational contexts that maintains a commitment to objectivity and neutrality albeit with particular nuances. Their dispute with mainstream positivists who reject *verstehen* in favour of *erklaren* is therefore more about *what* is important in understanding human behaviour, what is *directly* observable in a neutral fashion, and how this may be accomplished. In other words, it is the source of this data that is different from mainstream positivism (see also Knights, 1992; Van Maanen, 1995a, b) in that they argue that they can neutrally access actors' subjective understandings by using particular methodologies. Hence, they share mainstream positivism's ontological idea that there is a world out there that awaits discovery and epistemological exploration in an objective manner by collecting data – the ostensibly 'positively' given. Nevertheless, as we have tried to explain, the above differences have often led to the articulation of alternative evaluation criteria to those usually deployed to assess the outputs of mainstream positivism.

However, within neo-empiricism there lurks a tension between their objectivist epistemological impulse that emphasizes how inductive descriptions of cultures should correspond with members' intersubjectivity and an interpretive impulse that suggests that people socially construct the versions of reality that drive their meaningful behaviour – culturally derived processes which somehow do not extend to the neo-empiricist's own research processes (see Hammersley, 1992). It is this epistemological assumption that is questioned by social constructionists through their claim that interpretation applies to both researchers and the researched. As Van Maanen (1995b: 74) argues, social constructionism dismisses the possibility of a neutral observational language because such a possibility can only be sustained through the (illegitimate) deployment of a rhetoric of objectivity that privileges the subjective consciousness of the researcher over that of the researched.

Social constructionist evaluation criteria

As we demonstrated in Chapter 8, the argument here is that when we engage with phenomena we inevitably interpret them using different cultural and linguistic tools that carry social bias emanating from our own cultural backgrounds. These ways of engaging influence everyone's perception of what we often take to be 'out there': including the researcher, no matter how well they may have been methodologically trained. The idea here is that we are not, and cannot be, passive receivers of sensory data no matter what methodology we might use to enable this in developing our theories. Hence, the positivist ideal of a neutral detached observer is a myth – and probably a dangerous one because it allows people to claim objectivity when none exists. Rather, according to this subjectivist epistemological challenge to positivism, we inevitably apply various inferences and assumptions which:

1 either mediate and shape what we see like a set of filters, or lens, which lead us to interpret the external social world in particular ways (a stance typical of critical theory): the social world might be 'out there' but we can never know it as we are stuck in socially constructed versions of reality;

2 or, we create what we see, in and through the very act of perception itself (a stance typical of a type of postmodernism often called 'affirmative' postmodernism): what we take to be the social world 'out there', is a projection of the discourses that are socially produced and reproduced in and through everyday social interaction.

Hence, the questioning of the researcher's ability to be a neutral conduit and presenter of actors' intersubjectivity creates a point of departure of two competing social constructionist approaches to qualitative management research that themselves have some degree of departure over ontological issues. These philosophical disputes have important implications for processes of research evaluation and the criteria that may be deployed. As examples of this variation within social constructionism, we shall now consider criteriological issues in critical theory and postmodernism.

Critical theory

In some cases, methodologists whose early criteriological work may be classified as neo-empiricist seem to articulate key social constructionist philosophical assumptions. For instance, in their original work, at one point Lincoln and Guba reject what they term 'naive realism' (1985: 293) in favour of 'multiple constructed realities' (ibid.: 295). However, such an enisteuological and ontological shift, as Seale (1999a) points out, seems at odds with their proposed evaluation criteria that try to judge the 'trustworthiness' of research because the social constructionist impulse is not simultaneously applied to research processes and outputs by being limited to the interpretive processes occurring in the people being investigated. Likewise Hammersley also argues for 'subtle realism' which ...

> ... retains from naive realism the idea that the researcher investigates independent, knowable phenomena. But it breaks with it in denying that we have direct access to those phenomena, in accepting that we must always rely on cultural assumptions ... Obversely, subtle realism shares with relativism a recognition that all knowledge is based upon assumptions and purposes and is a human construction, but rejects ... abandonment of the regulative ideal of independent and knowable phenomena ... subtle realism is distinct ... in its rejection of the notion that knowledge must be defined as beliefs whose validity is known with certainty. (Hammersley, 1992: 52)

In talking about the implications of this philosophical position, Hammersley, like Lincoln and Guba in their early work (1985), seems to underestimate the epistemological implications of his argument for evaluating research. Indeed, these writers fail to systematically translate this apparent philosophical shift towards social constructionism into a congruent set of evaluation criteria: the criteria they proposed still rely upon privileging the consciousness of the researcher relative to the researched.

In response to similar criticisms of their early work (1985), Guba and Lincoln (1989, 1994) seem to replace their earlier neo-empiricist evaluation criteria with ones that they claim overlap those of critical theory's social constructionism. In commenting upon the reasons for this development Guba and Lincoln (1994: 114) argue that their previous work represented 'an early effort to resolve the quality issue for constructivism; although these criteria have been well received, their parallelism to positivist criteria makes them suspect'. Elsewhere the critical theory origins of this epistemological shift are made more explicit by the expression of a commitment to the 'belief that a politics of liberation must always begin with the perspectives, desires, and dreams of those individuals who have been oppressed by the larger ideological, economic and political forces of a society, or a historical moment' (Lincoln and Denzin, 1994: 575). This stance is articulated alongside an appeal to what amounts to a consensus view of truth and is expressed through new criteria of different types of 'authenticity' wherein a key issue is that research findings should represent an agreement about what is considered to be true.

Hence, they argue that in order to demonstrate authenticity (1994: 114) researchers must show how in any social setting:

1 different members' realities have been included and represented in any account (fairness);
2 they have helped those members to develop a range of understandings of the phenomenon being investigated thereby enlarging their personal constructions (ontological authenticity);

3 they have helped those members appreciate and understand the constructions of others (educative authenticity);

4 they have helped to stimulate action on the part of those members to change their situation based upon their new understandings (catalytic authenticity);

5 they have helped members to undertake those actions to change their circumstances through their research empowering them (tactical authenticity).

Thus, as Guba and Lincoln seem to admit, their social constructionist criteriology has a parallel with the development of critical theory, inspired by the Frankfurt School, in management research. As we illustrated in Chapter 8, critical theory has grown out of an overt rejection of positivist philosophical assumptions and by implication a critique of management prerogative, to articulate a consensus theory of truth intimately linked to highly participatory approaches to management research where the aim is the empowerment and emancipation of the disenfranchized through facilitating their development of a critical consciousness to transform organizational relationships and practices. Here an array of different critical theorists have attempted to specify evaluation criteria that may be seen as further elaborating those put forward by Guba and Lincoln above.

In outlining these criteria it is firstly useful to note the problem posed for critical theorists by their philosophical stance. Here Kincheloe and McLaren pose the problem ...

How do you determine the validity of information if you reject the notion of methodological correctness and your purpose is to free men and women from sources of oppression and domination? Where traditional verifiability rests on a rational proof built upon literal intended meaning, a critical qualitative perspective always involves a less certain approach characterized by participant reaction and emotional involvement ... Trustworthiness, many have argued, is a more appropriate word to use in the context of critical research. It is helpful because it signifies a different set of assumptions about research purposes than does validity. (1998: 287)

In developing the notion of what they seem to call *'critical trustworthiness'* (ibid.: 288) which is significantly different from Lincoln and Guba's original formulation of 'trustworthiness' (1985) and is much closer to their later specification of 'authenticity' (1989, 1994), Kincheloe and McLaren outline several key criteria that may be used to assess the critical trustworthiness of research inspired by critical theory and some associated forms of postmodernism. These centre on five interrelated issues:

1 Because there is no such thing as a neutral observational language, and thus all knowledge is a product of particular values and interests, researchers must 'enter into an investigation with their assumptions on the table so no one is confused concerning the epistemological and political baggage they bring with them' (Kincheloe and McLaren, 1998: 265). So, for instance, critical theorists need to be self-consciously critical of the philosophical assumptions they are making, reflexively interrogate those assumptions and present and justify those assumptions to others in their dissemination of any findings: to do otherwise is an abdication of intellectual responsibility (see also Johnson and Duberley, 2003).

2 Through 'critical interpretation' (Denzin, 1998: 332) and what amounts to a structural phenomenology (Forrester, 1993) or 'critical ethnography' (Thomas,

1993; Morrow and Brown, 1994), researchers attempt to sensitize themselves and participants to how hegemonic regimes of truth impact upon the subjectivities of the disadvantaged (Marcus and Fisher, 1986; Putnam et al., 1993). Thus, for Kincheloe and McLaren researchers must 'struggle to expose the way ideology constrains the desire for self-direction, and ... confront the way power reproduces itself in the construction of human consciousness' (1998: 288) in doing so they 'undermine what appears natural, and open to question what appears obvious' (ibid.: 293).

3 Here positivist conceptions of validity are overtly rejected and replaced by democratic research designs to generate conditions that approximate Habermas's ideal speech situation (e.g. Broadbent and Laughlin, 1997) and are dialogical (Schwandt, 1996: 66–7). Here what is important is what is termed the 'credibility' of the constructed realities to those who have participated in their development. However this, and consequently the critical trustworthiness of research, can be difficult to establish. As Kincheloe and McLaren observe, 'critical researchers award credibility only when the constructions are plausible to those who constructed them, and even then there may be disagreement, for the researcher may see effects of oppression in the constructs of those researched – effects that those researched may not see' (ibid.: 288).

4 Fourth, positivist concerns with generalizability are rejected in favour of what Kincheloe and McLaren (ibid.: 288) call 'anticipatory accommodation' where 'through their knowledge of a variety of comparable contexts, researchers begin to learn their similarities and differences – they learn from their comparisons of different contexts'.

5 Fifth is what Kincheloe and McLaren (ibid.: 289) call 'catalytic validity'. This is the extent to which 'research moves those it studies so that they understand the world and the way it is shaped in order to transform it'. Hence, catalytic validity refers to the way in which research processes enable the researched to understand themselves and their experiences in new ways and based upon that new understanding, challenge previously taken-for-granted discourse and practices (see also Freire, 1972a, b; Schwandt, 1996: 67).

In sum, it is evident that the evaluation criteria deriving from Kincheloe and McLaren's and supported by an array of critical theorists, closely parallel Guba and Lincoln's (1989, 1994) own increasing emphasis on authenticity. Here a social constructionist stance redirects management research into a more processual form that emphasizes researchers' encouragement in the researched of reflexive and dialogical interrogation of their own understandings to produce new democratically grounded self-understandings to challenge that which was previously taken to be unchallengeable thereby reclaiming the possibility of transformative organizational change (see also Unger, 1987; Beck, 1992; Alvesson, 1996; Gaventa and Cornwall, 2006; Park, 2006).

In their work, Kincheloe and McLaren claim that their evaluation criteria are equally suitable to both critical theory and postmodernism. However, as they explain in some detail, the type of postmodernism they refer to is commensurable with critical theory because it shares a realist ontology where discourse are played out and 'politicized by being situated in real social and historical conditions' (ibid.: 272). This 'resistant' (ibid.) form of postmodernism shares with critical theory a concern with an 'interventionist and transformative critique of Western culture' (ibid.). Thus, it is quite different from what might be termed labelled 'hard', 'affirmative' or 'reactionary' postmodernism (Rosenau, 1992; Tsoukas, 1992; Alvesson and Deetz, 1996, 2000; Kilduff and Mehra, 1997) which we described in Chapter 8.

According to Alvesson and Deetz (1996, 2000) both critical theory and resistant postmodernism, through critique and reflexivity, seek to denaturalize and challenge repressive discursive practices whilst avoiding relativism through using democracy as an epistemic standard. However, this is not the case with 'hard', 'affirmative' or 'reactionary' postmodernism where a subjectivist ontology comes to the fore and a demarcation with critical theory becomes clearer (see Alvesson and Deetz, 1996: 210). It is to this form of postmodernism and the possibility of its evaluation we now turn.

Affirmative postmodernism

As we have indicated, affirmative postmodernists think that discourses actively create and naturalize, rather than discover, the objects (i.e. simulacra) which seem to populate our (hyper) realities (Baudrillard, 1983). The result is that knowledge, truth and reality become construed as discursive productions potentially always open to revision but which are often stabilized through scientists', and other actors', 'performative' ability that persuades others to accept those renditions, as objective, as truthful, as normal, as therefore unchallengeable (Lyotard, 1984) and thereby accomplish what is called discursive closure. However, given this subjectivist ontological and epistemological stance, the affirmative postmodernist must accept that there are no good reasons for preferring one intersubjectively accomplished discursive representation over any other – including those that have been ostensibly democratically formulated. However, alternative discursive productions to those that have been stabilized are always possible and may always be immanent in any situation. Indeed, encouraging those silent but immanent potential 'voices' without specifying them, in order avoid discursive closure, wherein lies what amounts to evaluation criteria particular to affirmative postmodernism.

For some affirmative postmodernists (e.g. Smith, 1990; Mulkay, 1991; Smith and Deemer, 2000), a commitment to avoiding discursive closure means that the development of specific evaluative criteria should not be pursued since such criteria can only be rhetorical devices which operate to performatively hide the precarious subjectivity of both the researcher and the evaluator. Hence, any evaluation criteria are themselves merely discursively constituted regimes of power that produce truth-effects and must therefore be subverted by ending criteriological debate. Nevertheless, there is some irony here for there seems to be a largely tacit evaluative agenda embedded within affirmative postmodernists' own stance that promotes research practices aimed at understanding the ways in which discourses are sustained and undermined, in order to encourage discursive plurality and indeterminacy, rather than making claims about a reality independent of human cognition (see, for example, Edwards et al., 1995). These evaluative issues seem to be concerned with how this form of research unsettles those dominant discourses that have become more privileged than others by helping people to think about their own and others' thinking so as to question the familiar and taken-for-granted and thereby encouraging resistance and space for alternative discourses without advocating any preference which might impose discursive closure (see, for example, Gergen and Thatchenkerry, 1996; Barry, 1997; Barry and Elmes, 1997; Ford, 1999; Boje, 2001; Treleaven, 2001; Currie and Brown, 2003). In other words, these criteria may well be about how to establish, maintain and encourage relativism through methodologically avoiding the perceived anathema of discursive closure.

If a key aim of affirmative postmodernists is to open up any attempted discursive closure to a multiplicity of divergent possibilities that are thought to be always potentially present (see Baudrillard, 1983, 1993; Jeffcutt, 1994; Chia, 1995) by subverting established discourses, affirmative postmodernists must consistently deny that any linguistic construction, including their own (see Clifford and Marcus, 1986), produced in any social setting, can be ever settled or stable. Any discourse can be reflexively questioned as layers of meaning are removed to reveal those meanings which have been suppressed, sublimated or forgotten (Chia, 1995) in the act of speaking or writing. Therefore, a key task is to display and unsettle the discursive 'rules of the game' through deconstruction: the dismantling of such texts so as to reveal their internal contradictions, assumptions and different layers of meaning, which are hidden from the naive reader/listener and unrecognized by the author/speaker as they strive to maintain unity and consistency (see also Cooper, 1990; Martin, 1990; Kilduff, 1993; Linstead, 1993a; Czarniawaska-Joerges, 1996; Boje, 2001). However, at most, such deconstruction can only invoke alternative discursive social constructions of reality which are themselves amenable to further interrogation so as to expose their underlying narrative logic – and so on. In other words, any deconstruction is itself a discursive product that can be deconstructed – and presumably should be in order to promote plurality and instability and to simultaneously avoid the dangers of discursive closure.

One key means of destabilizing their own narratives used by some postmodernists is to avoid the dominant conventions of writing academic texts by purposefully promoting an awareness of the author(s) behind the text thereby undermining what they see as the asymmetrical authority relations between author and reader promoted by conventional forms of writing which create a illusion of objectivity on the part of the author. According to Putnam (1996: 386) the aim here is to encourage multiple readings 'to decentre authors as authority figures; and to involve participants, readers and audiences in the production of research'. For Ashmore (1989; Ashmore et al., 1995) these decentring processes involve hyper-reflexivity: the deconstruction of deconstructions and the development of new literary forms which repudiate any claim to textual and authorial authority. Here the conventional mode of writing, exemplified by the authoritative monologue of the single official writer, is abandoned. Instead a number of different voices appear, disappear and reappear in the text, interrupting and disrupting each other by debating each other in a potentially endless series of introspective iterations which purposefully surface various discursive possibilities in any social context. Alternatively researchers may articulate key aspects of themselves in the texts to display how they have personally influenced the presentation of their work by demonstrating 'their historical and geographical situatedness, their personal investments in the research, various biases they bring' (Gergen and Gergen, 2000: 1027). In this manner the author's authority is undermined and how the account they present is merely just one amongst many different possibilities is illustrated to avoid discursive closure. Indeed, the resultant unsettling, or paralogy (see Lyotard, 1984), is pivotal since it avoids the authorial privileging upon which any discursive closure depends (Ashmore et al., 1995) and encourages the proliferation of discursive practices which postmodernists call heteroglossia (see Gergen, 1992). Therefore, a further key evaluation criterion for this type of research relates to how the author is decentred, through hyper-reflexivity, to avoid any authorial privileging which would result in discursive closure.

Conclusions

At the beginning of this chapter we used several widely used evaluation criteria to identify the varying strengths and weaknesses of the different methods
we have reviewed in this book. We used this to illustrate how the making of
methodological choices involves a consideration of the inevitable trade-offs
that occur when issues such as internal validity, measurement validity, ecological validity, population validity and reliability are considered. As we have
seen, such trade-offs occur because of the various strengths and weaknesses
the different approaches have built into them. While we were trying to make
a serious point it was also slightly mischievous since the evaluation criteria
deployed, save perhaps for ecological validity (and even that might be suspect),
are legitimated by an underlying positivist epistemology. Hopefully it should
be evident now that the use of such criteria may be appropriate when it comes
to hypothetico-deductive research but it would be completely inappropriate
to extend their usage, say to neo-empiricism, or affirmative postmodernist
research, or action research that is inspired by critical theory and so on. These
alternatives to the positivist mainstream philosophically vary and thus have
different modes of evaluation which are appropriate. These different modes
of evaluation are primarily relevant to qualitative management research which
does not possess the relative philosophical homogeneity evident in quantitative
management research where a tacit consensus has enabled the development of
explicit evaluative criteria and has largely limited any controversy to debates
about how to most effectively meet those benchmarks (Schwandt, 1996;
Scheurich, 1997): a veritable discursive closure! Nevertheless, different evaluation criteria need to be used within different epistemological approaches and
it is crucial that management researchers develop the skills to be able to assess
the quality of management research using the appropriate criteria in a self-
conscious manner. Unfortunately this 'contingent' approach to research evaluation, based upon the idea that 'it all depends', is not always used in practice
and we must be alert to the dangers of criteriological misappropriation which
are often present. So whilst the different approaches to management research
that we have illustrated in this book all have something to offer, the point is
that what that 'something' is, and how it is valued and evaluated, varies considerably according to the underlying philosophical dispositions that lead us
to engage with our areas of interest in different ways.

Methodological differences and controversies continue to pervade management research – issues that tacitly influence how management research is
variably constituted and evaluated by its own practitioners. As Kuhn (1970)
noted, scientists will often first learn their trade by examining and copying how
exemplars of their discipline went about research. Here Kuhn was referring to
the security afforded by the protocols and 'puzzle-solving' of 'normal science'
practice within a well established paradigm where philosophical questions were
not open to dispute by practitioners. Instead they were largely accepted without question. However such consensus about how to do management research
is not so evident, for as with the rest of social sciences, it remains a philosophically contested terrain. Therefore who to turn to for guidance and inspi-
ration always is a somewhat problematic issue, for the direction provided by

established scholars will send any aspirant researcher upon different trajectories which articulate different sets of philosophical assumptions.

Therefore, in this book we have included an array of exemplars of different management research approaches. Although we have largely concentrated upon mainstream positivist methodologies, we have tried to use this as an heuristic foil to illustrate how, in recent years, an increasing diversity has become evident amongst management researchers which, in different ways, has challenged the established positivistic mainstream. Nevertheless, positivism remains pivotal to many researchers especially since its philosophical stance supports the possibility of managerial prerogative and moral authority through presenting a persuasive claim to expertise grounded in objective knowledge. Of course it is precisely this claim that is undermined by the development of various social constructionist stances, such as postmodernism and critical theory, since the possibility of neutral apprehension of reality is dismissed as naive and quixotic (see Thomas, 1997; Fournier and Grey, 2000; Grey and Willmott, 2002). From the philosophical stances of these alternatives to positivism, notions of truth and objectivity are dismissed as being outcomes of prestigious discursive practices which mask an inevitable partiality that must always operate. The result is not only the evolution of different methodologies and criteriologies but also the constitution of different research questions about the management terrain.

Despite the above developments, the role of philosophy in constituting how we do things and how we ask questions often remains unnoticed especially from the orientation of those who occupy the positivist mainstream. Philosophical introspection does not usually sit easily with the technical imperative that tends to dominate positivist research to improve the efficiency and effectiveness of management (see Grey and Mitev, 1995). However philosophical assumptions are always present in, and articulated by, any mode of engagement. Adopting a philosophical stance, no matter how tacitly, is always unavoidable: some philosophical position always guides what we do in research yet it is always contestable. So in understanding management research methodologies the issue is not about whether or not our research should be philosophically informed, it is about how well we reflexively interrogate our inevitable philosophical choices and are able to defend them in relation to their ever-present alternatives. This applies as much to positivists as it does to neo-empiricists, critical theorists, postmodernists and so on: – so dear reader – read carefully!

Further reading

Bochner (2000) lays out some of the problems inherent in criteriology. In doing so he argues that the philosophical diversity evident in the social sciences suggests a need for caution since there may be a tendency to universally apply evaluation criteria constituted by particular philosophical conventions. In contrast, Scandura and Williams (2000) provide an interesting review of research in three top-tier American business and management journals and examine changing practices in the triangulation of methods and how different forms of validity have been addressed. Their research suggests that business and management research may be 'moving even further away from rigour' (2000: 1259) by failing to methodologically triangulate findings – something which has resulted in a decrease in the internal, external and construct validity of studies. Whilst the evaluation criteria they propose are appropriate to positivist hypothetico-deductive research, they could be inadvertently applied in a universalistic manner and thereby would be open to the charge of being philosophically parochial. Lecompte and Goetz (1982) provide a good example of the idea that qualitative research is not philosophically distinct from quantitative research and apply relatively unreconstructed positivist evaluation criteria to ethnographic research whilst identifying some methodological strategies qualitative researchers could use to ameliorate possible weaknesses. In contrast, Seale (1999b) considers how philosophical differences are significant and therefore he traces the evolution and proliferation of various alternative sets of evaluation criteria with regard to different forms of qualitative research and their underlying philosophical commitments. However Seale is not content to just review others' work, therefore he develops his own ideas around criteriology to present a form of triangulation as a pragmatic device to ensure quality in qualitative research which seems to articulate a form of methodological pluralism. The theme that qualitative research is philosophically different to quantitative research is also evident in the work of Guba and Lincoln (1989, 1994) where they interrogate the philosophical underpinnings of both quantitative and qualitative approaches to undertaking research and propose that different evaluation criteria must be deployed depending on the paradigmatic location of the researcher whose research is being evaluated. This philosophical shift away from neo-empiricist assumptions is also provided by Kichenloe and McLarens' (1998) consideration of evaluation criteria appropriate to critical theory. Within this mode of engagement they argue that critical trustworthiness is a more appropriate concept to use to evaluate research since it signifies very different philosophical assumptions about the research process in comparison to positivist approaches. They proceed to identify how trustworthiness may be assessed and produce three key criteria which fit the critical theory's emancipatory agenda: the credibility of the portrayals of constructed realities; anticipatory accommodation; and catalytic validity. This can be compared with Schwandt's (1996) attempt to redefine social inquiry as a practical philosophy, with a post-foundationalist epistemology that derives also from critical theory. This project entails dialogue, critique and democracy, without recourse to criteriology as it abandons 'any indisputable criteria for distinguishing legitimate from not so legitimate scientific knowledge' (ibid.: 70). Although not specifically concerned with criteriology *per se*, Mabry (2002) is concerned with the possibilities and problems of evaluation from what she considers to be two different postmodern stances – a rupture primarily due to the different ontologies she sees to be at play.

These journal articles are freely available on the companion website (www.sagepub.co.uk/gillandjohnson):

Schwandt, T.A. (1996) Farewell to criteriology, *Qualitative Inquiry*, 2(1): 58–72.

Seale, C. (1999) Quality in qualitative research, *Qualitative Inquiry*, 5(4): 465–78.

Glossary

action learning A form of management development which, in essence, involves 'learning to learn-by-doing with and from others who are also learning-to-learn by doing' (Revans, 1980: 288). The process is inductive rather than deductive as managers are asked to solve actual organizational problems. It crucially depends upon the 'set' or group as a vehicle for learning by its members with a 'set adviser' to facilitate progress. Its variants in situations throughout the world are described by Revans (1980).

analysis The processes by which a phenomenon (e.g. a managerial problem) is conceptualized so that it is separated into its component parts and the interrelationships between those parts, and their contribution to the whole, elucidated.

analytic induction A research methodology concerned with the inductive development and testing of theory.

a priori Prior to, and independent of, experience or observation.

cognition The act or process of knowing.

concepts Abstractions which allow us to order our impressions of the world by enabling us to identify similarities and differences in phenomena and thereby classify them.

consensus theory of truth The notion that the veracity of an account or theory is determinable only through agreement between the researcher and his or her professional peers, or between the researcher and the subjects of his or her research.

control group A group of subjects in an experiment who do not experience the action of the independent variable or experimental treatment.

conventionalism Another term to describe the consensus theory of truth.

correspondence theory of truth A notion that the truthfulness of an account or a theory is determinable by direct comparison with the facts of an external and accessible reality. If they fail to correspond the theory or account must be rejected.

deduction The deduction of particular instances from general inferences. It entails the development of a conceptual and theoretical structure which is then tested by observation.

dependent variable The phenomenon whose variation the researcher is trying to explain or understand.

emic A form of explanation of a situation or events that relies upon elucidation of actors' internal logics or subjectivity.

empiricism The idea that valid knowledge is directly derived from sense-data and experience.

epistemology The branch of philosophy concerned with the study of the criteria by which we determine what does and does not constitute warranted or valid knowledge.

etic A form of analysis which relies upon explanations that impose an external logic or frame of reference upon subjects so as to explain their behaviour.

experimental group A group of subjects in an experiment who experience the action of the independent variable or experimental treatment.

extraneous variable A phenomenon whose variation might cause some variation in the dependent variable and thus provide rival explanations of any observed variability in the dependent variable to that suggested by the independent variable.

grounded theory The outcome of inductive research, that is, theory created or discovered through the observation of particular cases.

hermeneutic circle The notion that no observation or description is free from the observer's interpretation based upon his or her presuppositions and projection of his or her values, theories, etc., on to phenomena.

hypothesis A tentative proposal that explains and predicts the variation in a particular phenomenon.

ideographic An approach to social science that emphasizes that explanation of human behaviour is possible only through gaining access to actors' subjectivity or culture.

independent variable A phenomenon whose variation notionally explains or causes changes in the dependent variable.

indexicality The problem that people vary their behaviour according to their interpretation of the situation in which they find themselves.

induction General inferences induced from particular instances, or the development of theory from the observation of empirical reality.

methodology The study of the methods or procedures used in a discipline so as to gain warranted knowledge.

multivariate analysis A generic term for the use of various statistical procedures to indicate the amount of variance in the dependent variable which can be attributed to the action of each independent and extraneous variable.

naturalism This term can have two opposing meanings:

1 That the methodologies of the natural and physical sciences (e.g. physics) provide a blueprint that should be followed by the social sciences.
2 The necessity to investigate human action in its natural or everyday setting and that the researcher must avoid disturbing that setting.

nomothetic Approaches to social science that seek to construct a deductively tested set of general theories that explain and predict human behaviour.

objectivism *See* realism.

ontology The study of the essence of phenomena and the nature of their existence.

operationalization The creation of rules which indicate when an instance of a concept has empirically occurred.

paradigm Usually taken to mean a way of looking at some phenomenon. A perspective from which distinctive conceptualizations and explanations of phenomena are proposed.

phenomenology A study of how things appear to people – how people experience the world.

positivism Often classified as an approach that emphasizes the use of the methods presumed to be used in the natural sciences in the social sciences: the philsophical view that the social sciences should copy the natural sciences methodologically is often also called methodological monism. However, this type of definition of positivism rather misses the key characteristic of positivism – that positivists assume that it is possible to neutrally apprehend reality provided that the appropriate methods are used. In other words, positivism is best associated with the idea that scientists must only deal with the positively given – data that can be neutrally accessed through the deployment of a neutral observational language. It is precisely this assumption that is contested by those (for example, critical theorists, etc.) who wish to distance themselves from positivism, but it is an assumption often accepted by some of those who also use qualitative methods (i.e. qualitative positivists) and thereby have also rejected methodological monism.

practical adequacy Criterion that determines the truthfulness of knowledge through consideration of the extent to which such knowledge generates explanations regarding the results of human action that are actually realized. In other words, the extent to which knowledge is practically useful.

random sample A sample in which all members of the specific populations from which the sample is drawn have an equal chance of selection.

realism May be divided into ontological/ metaphysical realism and epistemological realism. Ontological/metaphysical realism considers that reality exists independently of the cognitive structures of observers, while epistemological realism considers that reality to be cognitively accessible to observers. Much of realism entails both views and where it does it is often called 'objectivism', i.e. there is a real social and natural world existing independently of our cognitions which we can neutrally apprehend through observation. However, other realists would claim that while reality does exist independently of our efforts to understand it, it is not cognitively accessible in a neutral manner. In other words, they accept metaphysical realism but combine it with a subjectivist view of epistemology which denies the possibility of a theory-neutral observational language.

reflexivity The monitoring by an ethnographer of his or her impact upon the social situation under investigation. This may be called situational reflexivity and can be contrasted with epistemological reflexivity where the observer attempts hermeneutically to reflect upon and articulate the assumptions he or she deploys in apprehending and interpreting his or her own observations.

relativism The notion that how things appear to people, and individuals' judgement about truth, are relative to their particular paradigm or frame of reference.

reliability A criterion that refers to the consistency of the results obtained in research.

theory A formulation regarding the cause-and-effect relationships between two or more variables, which may or may not have been tested.

theory-dependent This term refers to the way in which human practical activities entail acting upon the imperatives deriving from theoretical conjectures about, and explanations of, phenomena.

theory-laden This term refers to the way in which the prior values, knowledge and theories of an observer influence what he or she sees during observation.

theory-neutral observation language The idea that it is possible to test precisely a theory through observation of empirical reality which is readily open to neutral inspection by the observer.

triangulation

1   The use of different research methods in the same study to collect data so as to check the validity of any findings.
2   The collection of different data upon the same phenomena, sometimes using different researchers so as to validate any findings.
3   Collecting data upon the same phenomenon at different times and places within the same study.

validity There are three types of validity:

1   Internal validity is the extent to which the conclusions regarding cause and effect are warranted.
2   Population validity is the extent to which conclusions might be generalized to other people.
3   Ecological validity is the extent to which conclusions might be generalized to social contexts other than those in which data have been collected.

verstehen A term used to refer to explanations of the actions of subjects by understanding the subjective dimensions of their behaviour.

References

Abel, T. (1958) The operation called verstehen, *American Journal of Sociology*, 54: 211–18.

Adair, J. G. (1984) The Hawthorne Effect: a reconsideration of the methodological artifact, *Journal of Applied Psychology*, 69: 334–45.

Adler, P. A. and Adler, P. (1987) *Membership Roles in Field Research*, Sage University Paper Series on Qualitative Research Methods, Vol. 6. Beverly Hills, CA: Sage.

Adler, P. A. and Adler, P. (1994) Observation techniques, in N. K. Denzin and Y. S. Guba (eds), *Handbook of Qualitative Research*. Thousand Oaks, CA: Sage.

Aguinis, H. (1993) Action research and scientific method: presumed discrepancies and actual similarities, *Journal of Applied Behavioural Science*, Special Issue, 29 (4): 416–31.

Ahlgren, A. and Walberg, H. J. (1979) Generalised regression analysis, in J. Bynner and K. M. Stribley (eds), *Social Research, Principles and Procedures*. London: Longman.

Alderfer, C. (1968) Organizational diagnosis from initial client reactions to a researcher, *Human Relations*, 27: 260–5.

Allen, T. D., Freeman, T. M., Russell, J. E. A., Reizenstein, R. C. and Rentz, J. D. (2001) Survivor reactions to organisational downsizing: does time ease the pain? *Journal of Organisational and Occupational Psychology*, 74 (2): 145–64.

Alvesson, M. (1996) *Communication, Power and Organization*. Berlin/New York: Walter de Gruyter.

Alvesson, M. and Deetz, S. (1996) Critical theory and postmodernism approaches to organization studies, in S. R. Clegg, C. Hardy, and W. R. Nord (eds), *Handbook of Organization Studies*. London: Sage.

Alvesson, M. and Deetz, S. (2000) *Doing Critical Management Research*. London: Sage.

Alvesson, M. and Skoldberg, K. (2000) *Reflexive Methodology: New Vistas for Qualitative Research*. London: Sage.

Alvesson, M. and Willimott, H. C. (1996) *Making Sense of Management: A Critical Introductiion*. London: Sage.

Alvesson, M. and Willmott, H. C. (1992) (eds) *Critical Management Studies*. London: Sage.

Arbib, M. A. and Hesse, M. B. (1986) *The Construction of Reality*. Cambridge: Cambridge University Press.

Argyle, M. (1969) *Social Interaction*. London: Methuen.

Argyris, C. (1993) *Knowledge for Action*. San Francisco, CA: Jossey-Bass.

Argyris, C. and Schon, D. A. (1989) Participatory action research and action science compared, *American Behavioural Scientist*, 32 (5): 612–23.

Argyris, C. and Schon, D. (1991) Participatory action research and action science compared, in W. F. Whyte (ed.), *Participatory Action Research*. Newbury Park, CA: Sage.

Argyris, C., Putman, R. and Smith, D. M. (1985) *Action Science*. San Francisco, CA: Jossey-Bass.

Asch, S. E. (1951) Effect of group pressure upon the modification and distortion of judgements, in M. Guetzkow (ed.), *Groups, Leadership and Men*. Pittsburg, PA: Carnegie Press.

Ashmore, M. (1989) *The Reflexive Thesis: Wrighting the Sociology of Scientific Knowledge*. Chicago, IL: University of Chicago Press.

Ashmore, M., Myres, G. and Potter, J. (1995) Discourse, rhetoric and reflexivity: seven days in the library, in G. E. Markle, J. C. Petersen and J. Pinch (eds), *Handlook of Science and Technology Studies*. London: Sage.

Ashworth, A.E. (1968) The sociology of trench warfare 1914–18, *The British Journal of Sociology*, XIX (4): 407–23.

Atkinson, P. (1990) *The Ethnographic Imagination: Textual Constructions of Reality*. London: Routledge.

Ayer, A. J. (1971) *Language, Truth and Logic*. Harmondsworth: Penguin.

Baggaley, A.R. (1981) Multivariate analysis: an introduction for consumers of behavioral research, *Evaluation Review*, 5: 123–31.

Ball, K. and Wilson, D. C. (2000) Power, control and computer-based performance monitoring: repertoires, resistance and subjectivities, *Organization Studies*, 21 (3): 539–65.

Bansal, P. and Roth, K. (2000) Why companies go green: a model of ecological responsiveness, *Academy of Management Review*, 13 (4): 717–36.

Barnes, B. (1974) *Scientific Knowledge and Sociological Theory*. London: Routledge.

Barnes, B. (1977) *Interests and the Growth of Knowledge*. London: Routledge.

Barnes, J. A. (1979) *Who Should Know What?* Harmondsworth: Penguin.

Barry, D. (1997) Telling changes: from narrative family therapy to organizational change and development, *Journal of Organizational Change Management*, 10 (1): 30–46.

Barry, D. and Elmes, M. (1997) Strategy retold: toward a narrative view of strategic discourse, *Academy of Management Review*, 22 (2): 429–52.

Bartlett, J. E., Kotrlik, J. W. and Higgins, C. C. (2001) Organizational research: determining appropriate sample size in survey research, *Learning and Performance Journal*, 19 (1), Spring.

Baudrillard, J. (1983) *Simulations*. New York: Semiotext(e).

Baudrillard, J. (1993) *Baudrillard Live: Selected Interviews* (ed. M.Gane). London: Routledge.

Bauman, Z. (1995) *Life in Fragments: Essays in Postmodern Morality*. Oxford: Blackwell.

Bazeley, P. and Richards, L. (2000) *The Nvivo Qualitative Project Book*. London: Sage.

Bearden, W., Netermeyer, R. and Mobley, M. (1993) *Handbook on Marketing Scales*. London: Sage.

Bechhofer, F. (1974) Current approaches to empirical research: some central ideas, in J. Rex (ed.), *Approaches to Sociology*. London: Routledge.

Bechhofer, F., Elliott, B. and McCrone, D. (1984) Safety in numbers: on the use of multiple interviewers, *Sociology*, 18 (1): 97–100.

Beck, U. (1992) *The Risk Society: Towards a New Modernity*. Cambridge: Polity Press.

Beck, U. (1996) World risk society as cosmopolitan society? Ecological questions in a framework of manufactured uncertainties, *Theory, Culture and Society*, 13 (4): 1–32.

Becker, H. S. (1965) Review of P. E. Hammond's *Sociologists at Work*, *American Sociological Review*, 30: 602–3.

Becker, H. S. (1970) *Sociological Work*. Chicago, IL: Aldine.

Beer, M. and Walton, A. (1987) Organizational change and development, *Annual Review of Action Research Psychology*, 38: 339–67.

Behling, O. (1980) The case for the natural science model for research in organizational behaviour and organization theory, *Academy of Management Review*, 5 (4): 483–90.

Bell, J. (2005) *Doing Your Research Project: A Guide for First-time Researchers in Education and the Social Science*, 4th edn. Buckingham: Open University.

Berger, P. L. and Luckmann, T. (1967) *The Social Construction of Reality*. Harmondsworth: Penguin.

Berreman, G. D. (1962) Behind many masks: ethnography and impression management in a Himalayan village, *Monograph No. 4, Society for Applied Anthropology*. Ithaca, NY: Cornell University Press.

Block, P. (1987) *The Empowered Manager: Positive Political Skills at Work*. San Francisco, CA: Jossey-Bass.

Bloor, D. (1976) *Knowledge and Social Imagery*. London: Routledge.

Bloor, M. (1976) Bishop Berkeley and the adenotonsillectomy enigma: an explanation of variation in the social construction of medical disposals, *Sociology*, 10: 43–61.

Bloor, M. (1978) On the analysis of observational data: a discussion of the worth and uses of inductive techniques and respondent validation, *Sociology*, 12: 542–5.

Blumer, H. (1954) What is wrong with social theory, *American Sociological Review*, 19 (13): 3–10.

Blumer, H. (1967) *Symbolic Interactionism*. Englewood Cliffs, NJ: Prentice-Hall.

Bobko, P. (2001) *Correlation and Regression: Applications for Industrial Psychology and Management*. London: Sage.

Bochner, A. P. (2000) Criteria against ourselves, *Qualitative Inquiry*, 6 (2): 266–72.

Boje, D. M. (2001) *Narrative Methods for Organizational and Communication Research*. London: Sage.

Boyd, W. B. and Westfall, R. (1970) Interviewer bias once more revisited, *Journal of Marketing Research*, 7: 249–53.

Bracht, G. H. and Glass, G. U. (1968) The external validity of experiments, *American Education Research Journal*, 5 (5): 537–74.

Braithwaite, J. (1985) Corporate crime research: why two interviewers are needed, *Sociology*, 19 (1): 136–8.

Braverman, H. (1974) *Labor and Monopoly Capital: the Degradation of Work in the Twentieth Century*. New York: Monthly Review Press.

Brewer, D. (2000) *Ethnography*. Buckingham: Open University Press.

Brewer, D. (2004) Ethnography, in C. Casell and G. Symon (eds), *Essential Guide to Qualitative Methods in Organizational Research*. London: Sage.

Brewer, J. and Hunter, A. (1989) *Multimethod Research: A Synthesis of Styles*, Sage Library of Social Research, Vol. 175. Beverley Hills, CA: Sage.

Brewerton, P. and Millward, L. (2001) *Organizational Research Methods*. London: Sage.

Brief, A. P. and Dukerich, J. M. (1991) Theory in organizational behavior: can it be useful? *Research in Organizational Behavior*, 13: 327–52.

Broadbent, J. and Laughlin, R. (1997) Developing empirical research: an example informed by a Habermasian approach, *Accounting, Auditing and Accountability*, 10 (5): 622–48.

Brown, D. (1993) Social change through collective reflection with Asian non-governmental development organizations, *Human Relations*, 46 (2): 249–73.

Brown, R. (1965) *Social Psychology*. Glencoe, IL: Free Press.

Brown, R. B. (1997) You can't expect rationality from pregnant men: reflections on multi-disciplinarity in management research, *British Journal of Management*, 8 (1): 23–30.

Brunswick, E. C. (1956) *Perception and the Representative Design of Psychological Experiments*. Berkeley, CA: University of California Press.

Bryant, A. and Charmaz, K. (2006) *The Sage Handbook of Grounded Theory*. London: Sage

Bryman, A. (1989) *Research Methods and Organization Studies*. London: Routledge.

Bryman, A. and Bell, E. (2003) *Business Research Methods*, 2nd edn. Oxford: Oxford University Press.

Bryman, A. and Cramer, D. (2004) *Quantitative Data Analysis with SPSS 12 and 13: A Guide for Social Scientists*. London: Routledge.

Buchanan, D. A. and Bryman, A. (2007) Contextualizing methods choice in organizational research, *Organizational Research Methods*, 10 (3): 483–501.

Burnes, B. (2004) Kurt Lewin and the planned approach to change: a re-appraisal, *Journal of Management Studies*, 41 (6): 977–1002.

Burns, R. P. and Burns, R. (2008) *Business Research Methods and Statistics Using SPSS*. London: Sage.

Burr, V. (1995) *Introduction to Social Constructionism*. London: Routledge.

Burrell, G. (1997) *Pandemonium: Towards a Retro-organization Theory*. London: Sage.

Burrell, G. and Morgan, G. (1979) *Sociological Paradigms and Organizational Analysis*. London: Heinemann.

Bygrave, W. D. (1989) The entrepreneurship paradigm: a philosophical look at its research methodologies, *Entrepreneurship: Theory and Practice*, 14 (1): 7–26.

Bynner, J. and Stribley, K. M. (eds) (1978) *Social Research, Principles and Procedures*. London: Longman.

Calas, M. B. and Smircich, L. (1991) Voicing seduction to silence leadership, *Organization Studies*, 12 (4): 567–602.

Campbell, D. T. (1969) Reforms as experiments, in J. Bynner and K. M. Stribley (eds), *Social Research, Principle and Procedures*. London: Longman.

Campbell, D. T. and Fiske, D. W. (1959) Convergent and discriminant validation by the multitrait–multimethod matrix, *Psychological Bulletin*, 56: 81–5.

Campbell, D. T. and Ross, H. L. (1968) The Connecticut crackdown on speeding: time series data in quasi-experimental analysis, *Law and Society Review*, 3 (1): 33–53.

Campbell, D. T. and Stanley, J. C. (1963) *Experimental and Quasi-Experimental Designs for Research*. Chicago, IL: Rand McNally.

Cappelli, P., Bassi, L., Kahtz, H., Knoke, D., Osterman, P. and Useem, M. (1997) *Change at Work*. Oxford University Press: Oxford.

Capra, F. (1975) *The Tao of Physics*. London: Wildwood.

Carchedi, G. (1983) Class analysis and social forms, in G. Morgan (ed.), *Beyond Method*. London: Sage.

Cassell, C. and Fitter, M. (1992) Responding to a changing environment: an action research case study, in D. Hoskin and N. R. Anderson (eds), *Organizational Change and Innovation*. London: Routledge.

Cassell, C. and Johnson, P. (2006) Action research: explaining the diversity, *Human Relations*, 59 (6): 783–814.

Cassell, C. and Symon, G. (2004) *Essential Guide to Qualitative Methods in Organizational Research*. London: Sage.

Charmaz, K. (2006) *Constructing Grounded Theory*. London: Sage.

Checkland, P. (1981) *Systems Thinking, Systems Practice*. Chichester: Wiley.

Checkland, P. (1991) From framework through experience to learning: the essential nature of action research, in H. E. Nissen, H. K. Klein and R. Hirscheim (eds), *Information Systems Research: Contemporary Approaches and Emergent Traditions*. B. V. North-Holland: Elsevier Science Publishers.

Chia, R. (1995) From modern to postmodern organizational analysis, *Organization Studies*, 16 (4): 579–604.

Chia, R. (1996) 'Metaphors and metaphorization in organizational analysis: thinking beyond the thinkable', in D. Grant, and C. Oswick (eds), *Metaphor and Organizations*. London: Sage.

Chia, R. and Morgan, S. (1996) Educationing the philosopher manager, *Management Learning*, 27 (1): 37–64.

Chisholm, R. F. and Eden, M. (1993) Features of emerging action research, *Human Relations*, 46 (2): 275–98.

Chubin, D. E. and Restivo, S. (1983) The 'mooting' of social studies: research programmes and science policy, in K. D. Knorr-Cetina and M. Mulkay (eds), *Science Observed: Perspectives on the Social Study of Science*. London: Sage.

Cicourel, A. V. (1982) Interviews surveys and the problem of ecological validity, *The American Sociologist*, 17: 11–20.

Clifford, J. and Marcus, G. (1986) *Writing Culture: The Poetics and Politics of Ethnography*, Berkeley: University of California Press.

Cloke, K. and Goldsmith, J. (2002) *The End of Management and the Rise of Organizational Democracy*. San Francisco, CA: Jossey-Bass.

Clutterbuck, D. (1994) *The Power of Empowerment*. London: Kogan Page.

Cochran, W. G. (1977) *Sampling Techniques*, 3rd edn. New York: Wiley & Sons.

Coghlan, D. and Brannick, T. (2004) *Doing Action Research in Your Own Organization*, 2nd edn. London: Sage.

Comte, A. (1853) *The Positive Philosophy of Auguste Comte*. London: Chapman.

Cook, T. D. (1983) Quasi-experimentation: its ontology, epistemology and methodology, in G. Morgan (ed.), *Beyond Method*. London: Sage.

Cooper, H. M. (1989) *Integrating Research: A Guide for Literature Reviews*, 2nd edn. Applied Social Research Methods Series, Vol. 2. London: Sage.

Cooper, R. (1990) Organization/disorganization, in J. Hassard and D. Pym (eds), *The Theory and Philosophy of Organizations: Critical Issues and New Perspectives*. London: Routledge.

Cooper, R. and Burrell, G. (1988) Modernism, postmodernism and organisational analysis: an introduction, *Organization Studies*, 9: 91–112.

Cooperrider, D. L. and Srivastva, S. (1987) Appreciative inquiry in organizational life, in R. Woodman and W. Pasmore (eds), *Research in Organizational Change and Development*. Greenwich, CT: JAI.

Covin, J. B. and Slevin, D. P. (1988) The influence of organisation structure on the utility of an entrepreneurial top management style, *Journal of Management Studies*, 23 (3): 217–34.

Cressey, D. (1950) The criminal violation of financial trust, *American Sociological Review*, 15: 738–43.

Cresswell, J. W. (1994) *Research Design: Qualitative and Quantitative Approaches*. London: Sage.

Cresswell, J. W. (1998) *Qualitative Inquiry and Research Design: Choosing Among Five Traditions*. Thousand Oaks, CA: Sage.

Cronbach, L. J. and Meehl, P. E. (1978) Construct validity in psychological tests, in J. Bynner and K. M. Stribley (eds), *Social Research, Principles and Procedures*. London: Longman.

Cummings, T. G. and Worley, C. (1993) *Organization Development and Change*, 5th edn. West: New York.

Cunnison, S. (1966) *Wages and Work Allocation*. London: Tavistock.

Currall S. C., Hammer, T. H., Baggett, L. S. and Doniger, G. M. (1999) Combining qualitative and quantitative methodologies to study group processes, *Organizational Research Methods*, 2 (1): 5–36.

Currie, G. and Brown, A. D. (2003) A narratological approach to understanding processes of organizing in a UK hospital, *Human Relations*, 56 (5): 563–86.

Czarniawaska-Joerges, B. (1996) *Narrating the Organization: Dramas of Institutional Identity*. Chicago, IL: Chicago University Press.

Dalton, M. (1959) *Men Who Manage*. New York: Wiley.

Dalton, M. (1964) Preconceptions and methods in *Men who Manage*, in P. E. Hammond, *Sociologists, at work: Essays on the Craft of Social Research*. New York: Basic Books.

Darwin, J., Johnson, P. and McAuley, J. (2002) *Developing Strategies for Change*. London: Financial Times/Prentice Hall.

De Bono, F. (1971) *Lateral Thinking for Management*. London: McGraw-Hill.

Delbridge, R. (1998) *Life on the Line: The Workplace Experience of Lean Production and the 'Japanese' Model*. Oxford: Oxford University Press.

Denzin, N. K. (1970) *The Research Act: A Theoretical Introduction to Sociological Methods*. Chicago, IL: Aldine.

Denzin, N. K. (1971) *The Logic of Scientific Naturalistic Inquiry, Social Forces*, 50: 166–82.

Denzin, N. K. (1978) *Sociological Methods: A Sourcebook*. New York: McGraw-Hill.

Denzin, N. K. (1998) The art and politics of interpretation, in N. K. Denzin and Lincoln, Y. (eds), *Collecting and Interpreting Qualitative Materials*. London: Sage.

Denzin, N. K. and Lincoln, Y. (1998) Introduction: entering the field of qualitative research, in N. K. Denzin and Y. Lincoln (eds), *The Landscape of Qualitative Research*. Thousand Oaks: Sage.

Denzin, N. K. and Lincoln, Y. (2000) Introduction: entering the field of qualitative research, in N. K. Denzin and Y. Lincoln (eds), *Handbook of Qualitative Research*. London: Sage.

Denzin, N. K. and Lincoln, Y. (eds) (2003) *Collecting and Interpreting Qualitative Materials*. London: Sage.

Dey, I. (1993) *Qualitative Data Analysis: A User-Friendly Guide for Social Scientists*. London: Routledge.

Dickens, L. and Watkins, K. (1999) Action research: rethinking Lewin, *Management Learning*, 30 (2): 127–40.

Dingwall, R. (1980) Ethics and ethnography, *Sociological Review*, 28 (4): 871–91.

Donaldson, L. (1996) *For Positivist Organization Theory*. London: Sage.

Douglas, J. D. (ed.) (1970) *Understanding Everyday Life*. London: Routledge.

Douglas, J. D. (1976) *Investigative Social Research: Individual and Team Field Research*. London: Sage.

Douglas, J. D. (1985) *Creative Interviewing*. London: Sage.

Drummond, H. (1989) A note on applying lateral thinking to data collection, *Graduate Management Research*, Summer: 4–6.

Dryzek, J. S. (1995) Critical theory as a research programme, in S. K. White (ed.), *The Cambridge Companion to Habermas*. Cambridge: Cambridge University Press.

Du Gay, P. (1996) *Consumption and Identity at Work*. London: Sage.

Du Gay, P. (2000) *In Praise of Bureaucracy*. London: Sage.

Easterby-Smith, M., Thorpe, R. and Jackson, P. R. (2008) *Management Research*, 3rd edn. London: Sage.

Eden, M. and Huxham, C. (1996) Action research for management research, *British Journal of Management*, 7 (1): 75–86.

Edwards, D., Ashmore, M. and Potter, J. (1995) Death and furniture: the rhetoric, politics and theology of bottom line arguments against relativism, *History of the Human Sciences*, 8 (2): 25–49.

Eisenhardt, K. M. (1989) Building theories from case study research, *Academy of Management Review*, 14 (4): 532–50.

Ely, R. J. (1995) The power in demography: women's social construction of gender identity at work, *Academy of Management Journal*, 38: 589–634.

Fay, B. (1975) *Social Theory and Political Practice*. London: Allen & Unwin.

Fetterman, D. M. (1989) *Ethnography: Step by Step*, Applied Social Research Methods Series, Vol. 17. Beverly Hills, CA: Sage.

Fielding, N. G. (1988) Between micro and macro, in N. G. Fielding (ed.), *Actions and Structure*. London: Sage.

Fielding, N. G. (2002) Automating the ineffable: qualitative software and the meaning of qualitative research, in T. May (ed.), *Qualitative Research in Action*. London: Sage.

Fielding, N. G. and Fielding, J. L. (1986) *Linking Data*, Sage University Paper Series on Qualitative Research Methods, Vol. 4. Beverly Hills, CA: Sage.

Ford, J. D. (1999) Organizational change as shifting conversations, *Journal of Organizational Change Management*, 12: 480–500.

Flyvbjerg, B. (2006) Five misunderstandings about case-study research, *Qualitative Inquiry*, 12 (2): 219–45.

Forrester, J. (1983) Critical theory and organizational analysis, in G. Morgan (ed.), *Beyond Method*. London: Sage.

Forrester, J. (1992) Critical ethnography: on fieldwork in a Habermasian way, in M. Alvesson and H. Willmott, *Critical Management Studies*. London: Sage.

Forrester, J. (1993) *Critical Theory, Public Policy and Planning Practice*. Albany, NY: University of New York Press.

Forrester, J. (2003) On fieldwork in a habermasian way: critical ethnography and the extra-ordinary character of ordinary professional work, in M. Alvesson and H. Willmott, *Studying Management Critically*. London: Sage.

Forrester, J., Fournier, V. and Grey, C. (2000) At the critical moment: conditions and prospects for critical management studies, *Human Relations*, 53 (1): 7–32.

Fournier, V. and Grey, C. (2000) At the critical moment: conditions and prospects for critical management studies, *Human Relations*, 53 (1): 7–32.

Fowler, F. J. (2002) *Survey Research Methods,* 3rd edn. Newbury Park, CA: Sage.

French, W. L. and Bell, C. H. (1984) *Organization Development*. Englewood Cliffs, NJ: Prentice-Hall.

Frey, J. H. (1989) *Survey Research by Telephone,* 2nd edn. London: Sage.

Friedman, M. (1953) *Essays in Positive Economics*. Chicago, IL: University of Chicago Press.

Friedman, V. J. (2006) Action science: creating communities of inquiry in communities of practice, in P. Reason and H. Bradbury (eds), *Handbook of Action Research*. London: Sage.

Freire, P. (1972a) *Pedagogy of the Oppressed*. Harmondsworth: Penguin.

Freire, P. (1972b) *Cultural Action for Freedom*. Harmondsworth: Penguin.

Gadamer, H. (1975) *Truth and Method*. London: Sheed & Ward.

Gauld, A. and Shotter, J. (1977) *Human Action and the Psychological Investigation*. London: Routledge.

Gaventa, J. and Cornwall, A. (2006) Power and knowledge, in P. Reason and H. Bradbury (eds), *Handbook of Action Research: Concise Paperback Edition*. London: Sage.

Geertz, C. (1973) *The Interpretation of Cultures*. New York: Basic Books.

Gephart, R. (2004) Qualitative research and *The Academy of Management Journal*, *Academy of Management Journal*, 47 (4): 454–62.

Gergen, K. (1992) Organization theory in the postmodern era, in M. Reed and M. Hughes (eds), *Rethinking Organization*. London: Sage.

Gergen, K. and Thatchenkerry, T. J. (1996) Organization science as social construction: postmodern potentials, *Journal of Applied Behavioural Science*, 32 (4): 356–77.

Gergen, M. and Gergen, K. (2000) Qualitative inquiry: tensions and transformations, in N. K. Denzin and Y. Lincoln (eds), *Handbook of Qualitative Research*, 2nd edn. Thousand Oaks, CA: Sage.

Giddens, A. (1976) *New Rules of Sociological Method*. London: Hutchinson.

Giddens, A. (ed.) (1979) *Positivism and Sociology*. London: Heinemann Educational.

Giddens, A. (1984) *The Construction of Society*. London: Polity Press.

Gill, J. (1986) Research as action: an experiment in utilising the social sciences, in F. Heller (ed.), *The Use and Abuse of Social Science*. London: Sage.

Gill, J., Golding, D. and Angluin, D. (1989) Management development and doctoral research, *Management Education and Development*, 20 (1): 77–84.

Giroux, H. A. (1992) *Border Crossings: Cultural Workers and the Politics of Education*. New York: Routledge.

Gladwin, C. H. (1989) *Ethnographic Decision Tree Modelling*, Sage University Paper Series on Qualitative Research Methods, Vol. 19. Beverly Hills, CA: Sage.

Glaser, B. G. and Strauss, A. L. (1967) *The Discovery of Grounded Theory*. Chicago, IL: Aldine.

Glesne, C. and Peshkin, A. (1992) *Becoming Qualitative Researchers: An Introduction*. London: Longman.

Glidewell, J. C. (1959) The entry problem in consultation, *Journal of Social Issues*, 15 (2): 1–59.

Godsland, J. M. and Fielding, N. G. (1985) Children convicted of grave crimes, *Howard Journal of Criminal Justice*, 24 (3): 282–97.

Goffman, E. (1961) *Asylums: Essays on the Social Situation of Mental Patients and Other Inmates*. Harmondsworth: Penguin.

Goffman, E. (1969) *The Presentation of Self in Everyday Life*. Harmondsworth: Penguin.

Gold, R. (1958) Roles in sociological field observation, *Social Forces*, 36 (3): 217–23.

Golding, D. (1979) Some symbolic manifestations of power in industrial organizations. Unpublished PhD thesis, Sheffield City Polytechnic.

Gorman, R. A. (1977) *The Dual Vision*. London: Routledge.

Goulding, C. (2002) *Grounded Theory: A Practical Guide for Mangement, Business, and Marketing Researchers*. London: Sage.

Gouldner, A. W. (1954a) *Wildcat Strike*. New York: Harper & Row.

Gouldner, A. W. (1954b) *Patterns of Industrial Bureaucracy*. Glencoe, NY: Free Press.

Grafton-Small, R. (1985) Marketing managers: the evocation and structure of socially negotiated meaning. Unpublished PhD thesis, Sheffield City Polytechnic.

Greenwood, D. and Levin, M. (1998) *Introduction to Action Research*. London: Sage.

Grey, C. (1997) Management as a technical practice: professionalization or responsibilization, *Systems Practice*, 10 (6): 703–26.

Grey, C. and Mitev, N. (1995) Management education: a polemic, *Management Learning*, 26 (1): 73–90.

Grey, C. and Willmott, H. (2002) Contexts of CMS, *Organization*, 9 (3): 411–18.

Grey, C. and Willmott, H. (2005) Introduction, in C. Grey and H. Willmott (eds), *Critical Management Studies*. Oxford: Oxford University Press.

Griseri, P. (2002) *Management Knowledge: A Critical View*. Basingstoke: Palgrave.

Grubbs, B. W. (2001) A community of voices: using allegory as an interpretive device in action research on organizational change, *Organizational Research Methods*, 4 (4): 276–392.

Grundy, S. (1987) *Curriculum: Product or Praxis*. Lewes: Falmer Press.

Guba, E. and Lincoln, Y. S. (1989) *Fourth Generation Evaluation*. Newbury Park: Sage.

Guba, E. and Lincoln, Y. S. (1994) Competing paradigms in qualitative research, in N. K. Denzin and Y. S. Lincoln (eds), *Handbook of Qualitative Research*. Newbury Park: Sage.

Gubrium, J. F. and Silverman, D. (eds) (1989) *The Politics of Field Research*. London: Sage.

Gummesson, E. (2000) *Qualitative Methods in Management Research*, 2nd edn. London: Sage.

Gustavsen, A. (2006) Theory and practice: the mediating discourse, in P. Reason and H. Bradbury (eds), *Handbook of Action Research*. London: Sage.

Habermas, J. (1974a) *Theory and Practice*. London: Heinemann.

Habermas, J. (1974b) Rationalism divided in two: a reply to Albert, in A. Giddens (ed.), *Positivism and Sociology*. London: Heineman Educational.

Hammersley, M. (1989) *The Dilemma of Qualitative Method: Herbert Blumer and the Chicago Tradition*. London: Routledge.

Hammersley, M. (1990) *Reading Ethnographic Research: A Critical Guide*. London: Longman.

Hammersley, M. (1992) *What's Wrong with Ethnography?* London: Routledge.

Hammersley, M. and Atkinson, P. (1995) *Ethnography: Principles in Practice*, 2nd edn. London: Routledge.

Hancock, P. and Tyler, M. (2001) *Work, Postmodernism and Organization: A Critical Introduction*. London: Sage.

Hanson, N. R. (1958) *Patterns of Discovery*. Cambridge: Cambridge University Press.

Hardy, C. and Clegg, S. (1997) Relativity without relativism: reflexivity in post-paradigm studies, *British Journal of Management*, Special Issue 8: 5–17.

Hart, C. (1998) *Doing a Literature Review*. London: Open University/Sage.

Hart, C. (2001) *Doing a Literature Search*. London: Sage.

Hartley, J. (1994) Case studies in organizational research, in C. Cassell and G. Symon *Qualitative Methods in Organizational Research: A Practical Guide*. London: Sage.

Hartley, J. (2001) Employee surveys: strategic aid or hand-grenade for organisational and cultural change? *International Journal of Public Sector Management*, 14 (3): 184–204.

Hartley, J. (2004) Case study research, in C. Cassell and G. Symon (eds), *Essential Guide to Qualitative Methods in Organizational Research*. London: Sage.

Hartley, J. and Barling, J. (1998) The use of employee attitude surveys in researching the world of work, in K. Whitfield and G. Strauss, G. (eds), *Researching the World of Work*. Ithaca, NY: Cornell University Press.

Harvey-Jones, J. (1989) *Making it Happen: Reflections on Leadership*. London: Fontana.

Hassard, J. (1991) Multiple paradigms and organizational analysis: a case study, *Organization Studies*, 12(2): 275–99.

Hassard, J. and Parker, M. (eds) (1993) *Postmodernism and Organisations*. London: Sage.

Heckscher, C. (1994) Defining the post-bureaucratic type, in C. Hechsher and A. Donnelon (eds), *The Post-Bureaucratic Organization*. London: Sage.

Heller, F. (1976) Group feedback analysis as a method of action research, in A. Clark (ed.), *Experimenting with Organizational Life: The Action Research Approach*. New York: Plenum Press.

Heller, F. (ed.) (1986) *The Use and Abuse of Social Science*. London: Sage.

Heller, F. (1993) Another look at action research, *Human Relations*, 46 (10): 1235–42.

Heller, F. (2004) Action research and research action: a family of methods, in C. Cassell and G. Symon (eds), *Essential Guide to Qualitative Methods in Organizational Research*. London: Sage.

Hendry, J. (2006) Educating managers for post-bureaucracy: the role of the humanities, *Management Learning*, 37 (3): 267–81.

Herbelein, T. H. and Baumgarter, R. (1978) Factors affecting response rates to mailed questionnaires: a quantitative analysis of the published literature, *American Sociological Review*, 43 (4): 447–62.

Heron, J. (1996) *Co-operative Inquiry: Research into the Human Condition*. London: Sage.

Herr, K. and Andersen, G. L. (2005) *The Action Research Dissertation: A Guide to Faculty and Students*. London: Sage.

Hindess, B. (1977) *Philosophy and Methodology in Social Science*. Hassocks: Harvester.

Hirschheim, R. A. (1985) Information systems epistemology: an historical perspective, in E. E. Mumford, R. Hirschheim, G. Fitzgerald and A. T. Wood-Harper (eds), *Research Methods in Information Systems*. Amsterdam: Elsevier.

Hogan, R. and Sinclair, R. (1996) Intellectual, ideological and political obstacles to the advancement of organizational science, *The Journal of Applied Behavioural Science*, 32 (4): 378–89. NTL Institute.

Holland, R. (1999) Reflexivity, *Human Relations*, 52 (4): 463–83.

Horowitz, R. (1986) Remaining an outsider: membership as a threat to research rapport, *Urban Life*, 14: 409–30.

House, R. J. (1970) Scientific investigation in management, *Management International Review*, 4/5 (10): 139–50.

Howard, K. and Sharp, J. A. (1983) The *Management of a Student Research Project*. Aldershot: Gower.

Huczynski, A. A. (1993) *Management Gurus: What Makes Them and How to Become One*. London: Routledge.

Hume, D. (1739–40/1965) *A Treatise of Human Nature*. Oxford: Clarendon Press.

Hunt, J. C. (1979) *Psychoanalytic Aspects of Fieldwork*, Sage University Paper Series on Qualitative Research Methods, Vol. 18. Newbury Park, CA: Sage.

Introna, L. D. and Whitley, E. A. (2000) About experiments and style: a critique of laboratory research in information systems, *Information, Technology and People*, 13 (3): 161–73.

Jackall, R. (1988) *Moral Mazes: The World of Corporate Managers*. Oxford: Oxford University Press.

Janis, I. L. (1972) *Victims of Groupthink*. Boston, MA: Houghton Mifflin.

Jantsch, E. (1967) *Technological Forecasting in Perspective*. Paris: OECD.

Jaques, E. (1951) *The Changing Culture of a Factory*. London: Tavistock.

Jeffcutt, P. (1994) The interpretation of organization: a contemporary analysis and critique, *Journal of Management Studies*, 31: 225–50.

Jermier, J. M. (1998) Introduction: critical perspectives on organizational control, *Administrative Science Quarterly*, 43 (2): 235–56.

Jick, T. J. (1979a) Mixing qualitative and quantitative methods: triangulation in action, *Administrative Science Quarterly*, 24, December: 602–11.

Jick, T. J. (1979b) Process and impacts of merger: individual and organizational perspectives. Unpublished doctoral dissertation, New York State School of Industrial and Labor Relations, Cornell University.

Johnson, P. (1995) Towards an epistemology for radical accounting: beyond objectivism and relativism, *Critical Perspectives on Accounting*, 6: 485–509.

Johnson, P. and Clark, M. (2006) *Business and Management Research Methodologies*, Volumes 1–6. London: Sage.

Johnson, P. and Duberley, J. (2000) *Understanding Management Research: An Introduction to Epistemology*. London: Sage.

Johnson, P. and Duberley, J. (2003) Reflexivity in management research, *Journal of Management Studies*, 40 (6): 1279–303.

Johnson, P. and Gill, J. (1993) *Management Control and Organization Behaviour*. London: Sage.

Johnson, P., Duberley, J., Close, P. and Cassells, C. (1999) Negotiating field roles in manufacturing management research: the need for reflexivity, *International Journal of Operations and Production Management*, 19 (12): 1234–54.

Johnson, P., Cassell, C., Buehring, A. and Symon, G. (2006) Evaluating qualitative management research: towards a contingent criteriology, *International Journal of Management Reviews*, 8 (3): 131–56.

Johnson, P., Buehring, A., Cassell, C. and Symon, G. (2007) Defining qualitative management research: an empirical investigation, *Qualitative Research in Organization and Management*, 2 (1): 23–42.

Johnson, P., Wood, G., Brewster, C. and Brookes, M. (2009) The rise of post-bureaucracy: theorists' fancy or organizational praxis? *International Sociology*, 24 (1): 37–61.

Junker, B. H. (1960) *Fieldwork*. Chicago, IL: University of Chicago Press.

Kalleberg, A. L. (2001) Organizing flexibly: the flexible firm in a new century, *British Journal of Industrial Relations*, 39 (4): 479–504.

Keat, R. and Urry, J. (1975) *Social Theory as Science*. London: Routledge.

Keleman, M. and Bansal, P. (2002) The conventions of management research and the relevance to management practice, *British Journal of Management*, 13: 97–108.

Keleman, M. and Rumens, N. (2008) *An Introduction to Critical Management Research*. London: Sage.

Kemmis, S. (2006) Exploring the relevance of critical theory for action research: emancipatory action research in the footsteps of Jurgen Habermas, in P. Reason and H. Bradbury (eds), *Handbook of Action Research: Concise Paperback Edition*. London: Sage.

Kemmis, S. and McTaggart, R. (1988) *The Action Research Planner*. Victoria, Australia: Deakin University.

Kemmis, S. and McTaggart, R. (2000) Participatory action research, in N. K. Denzin and Y. S. Lincoln (eds), *Handbook of Qualitative Research*, 2nd edn. London: Sage.

Kidder, L. H. (1981) Qualitative research and quasi-experimental frameworks, in M. B. Brewer and B. E. Collins (eds), *Scientific Inquiry and the Social Sciences*. San Francisco, CA: Jossey-Bass.

Kidder, L. H. and Judd, C. M. (1986) *Research Methods in Social Relations*, 8th edn. London: Holt, Rinehart & Winston.

Kilduff, M. (1993) Deconstructing organizations, *Academy of Management Review*, 18 (1): 13–31.

Kilduff, M. and Mehra, A. (1997) Postmodernism and organizational research, *Academy of Management Review*, 22 (2): 453–81.

Kirk, J. and Miller, M. (1986) *Reliability and Validity in Qualitative Research*. London: Sage.

Kish, L. (1965) *Survey Sampling*. New York: Wiley.

Knights, D. (1992) Changing spaces: the disruptive impact of a new epistemological location for the study of management, *Academy of Management Review*, 17 (3): 514–36.

Knights, D. and Morgan, G. (1991) Strategic discourse and subjectivity, *Organization Studies*, 12 (2): 251–74.

Kolakowski, L. (1969) Karl Marx and the classical definition of truth, in L. Kolakowski (ed.), *Marxism and Beyond*. London: Pall Mall Press.

Kolb, D. A., Rubin, I. M. and Mcintyre, J. M. (1979) *Organizational Psychology: An Experiential Approach*. London: Prentice-Hall.

Kondo, D. (1990) *Crafting Ourselves: Power, Gender and Discourses of Identity in a Japanese Workplace*. Chicago, IL: Chicago University Press.

Krausz, E. and Miller, S. H. (1974) *Social Research Design*. London: Longman.

Kuhn, T. (1970) *The Structure of Scientific Revolutions*, 2nd edn. Chicago, IL: University of Chicago Press.

Kulka, R. A. (1982) Idiosyncrasy and circumstance: choices and constraints in the research process, in J. E. McGrath, J. Martin and R. A Kulka (eds), *Judgement Calls in Research*. London: Sage.

Kunda, G. (1992) *Engineering Culture: Control and Commitment in a High Tech Corporation*. Philadelphia: Temple University Press.

Laing, R. D. (1967) *The Politics of Experience and the Birds of Paradise*. Harmondsworth: Penguin.

Lau, F. (1999) Towards a framework for action research in information systems studies, *Information Technology and People*, 12 (2): 148–75.

Law, J. (2004) *After Method: Mess in Social Science Research*. London: Routledge.

Law, J. and Lodge, P. (1984) *Science for Social Scientists*. London: Macmillan.

Lawler, E. E. and Rhode, J. R. (1976) *Information and Control in Organizations*. London: Goodyear.

Lecompte, M. and Goetz, J. (1982) Problems of relability and validity in ethnographic research, *Review of Educational Research*, 52 (1): 31–60.

Lee, A.S. (1989) Case studies as natural experiments, *Human Relations*, 42(2): 117–37.

Lee, N. and Lings, I. (2008) *Doing Business Research: A Guide to Theory and Practice*. London: Sage.

Lehman, C. R. (1992) *Accounting's Changing Role in Social Conflict*. London: Paul Chapman.

Leininger, M. (1994) Evaluation criteria and critique of qualitative research studies, in J. M. Morse (ed.), *Critical Issues in Qualitative Research Methods*. London: Sage.

Lennon, A. and Wollin, A. (2001) Learning organisations: empirically investigating metaphors, *Journal of Intellectual Capital*, 2 (4): 410–22.

Lessnoff, M. (1974) *The Structure of Social Science*. London: Allen & Unwin.

Levin, M. and Greenwood, D. (2001) Pragmatic action research and the struggle to transform universities into learning communities, in P. Reason and H. Bradbury (eds), *Handbook of Action Research: Participative Inquiry and Practice*. London: Sage.

Lewin, K. (1946) Action research and minority problems, *Journal of Social Issues*, 2 (4): 34–46.

Lewin, K. (1948/1998) Group decision and social change, in M. Gold (ed.), *The Complete Social Scientist: A Kurt Lewin Reader*. Washington DC: American Psychological Association.

Lincoln, Y. S. and Denzin, N. K. (1994) The fifth moment, in N. K. Denzin and Y. Lincoln (eds), *Handbook of Qualitative Research*. London: Sage.

Lincoln, Y. S. and Guba, E. (1985) *Naturalistic Enquiry*. Beverly Hill, CA: Sage.

Lindesmith, A. (1947) *Opiate Addiction*. Bloomington, IN: Principia Press.

Linstead, S. (1993a) Deconstruction in the study of organizations in J. Hassard and M. Parker (eds), *Postmodernism and Organizations*. London: Sage.

Linstead, S. (1993b) From postmodern anthropology to deconstructive ethnography, *Human Relations*, 46: 97–120.

Locke, K. (1996) Rewriting the discovery of grounded theory after 25 years?, *Journal of Management Inquiry*, 5(3): 239–45.

Locke, K. D. (2000) *Grounded Theory in Management Research*. London: Sage.

Locke, K. D. (2001) *Grounded Theory in Management Research*. London: Sage.

Locke, L. F., Spirduso, W. W. and Silverman, S. J. (2007) *Proposals that Work: A Guide for Planning Dissertations and Grant Proposals*, 5th edn. London: Sage.

Loftland, J. (1970) Interactionist imagery and analytic interruptus, in T. Shibutani (ed.), *Human Nature and Collective Behavior*. Papers in Honor of Herbert Blumer. Englewood Cliffs, NJ: Prentice Hall.

Lowe, J., Morris, J. and Wilkinson, B. (2000) British factory, Japanese factory and Mexican factory: an international comparison of front line management and supervision, *Journal of Management Studies*, 37 (June): 541–62.

Ludema, J. D., Cooperider, D. L. and Barrett, F. J. (2006) Appreciative inquiry: the power of the unconditional positive question, in P. Reason and H. Bradbury (eds), *Handbook of Action Research*. London: Sage.

Lumley, R. (1978) A study of industrial relations on a large construction site. Unpublished PhD thesis, Sheffield City Polytechnic.

Lupton, T. (1963) *On the Shop Floor*. Oxford: Pergamon.

Lupton, T. (1971) *Management and the Social Sciences*. Harmondsworth: Penguin.

Lyotard, J-F. (1984) *The Postmodern Condition: A Report on Knowledge*. Manchester: Manchester University Press.

McAuley, J. M. (1985) Hermeneutics as a practical research methodology in management, *Management Education and Development*, 16 (3): 292–9.

McAuley, J. M., Duberley, J. and Johnson, P. (2007) *Organization Theory: Challenges and Perspectives*. London: Prentice Hall Financial Times.

McCall, G. J. and Simmons, J. L. (1969) *Issues in Participant Observation*. Wokingham: Addison-Wesley.

McCall, M. W. and Bobko, P. (1990) Research methods in the service of discovery, in M. D. Dunnette and L. M. Hough (eds), *Handbook of Industrial and Organizational Psychology*. Palo Alto, CA: Consulting Psychologists Press.

McDavid, J. C. and Hawthorn, L. R. (2005) *Program Evaluation and Performance Measurement: An Introduction to Practice*. London: Sage.

McKernan, J. (1996) *Curriculum Action Research*. London: Kogan Page.

McLennan, G. (1995) *Pluralism*. Buckingham: Open University Press.

McNiff, J. and Whitehead, J. (2005) *All You Need To Know About Action Research*. London: Sage.

Mabry, L. (2002) Postmodern evaluation – or not? *American Journal of Evaluation*, 23 (2): 141–57.

Madge, J. H. (1953) *The Tools of Social Science*. London: Longman.

Malim, T. and Birch, A. (1997) *Research Methods and Statistics*. London: MacMillan.

Malinowski, B. (1922) *Argonauts of the Western Pacific*. London: Routledge.

Mannheim, K. (1952) *Essays on the Sociology of Knowledge*. London: Routledge & Kegan Paul.

Mant, A. (1977) *The Rise and Fall of the British Manager*. London: Macmillan.

Maranell, G. M. (ed.) (1974) *Scaling: A Sourcebook for Behavioral Scientists*, Chicago, IL: Aldine.

Marcus, G. E. (1994) What comes just after 'post': the case of ethnography, in N. K. Denzin and Y. S. Lincoln (eds), *The Handbook of Qualitative Research*. London: Sage.

Marcus, G. E. and Fisher, M. (1986) *Anthropology as Cultural Critique*. Chicago, IL: University of Chicago Press.

Marrow, A. J. (1969) *The Practical Theorist: The Life and Works of Kurt Lewin*. New York: Basic Books.

Martin, J. (1990) Deconstructing organizational taboos: the suppression of gender conflict in organizations, *Organization Science*, 1 (4): 339–59.

Maslow, A. M. (1943) A theory of human motivation, *Psychological Review*, 50: 370–96.

Mattick, J. P. (1986) *Social Knowledge*. London: Hutchinson.

Maxwell, J. (2005). *Qualitative Research Design: An Interactive Approach*, 2nd edn. London: Sage.

May, T. (2002) (ed.) *Qualitative Research in Action*. London: Sage.

Mead, G. H. (1934) *Mind, Self and Society*. Chicago, IL: Chicago University Press.

Mead, M. (1943/1922) *Coming of Age in Samoa*. Harmondsworth: Penguin.

Merton, R. K. (1938/70) *Science Technology and Society in Seventeenth Century England*. New York: Harper & Row.

Meyerson, D. (1994) Interpretations of stress in institutions: the cultural production of ambiguity and burnout, *Administrative Science Quarterly*, 39: 628–53.

Mies, M. (1993) Towards a methodology for feminist research, in M. Hammersley (ed.), *Social Research: Philosophy, Politics and Practice*. London: Sage.

Miles, M. B. and Huberman, A. M. (1994) *Qualitative Data Analysis: An Expanded Sourcebook*, 2nd edn. London: Sage.

Milgram, S. (1963) Behavioural study of obedience, *Journal of Abnormal Social Psychology*, 67: 371–8.

Mill, J. S. (1874) *A System of Logic*. London: Longman Green.

Miller, E. J. (1983) *Work and Creativity*, Occasional Paper no. 6. London: The Tavistock Institute of Human Relations.

Miller, E. J. (1995) Dialogue with the client system: use of the 'working note' in organizational consultancy, *Journal of Managerial Psychology*, 10 (6): 27–30.

Mingers, J. (2000) Critical realism as the underpinning philosophy for OR/MS and systems, *Journal of the Operational Research Society*, 51 (11): 1256–70.

Mintzberg, H. (1973) *The Nature of Managerial Work*. New York: Harper & Row.

Mitchell, J. C. (1983) Case and situational analysis, *Sociological Review*, 31: 187–211.

Mitchell, T. R. (1985) An evaluation of the validity of correlation research conducted in organizations, *Academy of Management Review*, 2: 192–205.

Mitroff, I. I. (1974) *The Subjective Side of Science*. Amsterdam: Elsevier.

Mitroff, I. I. and Pondy, L. (1978) Afterthoughts on the leadership conference, in M. McCall and M. Lombardo (eds), *Leadership: Where Else Can We Go?* Durham: Duke University.

Morgan, D. H. J. (1972) The British Association scandal: the effect of publicity on a sociological investigation, *Sociological Review*, 20 (2): 185–206.

Morgan, G. (ed.) (1983) *Beyond Method*. London: Sage.

Morgan, G. (1986) *Images of Organisation*. London: Sage.

Morgan, G. (1993) *Imaginization*. London: Sage.

Morgan, G. and Smircich, L. (1980) The Case for Qualitative Research, *Academy of Management Review*, 5 (4): 491–500.

Morrow, R. and Brown, D. (1994) *Critical Theory and Methodology*. London: Sage.

Morse, J. M. (1994) Emerging from the data: the cognitive process of analysis in qualitative enquiry, in J. M. Morse (ed.), *Critical Issues in Qualitative Research Methods*. London: Sage.

Moser, C. A. and Kalton, G. (1971) *Survey Methods and Social Investigation*. London: Heinemann.

Mulkay, M. (1991) *Sociology of Science: A Sociological Prilgrimage*. Milton Keynes: Open University Press.

Myers, C. S. (1924) *Industrial Psychology in Great Britain*. London: Cape.

Nagel, E. (1961) *The Structure of Science*. Princeton: Princeton University Press.

Neimark, M. (1990) The King is dead, long live the King, *Critical Perspectives on Accounting*, 1 (1): 103–14.

Neurath, O. (1959) Sociology and physicalism, in A. J. Ayer (ed.), *Logical Positivism*. New York: Free Press.

Newton, T. (1999) Power, subjectivity and British industrial and organizational sociology: the relevance of the work of Norbert Elias, *Sociology*, 33 (2): 415–47.

Noble, F. (1989) Organizational design and the implementation of office information systems. Unpublished PhD proposal, Sheffield City Polytechnic.

O'Creevey, M. F. (1995) *Striking Off the Shackles: A Survey of Managers' Attitudes to Employee Involvement*. Corby: Institute of Management.

O'Dochartaigh, N. (2001) *The Internet Research Handbook: A Practical Guide for Students and Researchers in the Social Sciences*. London: Sage.

Ofori-Dankwa, J. and Julian S. D. (2005) From thought to theory to school: the role of contextual factors in the evolution of schools of management thought, *Organization Studies*, 26 (9): 1307–29.

Oliver, P. (2008) *Writing Your Thesis*, 2nd edn. London: Sage.

Oppenheim, A. N. (1966) *Questionnaire Design and Attitude Measurement*. London: Heinemann.

Orpen, C. (1979) The effects of job enrichment on employee satisfaction, motivation, involvement and performance: a field experiment, *Human Relations*, 32 (3): 189–217.

Osbourne, D. and Plastrik, D. (1998) *Banishing Bureaucracy: Five Strategies for Reinventing Government*. New York: Plume.

Outhwaite, W. (1975) *Understanding Social Life: The Method Called Verstehen*. London: George Allen Unwin.

Park, P. (2006) *Knowledge and Participatory Research*, in P. Reason and H. Bradbury (eds), *Handbook of Action Research*. London: Sage.

Parker, M. (2000) *Organization, Culture and Identity*. London: Sage.

Parnes, S. J., Noller, R. B. and Bondi, A. M. (1977) *Guide to Creative Action*. New York: Charles Scribner's Sons.

Partington, D. (2000) Building grounded theories of management action, *British Journal of Management*, 11: 91–102.

Passmore, W. (2006) Action research in the workplace: the socio-technical perspective, in P. Reason and H. Bradbury (eds), *Handbook of Action Research*. London: Sage.

Patton, M. (1990) *Qualitative Evaluation and Research Methods*. London: Sage.

Pawson, R. and Tilley, N. (1997) *Realistic Evaluation*. London: Sage.

Payne, S. (1951) *The Art of Asking Questions*. Princeton, NJ: Princeton University Press.

Perry, C. and Zuber-Skerritt, O. (1994) Doctorates by action research for senior practising managers, *Management Learning*, 25 (2): 113–24.

Peters, T. and Waterman, R. H. (1982) *In Search of Excellence*. London: Harper & Row.

Pettigrew, A. M. (1985a) Contextualist research: a natural way to link theory and practice, in E. E. Lawler, A. M. Mohrman, S. A. Mohrman, G. E. Ledford, T. G. Cummings and Associates (eds), *Doing Research that is Useful for Theory and Practice*. San Francisco, CA: Jossey-Bass.

Pettigrew, A. M. (1985b) *The Awakening Giant: Continuity and Change in ICI*. Oxford: Blackwell.

Pfeffer, J. (1993) Barriers to the advancement of organization science: paradigm development as a dependent variable, *Academy of Management Review*, 18 (4): 599–620.

Pfeffer, J. (1995) Mortality, reproducibility and the persistence of styles of theory, *Organization Science*, 6 (6): 681–93.

Phelps, R. Fisher, K. and Ellis, A. (2007) *Organizing and Managing Your Research*. London: Sage.

Phillips, E. M. and Pugh, D. S. (1987) *How to Get a PhD*. Milton Keynes: Open University Press.

Pollert, A. (1981) *Girls, Wives, Factory Lives*. London: Macmillan.

Pollner, M. and Emerson, R. M. (1983) The dynamics of inclusion and distance in fieldwork relations, in R. M. Emerson (ed.), *Contemporary Field Research*. Boston, MA: Little, Brown.

Popper, K. R. (1957) *The Poverty of Historicism*. London: Routledge.

Popper, K. R. (1967) *Conjectures and Refutations*. London: Routledge.

Popper, K. R. (1972a) *Objective Knowledge*. Oxford: Clarendon Press.

Popper, K. R. (1972b) *The Logic of Scientific Discovery*. London: Hutchinson.

Porter, S. (1993) Critical realist ethnography: the case of racism and professionalism in a medical setting, *Sociology*, 27 (4): 591–609.

Prasad, A. and Prasad, P. (2002) The coming age of interpretive organizational research, *Organizational Research Methods*, 5 (1): 4–11.

Prasad, P. (1993) Symbolic processes in the implementation of technological change: a symbolic interactionist study of work computerization, *Academy of Management Journal*, 36 (6): 1400–29.

Pratt, V. (1978) *The Philosophy of the Social Sciences*. London: Methuen.

Pugh, D. S. (ed.) (1971) *Organisation Theory: Selected Readings*. Harmondsworth: Penguin.

Punch, K. F. (2006) *Developing Effective Research Proposals*, 2nd edn. London: Sage.

Punch, M. (1986) *The Politics and Ethics of Fieldwork*, Sage University Paper Series on Qualitative Research Methods, Vol. 3. Beverly Hills, CA: Sage.

Putnam, L. (1996) Situating the author and text, *Journal of Management Inquiry*, 5: 382–6.

Putnam, L., Brantz, C., Deetz, S., Mumby, D. and Van Maanen, J. (1993) Ethnography versus critical theory, *Journal of Management Inquiry*, 2 (3): 221–35.

Quine, W. V. (1960) *World and Object*. Cambridge, MA: Harvard University Press.

Ragin, C. C. (1994) *Constructing Social Research: The Unity and Diversity of Method*. London: Sage.

Rapoport, R. N. (1970) Three dilemmas in action research, *Human Relations*, 23 (6): 499–513.

Reason, P. (ed.) (1994) *Participation in Human Inquiry*. London: Sage.

Reason, P. (1999) Integrating action and reflection through co-operative inquiry, *Management Learning*, 30 (2): 207–26.

Reason, P. and Bradbury, H. (eds) (2006) *Handbook of Action Research*. London: Sage.

Reed, M. and Hughes, M. (eds) (1992) *Rethinking Organization*. London: Sage.

Reeves, T. K. and Harper, D. (1981) *Surveys at Work: A Practitioner's Guide*. London: McGraw-Hill.

Revans, R. W. (1971) *Developing Effective Managers*. London: Longman.

Revans, R. W. (1980) *Action Learning: New Techniques for Management*. London: Blond & Briggs.

Richards, L. (2005) *Handling Qualitative Data: A Practical Guide*. London: Sage.

Ridley, D. (2008) *The Literature Review: A Step-by-step Guide for Students*. London: Sage.

Robinson, R. D. (1997) *The Empowerment Cookbook*. New York: McGraw-Hill.

Robinson, W. S. (1951) The logic and structure of analytic induction, *American Sociological Review*, 16: 192–208.

Robson, C. (1993) *Real World Research: A Resource for Social Scientists and Practitioner-Researchers*. Oxford: Blackwell.

Roethlisberger, F. J. and Dickson, W. J. (1939) *Management and the Worker*. Cambridge, MA: Harvard University Press.

Rorty, R. (1979) *Philosophy and the Mirror of Nature*. Princeton, NJ: Princeton University Press.

Rose, M. (1975) *Industrial Behaviour: Theoretical Developments Since Taylor*. Harmondsworth: Allen Lane.

Rosen, M. (1985) Breakfast at Spiro's: dramaturgy and dominance, *Journal of Management*, 11 (2): 31–48.

Rosenau, P. M. (1992) *Post-modernism and the Social Sciences: Insights, Inroads and Intrusions*. Princeton, NJ: Princeton University Press.

Rosenberg, M. J. (1968) *The Logic of Survey Analysis*. New York: Basic Books.

Rosenthal, R. (1966) *Experimenter Effects in Behavioral Research*. New York: Appleton Century Crofts.

Rosenthal, R. and Rosnow, R. L. (1975) *Primer Methods for the Behavioural Sciences*. London: Wiley.

Ross, D. (1991) *The Origins of American Social Science*. New York: Cambridge.

Rossi, P. H., Lipsey, M. W. and Freeman, H. E. (2003) *Evaluation: a Systematic Approach*. London: Sage.

Roy, D. (1960) 'Banana time' – job satisfaction and informal interactions, *Human Organisation*, 18 (2): 156–68.

Rudestam, K. E. and Newton, R. R. (1992) *Surviving your Dissertation: A Comprehensive Guide to Content and Process*. London: Sage.

Rummel, R. W. and Ballaine, W. C. (1963) *Research Methodology in Business*. New York: Harper & Row.

Ryan, A. (1970) *The Philosophy of the Social Sciences*. London: Macmillan.

Sanday, P. R. (1979) The ethnographic paradigm(s), *Administrative Science Quarterly*, 24, December: 527–38.

Sandberg, A. (1985) Socio-technical design, trade union strategies and action research, in E. Mumford, R. Hirscheim, G. Fitzgerald and T. Wood-Harper (eds), *Research Methods in Information Systems*, B.V. North-Holland: Elsevier Science Publishers. 79–92.

Sapsford, R. (2006) *Survey Research*, 2nd edn. London: Sage.

Sapsford, R. and Jupp, V. (1996) *Data Collection and Analysis*. London: Sage.

Sayer, A. (1981) Abstraction: a realist interpretation, *Radical Philosophy*, 28: 6–15.

Sayer, A. (1992) *Method in Social Science: A Realist Approach*. London: Routledge.

Sayles, L. (1958) *The Behavior of Industrial Work Groups*. New York: Wiley.

Sayles, L. (1964) *Managerial Behavior: Administration in Complex Organizations*. New York: McGraw-Hill.

Scandura, T. A. and Williams, E. A. (2000) Research methodology in management: current practices, trends, and implications for future research, *Academy of Management Journal,* 43 (6): 1248–64.

Schaubroeck, J. and Kuehn, K. (1992) Research design in industrial and organizational psychology, in C. L. Cooper and I. T. Robertson (eds), *International Review of Industrial and Organizational Psychology*, Vol. 7. Chichester: John Wiley.

Schein, E. H. (1970) *Organizational Psychology*, 2nd edn. Englewood Cliffs, NJ: Prentice-Hall.

Schein, E. H. (1987) *The Clinical Perspective in Fieldwork*, Sage University Paper Series on Qualitative Research Methods, Vol. 5. Beverly Hills, CA: Sage.

Schein, E. H. (1995) Process consultation, action research and clinical inquiry: are they the same?, *Journal of Managerial Psychology*, 10 (6): 14–19.

Schein, E. H. (1997) Organization learning: what is new? in M. A. Rahim et al. (eds), *Current Topics in Management*, Vol. 2. Greenwich, CT: JAI.

Scheurich, J. J. (1997) *Research Method in the Postmodern*. London: Falmer Press.

Schon, D. A. (1983) *The Reflective Practitioner: How Professionals Think in Action*. London: Temple Smith.

Schultz, M. and Hatch, M. J. (1996) Living with multiple paradigms: the case of multiple paradigms in organization culture studies, *Academy of Management Review*, 21: 529–57.

Schwandt, T. A. (1996) Farewell to criteriology, *Qualitative Inquiry*, 2 (1): 58–72.

Schwandt, T. A. (1999) On understanding understanding, *Qualitative Inquiry*, 5 (4): 451–64.

Schwartzman, H. B. (1993) *Ethnography in Organizations*. London: Sage.

Scott, C. (1961) Research on mail surveys, *Journal of the Royal Statistical Society*, 124: 143–205.

Scott, W. R. and Meyer, J. W. (1994) *Institutional Environments and Organizations*. London: Sage.

Seale, C. (1999a) *The Quality of Qualitative Research*. London: Sage.

Seale, C. (1999b) Quality in qualitative research, *Qualitative Inquiry*, 5 (4): 465–78.

Shalin, D. N. (1986) Pragmatism and social interaction, *American Sociological Review*, 51: 9–29.

Shotter, J. (1975) *Images of Man in Psychological Research*. London: Methuen.

Simons, R. (1987) Accounting control systems and business strategy: an empirical analysis, *Accounting, Organisations and Society*, 12 (4): 357–74.

Simsek, Z. and Veiga, J. F. (2000) The electronic survey technique: an integration and assessment, *Organizational Research Methods*, 3 (3): 92–114.

Simsek, Z. and Veiga, J. F. (2001) A primer on internet organizational surveys, *Organizational Research Methods*, 4 (3): 218–35.

Sirkin, R. M. (1994) *Statistics for the Social Sciences*. London: Sage.

Slife, B. D. and Williams, R. N. (1995) *What's Behind the Research? Discovering Hidden Assumptions in the Behavioural Sciences*. London: Sage.

Smart, B. (1975) *Marxism and Phenomenology*. London: Routledge.

Smircich, L. (1983) Studying organisations as cultures, in G. Morgan (ed.), *Beyond Method*. London: Sage.

Smith, G. M. (1975) Business and management studies: a guide to the information network, *Journal of Management Studies*, May: 194–209.

Smith, H. W. (1975) *Strategies of Social Research: The Methodological Imagination*. London: Prentice-Hall.

Smith, J. K. (1990) Goodness criteria: alternative research paradigms and the problem of criteria, in E. G. Guba (ed.), *The Paradigm Dialogue*. London: Sage.

Smith, J. K. and Deemer, D. (2000) The problem of criteria in the age of relativism, in N. K. Denzin and Y. Lincoln (eds), *Handbook of Qualitative Research*. London: Sage.

Smith, V. (2001) Ethnographies of work and the work of ethnographers, in P. Atkinson, A. Coffey, S. Delmont, J. Loftland and L. Loftland (eds), *Handbook of Ethnography*. London: Sage.

Snape, D. and Spencer, L. (2003) The foundations of qualitative research, in J. Ritchie and J. Lewis (eds), *Qualitative Research Practice*. London: Sage.

Sofer, C. (1961) *The Organisation from Within*. London: Tavistock.

Somekh, B. (1995) The contribution of action research to development in social endeavours: a position paper on action research methodology, *British Educational Research Journal*, 21 (3): 339–55.

Spencer, A. C. (1980) Some issues arising from the role relationships of the non-executive director. Unpublished PhD thesis, Sheffield City Polytechnic.

Spinelli, E. (1989) *The Interpreted World*. London: Sage.

Spreitzer, G. (1995) Psychological empowerment in the workplace: dimensions, measurement, and validation, *Academy of Management Journal*, 38 (5): 1442–65.

Stanton, J. M. (1998) An empirical assessment of data collection using the internet, *Personnel Psychology*, 51: 707–25.

Stanton, J. M. and Rogelberg, S. G. (2001) Using internet/intranet web pages to collect organizational research data, *Organization Research Methods*, 4 (3): 200–17.

Stone, E. F. (1982) In defence of rigorous research, *Contemporary Psychology*, 27: 581–95.

Strauss, A. and Corbin, J. (1998) *Basics of Qualitative Research*, 2nd edn. London: Sage.

Summers, G. F. (1970) *Attitude Measurement*. Chicago, IL: Rand McNally.

Susman, G. I. and Evered, R. D. (1978) An assessment of the scientific merits of action research, *Administrative Science Quarterly*, 23: 582–602.

Symon, G., Buering, A., Johnson, P. and Cassell, C. (2008) Positioning qualitative research as resistance to the institutionalization of the academic labour process, *Organization Studies*, 29 (10): 1315–36.

Symon, G., Cassell, C. and Dickson, R. (2000) Expanding our research and practice through innovative research methods, *European Journal of Work and Organizational Psychology*, 9 (4): 1–6.

Tenbrunsel, A. E., Galvin, T. L., Neale, M. A. and Bazerman, M. H. (1996) Cognitions in organizations, in S. R. Clegg, C. Hardy and W. R. Nord (eds), *Handbook of Organization Studies*. London: Sage.

Thomas, A. (1997) The coming crisis of western management education, *Systems Practice*, 10 (6): 681–702.

Thomas, J. (1993) *Doing Critical Ethnography*. London: Sage.

Tiles, M. (1987) A science of Mars or of Venus? *Philosophy*, 62 (241): 293–306.

Tinker, A. M. (1985) *Paper Prophets: A Social Critique of Accounting*. London: Holt, Rinehart & Winston.

Torbert, W. R. (1999) Distinctive questions developmental action inquiry tasks, *Management Learning*, 30 (2): 189–206.

Torres, R., Preskill, H. and Piontek, M. E. (2005) *Evaluation Strategies for Communication and Reporting*. London: Sage.

Townley, B. (1994) *Reframing Human Resource Management: Power, Ethics and the Subject at Work.* London: Sage.

Tranfield, D., Denyer, D. and Smart, P. (2003) Towards a methodology for developing evidence-informed management knowledge by means of systematic review, *British Journal of Management*, 14(3): 207–22.

Tranfield, D. and Starkey, K. (1998) The nature, social organization and promotion of management research: towards policy, *British Journal of Management*, 9: 341–53.

Treleaven, L. (2001) The turn to action and the linguistic turn: towards an integrated methodology, in P. Reason and H. Bradbury (eds), *Handbook of Action Research: Participative Inquiry and Practice.* London: Sage.

Trist, E. L., Higgin, G. W., Murray, H. and Pollock, A. B. (1963) *Organisational Choice: Capabilities of Groups at the Coal Face under Changing Conditions. The Loss, Rediscovery and Transformation of a Work Tradition.* London: Tavistock.

Trow, M. (1957) A comment on participant observation and interviewing: a comparison, *Human Organisation*, 16 (3): 33–5.

Tse, A. C. B. (1998) Comparing the response rate, response speed and response quality of two methods of sending questionnaires: e-mail vs mail, *Journal of the Market Research Society*, 40: 353–61.

Tsoukas, H. (1992) Postmodernism: reflexive rationalism and organization studies: a reply to Martin Parker, *Organization Studies*, 13 (4): 643–9.

Tucker, J. (1999) *The Theraputic Corporation.* New York: Oxford University Press.

Unger, R. (1987) *Politics: A Work in Constructive Social Theory: Its Situation and its Task.* Cambridge: Cambridge University Press.

Unwin, N. (1986) Beyond truth, *Mind*, XV: 300–17.

Uzzel, D. (1995) Ethnographic and action research, in G. M. Breakwell, S. Hammond and C. Fife-Shaw (eds), *Research Methods in Psychology.* London: Sage.

Van de Vall, M., Bolas, C. and Kang, T. S. (1976) Applied social research in industrial organisations. An evaluation of functions, theory and methods, *Journal of Applied Behavioural Science*, 12 (2): 158–77.

Van Maanen, J. (1991) The smile factory: work at Disneyland, in P. J. Frost, L. F. Moore, M. R. Louis, C. C. Lundberg and J. Martin (eds), *Reframing Organizational Culture.* London: Sage.

Van Maanen, J. (1995a) Style as theory, *Organization Science*, 7 (4): 641–52.

Van Maanen, J. (1995b) An end to innocence: the ethnography of ethnography, in J. Van Maanen (ed.), *Representation in Ethnography.* London: Sage.

Van Maanen, J. (1998) Different strokes: qualitative research in the *Administrative Science Quarterly* from 1956 to 1996, in J. Van Maanen (ed.), *Qualitative Studies of Organizations.* London: Sage.

Van Maanen, J. and Kolb, D. (1985) The professional apprentice: observations on field roles in two organizations, *Research in Organizations*, 4: 1–33.

Wall, T. D., Kemp, N. J., Jackson, P. R. and Clegg, C. W. (1986) The outcomes of autonomous workgroups: a long–term field experiment, *Academy of Management Journal*, 29 (2): 280–304.

Warmington, A. (1980) Action research: its methods and implications, *Journal of Applied Systems Analysis*, 7: 23–39.

Watson, T. J. (1977) *The Personnel Managers: A Study in the Sociology of Work and Employment.* London: Routledge.

Watson, T. J. (1994) *In Search of Management: Culture, Chaos and Control in Managerial Work.* London: Routledge.

Watson, T. J. (1997) Theorizing managerial work: a pragmatic pluralist approach to interdisciplinary research, *British Journal of Management*, 8 (1): 3–9.

Wax, R. H. (1971) *Doing Fieldwork.* Chicago, IL: University of Chicago Press.

Wayne, S. J. and Ferris, G. R. (1990) Influence tactics, affect and exchange quality in supervisor-subordinate interactions: a laboratory experiment and field study, *Journal of Applied Psychology*, 75 (5): 487–99.

Webb, E. J., Campbell, D. T., Schwartz, R. D. and Sechrest, L. (1969) *Unobtrusive Measures.* Chicago, IL: Rand McNally.

Webb, S. and Webb, B. (1932/1975) *Methods of Social Research.* Cambridge: Cambridge University Press.

Weick, K. E. (1989) Theory construction as disciplined imagination, *Academy of Management Review*, 14: 516–31.

Weick, K. E. (1999) Theory construction as disciplined reflexivity: trade offs in the 90s,

Academy of Management Review, 24 (4): 797–810.

Whitley, R. (1984a) The fragmented state of management studies: reasons and consequences, *Journal of Management Studies*, 21 (3): 331–48.

Whitley, R. (1984b) The scientific status of management research as a practically oriented social science, *Journal of Management Studies*, 21 (4): 369–90.

Whyte, W. F. (1948) *Human Relations in the Restaurant Industry*. New York: McGraw-Hill.

Whyte, W. F. (1984) *Learning from the Field*. London: Sage.

Whyte, W. F. (ed.) (1991) *Participatory Action Research*. London: Sage.

Willmott, H. C. (1998) Re-cognizing the other: reflections of a new sensibility in social and organization studies, in R. Chia (ed.), *In the Realm of Organization: Essays for Robert Cooper*. London: Routledge.

Willmott, H. and Knights, D. (1995) Culture and control in an insurance company, *Studies in Culture, Organizations and Society*, 1: 1–18.

Wilson, A. T. M. (1961) The manager and his world, *Industrial Management Review*, 3 (1): 1–26.

Wiseman, J. P. (1978) The research web, in J. Bynner and K. M. Stribley (eds), *Social Research Principles and Procedures*. London: Longman.

Wittgenstein, L. (1922) *Tractatus logico-philosophocus*. London: Routledge & Kegan Paul.

Wright, M. (1986) The make-buy decision and managing markets: the case of management buy-outs, *Journal of Management Studies*, 25 (4): 443–64.

Yin, R. K. (2003) *Case Study Research: Design and Methods*, 3rd edn. London: Sage.

Young, K., Fogarty, M. P. and McRae, S. (1987) *The Management of Doctoral Studies in the Social Sciences*, Occasional Paper no. 36. London: Policy Studies Institute.

Zikmund, W. G. (2002) *Business Research Methods*, 7th edn. Dryden: Thomson Learning.

Znaniecki, F. (1934) *The Method of Sociology*. New York: Farrar & Rinehart.

Index

Please note that page references to non-textual matter such as figures or tables will be in *italic* print. Titles of publications beginning with 'A' or 'The' will be sorted under the first significant word.

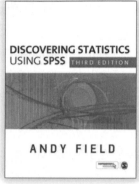
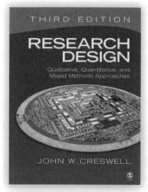

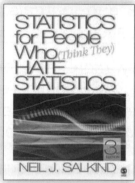

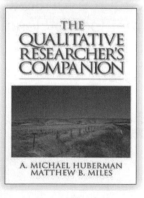

Supporting researchers for more than forty years

Research methods have always been at the core of SAGE's publishing. Sara Miller McCune founded SAGE in 1965 and soon after she published SAGE's first methods book, *Public Policy Evaluation*. A few years later, she launched the Quantitative Applications in the Social Sciences series – affectionately known as the 'little green books'.

Always at the forefront of developing and supporting new approaches in methods, SAGE published early groundbreaking texts and journals in the fields of qualitative methods and evaluation.

Today, more than forty years and two million little green books later, SAGE continues to push the boundaries with a growing list of more than 1,200 research methods books, journals, and reference works across the social, behavioural, and health sciences.

From qualitative, quantitative and mixed methods to evaluation, SAGE is the essential resource for academics and practitioners looking for the latest in methods by leading scholars.

www.sagepublications.com